THE·RING·OF
THE·NIBELUNG

• DEDICATION •

To Patrick Mason, who introduced me to The Ring.

To Mike Friedrich, who shepherded the project along for so many years.

And to Mike Richardson, for staying the course.

P.C.R.

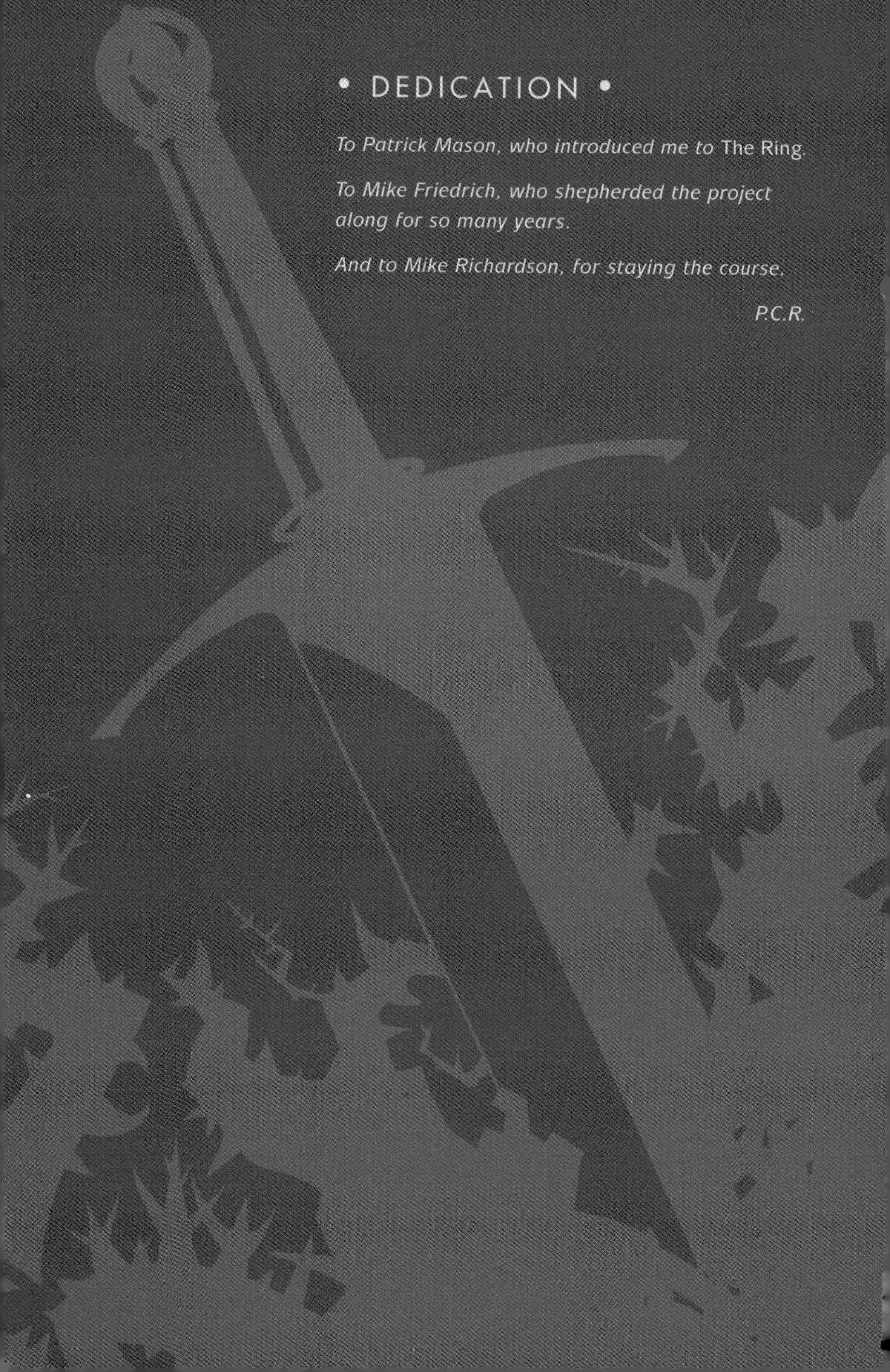

THE·RING·OF·THE·NIBELUNG

·VOLUME ONE·

BASED ON THE MUSIC DRAMAS OF RICHARD WAGNER

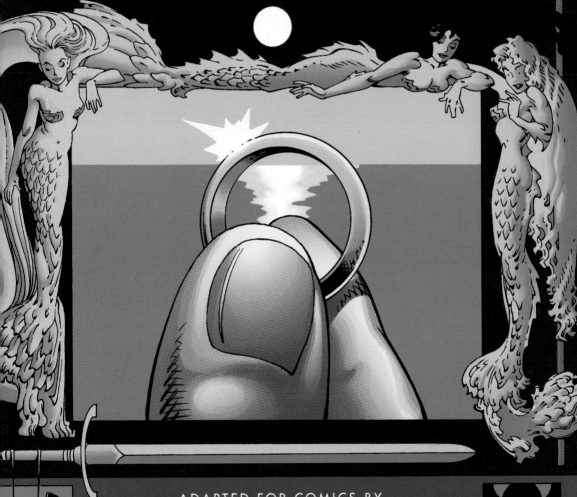

ADAPTED FOR COMICS BY

P. ⊂RAIG RUSSELL

translated by	*colored by*	*lettered by*
PATRICK	LOVERN	GALEN
MASON	**KINDZIERSKI**	**SHOWMAN**

editor
SCOTT ALLIE

assistant editors
ADAM GALLARDO & MIKE CARRIGLITTO

designers
DEBRA BAILEY & P. CRAIG RUSSELL

art director, Dark Horse Maverick
CARY GRAZZINI

publisher
MIKE RICHARDSON

special thanks to
RICH POWERS

Volume II: *Siegfried and Gotterdammerung,
The Twilight of the Gods*, coming in July 2002.

Published by
Dark Horse Comics, Inc.
10956 SE Main Street
Milwaukie, OR 97222

April 2002
First edition
ISBN: 1-56971-666-8

3 5 7 9 10 8 6 4 2

PRINTED IN CHINA

This book collects *The Ring of the Nibelung*: The Rhinegold #1-4 and
The Ring of the Nibelung: The Valkyrie #1-3, published by Dark Horse Comics.

• PREFACE •

Ever since it was first performed at Bayreuth in 1876, Wagner's *Der Ring des Nibelungen* has presented producers with visual problems. When does the action take place? In mythical times. How did people dress in mythical times? We don't know. But Wagner, in 1876, had his gods with horned helmets, and he tried as far as possible to follow his own stage directions: Fricka in *Die Walküre* arrives in a chariot drawn by two rams; Brünnhilde rides a horse named Grane; Fafner turns into a dragon; and so on, including at the very end the overflowing of the Rhine and the destruction of Valhalla. He must have known that he was asking for the impossible or the ludicrous.

Grappling with these problems has led in recent years to many divided approaches by stage directors. Some productions, like that at the New York Metropolitan, have tried to keep as closely as possible to the original stage instructions, only to be denounced by many critics as perpetuating a museum piece. Others, like Sir Peter Hall at Bayreuth, have found a modern way of coping with them, not to universal satisfaction at first. Others have given the four operas a contemporary or a 19th century setting, but this creates new problems. Wotan can be a frock-coated tycoon but he still has to carry his spear, Siegmund and Sieglinde need their swords, and Fafner has to be a dragon, because these elements are essential to the plot. You can't dispense with them.

How then can we come nearest to seeing *The Ring* as Wagner saw it in his mind as he composed it? Did he really think it could be staged as he visualized it, or did he think ahead to a time when a new technology such as the cinema could accomplish what he intended? A film of *The Ring* is the only way *all* the magical effects could be depicted, especially now in the age of the computer. Failing that, and with stage directors failing us, the best way of all, is through our own imaginations or an artist's imagination. In P. Craig Russell's graphic books of the whole cycle, we see *The Ring* almost as it might be seen through Wagner's eyes (and how thrilled he surely would have been

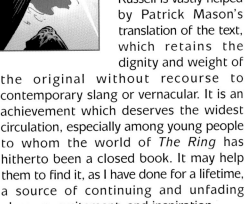

with the Ride of the Valkyries). Russell's drawings, like Arthur Rackham's many years ago, show us the gods and the mortals not as figures from some un-imaginable dark age, but as believable beings seen through modern eyes. In the world of Superman and Batman, Siegfried and Siegmund acquire a new dimension without losing their heroic stature. In this, Russell is vastly helped by Patrick Mason's translation of the text, which retains the dignity and weight of the original without recourse to contemporary slang or vernacular. It is an achievement which deserves the widest circulation, especially among young people to whom the world of *The Ring* has hitherto been a closed book. It may help them to find it, as I have done for a lifetime, a source of continuing and unfading pleasure, excitement, and inspiration.

Michael Kennedy
London

Michael Kennedy is the author of the *Oxford Dictionary of Music*, and is a music critic for the *London Telegraph*.

• INTRODUCTION •

P. Craig Russell is one of the world's greatest living comic-book artists and this, his impassioned and ambitious adaptation of Richard Wagner's epic *Ring of the Nibelung*, is a spectacular example of a maestro at the absolute height of his creative powers and skills. Craig has always been the sort of creator to follow his own muse, and consistent themes of passion, destiny, and retribution have long been the flesh and blood of his artistic endeavors. And, of course, there is opera. Seemingly alone amongst his host of talented contemporaries, Craig sees the obvious connection between the two art forms: opera, the grand marriage of music and words in order to stage a resounding narrative, and comics, the seamless partnership of pictures and words in order to achieve the same. For years, Craig has been producing brilliant adaptations of his favorite operatic selections, all of which have only honed his abilities for this, his most challenging effort yet.

Wagner's cycle of four continuous yet distinct operas is renowned for its powerful distillation of ancient German myth into a (relatively) more modern translation. While capturing the mythic majesty of these legends, Wagner's vision lets us see the personalities and motivations behind the personas of godhead and hero, villain and martyr. The structure of this famous musical saga is equally powerful, with each movement (*The Rhinegold*, *The Valkyrie*, *Siegfried*, and *Gotterdammerung*) comprising its own, separate opera and libretto, yet remaining intricately connected via various narrative motifs that eventually bring together all the elements into one cohesive whole. In the course of this marathon achievement Wagner attempts nothing less than to describe the endless tide of history, the sum of all earthly existence, and the tragic triumph of love.

This is the opera that most lay people think about when they think of opera. This is the one where the fat lady sings (although in Craig's version, she's justly striking). And this has proven to be the pinnacle of Craig Russell's creative quest.

Like his adaptive source, Craig understands the incredible magnitude of composition and the magical manipulation of symbols. His visual depictions proceed and progress with a musical pace and his cinematic staging is nothing short of astounding. I mean, the guy pulls off the creation of the universe on page one! Not a single element is wasted in Craig's art as colors, lines, balloons, and panels stylishly take the place of notes, chords, stage, and songs. His lush figure drawing combines with his keen graphic sensibility to create a singular staging that seems both beautifully grounded in reality, yet always seems to pays homage to the theatrical nature of what it is adapting.

And like his source, Craig understands the all-consuming nature of shadows and the all-pervasive presence of light. There's a lush sensuality that Craig perceives in the Ring cycle that usually gets lost in more sonorous interpretations. Be it in describing the gods' endless lust for power or the ultimately more triumphant, human longing for love, Craig's art is full of the throbbing pulse of creation and life. Seductively beckoning portals and powerfully phallic imagery abound with an awesome energy throughout all four books. Passions flare and emotion runs rampant as Craig's almost decadent depictions run vibrant and ecstatic across the page.

Life, they seem to convey, is born through the pulsating summation of love, the co-joined yin and yang. Set free of the singular, catastrophic effects of pride and greed, unbridled beauty reigns supreme in the eternal cycle of death and rebirth.

Craig Russell has attained a level of mastery that most artists only dream about. His obvious sense of passion and delight shines on every page of what must feel like an amazing achievement. *The Ring of the Nibelung* is the stunning realization of a vision made real, the resounding crescendo of a voice made whole.

Bravo, my friend.
Matt Wagner
(no relation that I know of)
Portland, Oregon

Matt Wagner is the Eisner Award-winning creator of *Grendel* and *Mage*.

· WHAT IS AN ADAPTATION? ·

P. Craig Russell

Since a composer can use a musical gesture to achieve an emotional response barely hinted at in the stage action, musical theatre, including opera, is possibly the most difficult form to adapt from, the most resistant to change. Paradoxically, it can be the very abstraction of music that allows the visual artist greater latitude to call on all the visual devices of symbolism, surrealism, and expressionism in designing a storytelling structure. And if the adaptation falls short of the brilliance of pure music, it will at least have become something more than a cut-and-paste editing job, illustrated by a series of talking heads — the approach seen in the old *Classics Illustrated* comics.

EXAMPLE ONE

In the opera *The Clowns* (*I Pagliacci*) by Leoncavallo, Canio delivers the following speech:

CANIO'S SPEECH IN ITALIAN	TRANSLATION BY MARC ANDREYKO
Recitar! Mentre preso dal delirio;	
Non so più quel che dico e quel che faccio.	How can I perform in this rage? I don't even know what I'm saying.
Eppur, è duopo — sforzati!	And yet I have to force myself on stage.
Bah, sei tu forse un uom? Ah! Ah!	Bah! Does that make me more of a man?
Tu se Pagliaccio!	Ha! You are Pagliaccio … the clown!
Vesti la giubba e la faccia infarina.	Put on your costume and make up your
La gente paga e rider vuole qua.	face! The people have paid and want to
E se Arlecchin t'invola Colombina,	laugh! And if Harlequino should steal
Ridi, Pagliaccio, e ognun applaudirà!	your Columbina … laugh … and all will
Tramuta in lazzi lo spasmo ed il pianto;	applaud. Turn your tears and your pain
In una smorfia il singhiozzo e'l dolor.	to a jest. Your agony and suffering to a
Ah!	grin … Ahhhh! Laugh, Pagliaccio.
Ridi, Pagliaccio, sul tuo amore infranto!	Laugh at the pain that poisons your heart.
Ridi del duol che t'avvelena il cor!	

Marc Andreyko's excellent work reads as a good translation should read, natural and unforced. It serves as a starting point for the adapting artist's blueprint for the visualization.

At this point, a mere series of pictures of Canio reciting this speech would cause the reader, no matter how good the artist's command of body language, to view the character's pain only from a distance, with little use of the graphic-story form's ability to allow us to participate. Something more is needed.

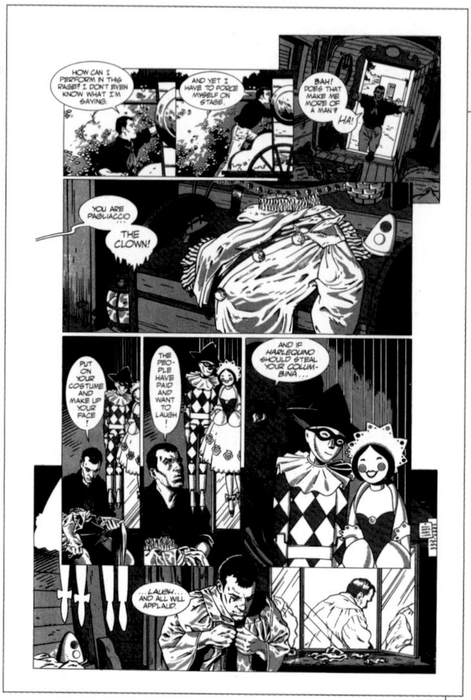

HOW CAN I PERFORM IN THIS RAGE? I DON'T EVEN KNOW WHAT I'M SAYING.
AND YET I HAVE TO FORCE MYSELF ON STAGE.
BAH! DOES THAT MAKE ME MORE OF A MAN?
HA!
YOU ARE PAGLIACCIO ...
THE CLOWN!
PUT ON YOUR COSTUME AND MAKE UP YOUR FACE!
THE PEOPLE HAVE PAID AND WANT TO LAUGH!
AND IF HARLEQUINO SHOULD STEAL YOUR COLUMBINA...
...LAUGH... AND ALL WILL APPLAUD.

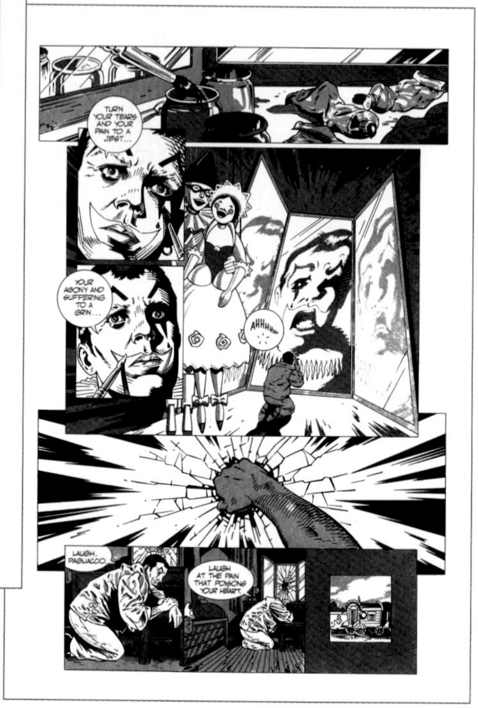

TURN YOUR TEARS AND YOUR PAIN TO A JEST...
YOUR AGONY AND SUFFERING TO A GRIN...
AHHHHH
LAUGH, PAGLIACCIO.
LAUGH AT THE PAIN THAT POISONS YOUR HEART.

In adapting the work for comics, I took advantage of what might be found inside a travelling performer's circus cart, and introduced marionettes dressed as Harlequin and Columbine. (Canio's unfaithful wife will later be seen dressed as Columbine alongside her onstage Harlequin.) Marionettes are nowhere mentioned in the original play, but I've used them as a visual metaphor, silently mocking Canio as he prepares for the evening's performance, growing larger each time we see them up to the moment of Canio's mental disintegration, at which point they seem to come to life. The marionettes, along with the larger-than-life distorted reflections and the shattered mirror, all become elements in creating a set piece which corresponds with the climax of the first act, in effect a sort of visual aria.

EXAMPLE TWO

Twelve drawings use their own interwoven set of visual motifs to illustrate an idea originally expressed in seven musical notes.

From this:

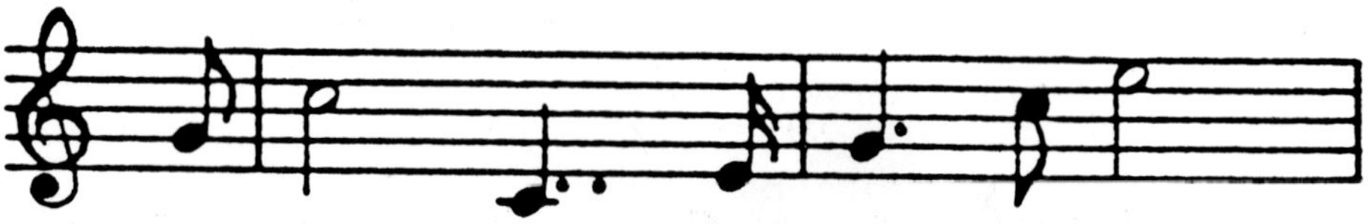

Came this:

WILL IT PROTECT US IN THE NIGHT THAT MUST COME?
YES

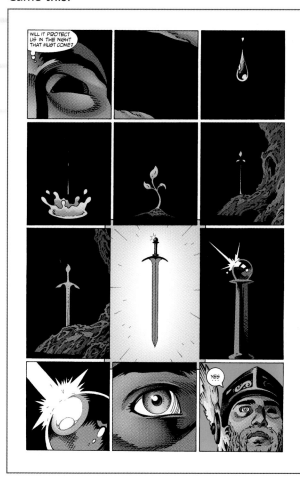

Much of the dramatic texture of *The Ring of the Nibelung* is expressed through the use of *leitmotifs*, a sort of musical signature — think of Darth Vader and his distinctive entrance music, the same through all three *Star Wars* films. Not just people (the Rhinemaidens, Siegfried, and Brunhilde), but objects (the sword, the spear, and the ring), and even ideas (love, power, and choice) have their own *motto*. By interweaving and evolving these musical ideas, Wagner could comment on the stage action or even indicate what a char acter was thinking.

Near the conclusion of *Rhinegold*, Voton — standing before Valhalla, wondering if it will shelter the gods from impending doom — conceives the idea of the sword, and of the hero sired by him to fight the fight his treaties disallow. In conceiving his idea, he believes he has finessed his way around a fate-ordained doom. Voton — always the operator.

At the moment Voton conceives his idea, the sword theme, heard for the first time, sounds deep in the orchestra. Though nothing is verbally expressed, the music lets us know that something important has just occurred. Wagner approached this moment with great subtlety, so the challenge in the adaptation became to show the moment of the sparking of an idea, as well as the idea itself. It was my hope that this could be done in a manner more sophisticated than the use of a light bulb in a word balloon and a line of explanatory dialogue ... "I know what I'll do!"

With seven notes Wagner teases us into thought and propels the action of the story. My challenge was to convey the same information in a way as unique to the visual form as Wagner's was to the musical.

The solution was to enter Voton's mind through the eye sacrificed for wisdom (inner vision). This leads to the interweaving of the visual motifs already established in *Rhinegold* (the primal elements of water and light) with motifs yet to come in *The Valkyrie* (the sword and the tree). The sequence ends with an exit, via the gleaming light of the sword, through Voton's good eye, the one which looks upon the outer world.

Ad•ap•ta•tion (ăd´ăp-ta´shən) *n.* **1.** the metamorphosis of one art form into another.

PN.8	Von der Abwendigen wend' ich mich ab; nicht wissen darf ich, was sie sich wünscht: die Strafe nur muss vollstreckt ich seh'n.	*I turn aside* *from her who is estranged from me;* *I may not know* *what is her wish:* *I must only see* *the sentence carried out.*
	BRÜNNHILDE Was hast du erdacht, dass ich erdulde?	**BRÜNNHILDE** *What have you planned* *that I should suffer?*
PN.9	**WOTAN** In festen Schlaf verschliess' ich dich: wer so die Wehrlose weckt, dem ward, erwacht, sie zum Weib.	**WOTAN** *I shall lock you* *fast in sleep:* *whoever wakes you thus defenceless* *shall have you, awakened, for his* *wife.*

Voton's judgment of Brunhildé, from page 21 of Valkyrie, Part Three. Here we see the original German/English version of the libretto from which P. Craig Russell worked, broken up into panels.

W (fiercly) ~~and~~ which I struck into ~~this~~ splinters!
(calming) Do not attempt to sway me girl. Your lot is cast. I must go from here. I've strayed too long./You have turned from me, now I must turn from you.

Br. What punishment have you decreed?

W I shall shut you in deepest sleep/, defenseless/, to be wived by your waker. THE FIRST MAN TO FIND YOU AND WAKE YOU.

Next, Patrick Mason's handwritten translation of the pertinent passages, with one of very few changes made by Russell.

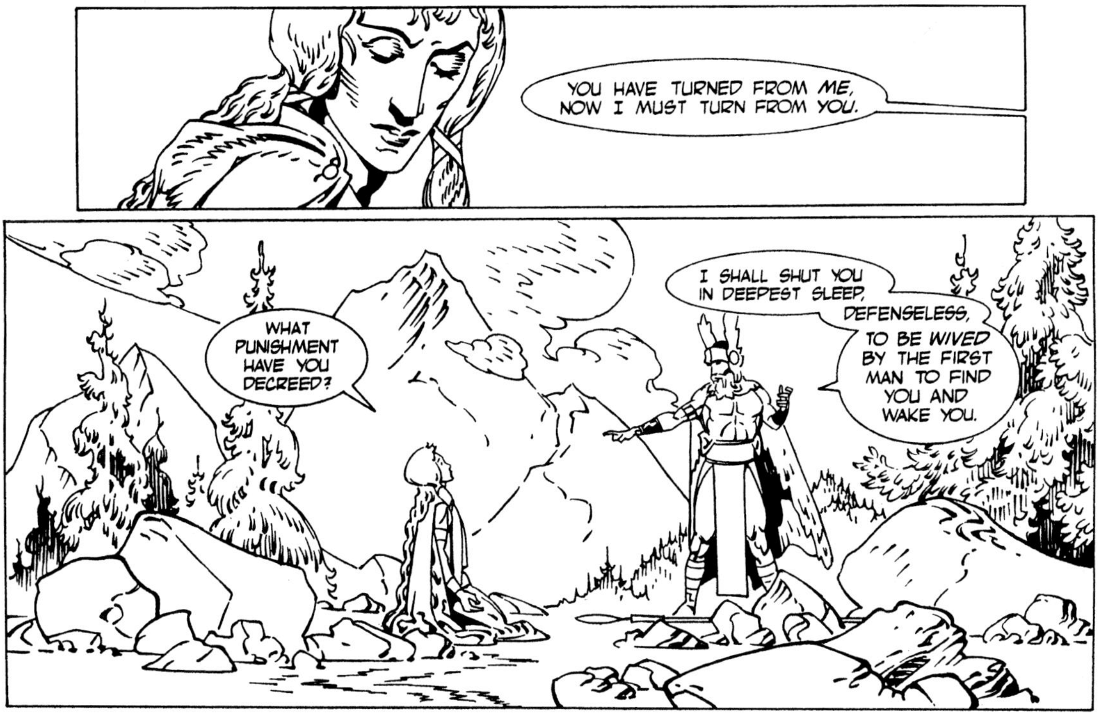
YOU HAVE TURNED FROM ME, NOW I MUST TURN FROM YOU.
WHAT PUNISHMENT HAVE YOU DECREED?
I SHALL SHUT YOU IN DEEPEST SLEEP, DEFENSELESS,
TO BE WIVED BY THE FIRST MAN TO FIND YOU AND WAKE YOU.

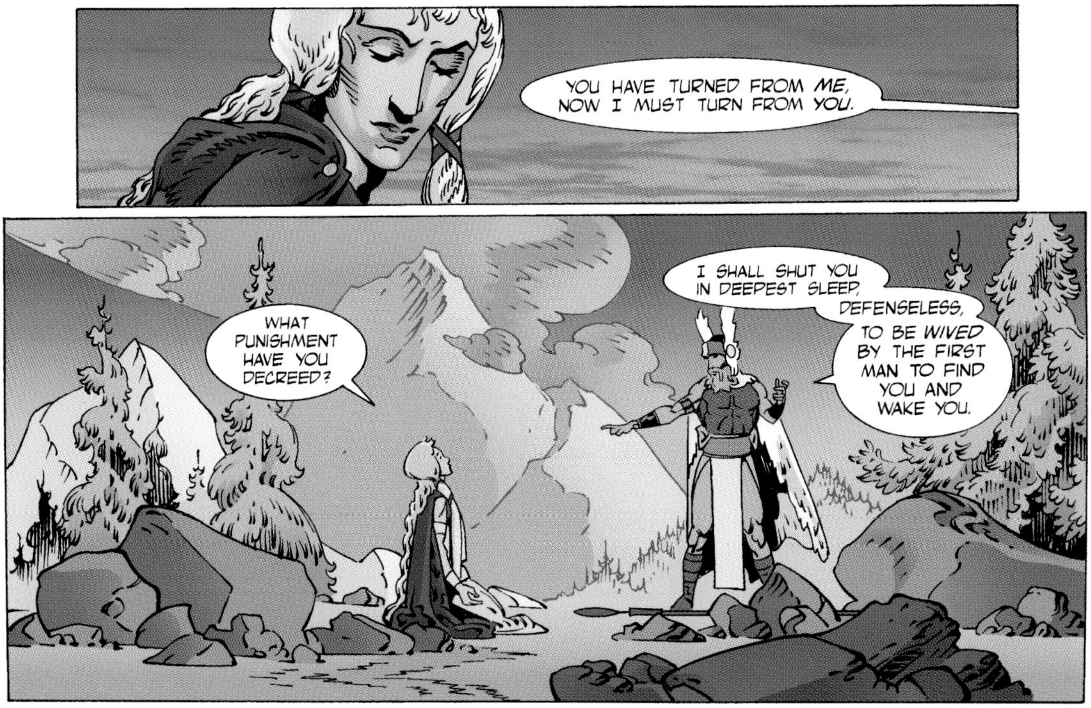
YOU HAVE TURNED FROM ME, NOW I MUST TURN FROM YOU.
WHAT PUNISHMENT HAVE YOU DECREED?
I SHALL SHUT YOU IN DEEPEST SLEEP, DEFENSELESS,
TO BE WIVED BY THE FIRST MAN TO FIND YOU AND WAKE YOU.

Finally, the finished panels as they appeared in this adaptation.

SIEGFRIED Nothung! Nothung! neidliches Schwert! jetzt haftest du wieder im Heft!	SIEGFRIED *Nothung! Nothung!* *Coveted Sword!* *Now you are hafted once more in your hilt!*
MIME . . . Dann wahrlich müht sich Mime nicht mehr.	MIME *. . . Then, indeed, Mime shall* *moil and toil no more!*

(They continue, each following his own train of thought oblivious of the other.)

SIEGFRIED Warst du entzwei ich zwang dich zu ganz; kein Schlag soll nun dich mehr zerschlagen.	SIEGFRIED *You were in bits—* *I have forced you to be whole;* *now no blow shall shatter you more.*
MIME Ihm schaffen And're den ew'gen Schatz.	MIME *Others produce the* *inexhaustible Treasure for him.*
SIEGFRIED Dem sterbenden Vater zersprang der Stahl, der lebende Sohn schuf ihn neu: nun lacht ihm sein heller Schein, seine Schärfe schneidet ihm hart.	SIEGFRIED *The steel once broke* *for the dying father,* *the living son* *has forged it anew.* *Now its clear lustre smiles at him,* *its sharp blade cuts clean for him.*
MIME Mime, der kühne, Mime ist König, Fürst der Alben, Walter des All's!	MIME *Mime the bold,* *Mime is king,* *prince of the elves,* *ruler of all.*
SIEGFRIED Nothung! Nothung! neidliches Schwert! zum Leben weckt' ich dich wieder. Tod lagst du in Trümmern dort,	SIEGFRIED *Nothung! Nothung!* *Coveted Sword!* *I have wakened you to life once more.* *You lay there dead* *in pieces;*
MIME Wer hätte wohl das gedacht?	MIME *Whoever would have thought it?*
SIEGFRIED Schlage den Falschen, fälle den Schelm! Schau, Mime, du Schmied: so schneidet Siegfrieds Schwert!	SIEGFRIED *Strike down the impostor,* *fell the rogue!* *Look, Mime, you smith—* *thus cleaves Siegfried's Sword!*

(He smites the anvil, which falls into two halves with a deafening crash, split from top to bottom.)

30

30

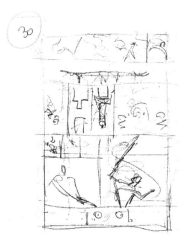

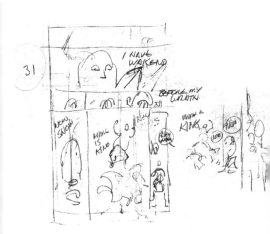

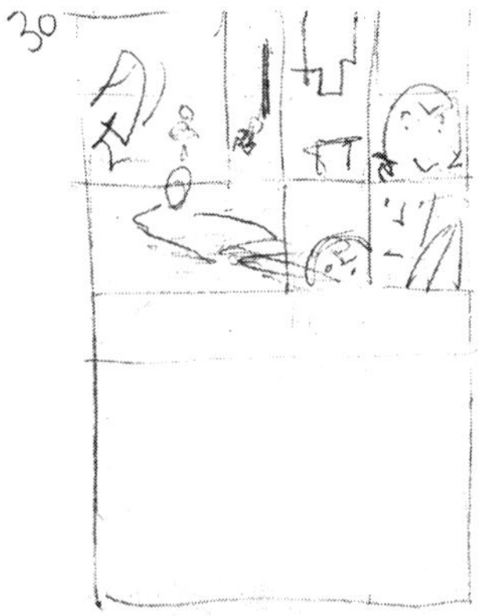

M (getting giddy) I can almost see the gold in my hand now... and Alberich will be my slave — yes, all men + gods will serve me

S (holding up the sword) Nothung! Now again in the hilt! Never to break again

M Never to toil again ... the whole earth will tremble at my least nod!

S All will tremble with fear ~~before you~~ who are knaves + false-hearted.

M Mime ~~is king~~ the bold! Mime is king!

S Noblest of weapons, Nothung the bold

M Prince of the dwarves, master of all !!

S Hey, Mime! Behold the sword of a hero! (Breaks the anvil in two. M. shrieks in fear. S. goes running off into the ~~[illegible]~~ woods) ~~Ha ha!~~ ~~Ha ha~~ (Mime follows)

Playing his horn

31
I HAVE WAKEND
MIME IS KING

Siegfried and Nothung. In this pivotal scene, when Siegfried reconstructs his father's sword, PCR took greater liberties with Mason's translation. After one failed attempt at laying out page 30, he hit upon a good design for the sequence, which required significant rewriting. It would be hard to match up the final script with Mason's translation or the original libretto, though the essence and action of the scene are perfectly evoked.

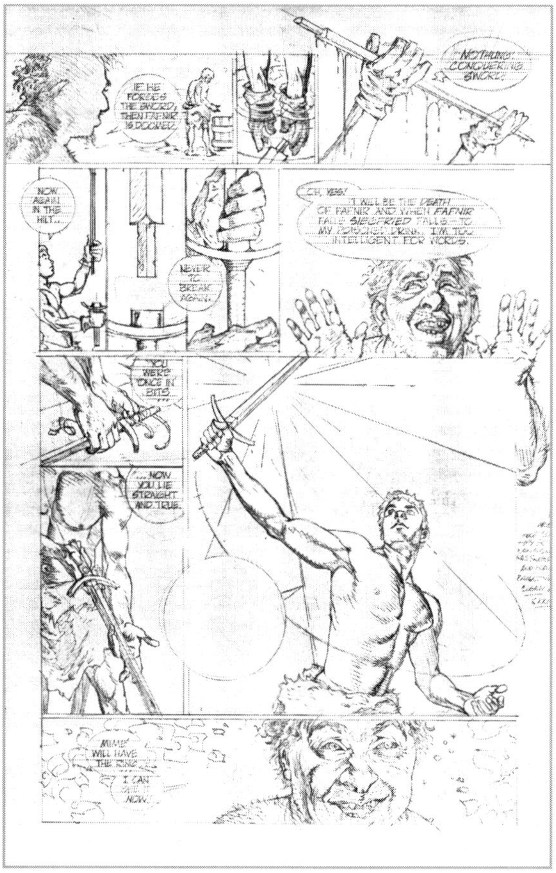

IF HE FORGES THE SWORD, THEN FAFNIR IS DOOMED.
NOTHUNG! CONQUERING SWORD!
NOW AGAIN IN THE HILT...
NEVER TO BREAK AGAIN.
OH, YES! IT WILL BE THE DEATH OF FAFNIR AND WHEN FAFNIR FALLS SIEGFRIED FALLS--TO MY POISONED DRINK. I'M TOO INTELLIGENT FOR WORDS.
YOU WERE ONCE IN BITS...
...NOW YOU LIE STRAIGHT AND TRUE.
MIME WILL HAVE THE RING... I CAN SEE IT NOW.

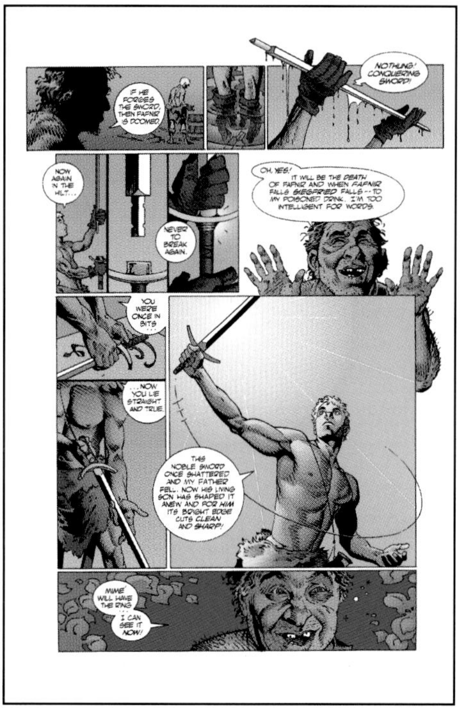

IF HE FORGES THE SWORD, THEN FAFNIR IS DOOMED.
NOTHUNG! CONQUERING SWORD!
NOW AGAIN IN THE HILT...
NEVER TO BREAK AGAIN.
OH, YES! IT WILL BE THE DEATH OF FAFNIR AND WHEN FAFNIR FALLS SIEGFRIED FALLS--TO MY POISONED DRINK. I'M TOO INTELLIGENT FOR WORDS.
YOU WERE ONCE IN BITS...
...NOW YOU LIE STRAIGHT AND TRUE.
THIS NOBLE SWORD ONCE SHATTERED AND MY FATHER FELL. NOW HIS LIVING SON HAS SHAPED IT ANEW AND FOR HIM ITS BRIGHT EDGE CUTS CLEAN AND SHARP!
MIME WILL HAVE THE RING... I CAN SEE IT NOW!

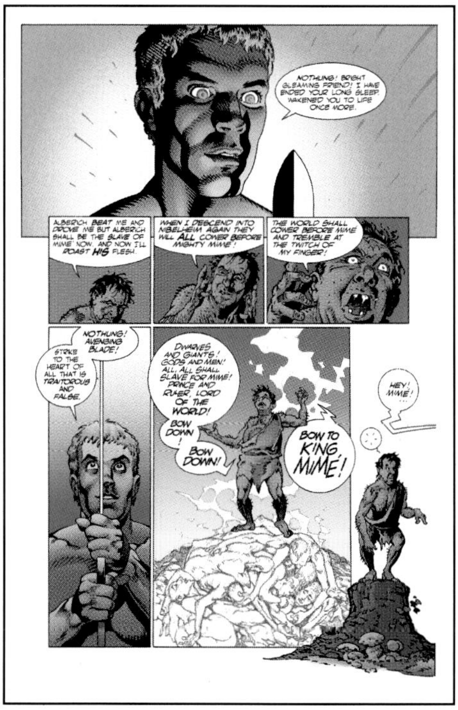

NOTHUNG! BRIGHT GLEAMING FRIEND! I HAVE ENDED YOUR LONG SLEEP. WAKENED YOU TO LIFE ONCE MORE.
ALBERICH BEAT ME AND DROVE ME BUT ALBERICH SHALL BE THE SLAVE OF MIME NOW. AND NOW I'LL ROAST HIS FLESH.
WHEN I DESCEND INTO NIBELHEIM AGAIN THEY WILL ALL COWER BEFORE MIGHTY MIME!
THE WORLD SHALL COWER BEFORE MIME AND TREMBLE AT THE TWITCH OF MY FINGER!
NOTHUNG! AVENGING BLADE!
STRIKE TO THE HEART OF ALL THAT IS TRAITOROUS AND FALSE.
DWARVES AND GIANTS! GODS AND MEN! ALL, ALL SHALL SLAVE FOR MIME! PRINCE AND RULER, LORD OF THE WORLD!
BOW DOWN!
BOW DOWN!
BOW TO KING MIME!
HEY! MIME!...

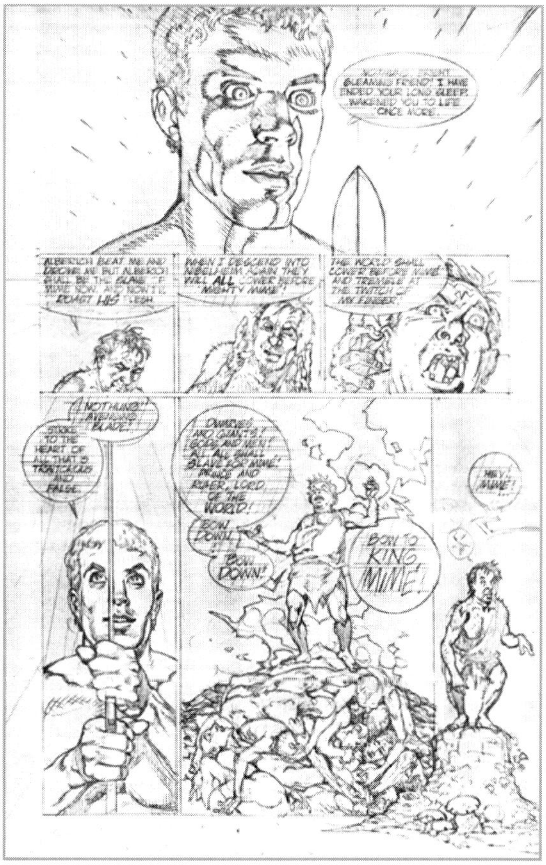

NOTHUNG! BRIGHT GLEAMING FRIEND! I HAVE ENDED YOUR LONG SLEEP. WAKENED YOU TO LIFE ONCE MORE.
ALBERICH BEAT ME AND DROVE ME BUT ALBERICH SHALL BE THE SLAVE OF MIME NOW. AND NOW I'LL ROAST HIS FLESH.
WHEN I DESCEND INTO NIBELHEIM AGAIN THEY WILL ALL COWER BEFORE MIGHTY MIME!
THE WORLD SHALL COWER BEFORE MIME AND TREMBLE AT THE TWITCH OF MY FINGER!
NOTHUNG! AVENGING BLADE!
STRIKE TO THE HEART OF ALL THAT IS TRAITOROUS AND FALSE.
DWARVES AND GIANTS! GODS AND MEN! ALL, ALL SHALL SLAVE FOR MIME! PRINCE AND RULER, LORD OF THE WORLD!
BOW DOWN!
BOW DOWN!
BOW TO KING MIME!
HEY! MIME!

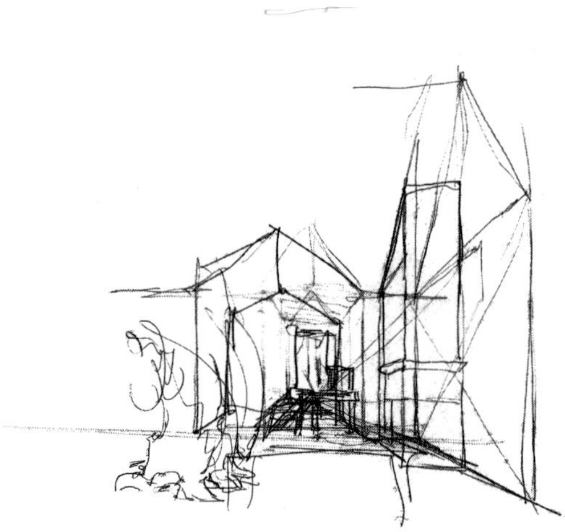

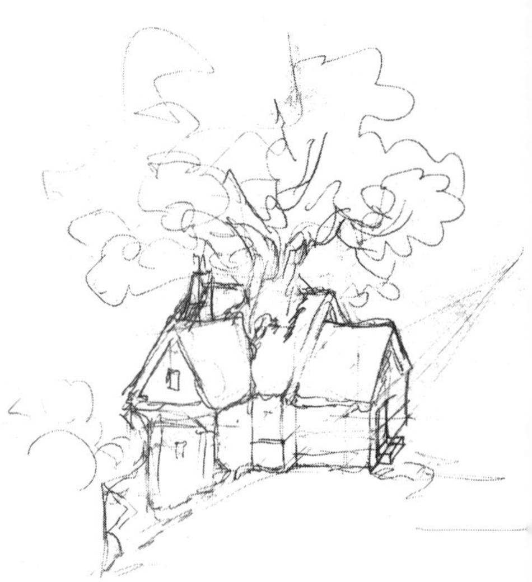

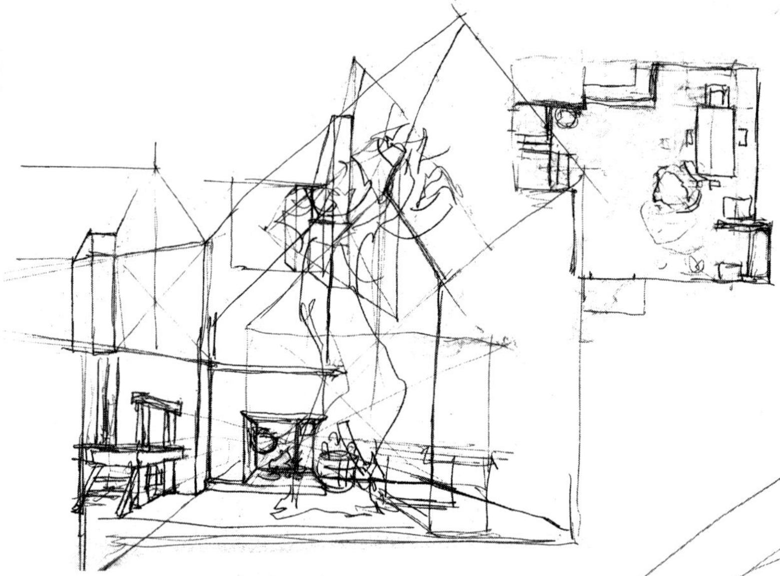

The first act of *The Valkyrie* takes place almost entirely in a one-room set: Hunding's Hut.

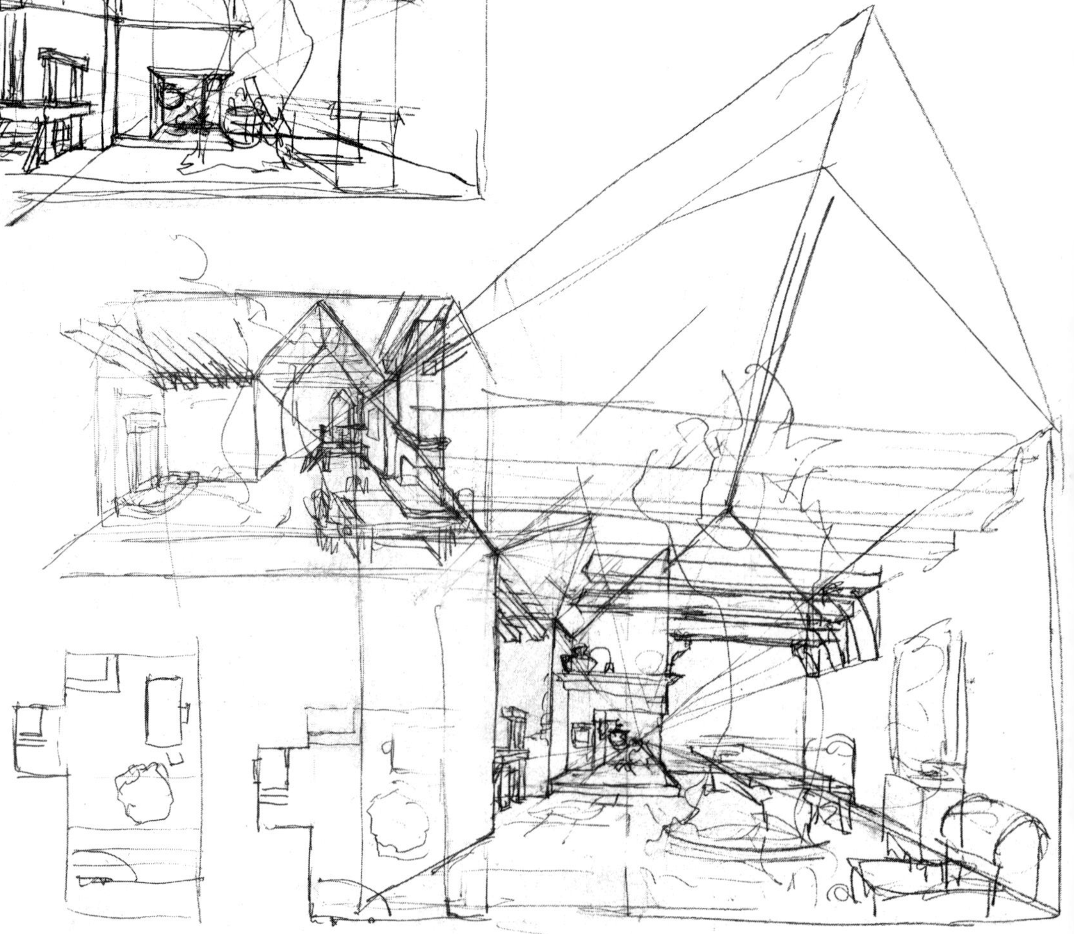

It was important for the room to be architecturally consistent, so the reader would grow familiar with the setting, and get the impression that it's a real place. To maintain dramatic tension, the artist also wanted to make sure that the readers would always know where the characters are in relation to the sword in the tree. Pictured here are just some of the floor plans and cut-away drawings with which the artist created the layout of the room. Below is the finished panel from VALKYRIE, Part One, when Siegmund first enters Hunding's Hut. All of the important elements are established in one shot: the table, the hearth, the bedroom door, and the tree into which Voton, long ago in his disguise as the wanderer, thrust the sword.

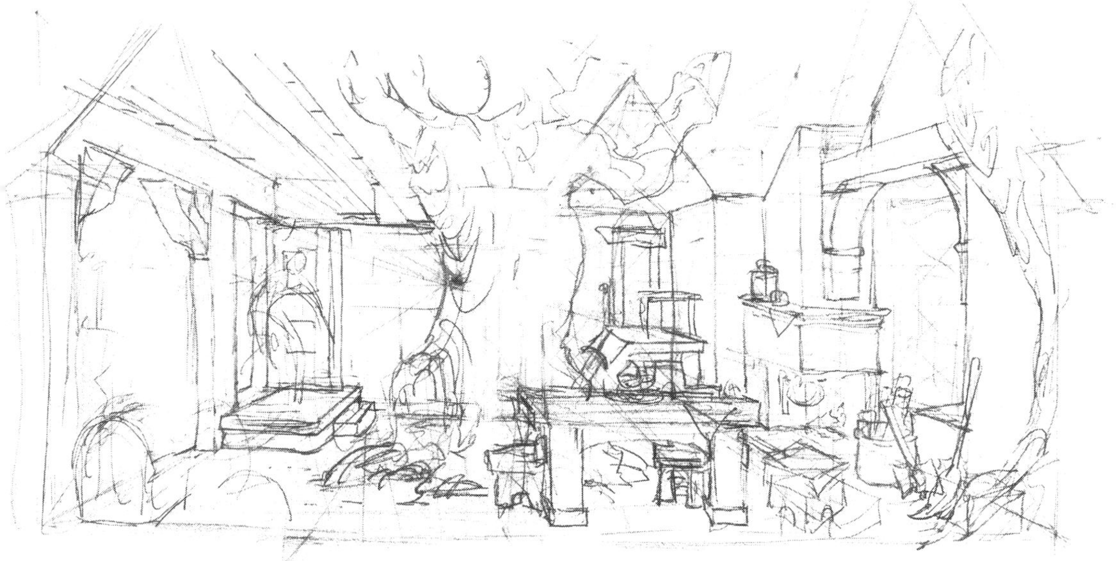

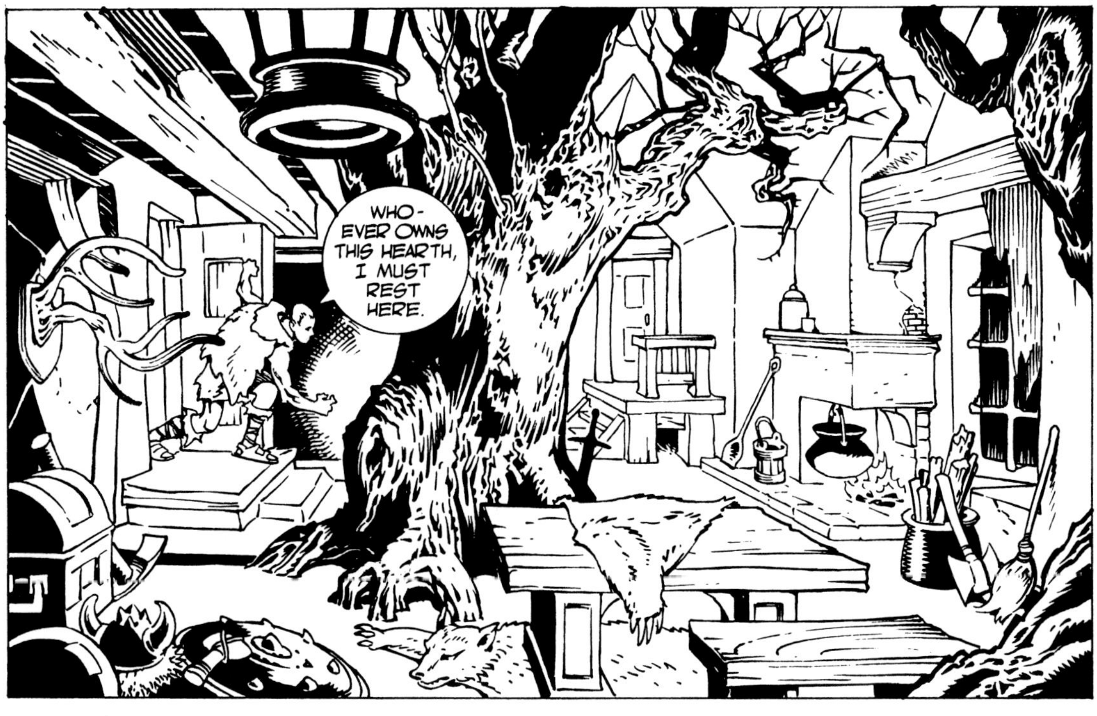
WHO-EVER OWNS THIS HEARTH, I MUST REST HERE.

Drawings of a younger Voton were done to render the mature character more credible and believable, giving the artist a more thorough grasp of the All Father. The original drawing is 11"x17".

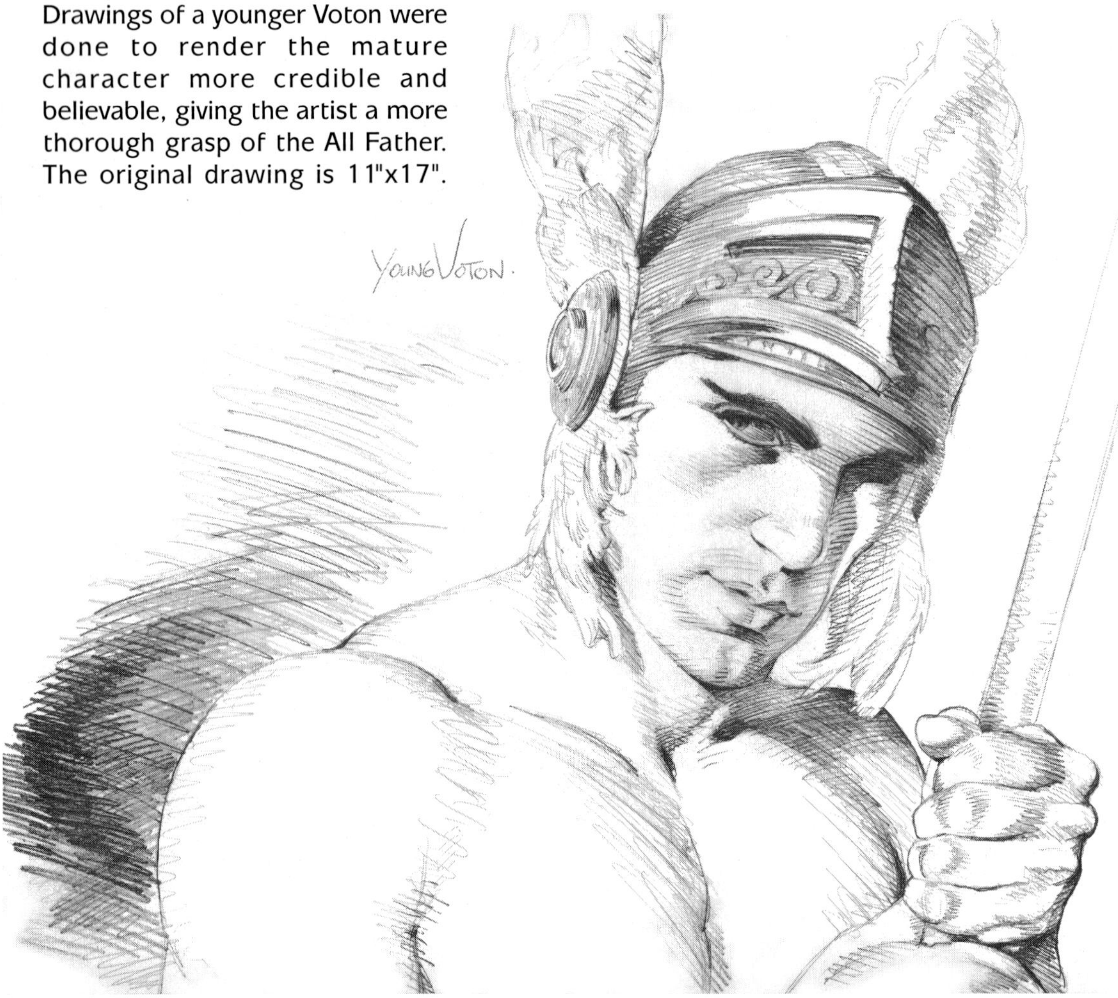
YOUNG VOTON.

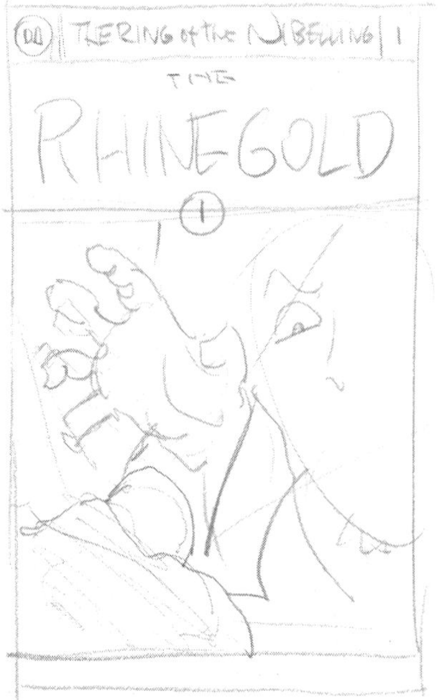
THE RING of the NIBELUNG 1
THE
RHINEGOLD
1

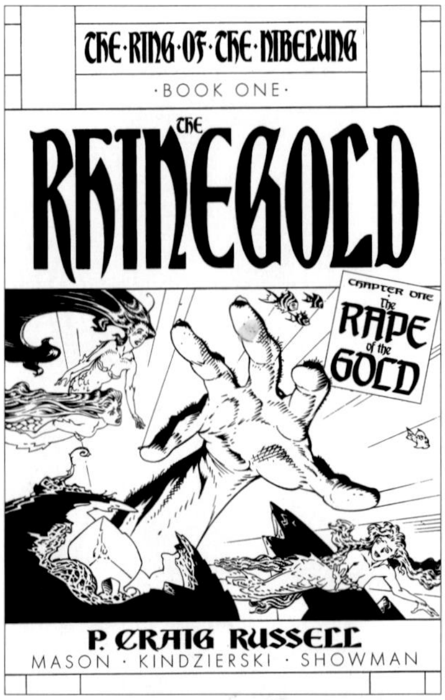
THE·RING·OF·THE·NIBELUNG
·BOOK ONE·
THE
RHINEGOLD
CHAPTER ONE
The
RAPE
of the
GOLD
P. CRAIG RUSSELL
MASON · KINDZIERSKI · SHOWMAN

Thumbnail sketches of covers provide a basic concept, which remains in the finished drawing, though greatly modified and expanded upon.

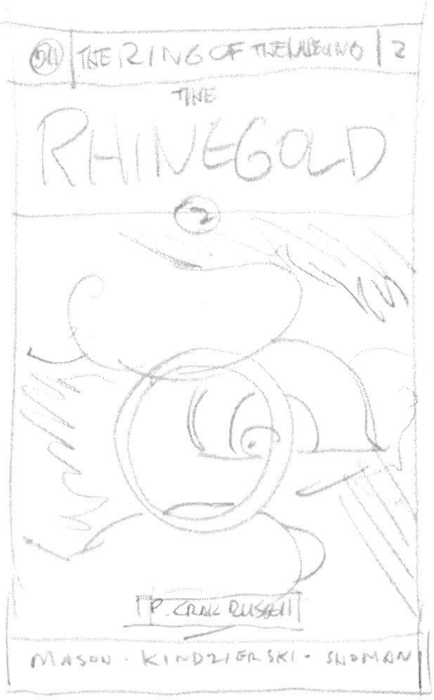
THE RING OF THE NIBELUNG
THE
RHINEGOLD
MASON · KINDZIERSKI · SHOWMAN

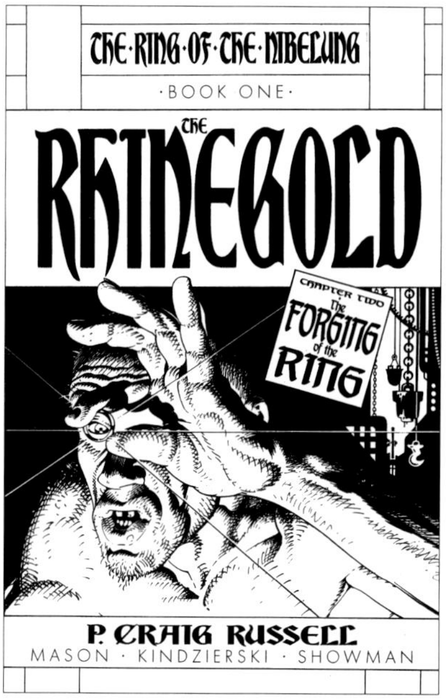
THE·RING·OF·THE·NIBELUNG
·BOOK ONE·
THE
RHINEGOLD
CHAPTER TWO
The
FORGING
of the
RING
P. CRAIG RUSSELL
MASON · KINDZIERSKI · SHOWMAN

P. Craig Russell prefers to produce the cover after the interiors have been completed. In this way a wealth of fully dramatized situations and characters can be drawn upon.

This is an early drawing of Donner, where the artist defined the look for his own God of Thunder.

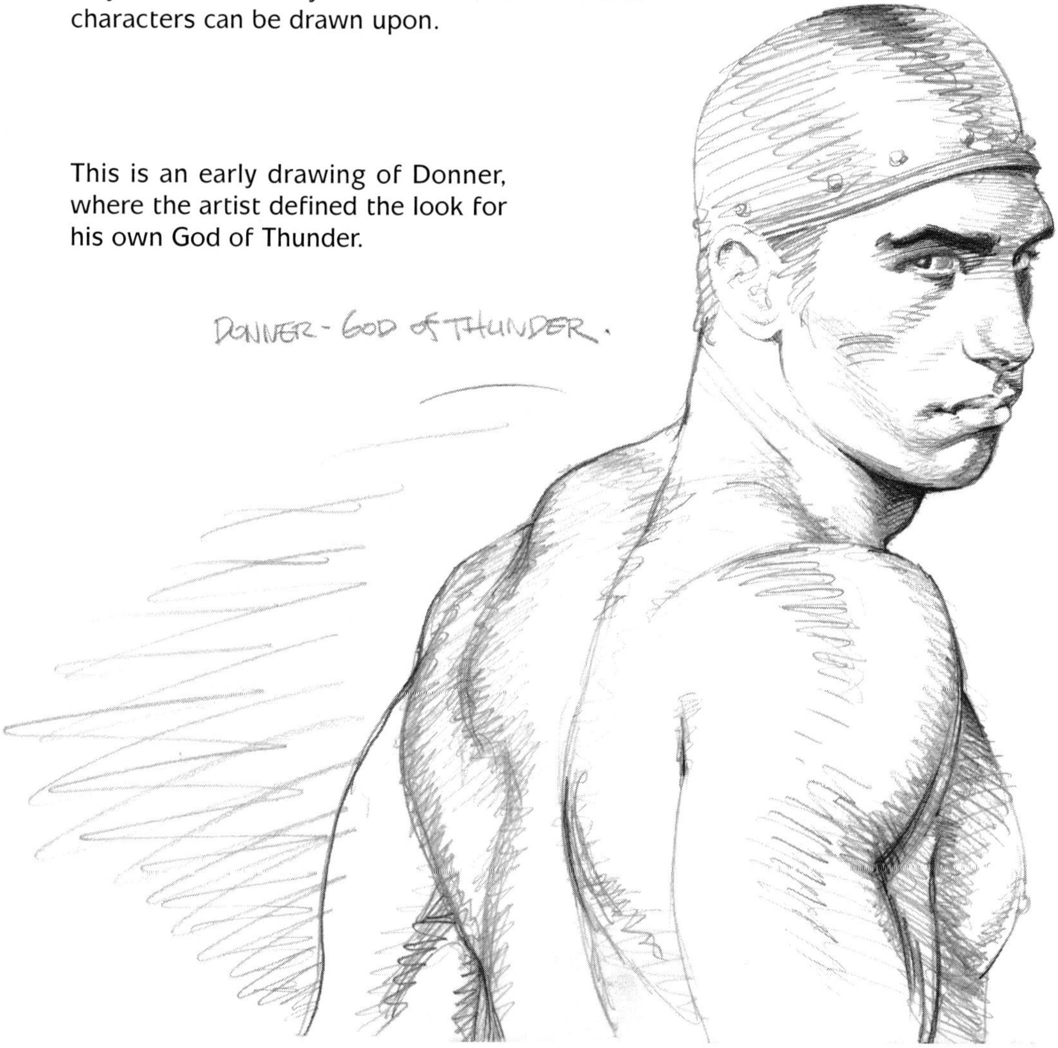
DONNER - GOD OF THUNDER.

THIS PAGE: These two drawings of Siegried were drawn not for practice or warm-ups, but were done after the pages were already drawn. That is, they were drawn for the fun of it.

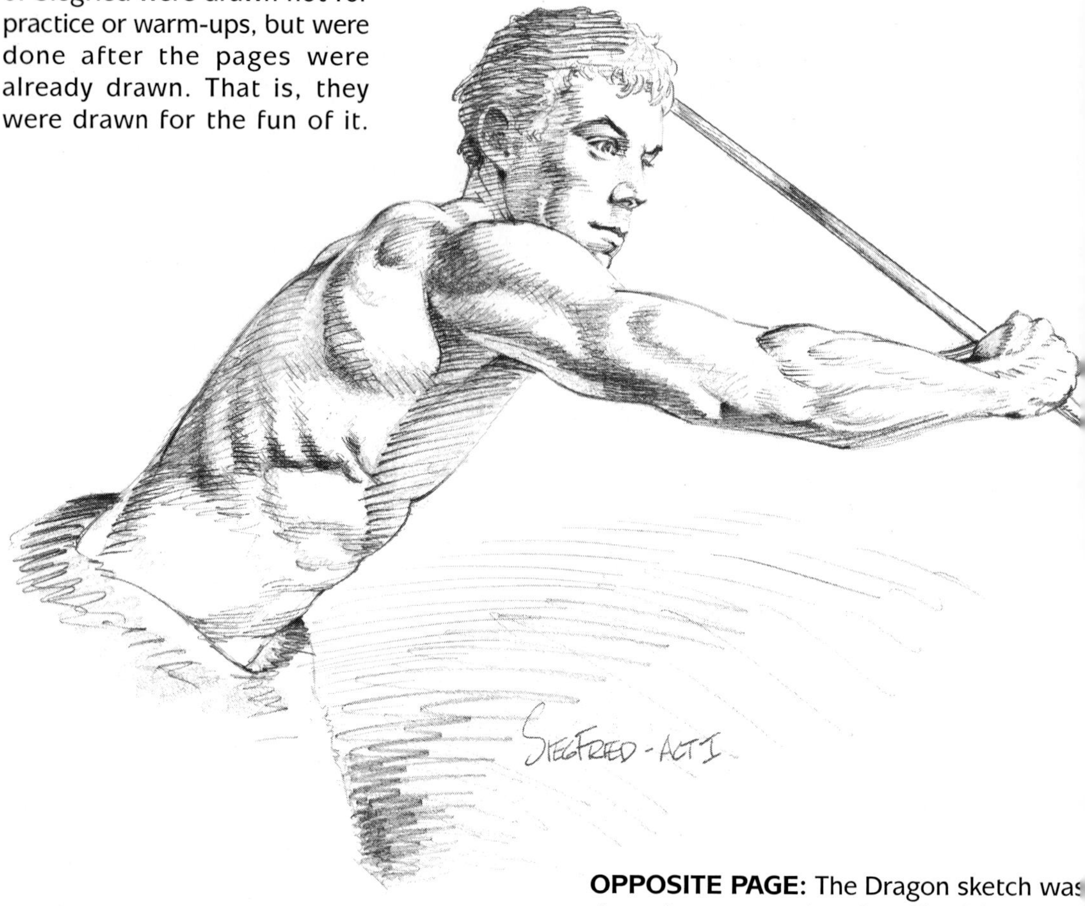
SIEGFRIED - ACT I

OPPOSITE PAGE: The Dragon sketch was done in preparation for *Siegfried*, Part One, in a flashback scene done in pencil. It also worked as an emblematic image to decorate the back cover, so the artist redrew and inked it.

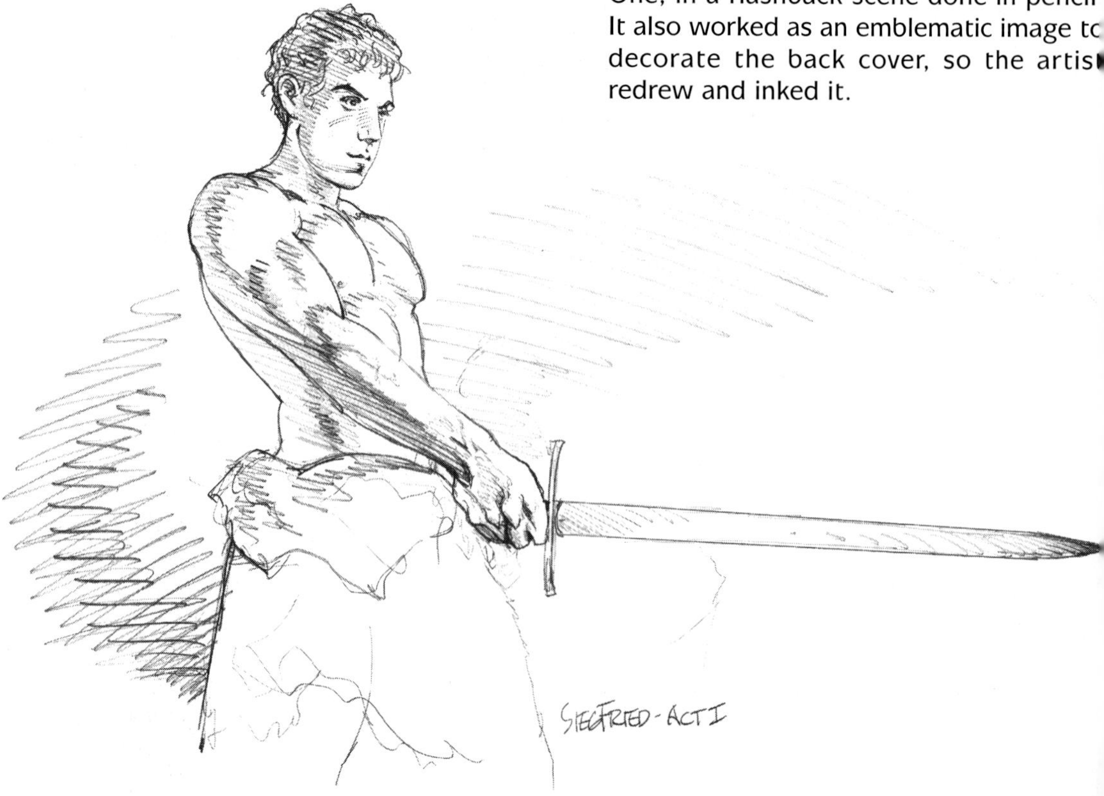
SIEGFRIED - ACT I

For dramatic poses, the artist often relies on models, so there is even an element of casting involved in *The Ring of the Nibelung*. Finding the right model is a combination of luck, friends of friends, and serendipity. P. Craig Russell had been trying to find a model for the giants Fasolt and Fafner for weeks, with several possibilities in mind. Any of them would do, but none were stellar. Then one day, as he stood talking to a friend in the local news shop, Frank, a "mountain" of a man, walked in.

"He stopped to listen, and I realized he knew the guy I was talking to," Russell recalls. "But it was only when I got home that I realized I'd met my giant." Several phone calls later, he'd made contact, and found an ex-cop comics fan who was quite willing to be twin giants, *and* turned out to be a natural actor.

"In working with models, I've occasionally drawn from life, but in a project of any scope it's impractical." Sometimes it's downright impossible to ask a model to hold a pose for the required length of time. So the camera becomes an essential tool. Through the course of *The Ring* project, the artist will take literally thousands of photos in preparation. In working with a camera, Russell will sometimes take several slightly different shots of the same pose. "Although I can do a lot to add expression in the final drawing, the model's ability to get into a role can be invaluable. Frank was great."

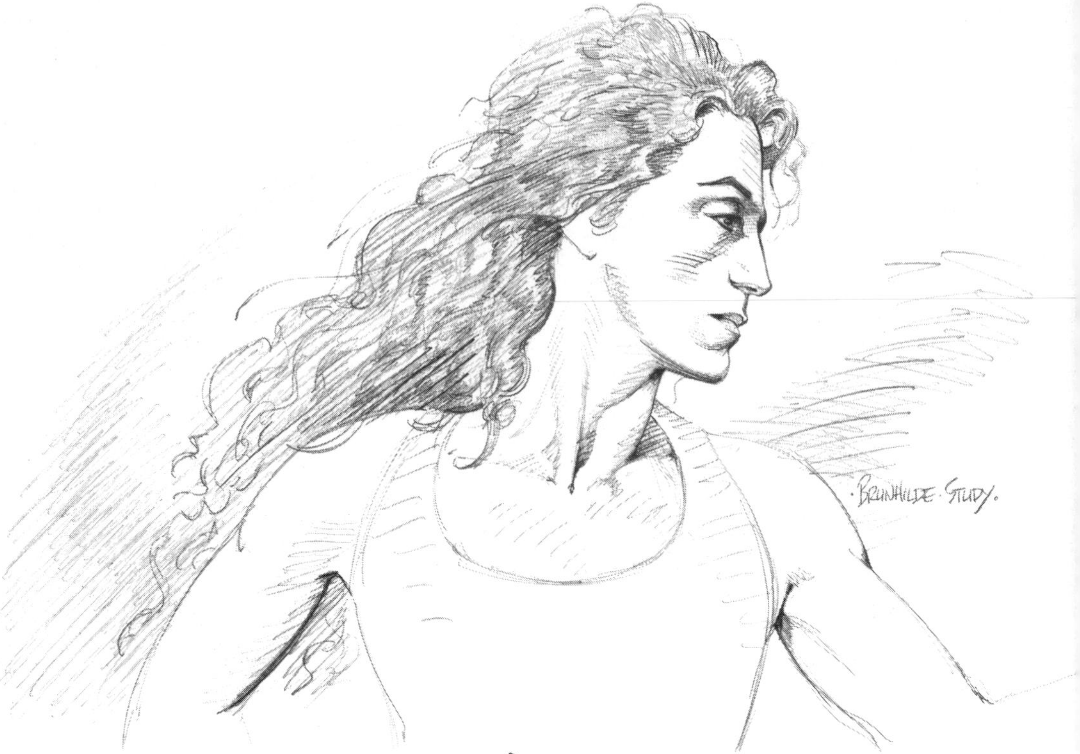
BRUNHILDE STUDY.

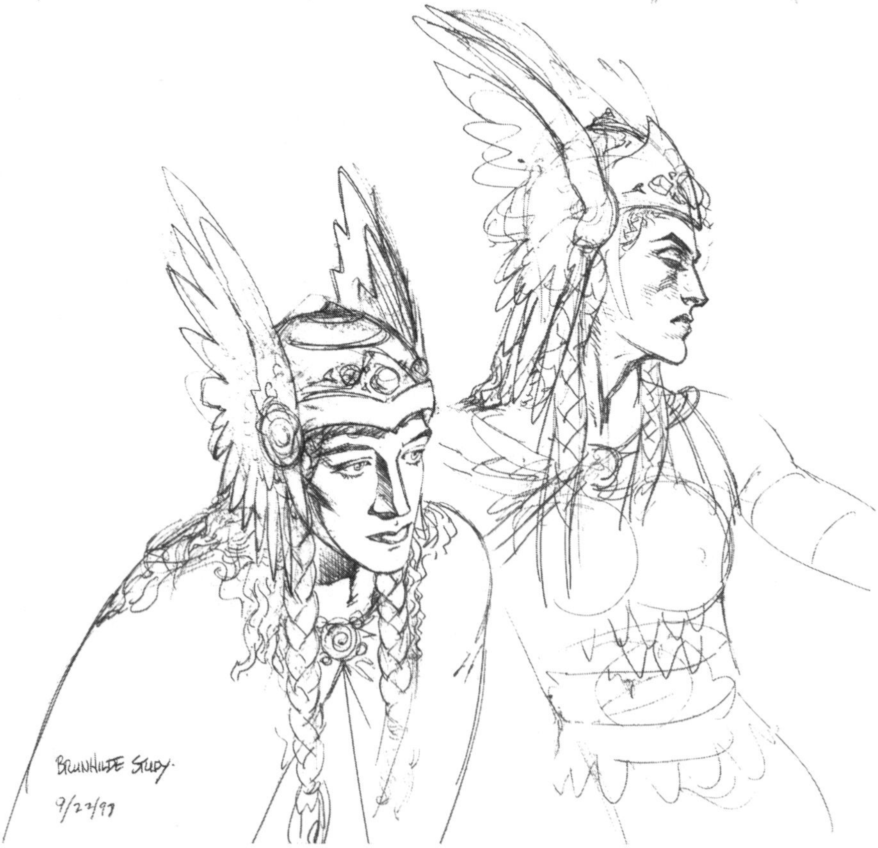
BRUNHILDE STUDY.
9/22/99

Casting about for a Brunhilde model, the artist hit upon Jill Thompson, the creator of *Scar* *Godmother*, a masterful combination comic/children's book from Sirius Publishing. Thompso was also the model for the Queen of the Night in Russell's adaptation of *The Magic Flute* and has "appeared" in other assorted projects. The studies above were the firs character/costume sketches produced for *The Ring of the Nibelung*.

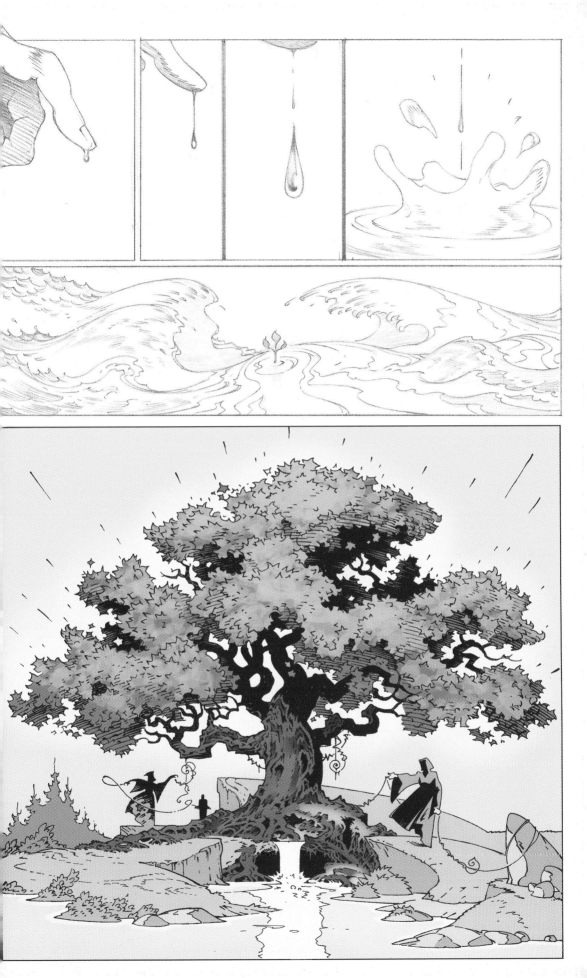

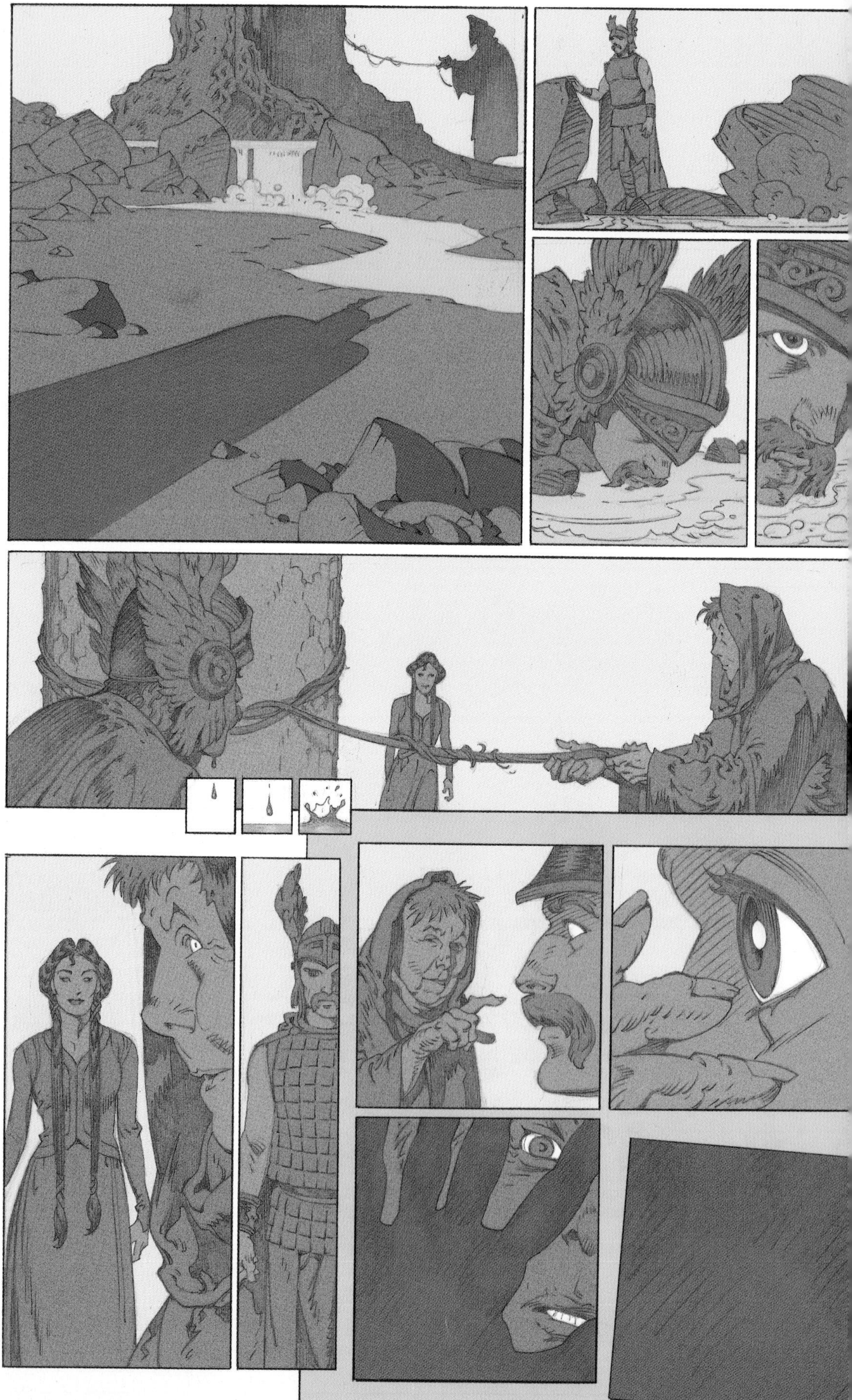

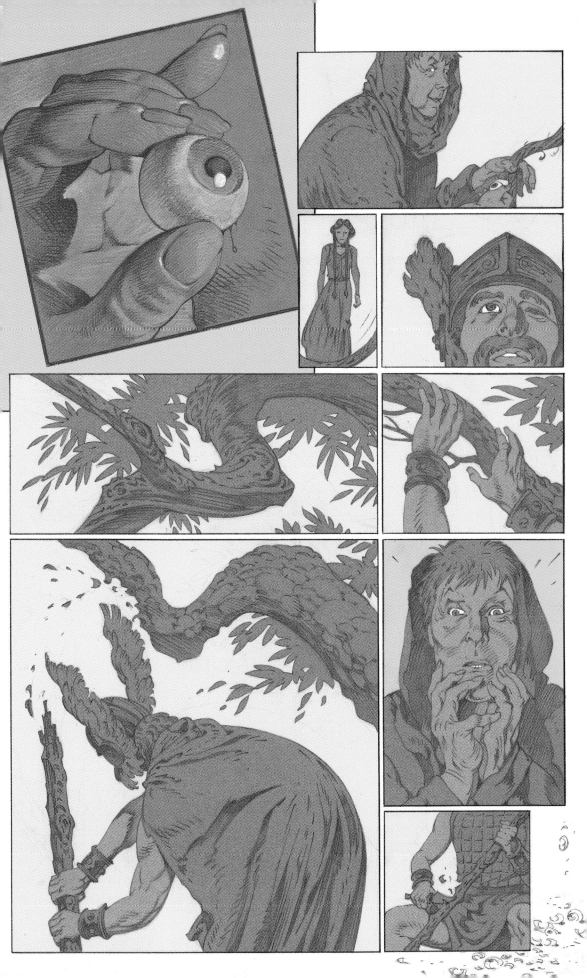

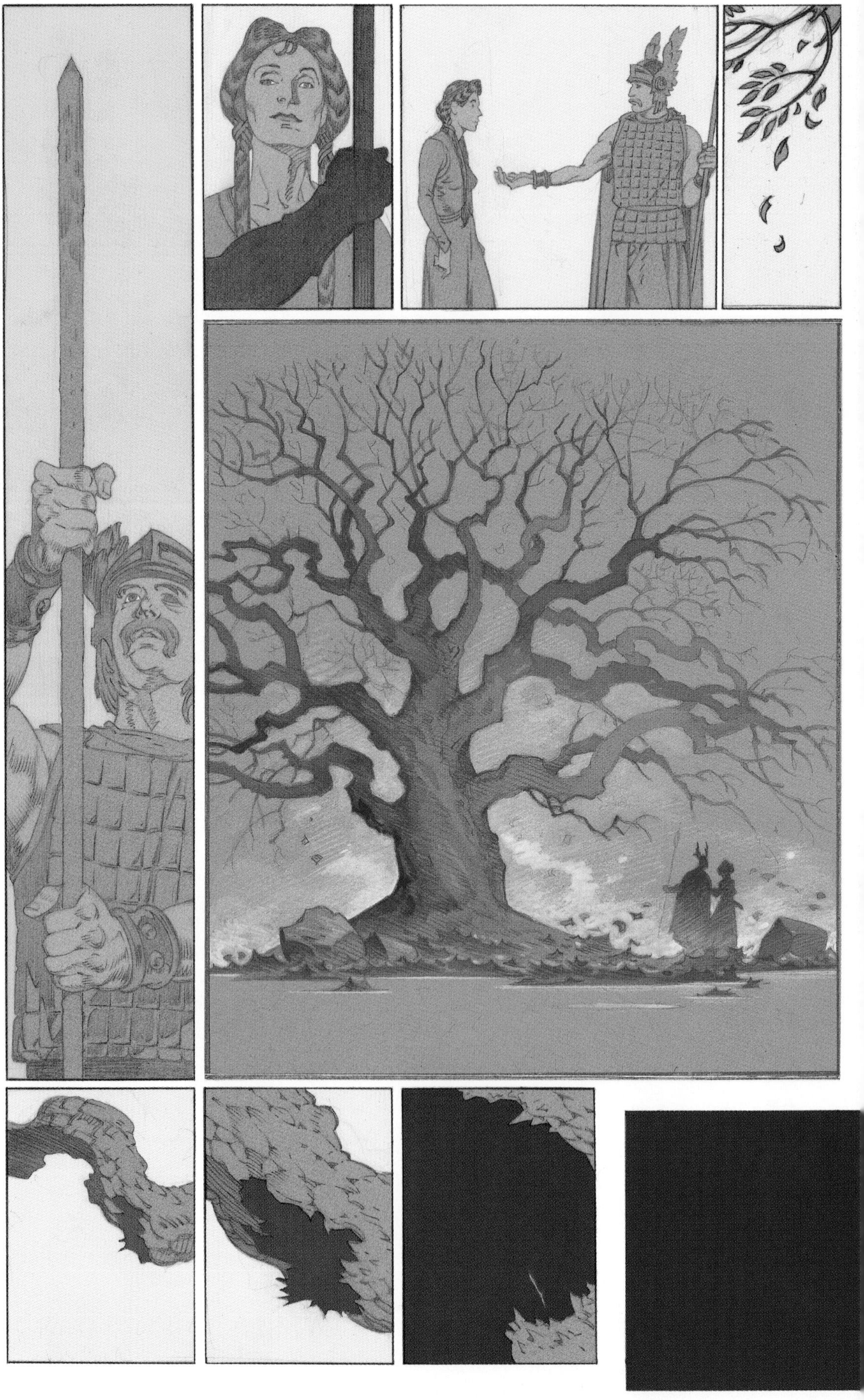

THE RING OF THE NIBELUNG

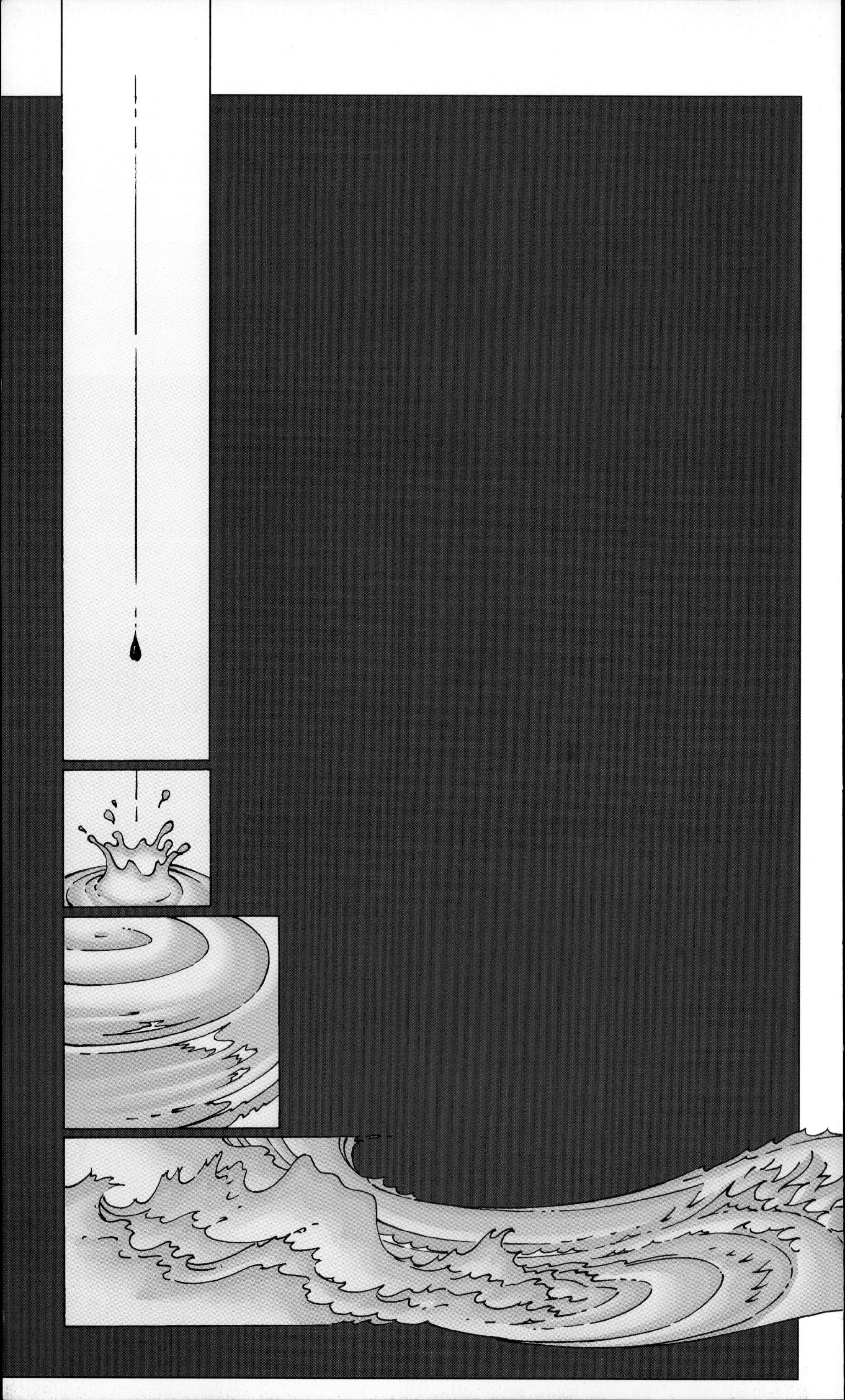

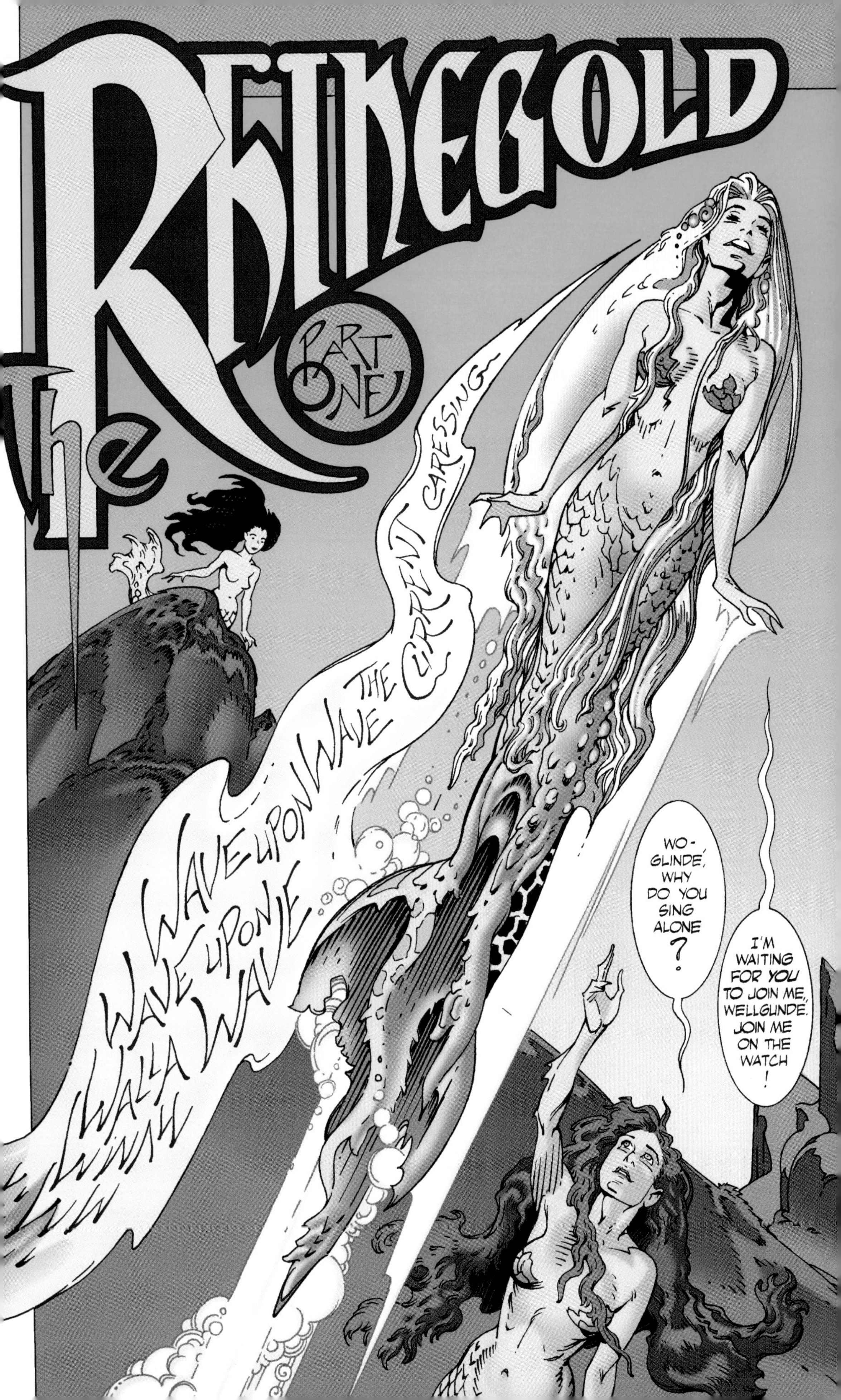

THE RHINEGOLD
PART ONE
WAVE UPON WAVE THE CURRENT CARESSING
WAVE UPON WAVE
WALLA WAVE
WO-GLINDE, WHY DO YOU SING ALONE?
I'M WAITING FOR *YOU* TO JOIN ME, WELLGUNDE. JOIN ME ON THE WATCH!

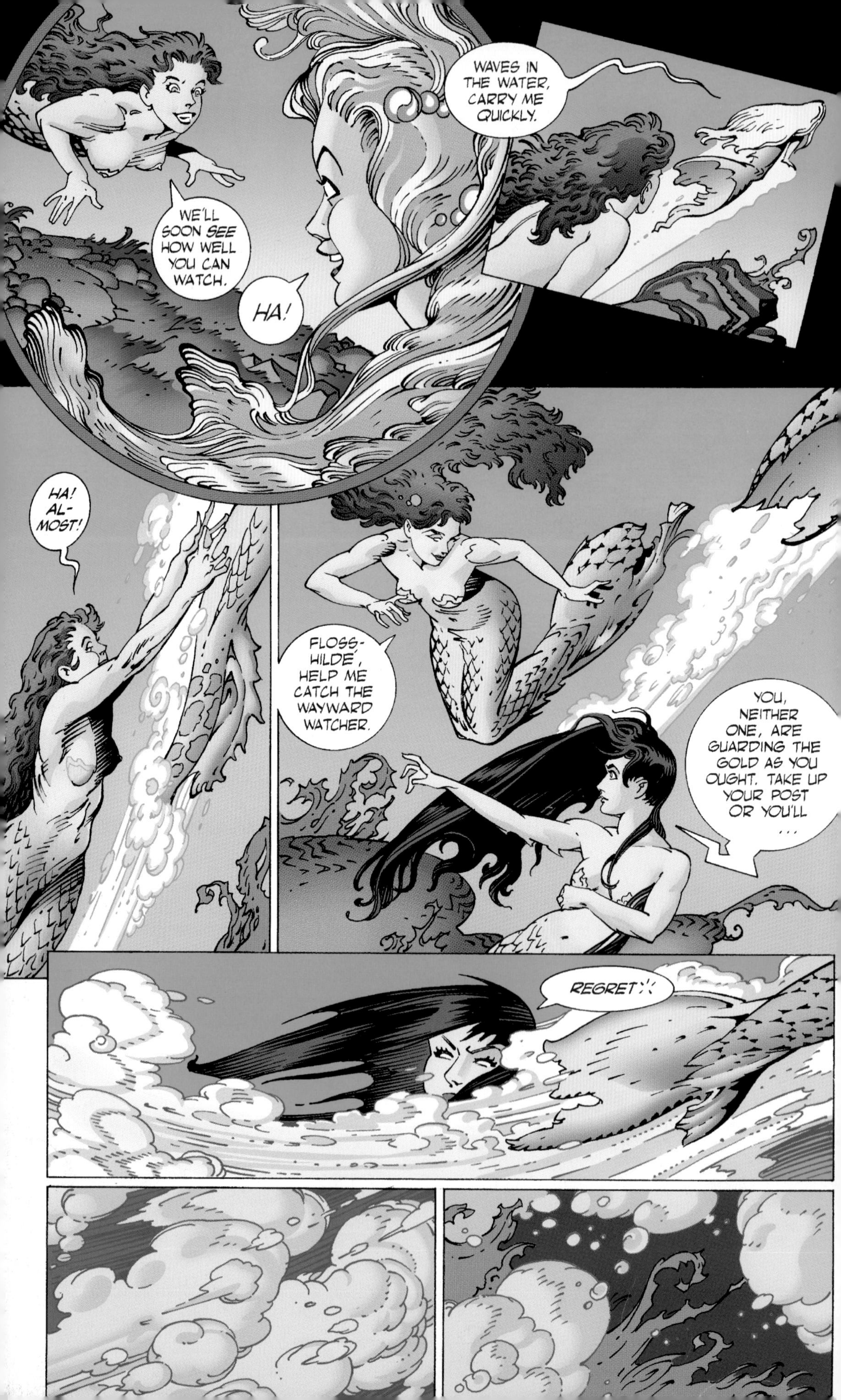
WAVES IN THE WATER, CARRY ME QUICKLY.
WE'LL SOON SEE HOW WELL YOU CAN WATCH.
HA!
HA! AL-MOST!
FLOSS-HILDE, HELP ME CATCH THE WAYWARD WATCHER.
YOU, NEITHER ONE, ARE GUARDING THE GOLD AS YOU OUGHT. TAKE UP YOUR POST OR YOU'LL ...
REGRET!

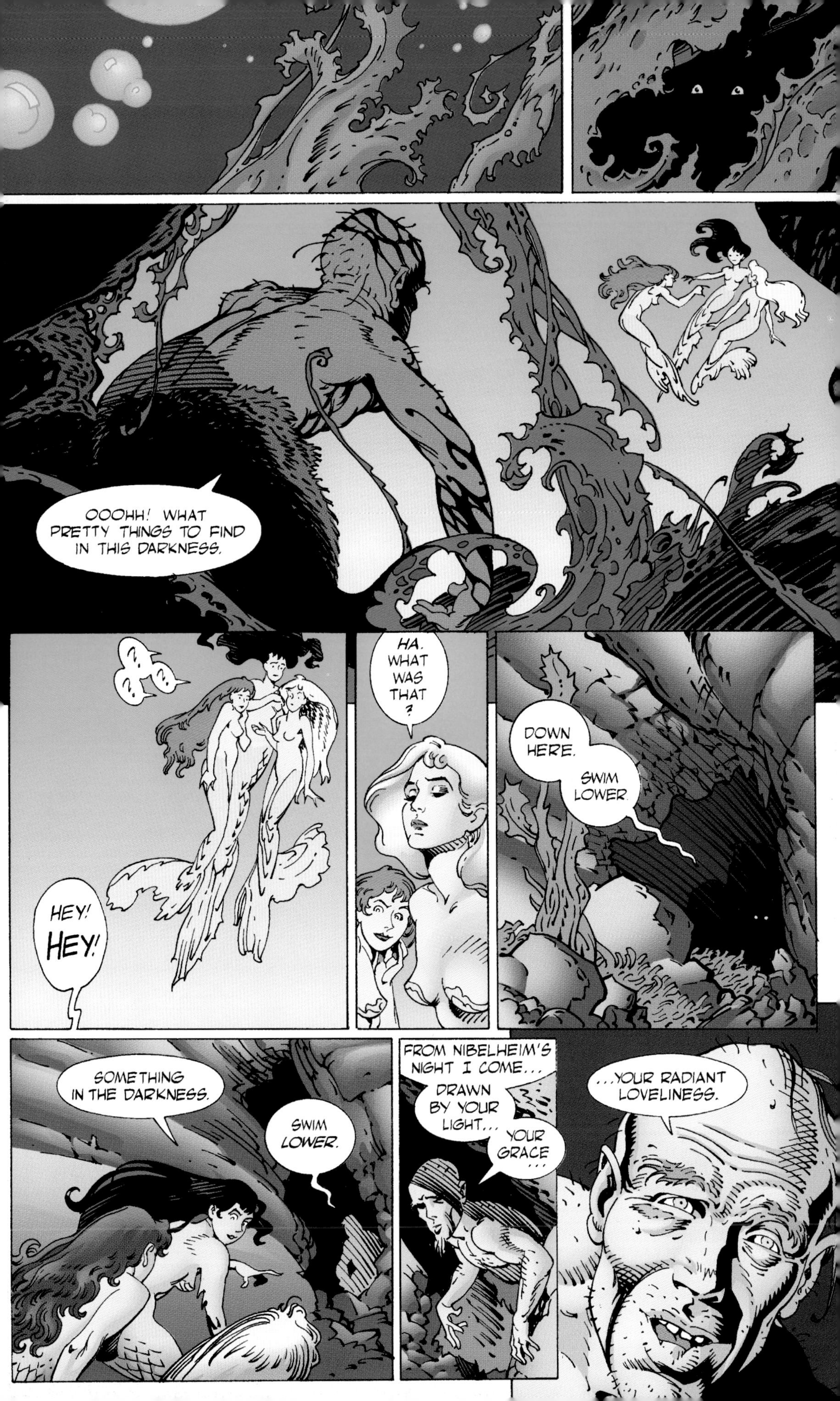
OOOHH! WHAT PRETTY THINGS TO FIND IN THIS DARKNESS.
? ? ?
HEY! HEY!
HA. WHAT WAS THAT ?
DOWN HERE.
SWIM LOWER.
SOMETHING IN THE DARKNESS.
SWIM LOWER.
FROM NIBELHEIM'S NIGHT I COME...
DRAWN BY YOUR LIGHT...
YOUR GRACE...
...YOUR RADIANT LOVELINESS.

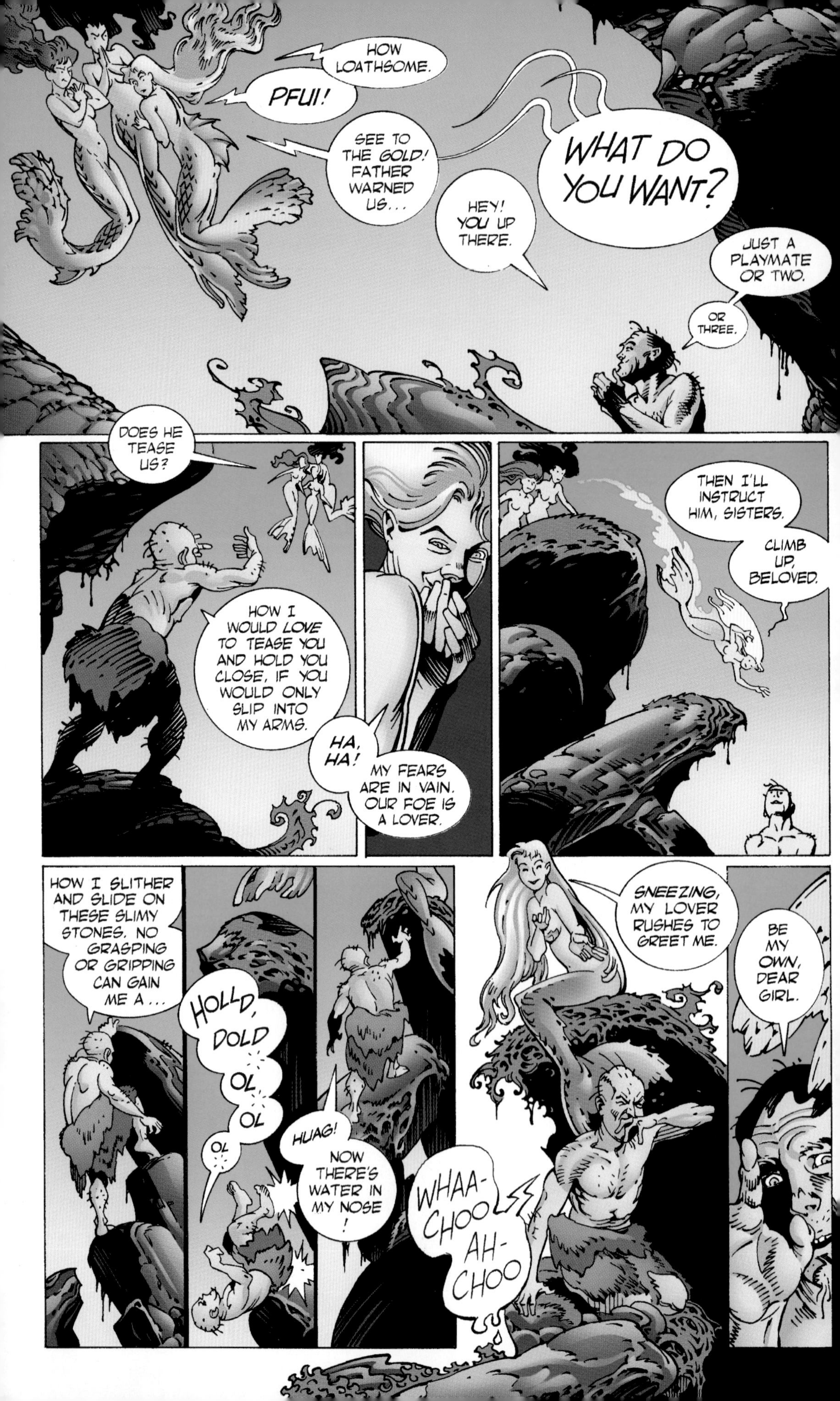
HOW LOATHSOME.
PFUI!
SEE TO THE GOLD! FATHER WARNED US...
HEY! YOU UP THERE.
WHAT DO YOU WANT?
JUST A PLAYMATE OR TWO.
OR THREE.
DOES HE TEASE US?
HOW I WOULD LOVE TO TEASE YOU AND HOLD YOU CLOSE, IF YOU WOULD ONLY SLIP INTO MY ARMS.
HA, HA!
MY FEARS ARE IN VAIN. OUR FOE IS A LOVER.
THEN I'LL INSTRUCT HIM, SISTERS.
CLIMB UP, BELOVED.
HOW I SLITHER AND SLIDE ON THESE SLIMY STONES. NO GRASPING OR GRIPPING CAN GAIN ME A...
HOLLD, DOLD OL OL OL
HUAG!
NOW THERE'S WATER IN MY NOSE!
WHAA-CHOO AH-CHOO
SNEEZING, MY LOVER RUSHES TO GREET ME.
BE MY OWN, DEAR GIRL.

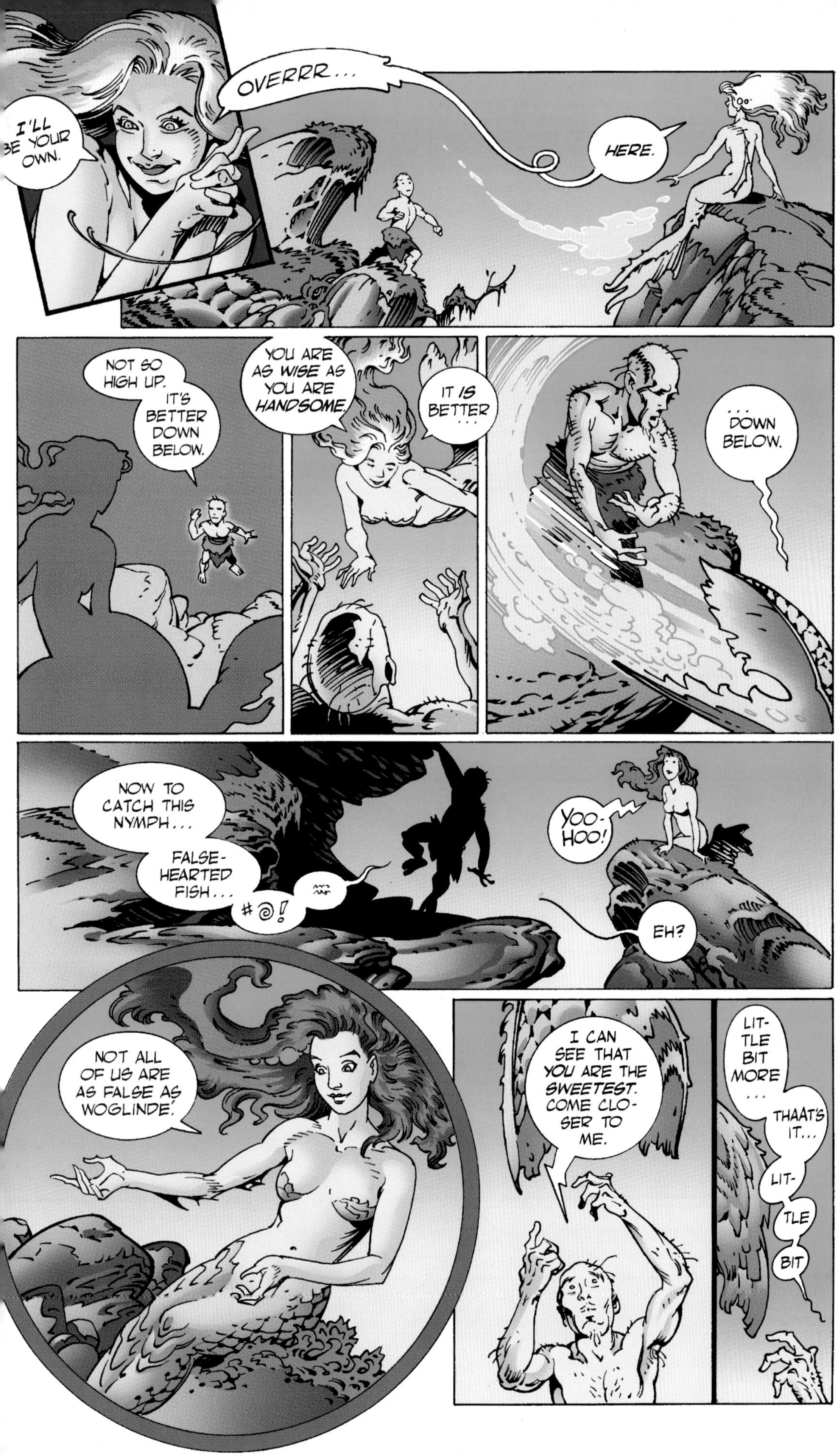

I'LL BE YOUR OWN.
OVERRR...
HERE.
NOT SO HIGH UP.
IT'S BETTER DOWN BELOW.
YOU ARE AS WISE AS YOU ARE HANDSOME.
IT IS BETTER ...
... DOWN BELOW.
NOW TO CATCH THIS NYMPH...
FALSE-HEARTED FISH...
#@!
YOO-HOO!
EH?
NOT ALL OF US ARE AS FALSE AS WOGLINDE.
I CAN SEE THAT YOU ARE THE SWEETEST. COME CLO-SER TO ME.
LIT-TLE BIT MORE ...
THAAT'S IT...
LIT-TLE BIT

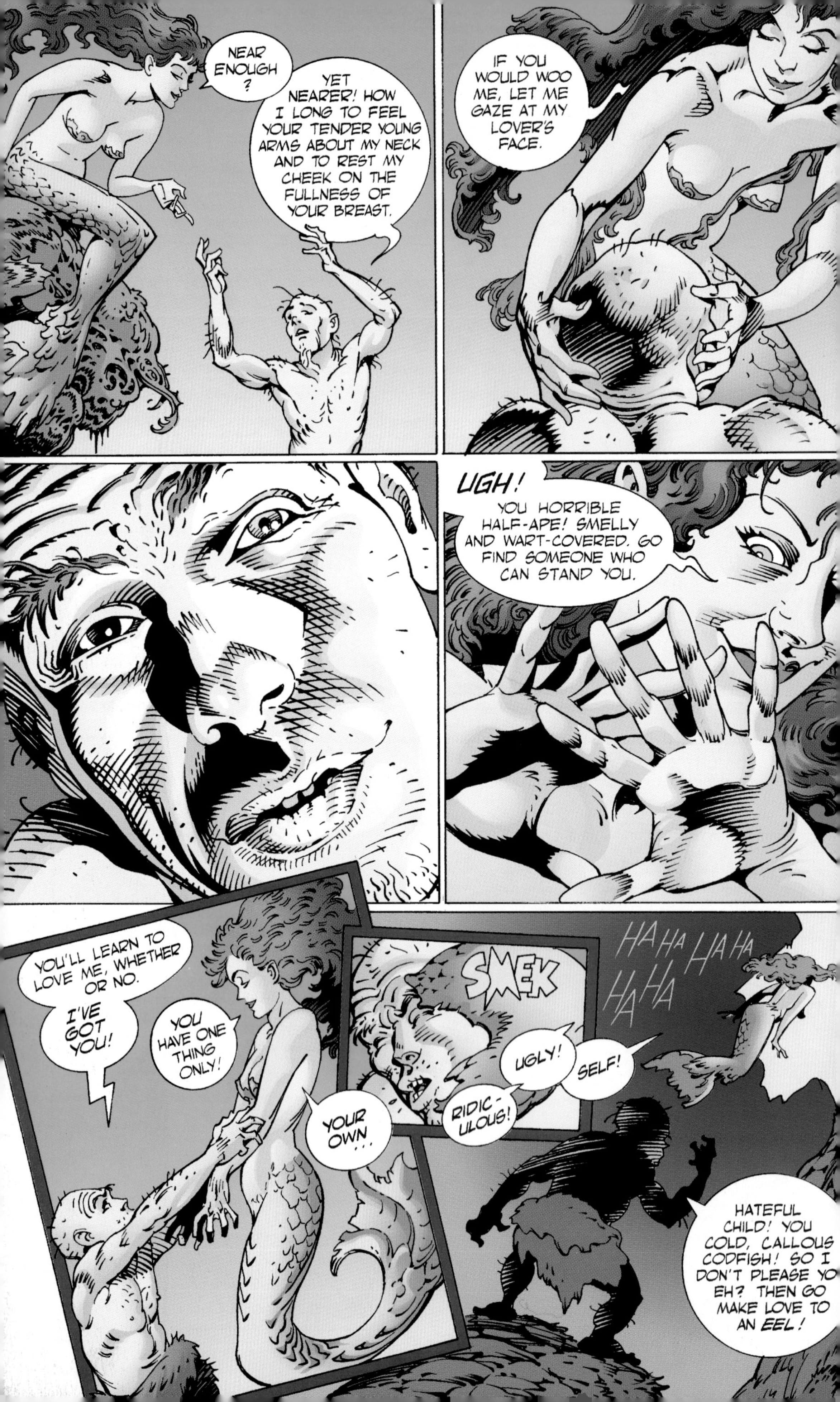

NEAR ENOUGH?
YET NEARER! HOW I LONG TO FEEL YOUR TENDER YOUNG ARMS ABOUT MY NECK AND TO REST MY CHEEK ON THE FULLNESS OF YOUR BREAST.
IF YOU WOULD WOO ME, LET ME GAZE AT MY LOVER'S FACE.
UGH!
YOU HORRIBLE HALF-APE! SMELLY AND WART-COVERED. GO FIND SOMEONE WHO CAN STAND YOU.
YOU'LL LEARN TO LOVE ME, WHETHER OR NO.
I'VE GOT YOU!
YOU HAVE ONE THING ONLY!
YOUR OWN...
SMEK
UGLY!
RIDIC-ULOUS!
SELF!
HA HA HA HA HA HA
HATEFUL CHILD! YOU COLD, CALLOUS CODFISH! SO I DON'T PLEASE YO EH? THEN GO MAKE LOVE TO AN EEL!

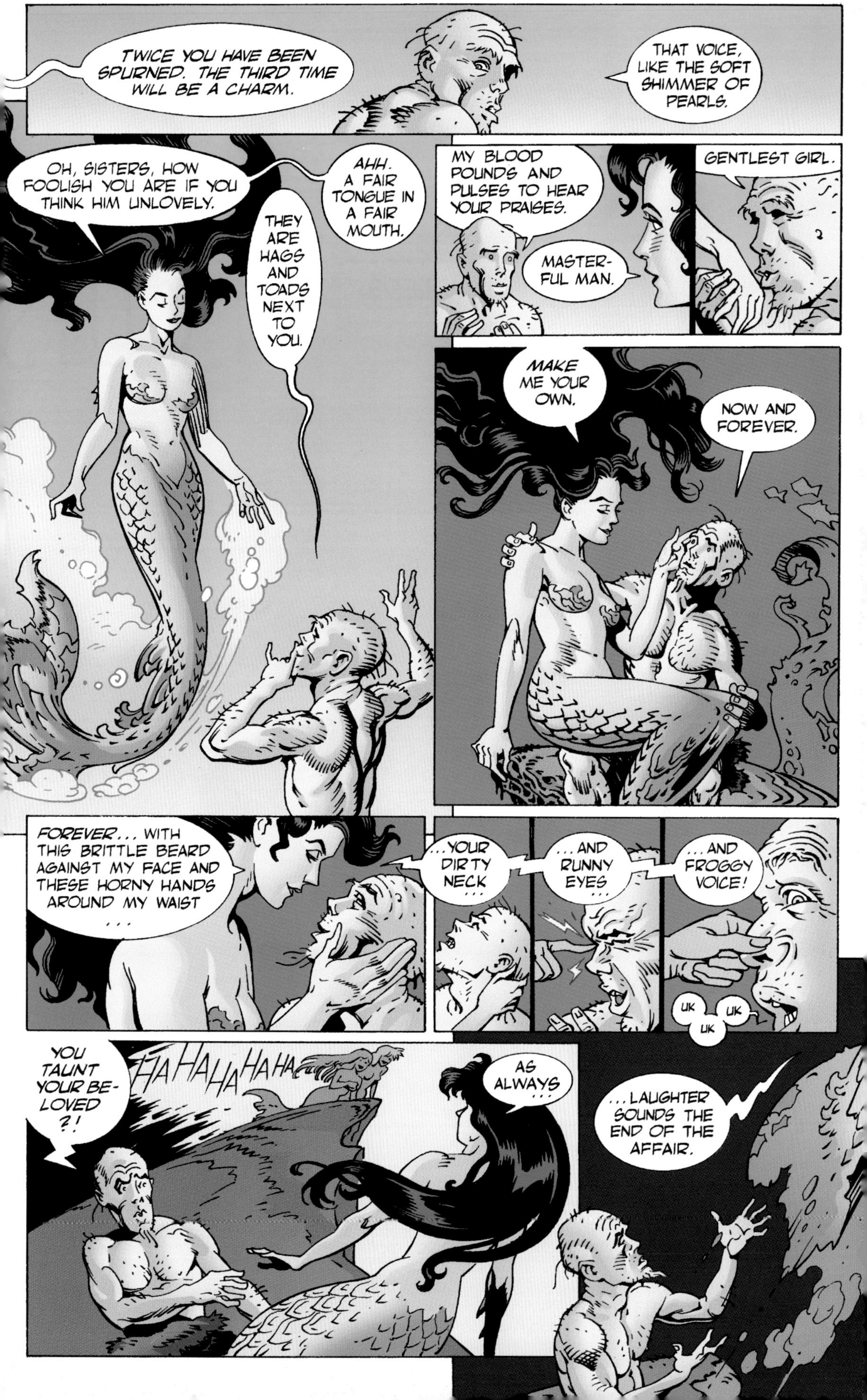
TWICE YOU HAVE BEEN SPURNED. THE THIRD TIME WILL BE A CHARM.
THAT VOICE, LIKE THE SOFT SHIMMER OF PEARLS.
OH, SISTERS, HOW FOOLISH YOU ARE IF YOU THINK HIM UNLOVELY.
AHH. A FAIR TONGUE IN A FAIR MOUTH.
THEY ARE HAGS AND TOADS NEXT TO YOU.
MY BLOOD POUNDS AND PULSES TO HEAR YOUR PRAISES.
MASTER-FUL MAN.
GENTLEST GIRL.
MAKE ME YOUR OWN.
NOW AND FOREVER.
FOREVER... WITH THIS BRITTLE BEARD AGAINST MY FACE AND THESE HORNY HANDS AROUND MY WAIST ...
...YOUR DIRTY NECK ...
...AND RUNNY EYES ...
...AND FROGGY VOICE!
UK
UK
UK
YOU TAUNT YOUR BE-LOVED ?!
HAHAHAHAHA
AS ALWAYS ...
...LAUGHTER SOUNDS THE END OF THE AFFAIR.

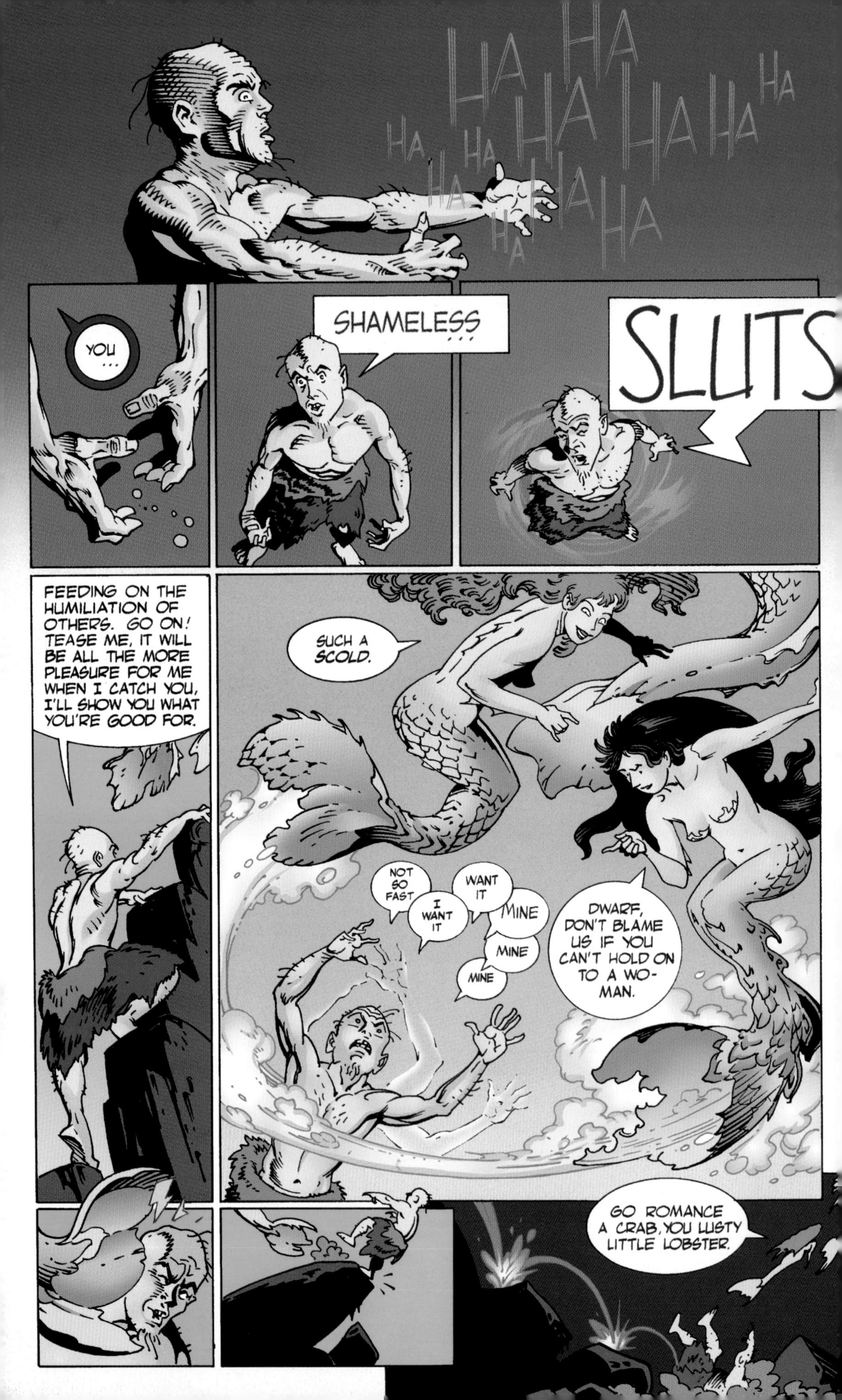

HA HA HA HA HA HA HA HA HA HA HA HA HA HA HA HA
YOU ...
SHAMELESS ...
SLUTS
FEEDING ON THE HUMILIATION OF OTHERS. GO ON! TEASE ME, IT WILL BE ALL THE MORE PLEASURE FOR ME WHEN I CATCH YOU, I'LL SHOW YOU WHAT YOU'RE GOOD FOR.
SUCH A SCOLD.
NOT SO FAST
I WANT IT
WANT IT
MINE
MINE
MINE
DWARF, DON'T BLAME US IF YOU CAN'T HOLD ON TO A WO-MAN.
GO ROMANCE A CRAB, YOU LUSTY LITTLE LOBSTER.

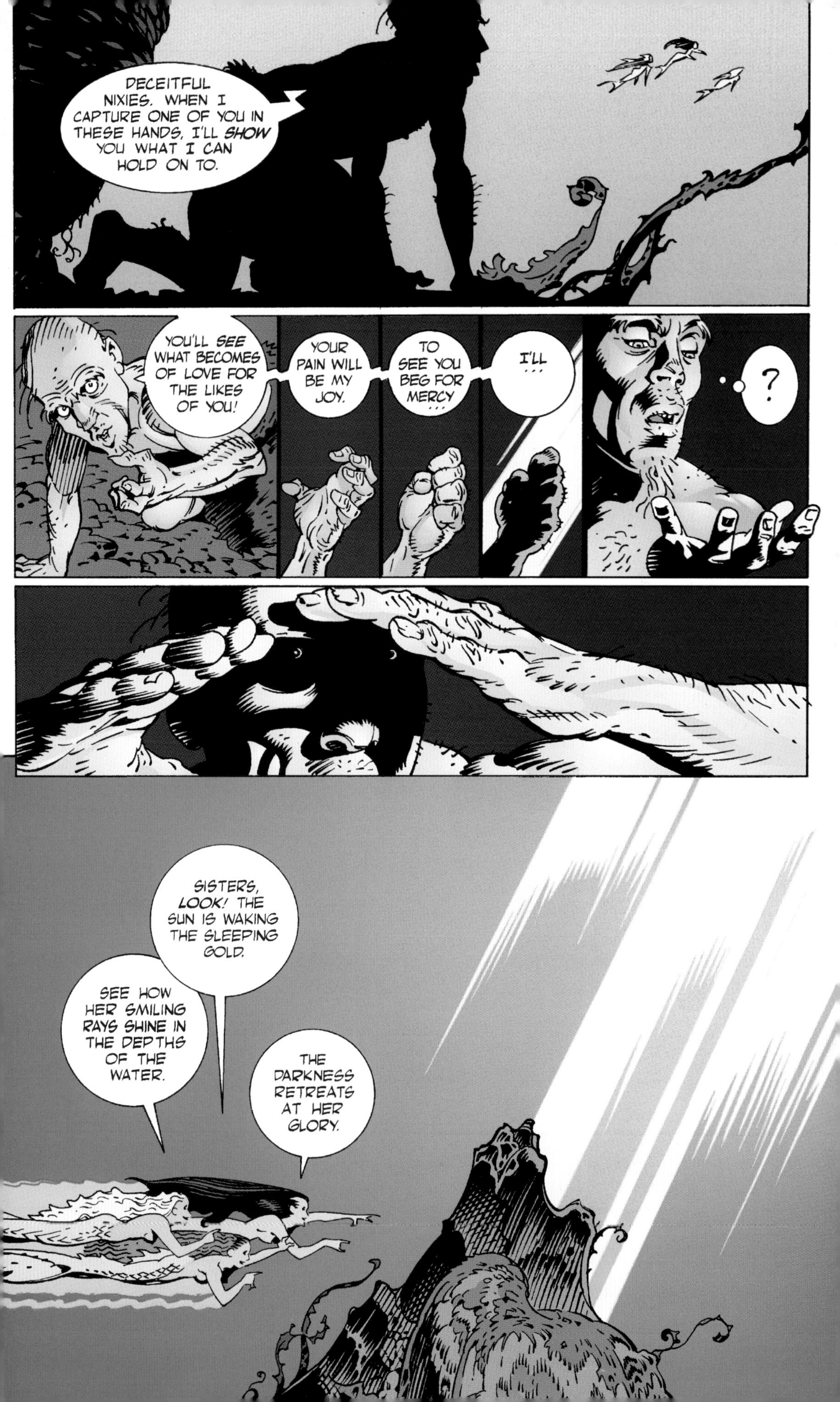
DECEITFUL NIXIES. WHEN I CAPTURE ONE OF YOU IN THESE HANDS, I'LL *SHOW* YOU WHAT I CAN HOLD ON TO.
YOU'LL *SEE* WHAT BECOMES OF LOVE FOR THE LIKES OF YOU!
YOUR PAIN WILL BE MY JOY.
TO SEE YOU BEG FOR MERCY...
I'LL...
?
SISTERS, *LOOK!* THE SUN IS WAKING THE SLEEPING GOLD.
SEE HOW HER SMILING RAYS SHINE IN THE DEPTHS OF THE WATER.
THE DARKNESS RETREATS AT HER GLORY.

NOW SHE KISSES THE SLEEPER'S EYES AWAKE...

"...SEE HOW HE SMILES AT HER TOUCH...

"...AND OPENING WIDE HIS ARMS, GREETS THE DAY WITH JOYFUL DELIGHT."

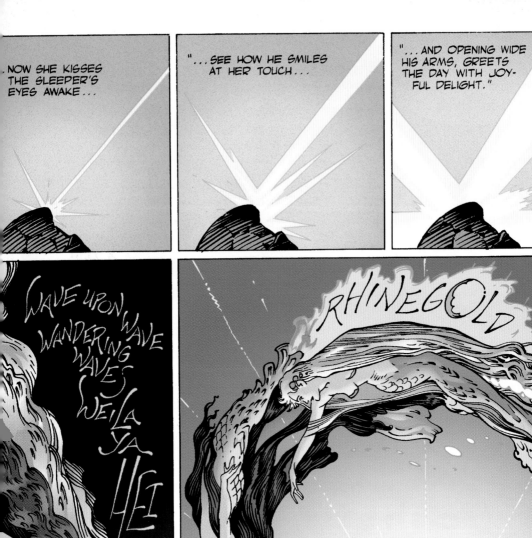

WAVE UPON WAVE WANDERING WAVES WEILA YA HEI

RHINEGOLD

RHINEGOLD

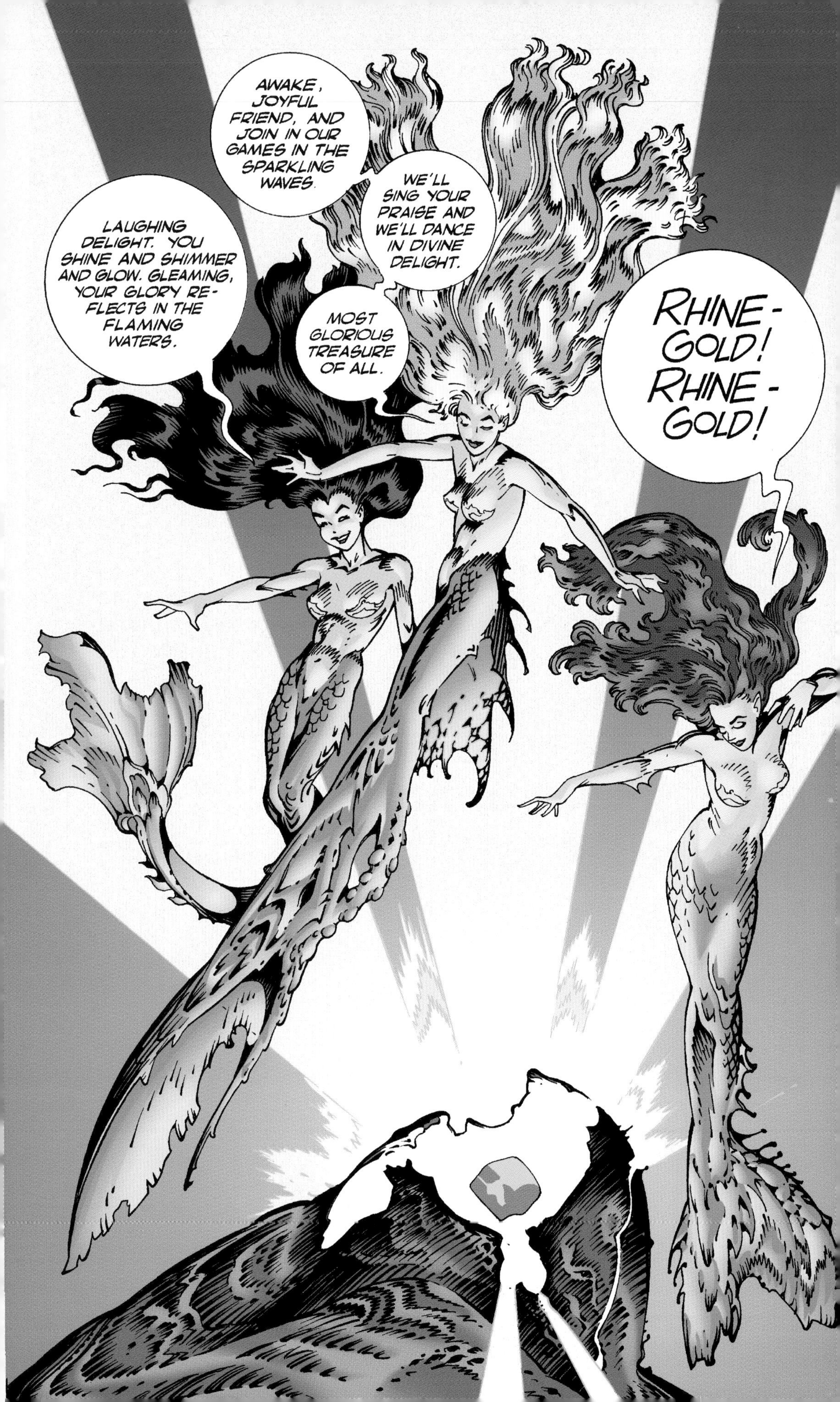
AWAKE, JOYFUL FRIEND, AND JOIN IN OUR GAMES IN THE SPARKLING WAVES.
WE'LL SING YOUR PRAISE AND WE'LL DANCE IN DIVINE DELIGHT.
LAUGHING DELIGHT. YOU SHINE AND SHIMMER AND GLOW. GLEAMING, YOUR GLORY RE-FLECTS IN THE FLAMING WATERS.
MOST GLORIOUS TREASURE OF ALL.
RHINE-GOLD! RHINE-GOLD!

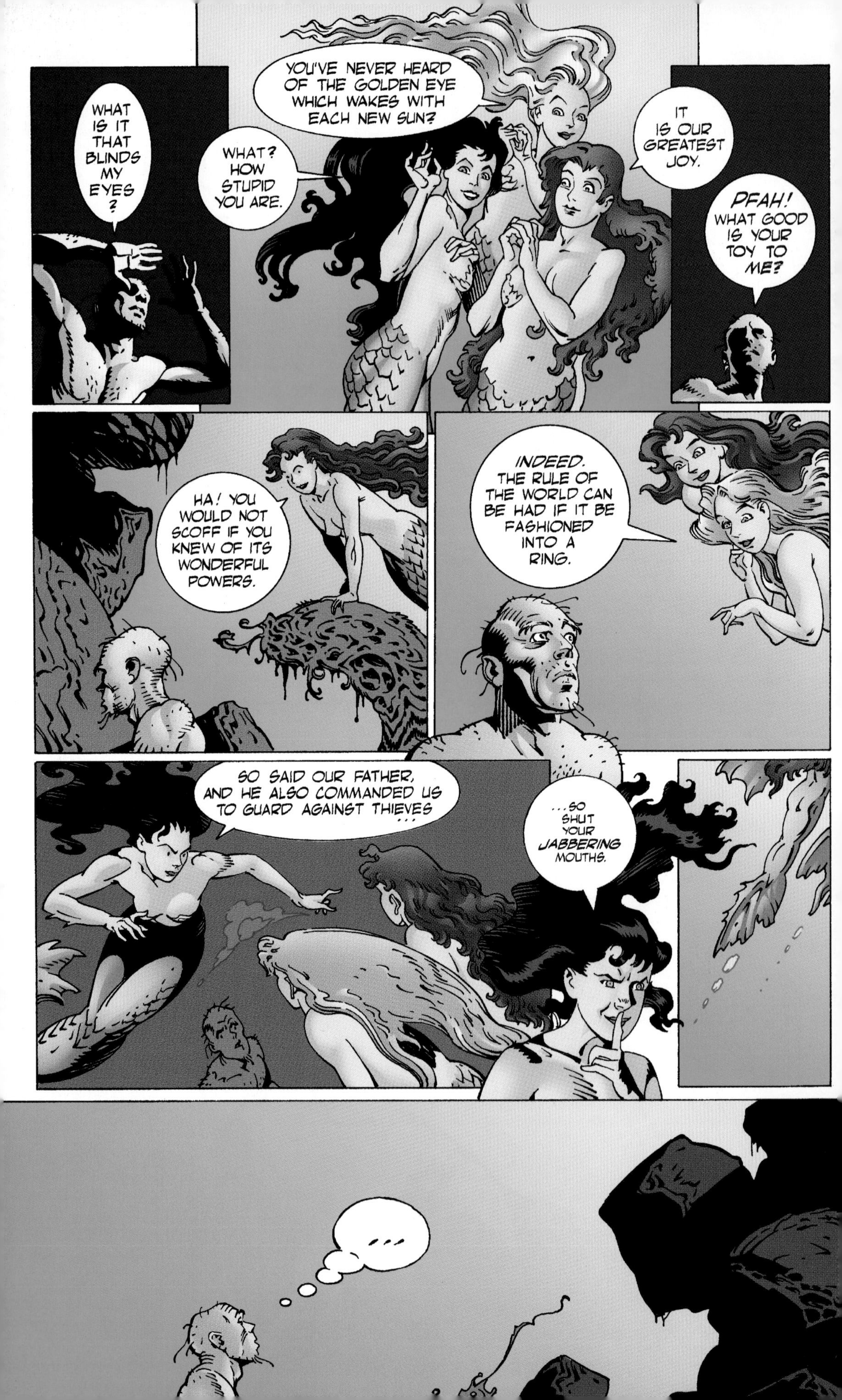

WHAT IS IT THAT BLINDS MY EYES?
YOU'VE NEVER HEARD OF THE GOLDEN EYE WHICH WAKES WITH EACH NEW SUN?
WHAT? HOW STUPID YOU ARE.
IT IS OUR GREATEST JOY.
PFAH! WHAT GOOD IS YOUR TOY TO ME?
HA! YOU WOULD NOT SCOFF IF YOU KNEW OF ITS WONDERFUL POWERS.
INDEED. THE RULE OF THE WORLD CAN BE HAD IF IT BE FASHIONED INTO A RING.
SO SAID OUR FATHER, AND HE ALSO COMMANDED US TO GUARD AGAINST THIEVES...
...SO SHUT YOUR JABBERING MOUTHS.
...

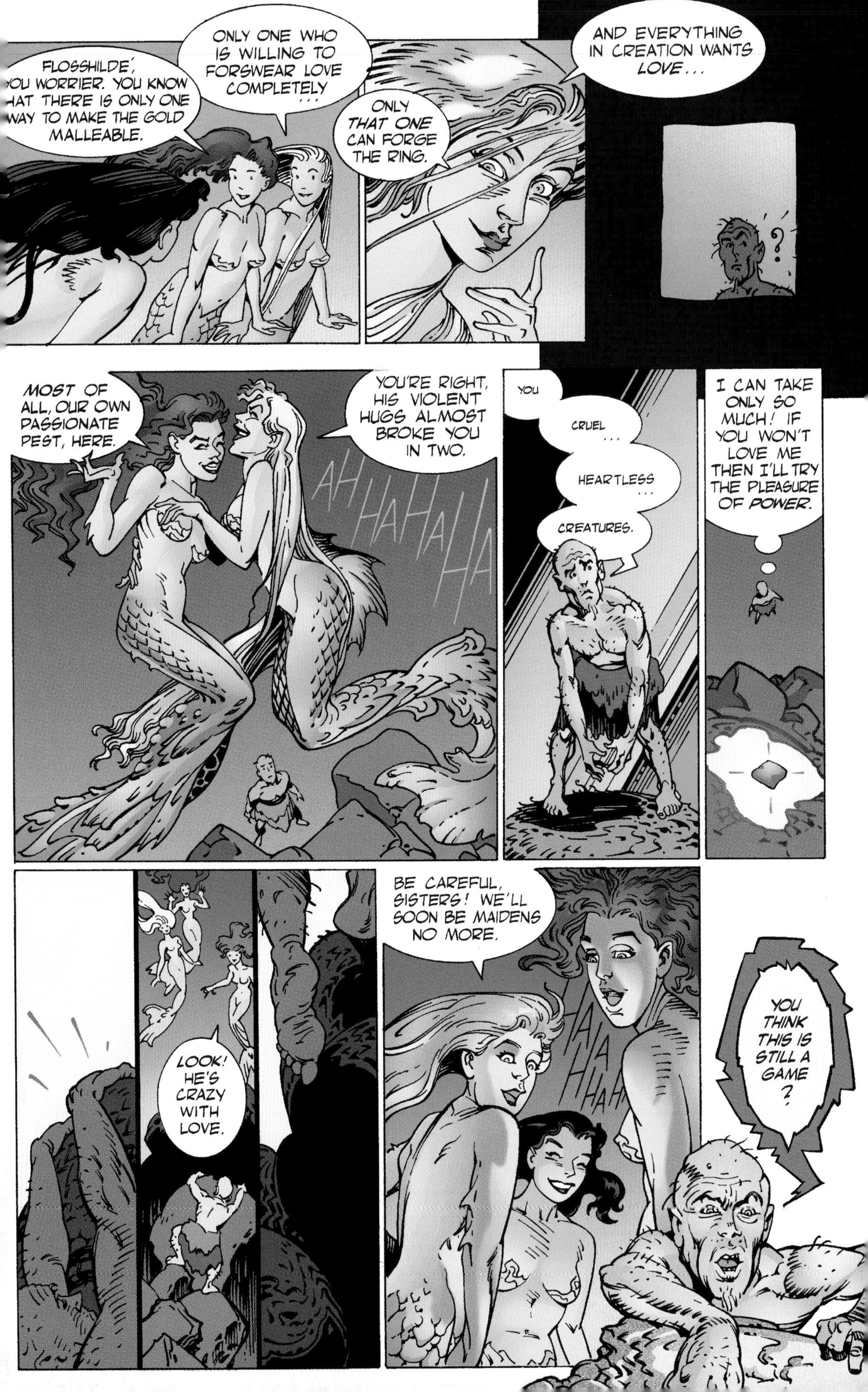
FLOSSHILDE, YOU WORRIER. YOU KNOW HAT THERE IS ONLY ONE WAY TO MAKE THE GOLD MALLEABLE.
ONLY ONE WHO IS WILLING TO FORSWEAR LOVE COMPLETELY . . .
ONLY THAT ONE CAN FORGE THE RING.
AND EVERYTHING IN CREATION WANTS LOVE . . .
?
MOST OF ALL, OUR OWN PASSIONATE PEST, HERE.
YOU'RE RIGHT, HIS VIOLENT HUGS ALMOST BROKE YOU IN TWO.
AH HA HA HA HA
YOU
CRUEL . . .
HEARTLESS . . .
CREATURES.
I CAN TAKE ONLY SO MUCH! IF YOU WON'T LOVE ME THEN I'LL TRY THE PLEASURE OF POWER.
LOOK! HE'S CRAZY WITH LOVE.
BE CAREFUL, SISTERS! WE'LL SOON BE MAIDENS NO MORE.
HA HA HA
YOU THINK THIS IS STILL A GAME ?

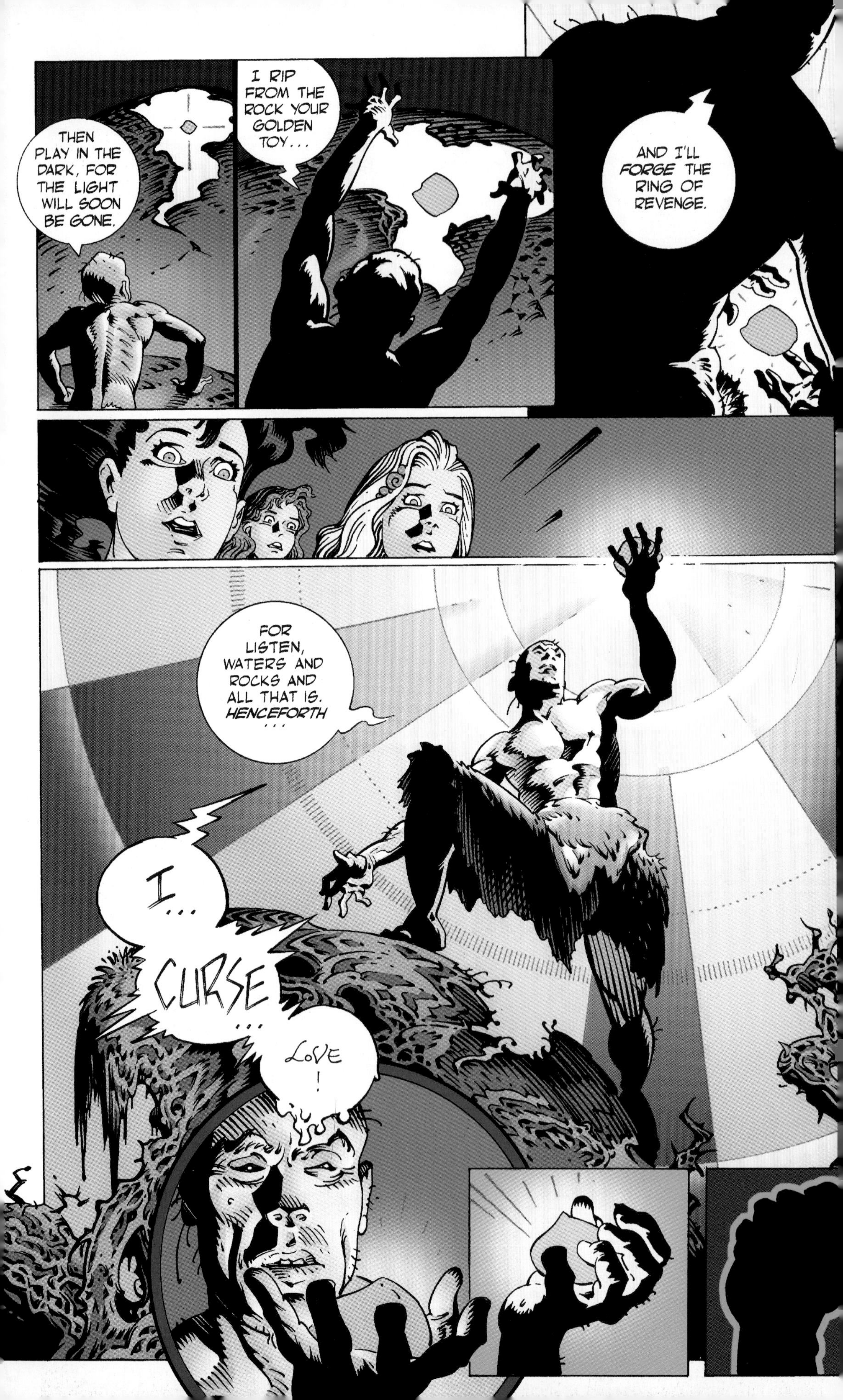
THEN PLAY IN THE DARK, FOR THE LIGHT WILL SOON BE GONE.
I RIP FROM THE ROCK YOUR GOLDEN TOY...
AND I'LL *FORGE* THE RING OF REVENGE.
FOR LISTEN, WATERS AND ROCKS AND ALL THAT IS. *HENCEFORTH* ...
I...
CURSE...
LOVE!

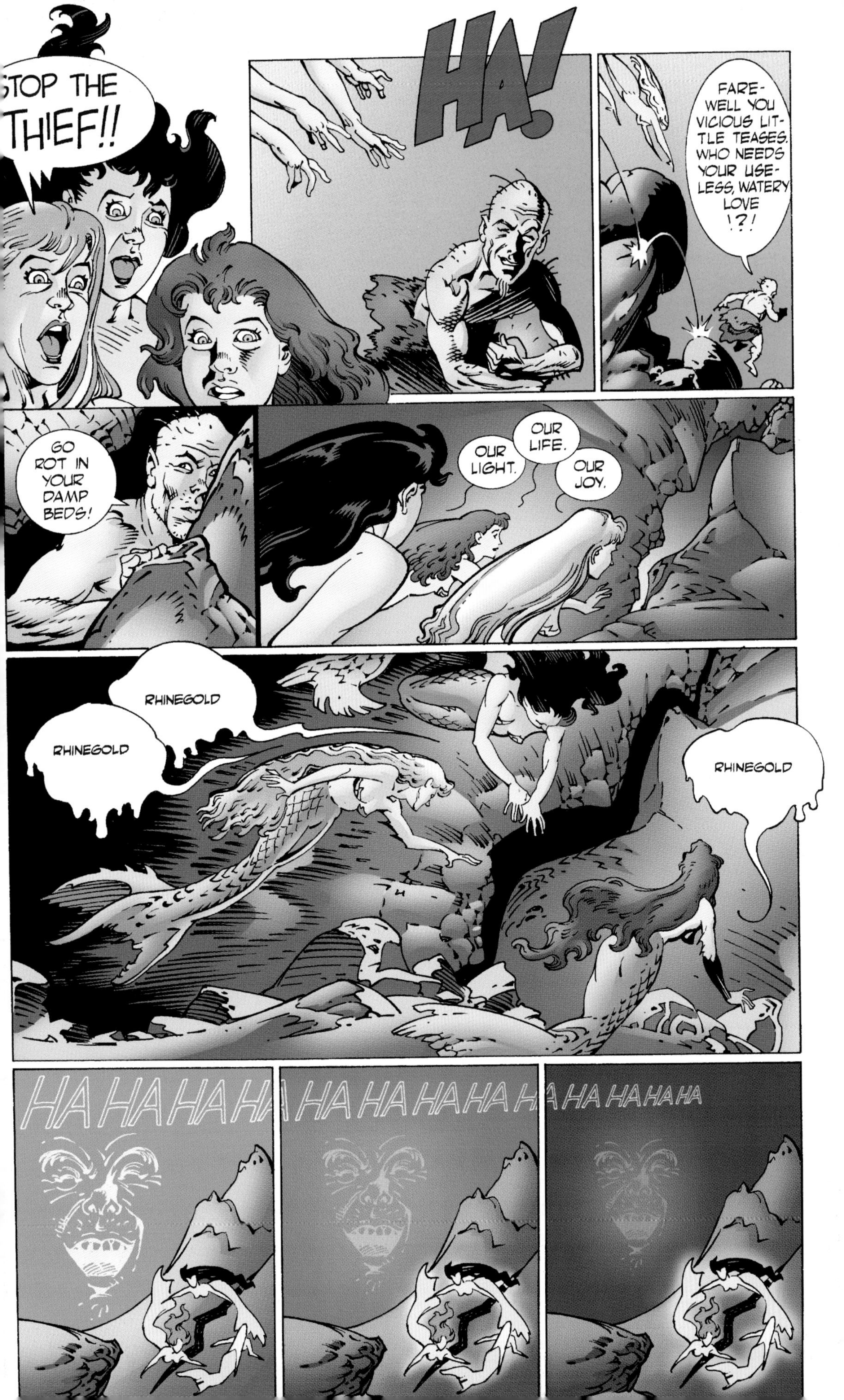
STOP THE THIEF!!
HA!
FARE-WELL YOU VICIOUS LIT-TLE TEASES. WHO NEEDS YOUR USE-LESS, WATERY LOVE !?!
GO ROT IN YOUR DAMP BEDS!
OUR LIGHT.
OUR LIFE.
OUR JOY.
RHINEGOLD
RHINEGOLD
RHINEGOLD
HA HA HA HA HA HA HA HA HA HA HA HA HA HA HA

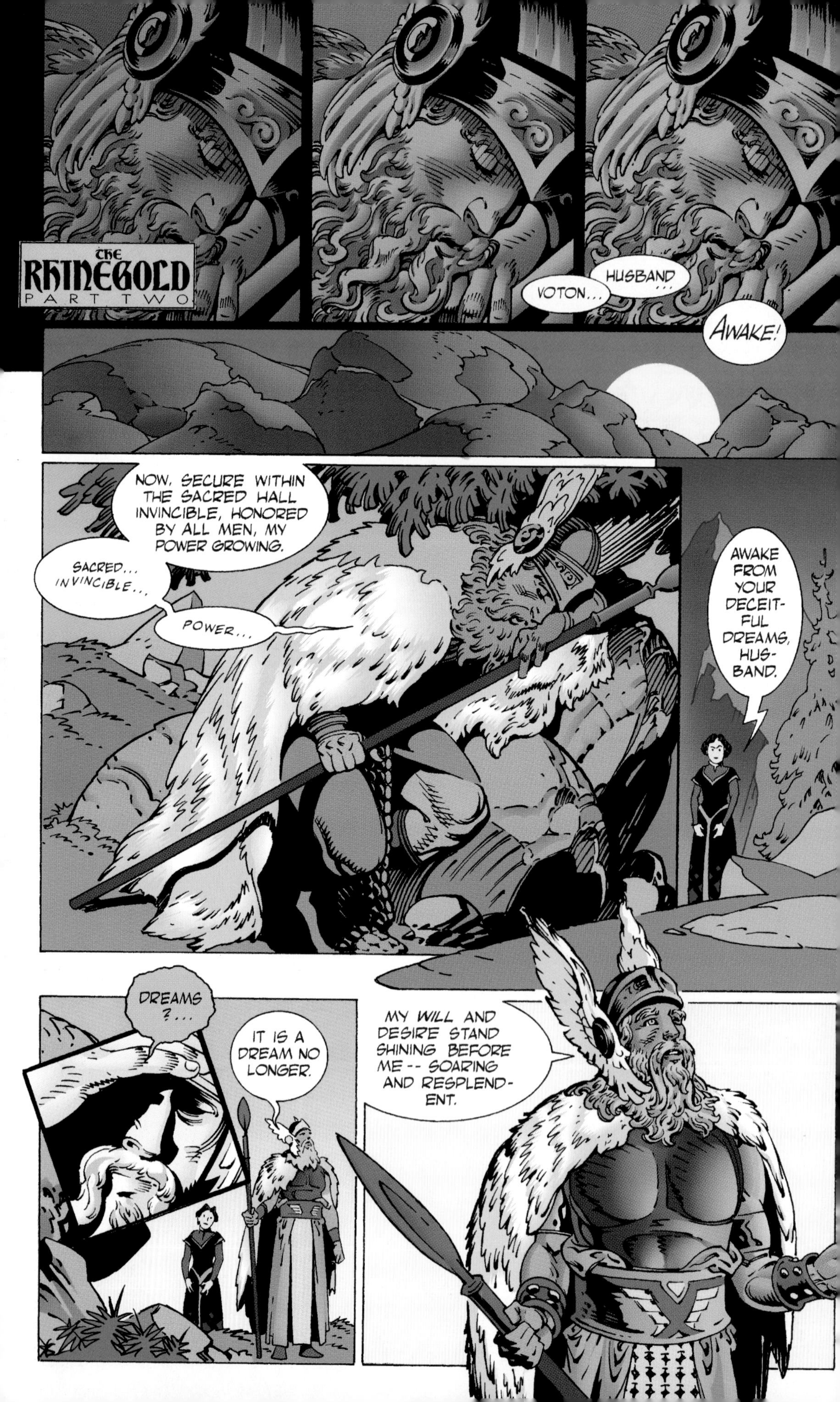

THE RHINEGOLD
PART TWO
VOTON...
HUSBAND...
AWAKE!
NOW, SECURE WITHIN THE SACRED HALL INVINCIBLE, HONORED BY ALL MEN, MY POWER GROWING.
SACRED... INVINCIBLE...
POWER...
AWAKE FROM YOUR DECEIT-FUL DREAMS, HUS-BAND.
DREAMS?...
IT IS A DREAM NO LONGER.
MY WILL AND DESIRE STAND SHINING BEFORE ME -- SOARING AND RESPLEND-ENT.

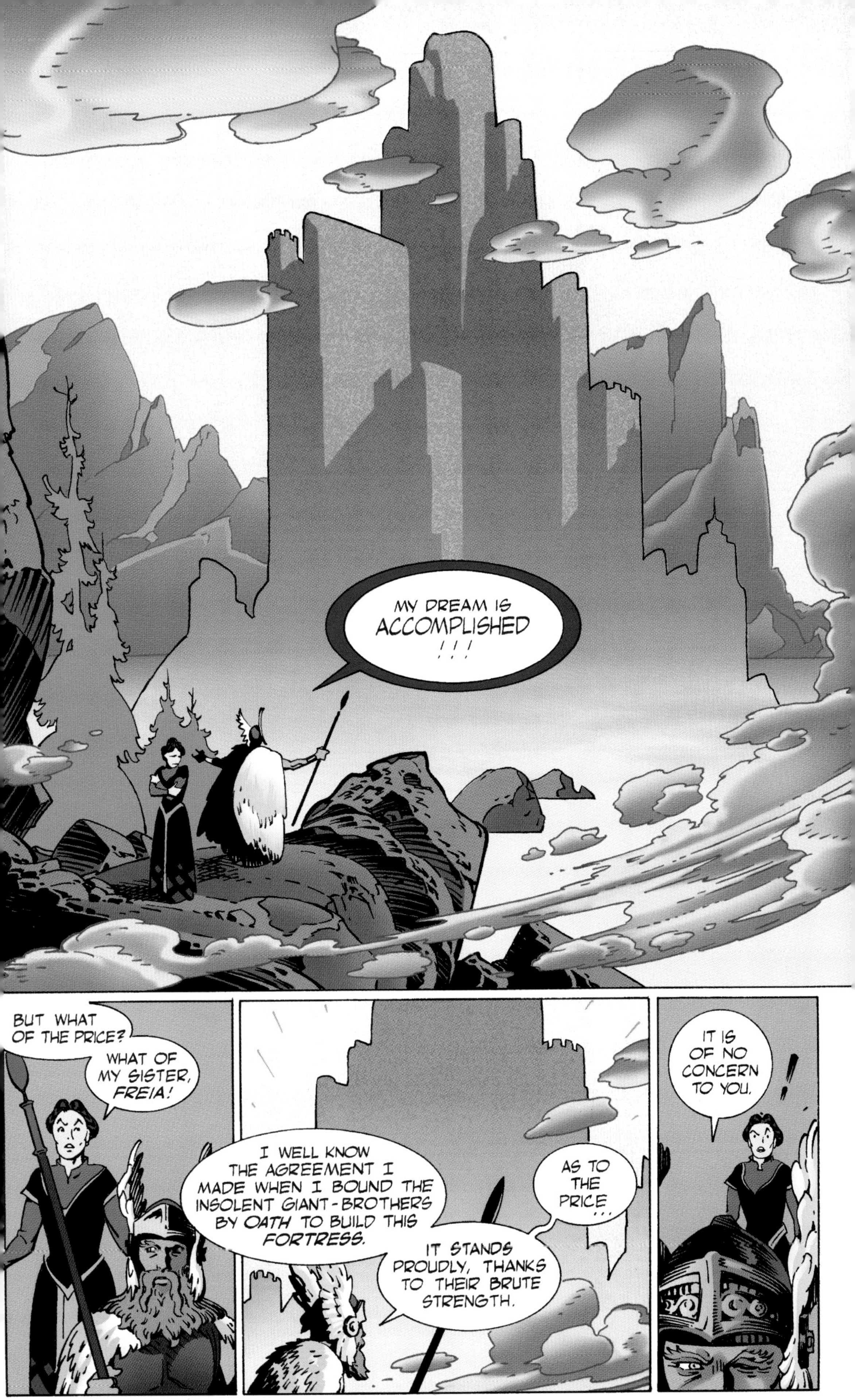
MY DREAM IS ACCOMPLISHED !!!
BUT WHAT OF THE PRICE?
WHAT OF MY SISTER, FREIA!
I WELL KNOW THE AGREEMENT I MADE WHEN I BOUND THE INSOLENT GIANT-BROTHERS BY OATH TO BUILD THIS FORTRESS.
IT STANDS PROUDLY, THANKS TO THEIR BRUTE STRENGTH.
AS TO THE PRICE...
IT IS OF NO CONCERN TO YOU.
!

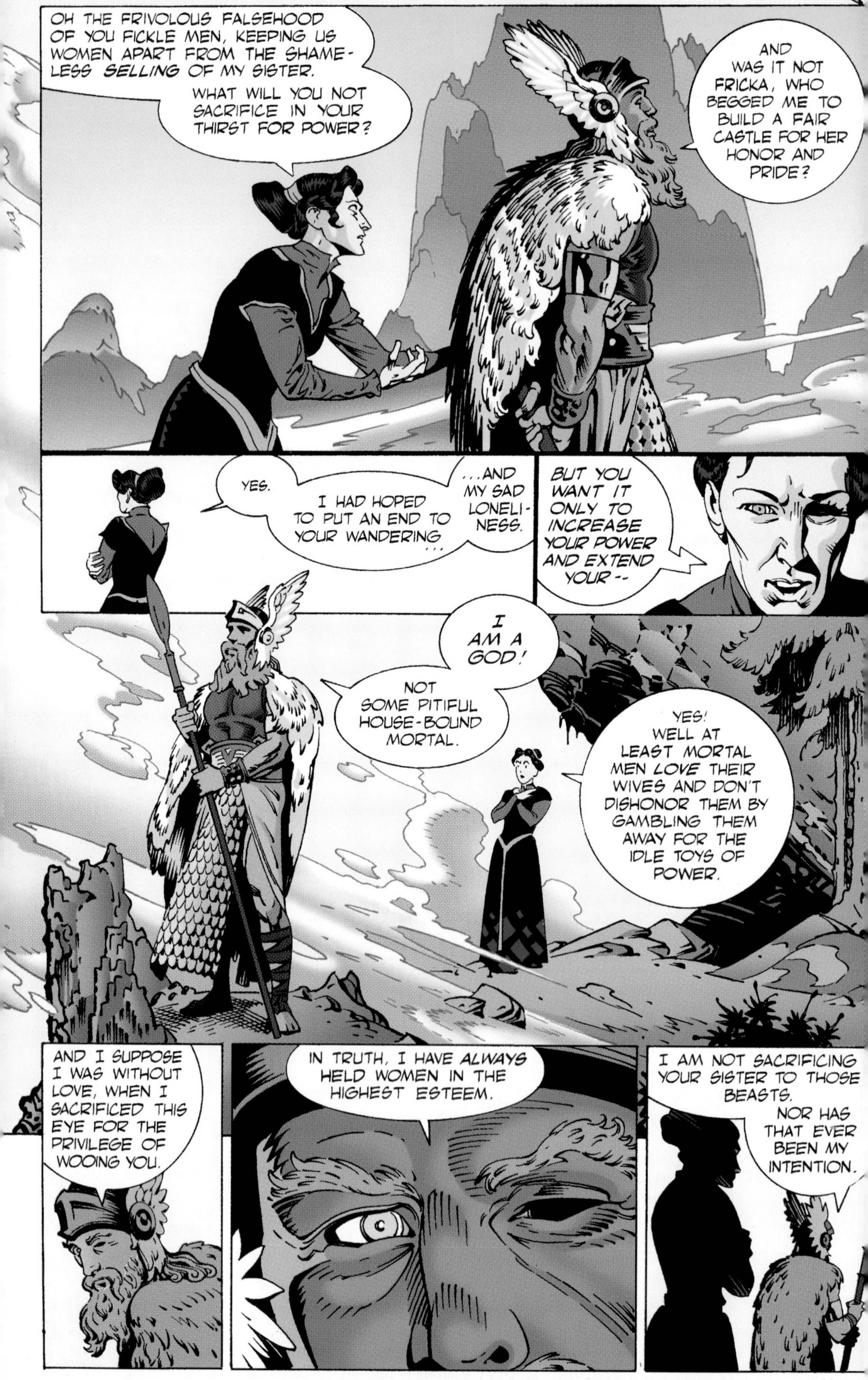
OH THE FRIVOLOUS FALSEHOOD OF YOU FICKLE MEN, KEEPING US WOMEN APART FROM THE SHAMELESS SELLING OF MY SISTER.
WHAT WILL YOU NOT SACRIFICE IN YOUR THIRST FOR POWER?
AND WAS IT NOT FRICKA, WHO BEGGED ME TO BUILD A FAIR CASTLE FOR HER HONOR AND PRIDE?
YES.
I HAD HOPED TO PUT AN END TO YOUR WANDERING . . .
. . .AND MY SAD LONELINESS.
BUT YOU WANT IT ONLY TO INCREASE YOUR POWER AND EXTEND YOUR --
I AM A GOD!
NOT SOME PITIFUL HOUSE-BOUND MORTAL.
YES! WELL AT LEAST MORTAL MEN LOVE THEIR WIVES AND DON'T DISHONOR THEM BY GAMBLING THEM AWAY FOR THE IDLE TOYS OF POWER.
AND I SUPPOSE I WAS WITHOUT LOVE, WHEN I SACRIFICED THIS EYE FOR THE PRIVILEGE OF WOOING YOU.
IN TRUTH, I HAVE ALWAYS HELD WOMEN IN THE HIGHEST ESTEEM.
I AM NOT SACRIFICING YOUR SISTER TO THOSE BEASTS.
NOR HAS THAT EVER BEEN MY INTENTION.

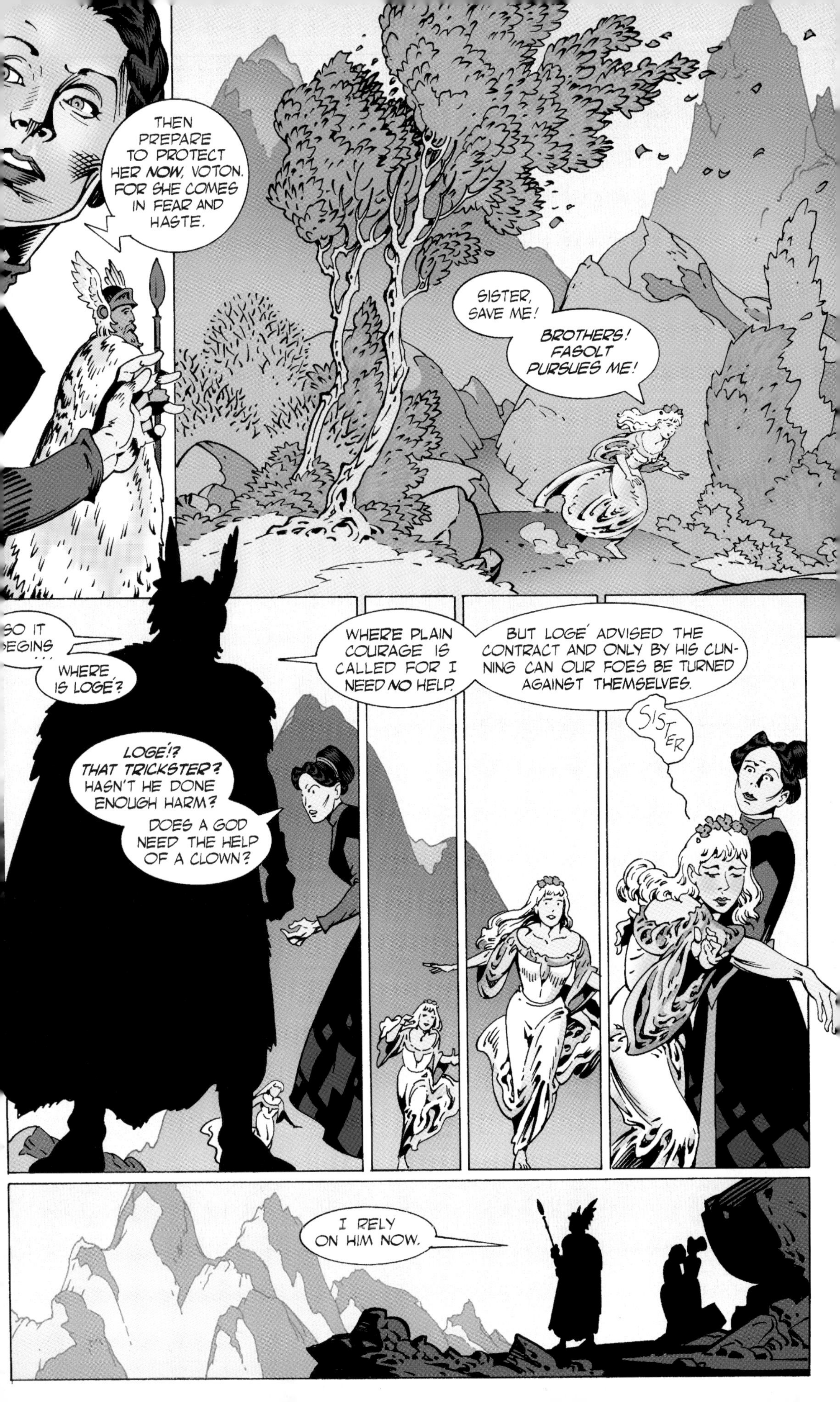
THEN PREPARE TO PROTECT HER NOW, VOTON. FOR SHE COMES IN FEAR AND HASTE.
SISTER, SAVE ME!
BROTHERS! FASOLT PURSUES ME!
SO IT BEGINS . . .
WHERE IS LOGE?
LOGE!? THAT TRICKSTER? HASN'T HE DONE ENOUGH HARM?
DOES A GOD NEED THE HELP OF A CLOWN?
WHERE PLAIN COURAGE IS CALLED FOR I NEED NO HELP.
BUT LOGE ADVISED THE CONTRACT AND ONLY BY HIS CUNNING CAN OUR FOES BE TURNED AGAINST THEMSELVES.
SISTER
I RELY ON HIM NOW.

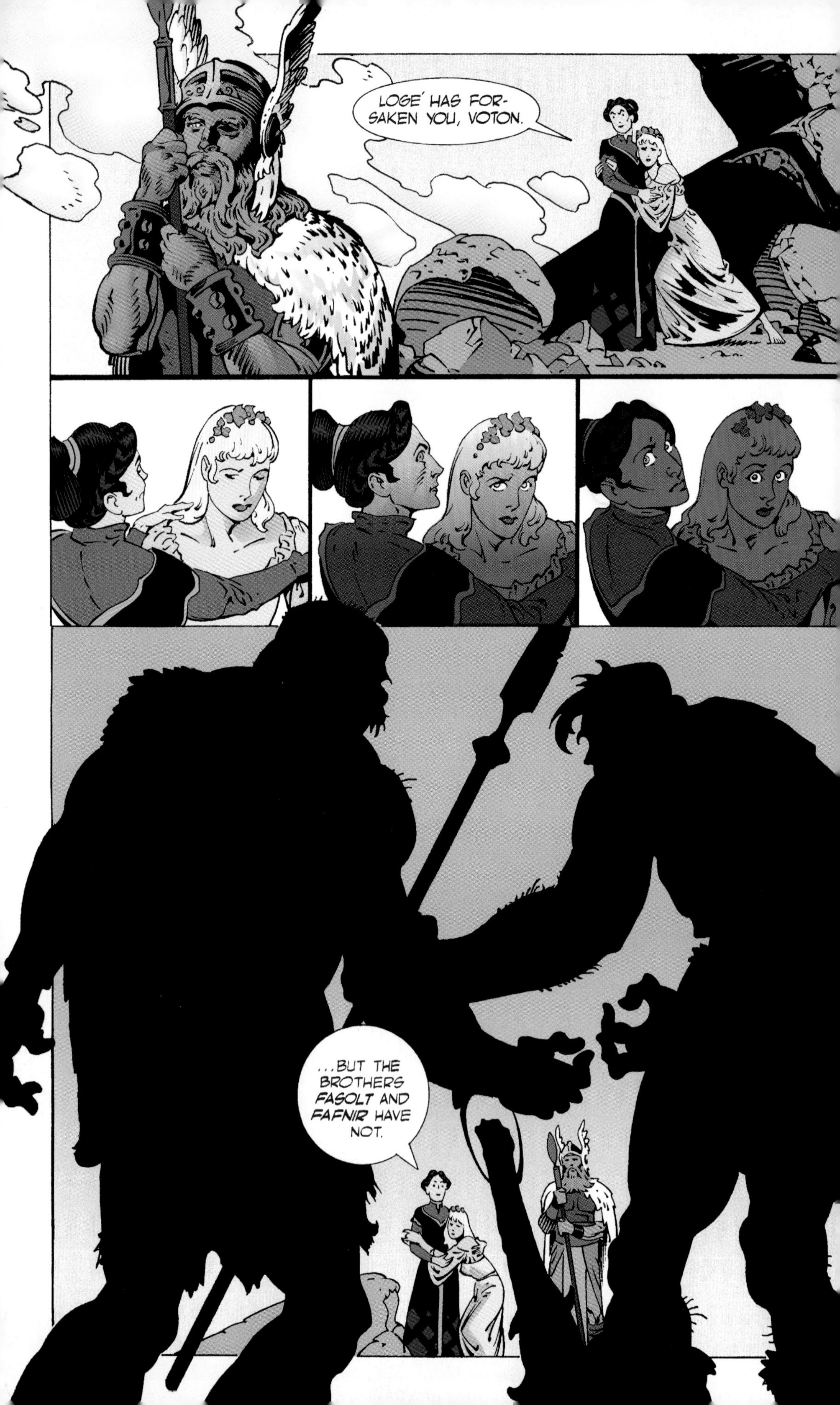
LOGE' HAS FORSAKEN YOU, VOTON.
...BUT THE BROTHERS FASOLT AND FAFNIR HAVE NOT.

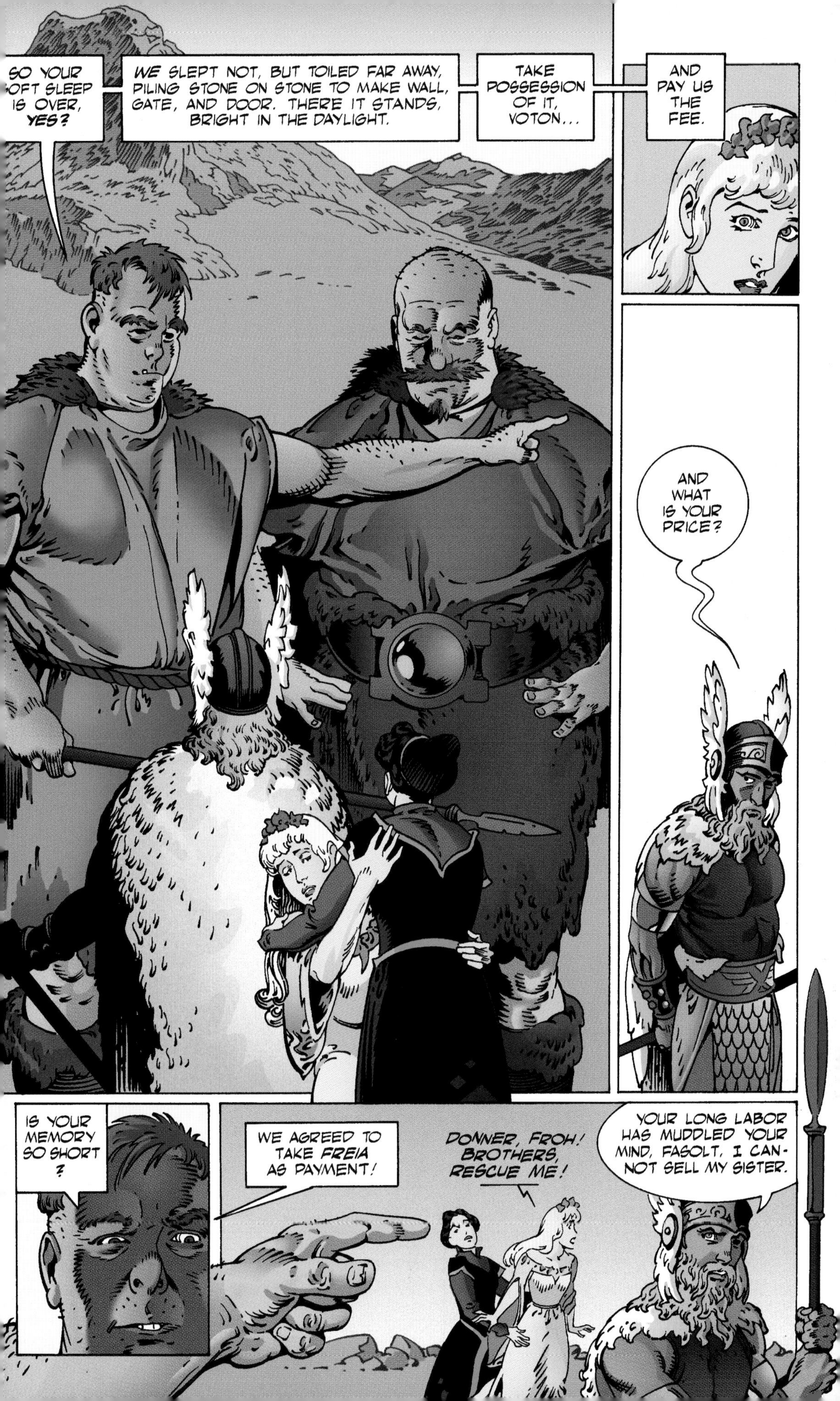
SO YOUR SOFT SLEEP IS OVER, YES?
WE SLEPT NOT, BUT TOILED FAR AWAY, PILING STONE ON STONE TO MAKE WALL, GATE, AND DOOR. THERE IT STANDS, BRIGHT IN THE DAYLIGHT.
TAKE POSSESSION OF IT, VOTON...
AND PAY US THE FEE.
AND WHAT IS YOUR PRICE?
IS YOUR MEMORY SO SHORT ?
WE AGREED TO TAKE FREIA AS PAYMENT!
DONNER, FROH! BROTHERS, RESCUE ME!
YOUR LONG LABOR HAS MUDDLED YOUR MIND, FASOLT, I CANNOT SELL MY SISTER.

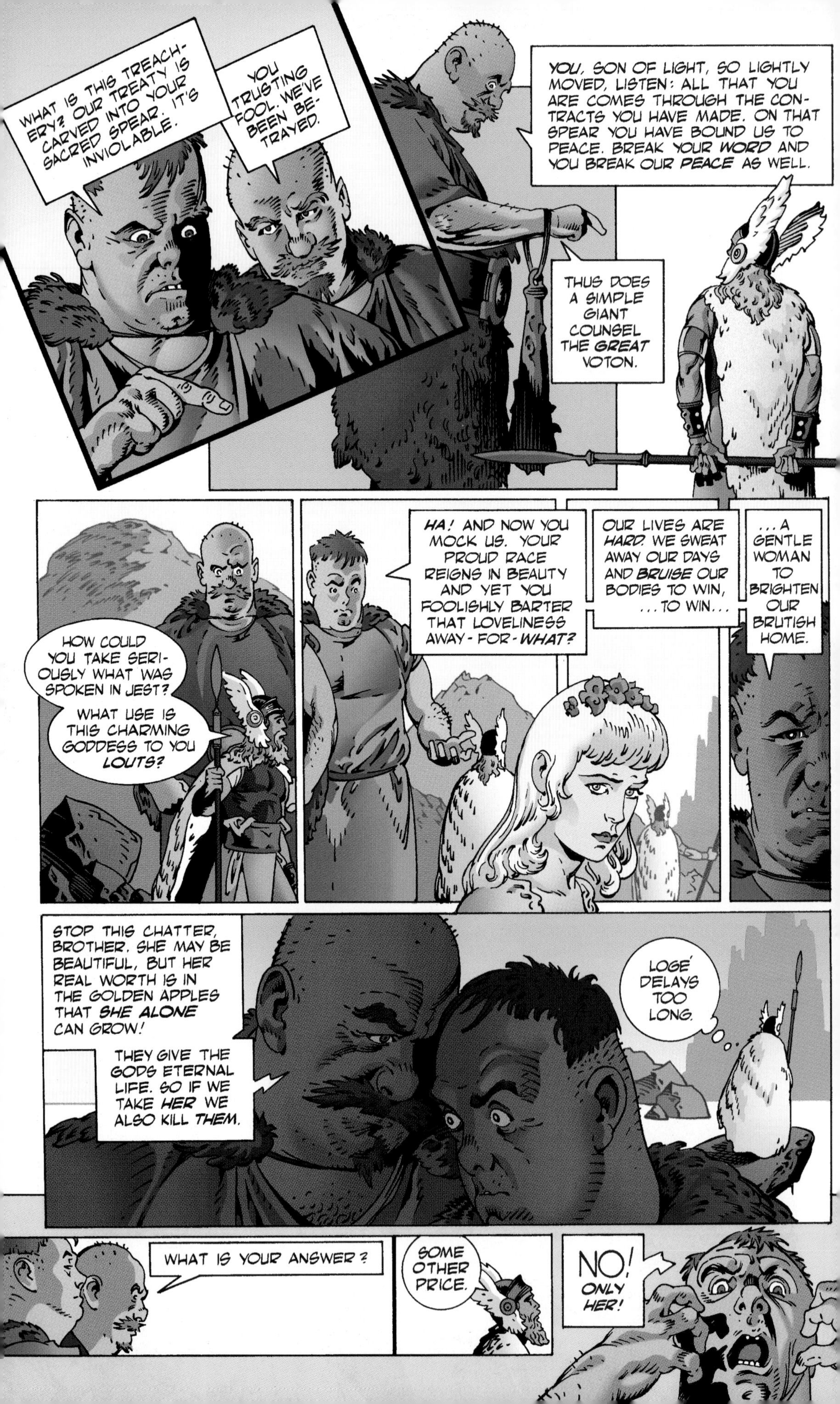
WHAT IS THIS TREACHERY? OUR TREATY IS CARVED INTO YOUR SACRED SPEAR. IT'S INVIOLABLE.
YOU TRUSTING FOOL. WE'VE BEEN BETRAYED.
YOU, SON OF LIGHT, SO LIGHTLY MOVED, LISTEN: ALL THAT YOU ARE COMES THROUGH THE CONTRACTS YOU HAVE MADE. ON THAT SPEAR YOU HAVE BOUND US TO PEACE. BREAK YOUR WORD AND YOU BREAK OUR PEACE AS WELL.
THUS DOES A SIMPLE GIANT COUNSEL THE GREAT VOTON.
HOW COULD YOU TAKE SERIOUSLY WHAT WAS SPOKEN IN JEST?
WHAT USE IS THIS CHARMING GODDESS TO YOU LOUTS?
HA! AND NOW YOU MOCK US. YOUR PROUD RACE REIGNS IN BEAUTY AND YET YOU FOOLISHLY BARTER THAT LOVELINESS AWAY- FOR- WHAT?
OUR LIVES ARE HARD. WE SWEAT AWAY OUR DAYS AND BRUISE OUR BODIES TO WIN, ...TO WIN...
...A GENTLE WOMAN TO BRIGHTEN OUR BRUTISH HOME.
STOP THIS CHATTER, BROTHER. SHE MAY BE BEAUTIFUL, BUT HER REAL WORTH IS IN THE GOLDEN APPLES THAT SHE ALONE CAN GROW!
THEY GIVE THE GODS ETERNAL LIFE. SO IF WE TAKE HER WE ALSO KILL THEM.
LOGE DELAYS TOO LONG.
WHAT IS YOUR ANSWER?
SOME OTHER PRICE.
NO! ONLY HER!

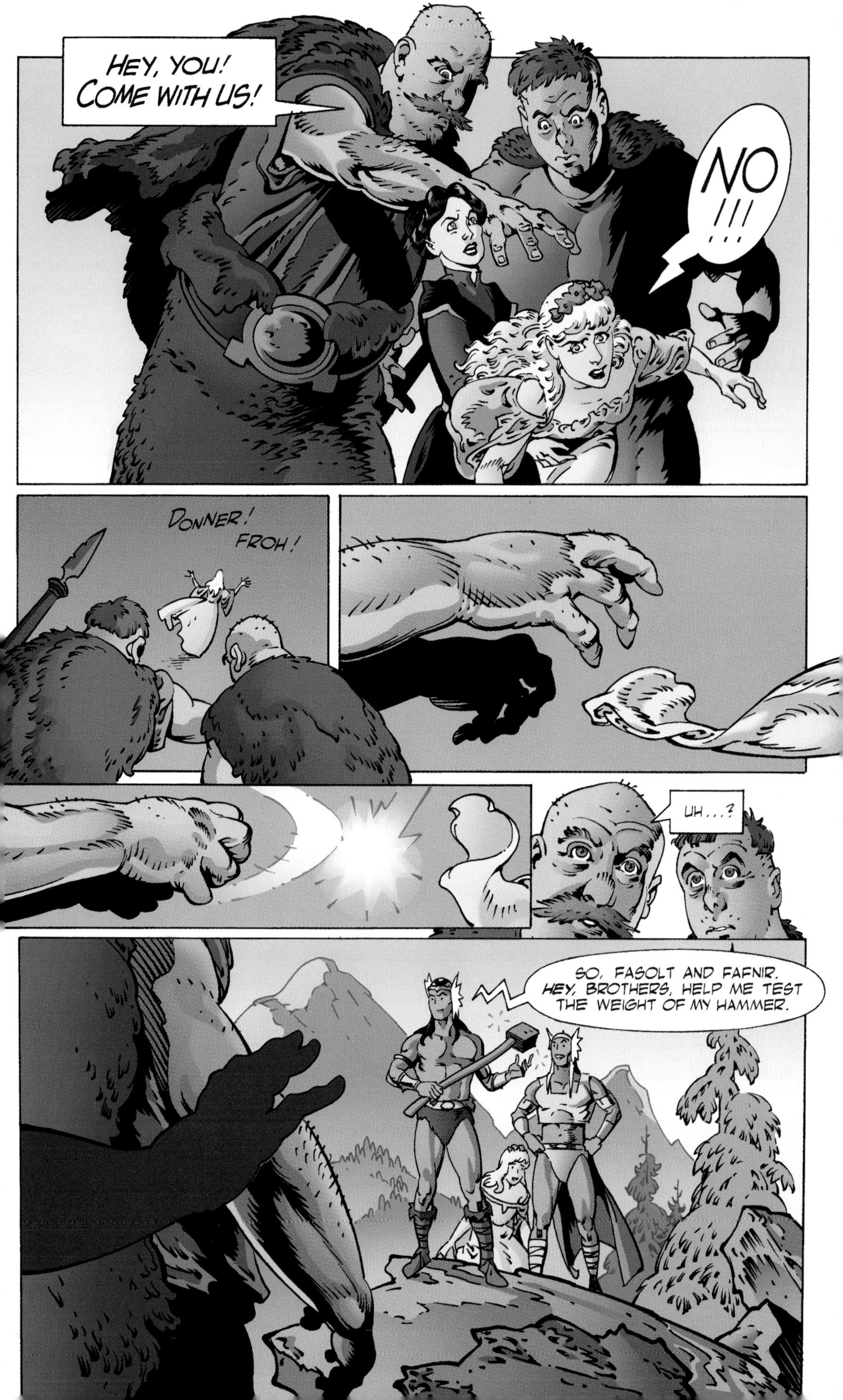
HEY, YOU! COME WITH US!
NO !!!
DONNER! FROH!
UH...?
SO, FASOLT AND FAFNIR. HEY, BROTHERS, HELP ME TEST THE WEIGHT OF MY HAMMER.

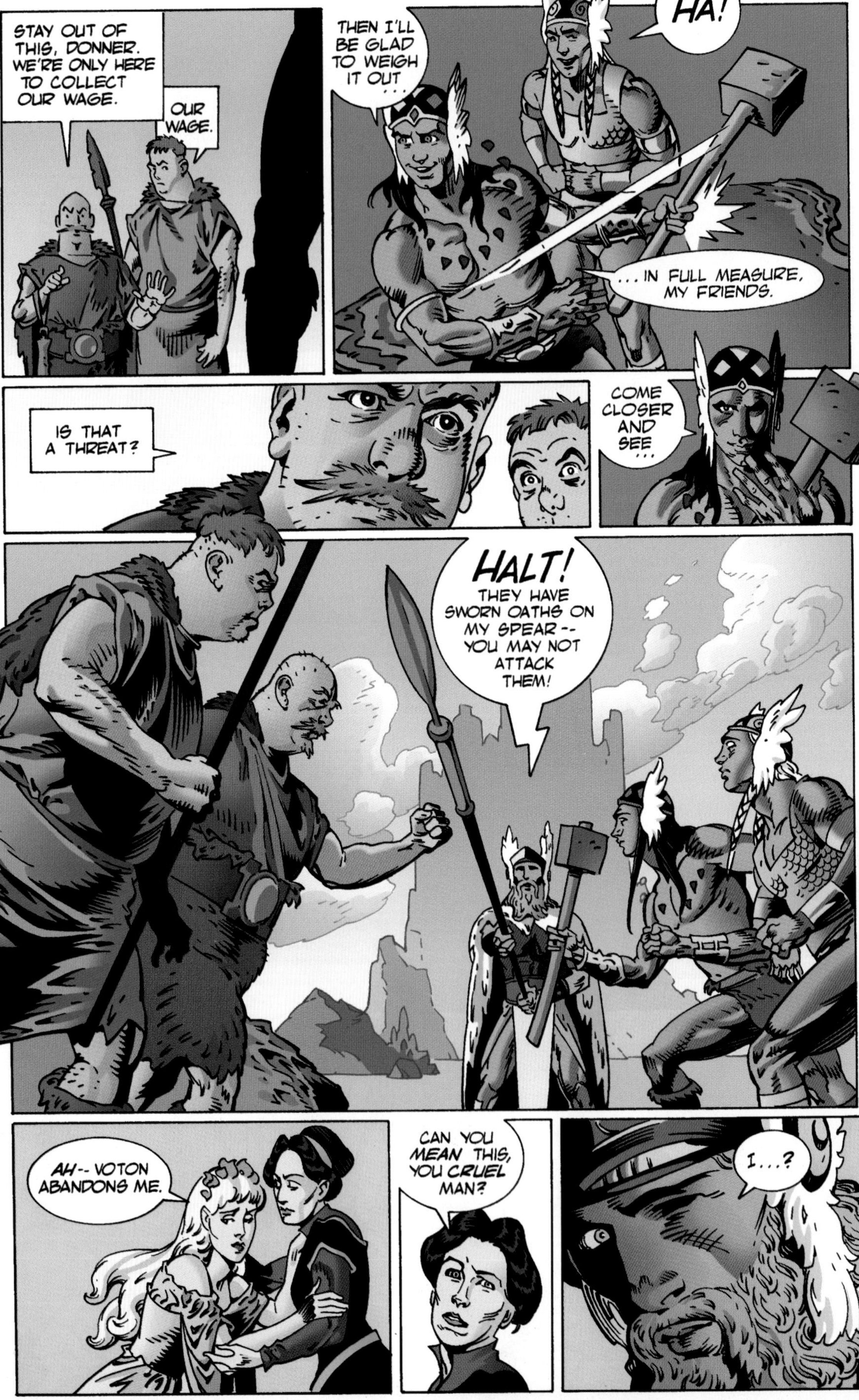
STAY OUT OF THIS, DONNER. WE'RE ONLY HERE TO COLLECT OUR WAGE.
OUR WAGE.
THEN I'LL BE GLAD TO WEIGH IT OUT . . .
HA!
. . . IN FULL MEASURE, MY FRIENDS.
IS THAT A THREAT?
COME CLOSER AND SEE . . .
HALT! THEY HAVE SWORN OATHS ON MY SPEAR -- YOU MAY NOT ATTACK THEM!
AH -- VOTON ABANDONS ME.
CAN YOU MEAN THIS, YOU CRUEL MAN?
I . . .?

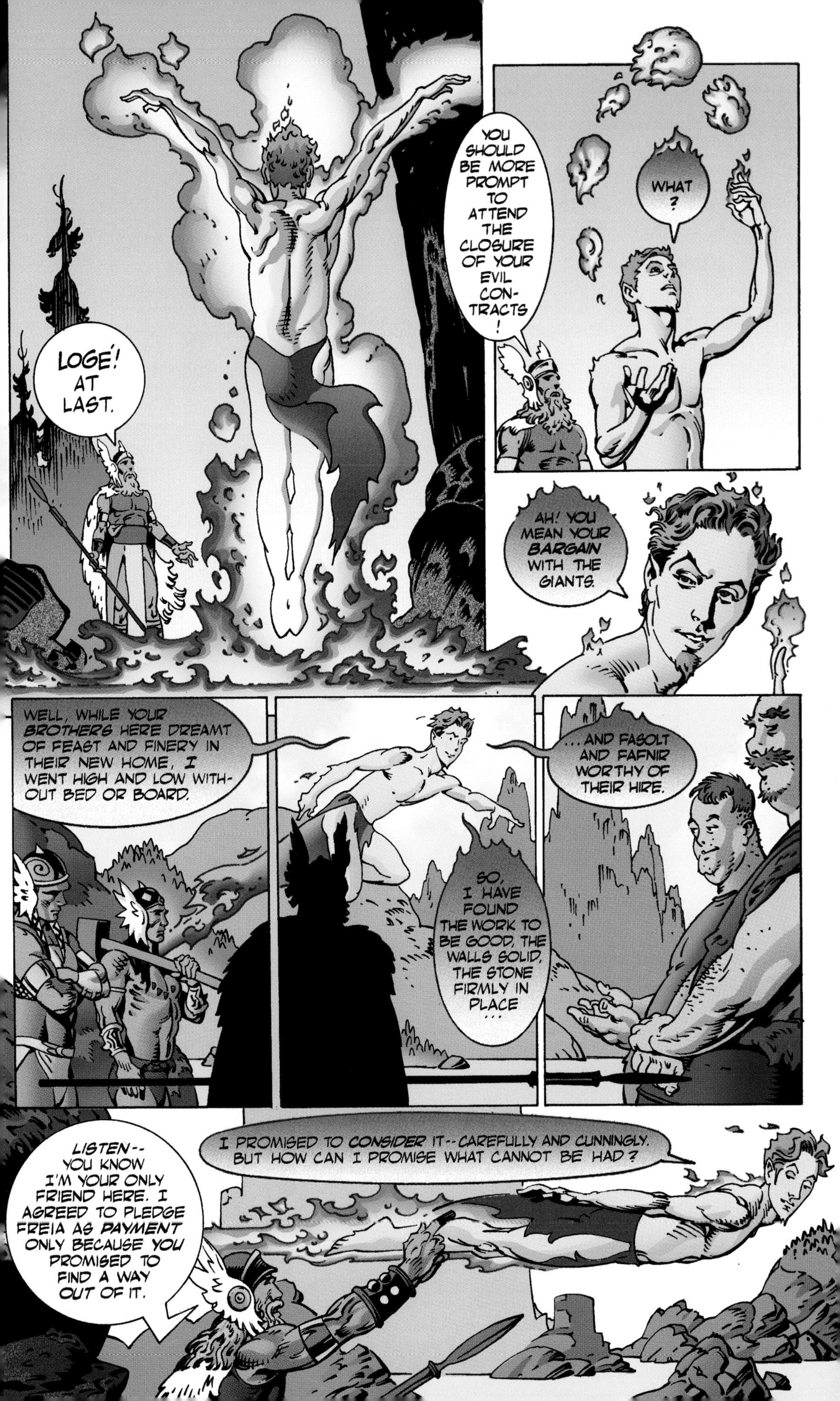
LOGE! AT LAST.
YOU SHOULD BE MORE PROMPT TO ATTEND THE CLOSURE OF YOUR EVIL CON-TRACTS!
WHAT?
AH! YOU MEAN YOUR BARGAIN WITH THE GIANTS.
WELL, WHILE YOUR BROTHERS HERE DREAMT OF FEAST AND FINERY IN THEIR NEW HOME, I WENT HIGH AND LOW WITH-OUT BED OR BOARD.
SO, I HAVE FOUND THE WORK TO BE GOOD, THE WALLS SOLID, THE STONE FIRMLY IN PLACE...
...AND FASOLT AND FAFNIR WORTHY OF THEIR HIRE.
LISTEN-- YOU KNOW I'M YOUR ONLY FRIEND HERE. I AGREED TO PLEDGE FREIA AS PAYMENT ONLY BECAUSE YOU PROMISED TO FIND A WAY OUT OF IT.
I PROMISED TO CONSIDER IT--CAREFULLY AND CUNNINGLY. BUT HOW CAN I PROMISE WHAT CANNOT BE HAD?

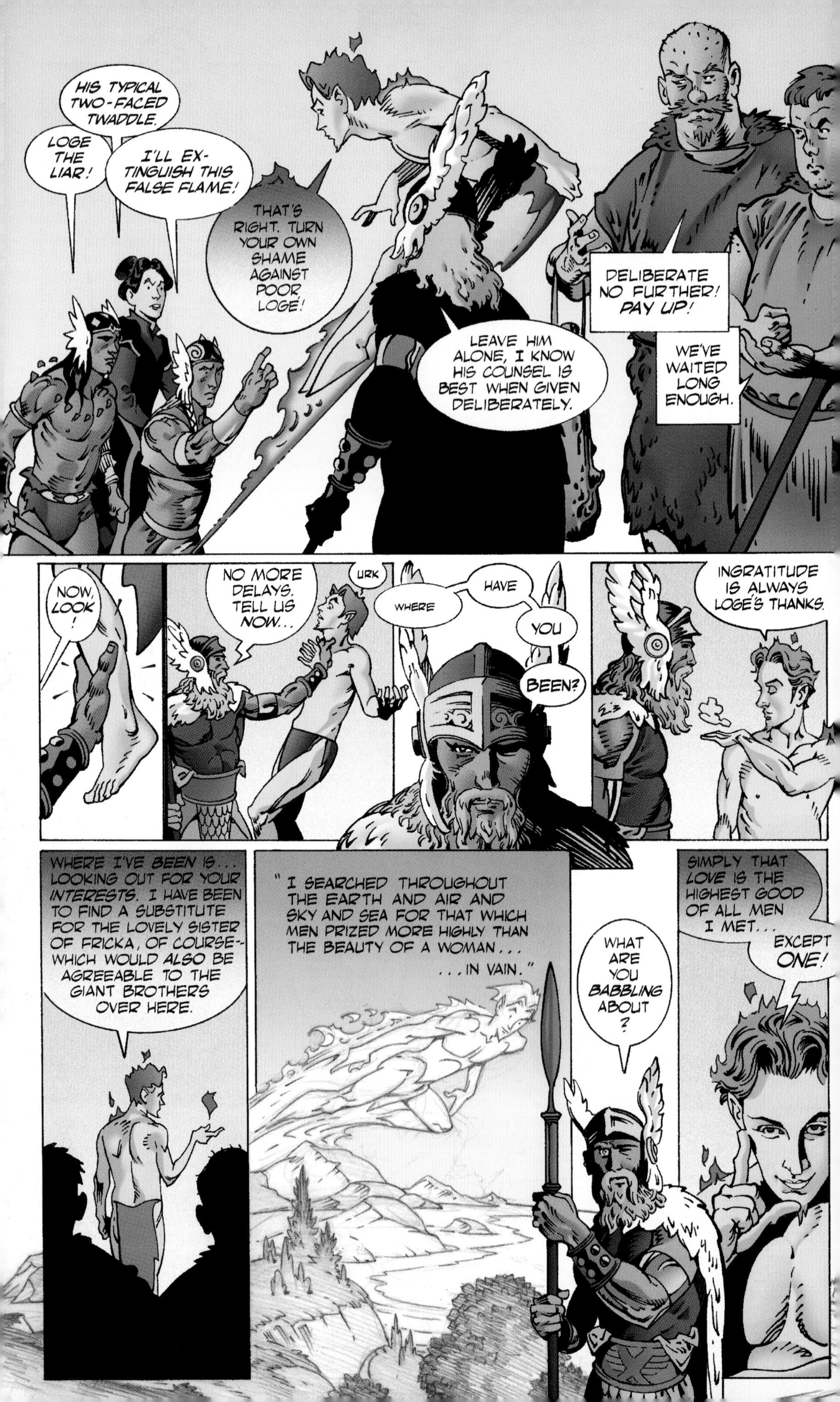
HIS TYPICAL TWO-FACED TWADDLE.
LOGE THE LIAR!
I'LL EX-TINGUISH THIS FALSE FLAME!
THAT'S RIGHT. TURN YOUR OWN SHAME AGAINST POOR LOGE!
LEAVE HIM ALONE, I KNOW HIS COUNSEL IS BEST WHEN GIVEN DELIBERATELY.
DELIBERATE NO FURTHER! PAY UP!
WE'VE WAITED LONG ENOUGH.
NOW, LOOK!
NO MORE DELAYS. TELL US NOW...
URK
WHERE
HAVE
YOU
BEEN?
INGRATITUDE IS ALWAYS LOGE'S THANKS.
WHERE I'VE BEEN IS... LOOKING OUT FOR YOUR INTERESTS. I HAVE BEEN TO FIND A SUBSTITUTE FOR THE LOVELY SISTER OF FRICKA, OF COURSE-- WHICH WOULD ALSO BE AGREEABLE TO THE GIANT BROTHERS OVER HERE.
"I SEARCHED THROUGHOUT THE EARTH AND AIR AND SKY AND SEA FOR THAT WHICH MEN PRIZED MORE HIGHLY THAN THE BEAUTY OF A WOMAN...
...IN VAIN."
WHAT ARE YOU BABBLING ABOUT?
SIMPLY THAT LOVE IS THE HIGHEST GOOD OF ALL MEN I MET...
EXCEPT ONE!

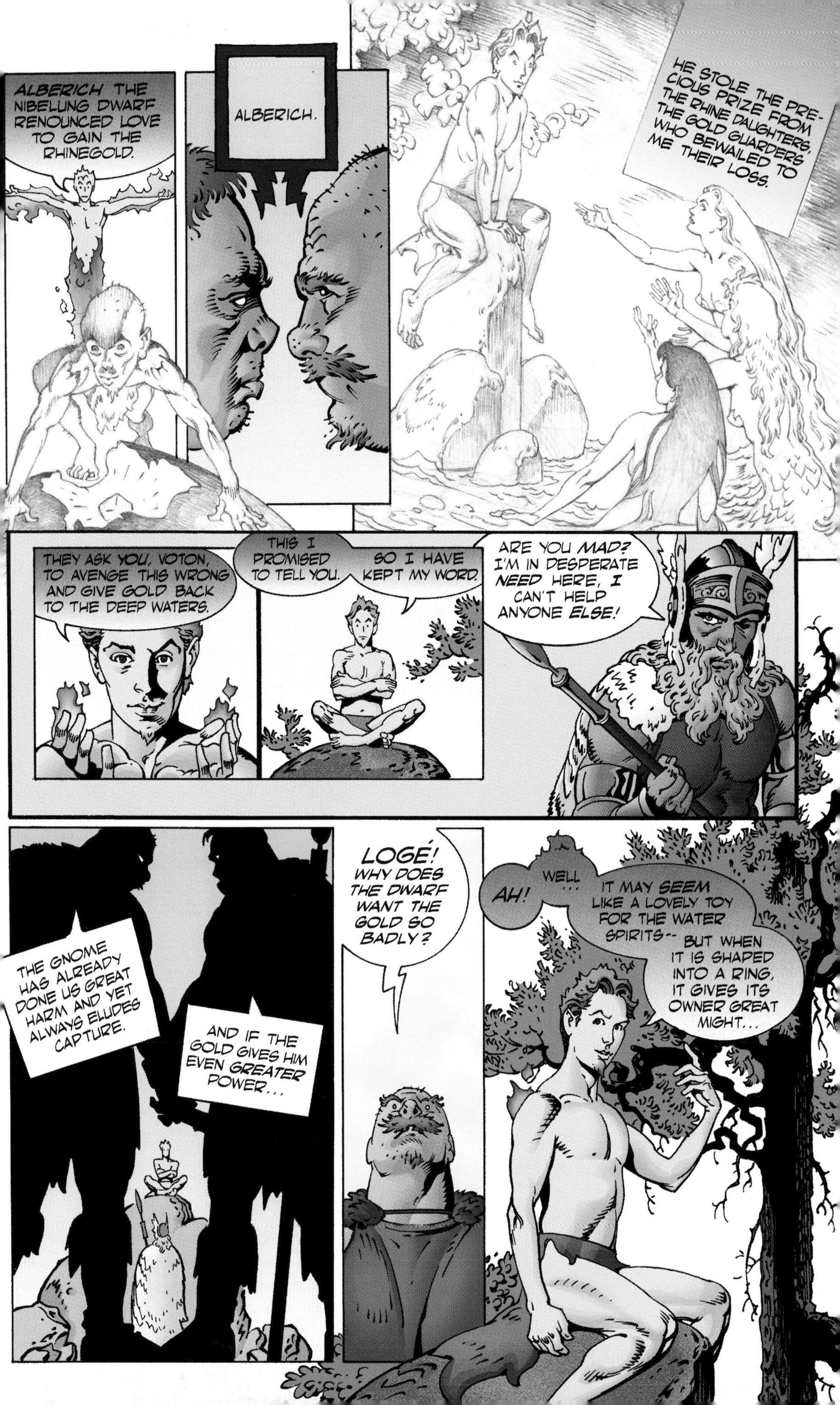
ALBERICH THE NIBELUNG DWARF RENOUNCED LOVE TO GAIN THE RHINEGOLD.
ALBERICH.
HE STOLE THE PRECIOUS PRIZE FROM THE RHINE DAUGHTERS, THE GOLD GUARDERS, WHO BEWAILED TO ME THEIR LOSS.
THEY ASK YOU, VOTON, TO AVENGE THIS WRONG AND GIVE GOLD BACK TO THE DEEP WATERS.
THIS I PROMISED TO TELL YOU.
SO I HAVE KEPT MY WORD.
ARE YOU MAD? I'M IN DESPERATE NEED HERE, I CAN'T HELP ANYONE ELSE!
THE GNOME HAS ALREADY DONE US GREAT HARM AND YET ALWAYS ELUDES CAPTURE.
AND IF THE GOLD GIVES HIM EVEN GREATER POWER...
LOGÉ! WHY DOES THE DWARF WANT THE GOLD SO BADLY?
AH!
WELL...
IT MAY SEEM LIKE A LOVELY TOY FOR THE WATER SPIRITS--
BUT WHEN IT IS SHAPED INTO A RING, IT GIVES ITS OWNER GREAT MIGHT...

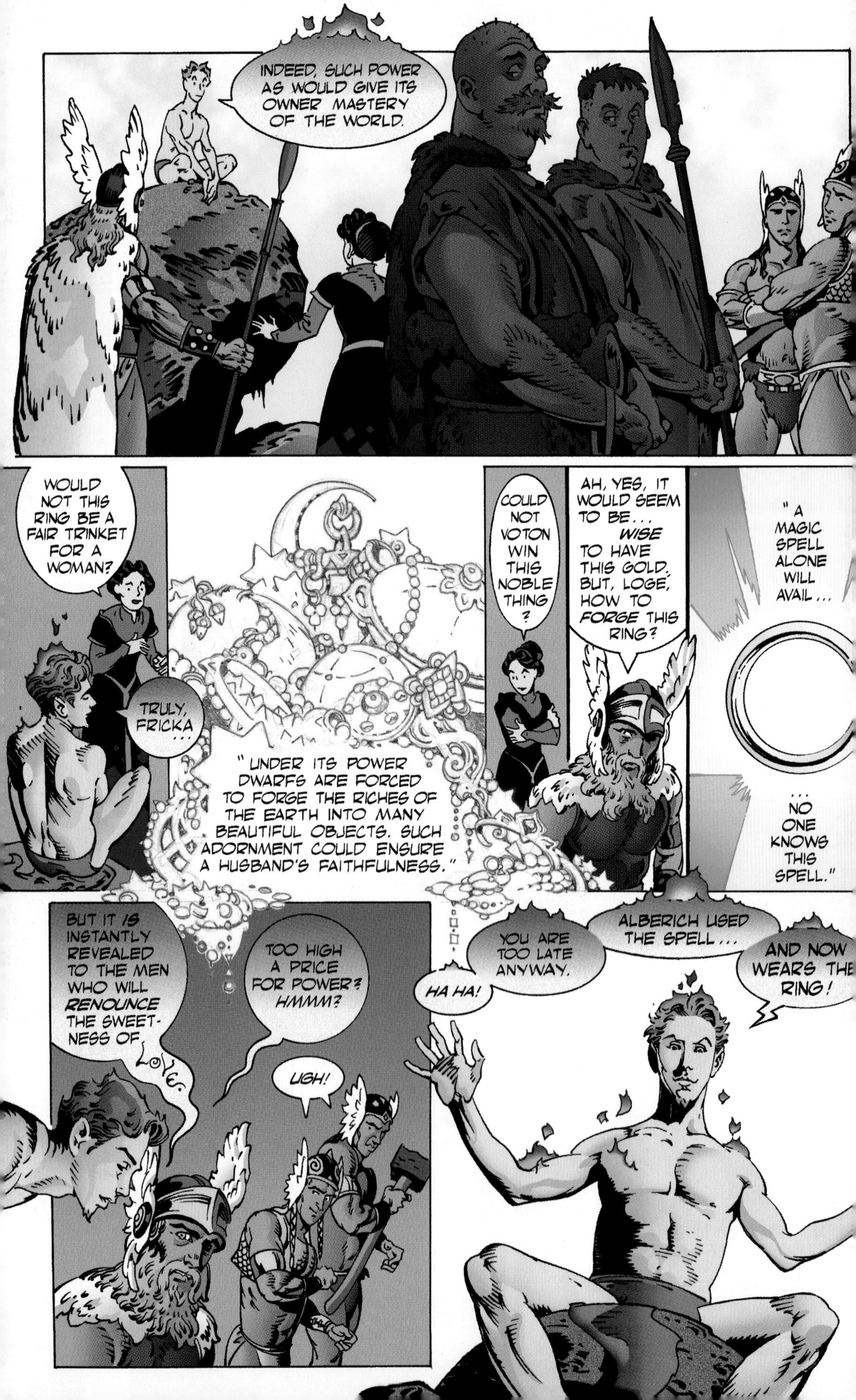

INDEED, SUCH POWER AS WOULD GIVE ITS OWNER MASTERY OF THE WORLD.
WOULD NOT THIS RING BE A FAIR TRINKET FOR A WOMAN?
TRULY, FRICKA ...
"UNDER ITS POWER DWARFS ARE FORCED TO FORGE THE RICHES OF THE EARTH INTO MANY BEAUTIFUL OBJECTS. SUCH ADORNMENT COULD ENSURE A HUSBAND'S FAITHFULNESS."
COULD NOT VOTON WIN THIS NOBLE THING?
AH, YES, IT WOULD SEEM TO BE... WISE TO HAVE THIS GOLD. BUT, LOGE, HOW TO FORGE THIS RING?
"A MAGIC SPELL ALONE WILL AVAIL...
... NO ONE KNOWS THIS SPELL."
BUT IT IS INSTANTLY REVEALED TO THE MEN WHO WILL RENOUNCE THE SWEETNESS OF LOVE.
TOO HIGH A PRICE FOR POWER? HMMM?
UGH!
HA HA!
YOU ARE TOO LATE ANYWAY.
ALBERICH USED THE SPELL...
AND NOW WEARS THE RING!

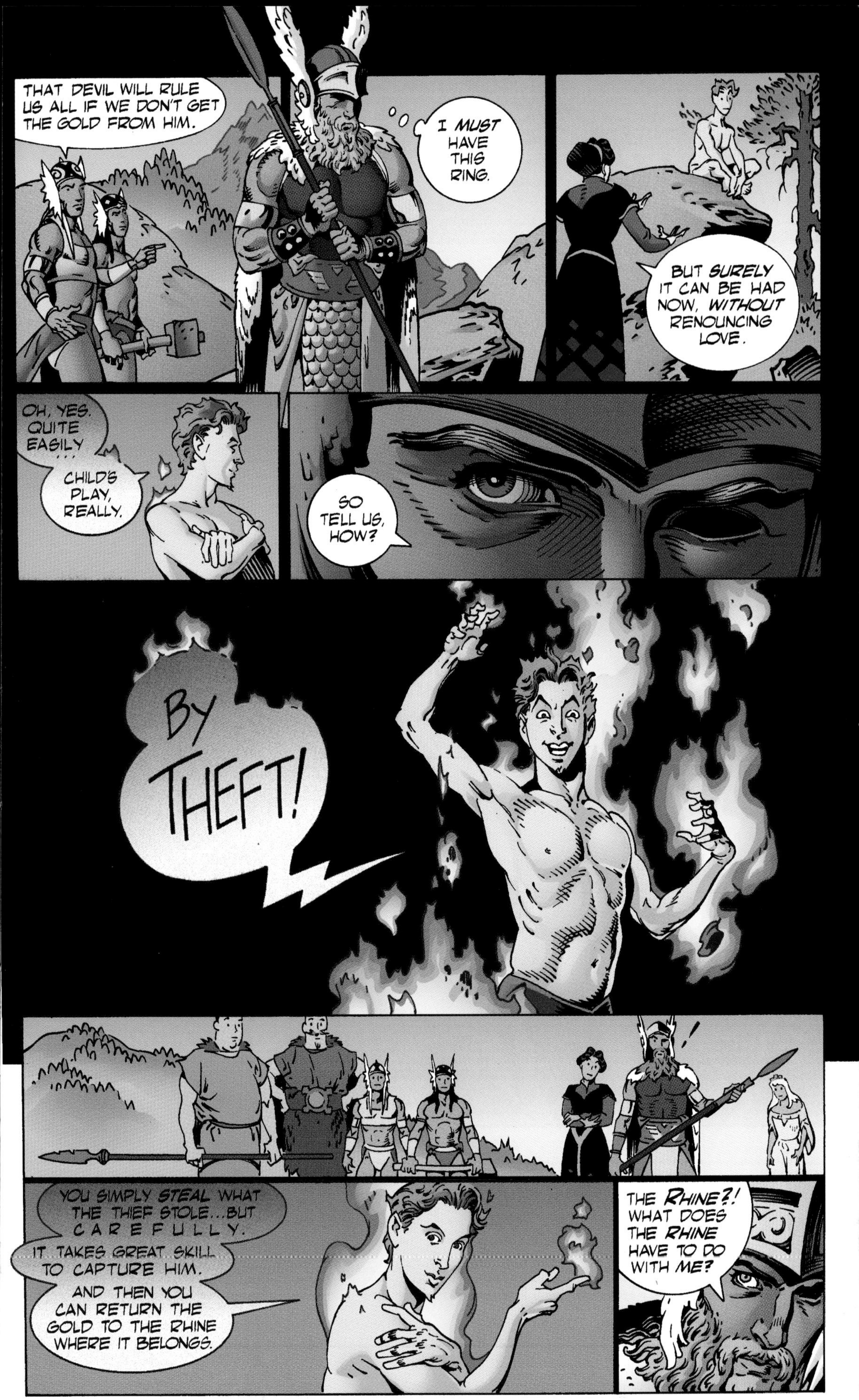
THAT DEVIL WILL RULE US ALL IF WE DON'T GET THE GOLD FROM HIM.
I MUST HAVE THIS RING.
BUT SURELY IT CAN BE HAD NOW, WITHOUT RENOUNCING LOVE.
OH, YES. QUITE EASILY . . .
CHILD'S PLAY, REALLY.
SO TELL US, HOW?
By THEFT!
YOU SIMPLY STEAL WHAT THE THIEF STOLE...BUT C A R E F U L L Y.
IT TAKES GREAT SKILL TO CAPTURE HIM.
AND THEN YOU CAN RETURN THE GOLD TO THE RHINE WHERE IT BELONGS.
THE RHINE?! WHAT DOES THE RHINE HAVE TO DO WITH ME?

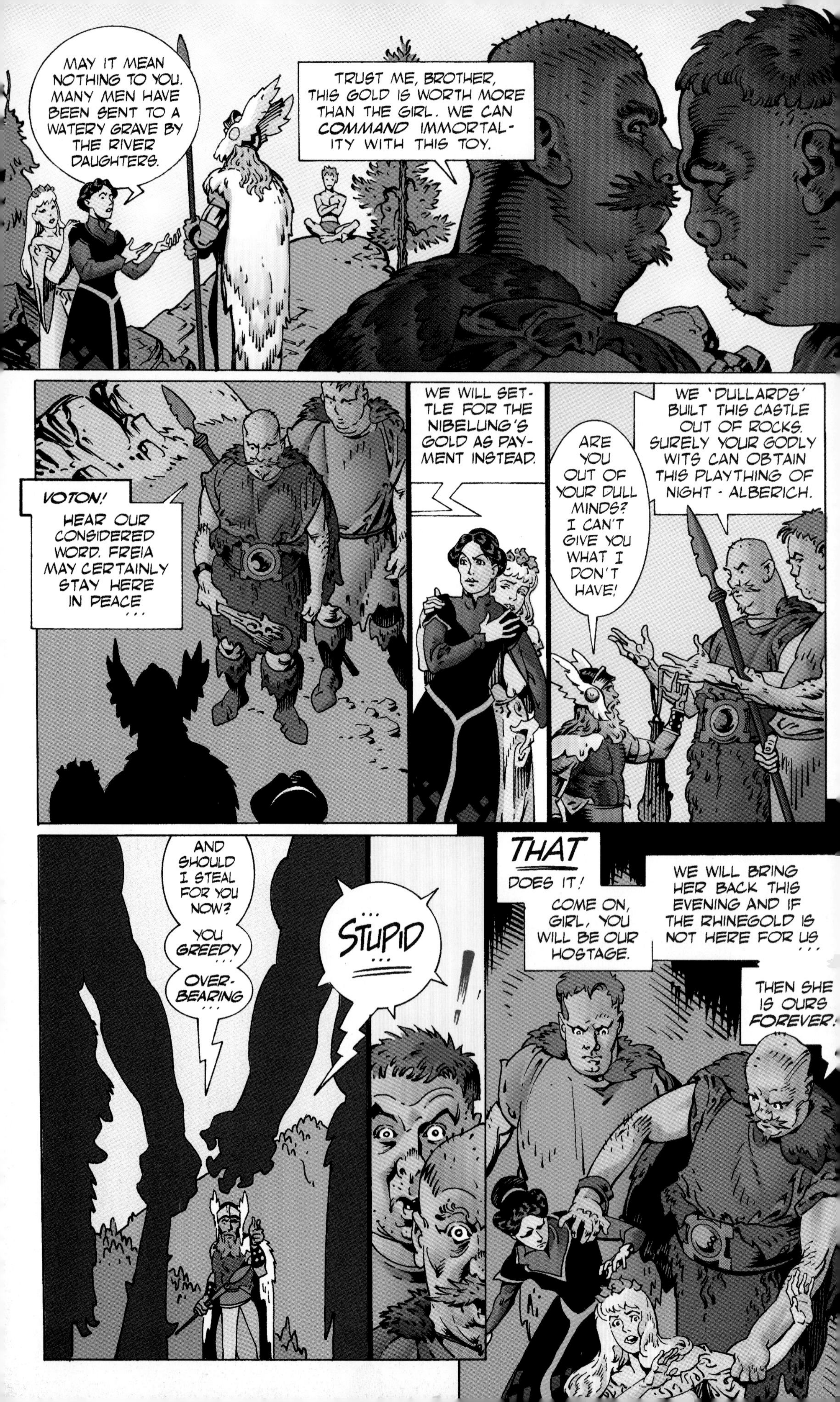

MAY IT MEAN NOTHING TO YOU. MANY MEN HAVE BEEN SENT TO A WATERY GRAVE BY THE RIVER DAUGHTERS.
TRUST ME, BROTHER, THIS GOLD IS WORTH MORE THAN THE GIRL. WE CAN COMMAND IMMORTALITY WITH THIS TOY.
VOTON!
HEAR OUR CONSIDERED WORD. FREIA MAY CERTAINLY STAY HERE IN PEACE . . .
WE WILL SETTLE FOR THE NIBELUNG'S GOLD AS PAYMENT INSTEAD.
ARE YOU OUT OF YOUR DULL MINDS? I CAN'T GIVE YOU WHAT I DON'T HAVE!
WE 'DULLARDS' BUILT THIS CASTLE OUT OF ROCKS. SURELY YOUR GODLY WITS CAN OBTAIN THIS PLAYTHING OF NIGHT - ALBERICH.
AND SHOULD I STEAL FOR YOU NOW?
YOU GREEDY . . .
OVERBEARING . . .
. . . STUPID . . .
THAT DOES IT!
COME ON, GIRL, YOU WILL BE OUR HOSTAGE.
WE WILL BRING HER BACK THIS EVENING AND IF THE RHINEGOLD IS NOT HERE FOR US . . .
THEN SHE IS OURS FOREVER.

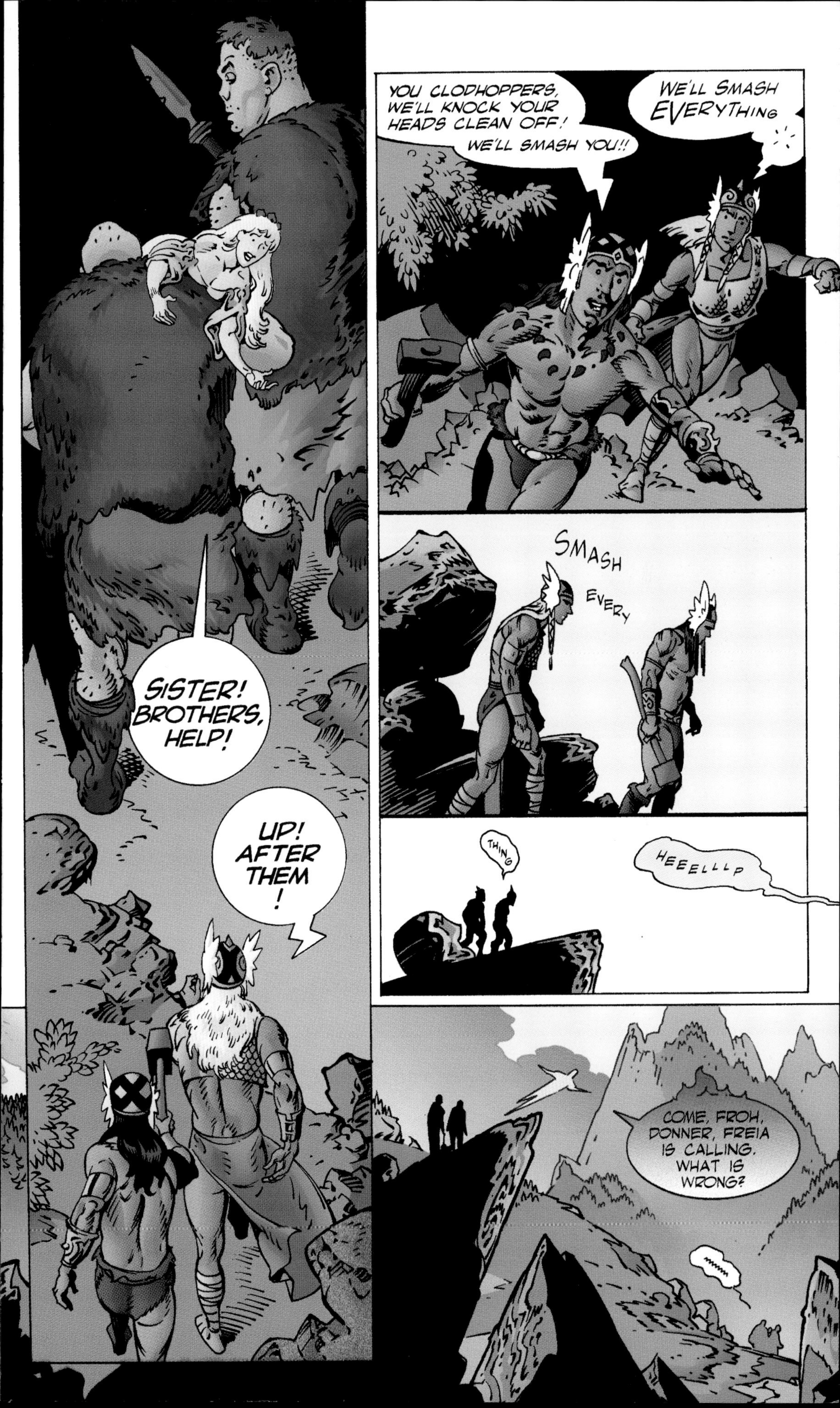

SISTER! BROTHERS, HELP!
UP! AFTER THEM!
YOU CLODHOPPERS, WE'LL KNOCK YOUR HEADS CLEAN OFF!
WE'LL SMASH YOU!!
WE'LL SMASH EVERYTHING
SMASH
EVERY
THING
HEEELLLP
COME, FROH, DONNER, FREIA IS CALLING. WHAT IS WRONG?

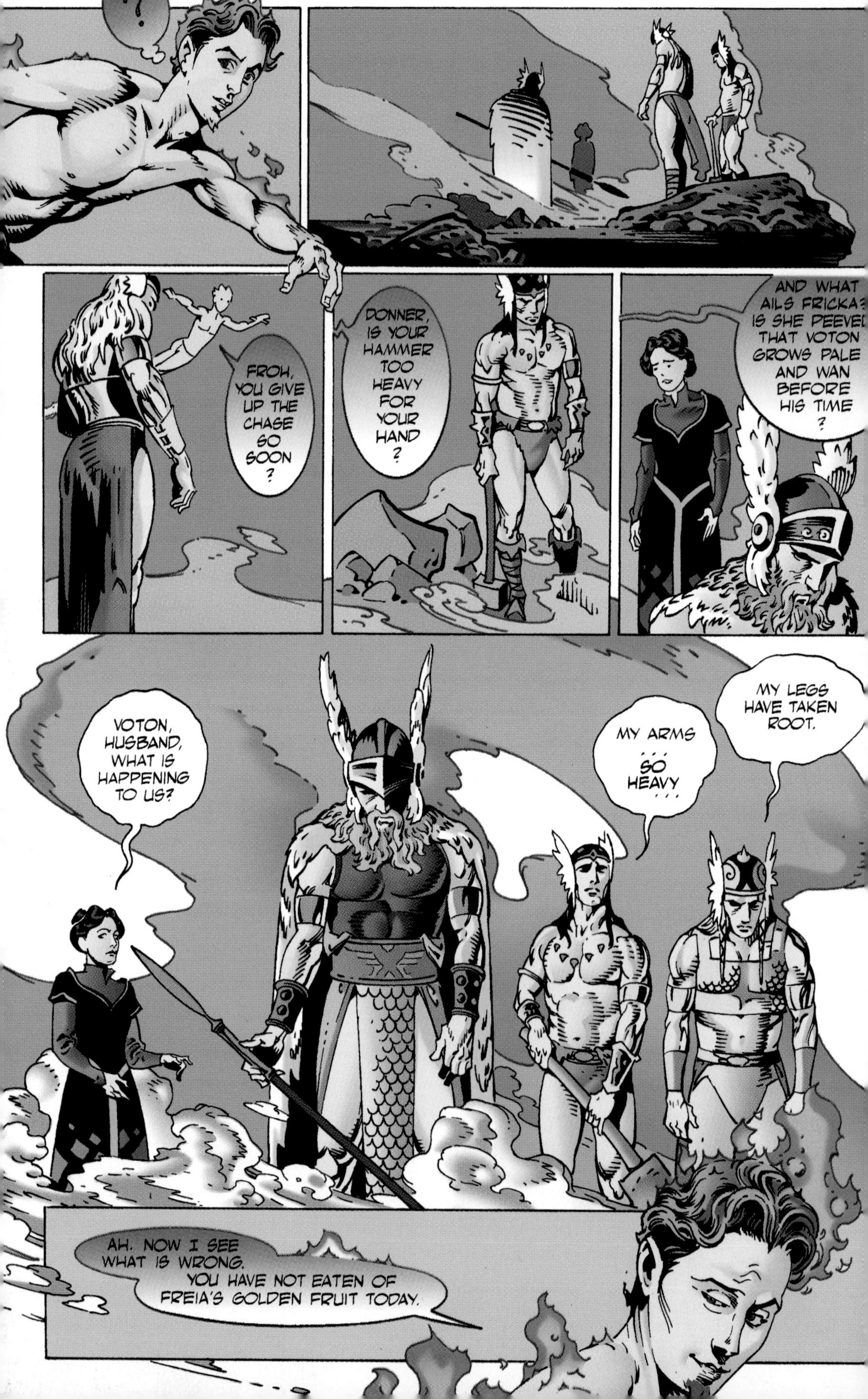
?
FROH, YOU GIVE UP THE CHASE SO SOON?
DONNER, IS YOUR HAMMER TOO HEAVY FOR YOUR HAND?
AND WHAT AILS FRICKA? IS SHE PEEVED THAT VOTON GROWS PALE AND WAN BEFORE HIS TIME?
VOTON, HUSBAND, WHAT IS HAPPENING TO US?
MY ARMS . . . SO HEAVY . . .
MY LEGS HAVE TAKEN ROOT.
AH. NOW I SEE WHAT IS WRONG. YOU HAVE NOT EATEN OF FREIA'S GOLDEN FRUIT TODAY.

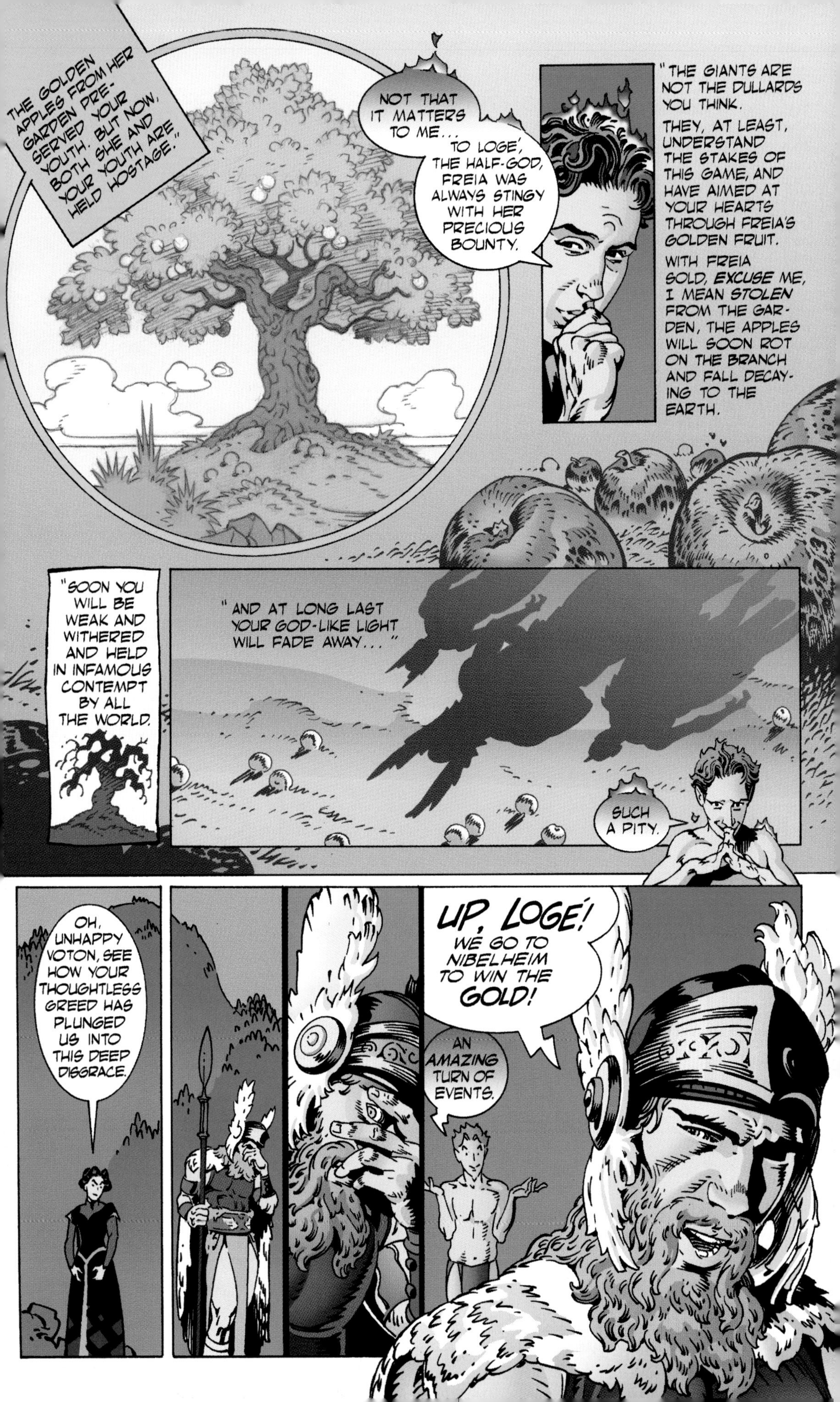

"THE GOLDEN APPLES FROM HER GARDEN PRE-SERVED YOUR YOUTH. BUT NOW, BOTH SHE AND YOUR YOUTH ARE HELD HOSTAGE."
NOT THAT IT MATTERS TO ME...
TO LOGE', THE HALF-GOD, FREIA WAS ALWAYS STINGY WITH HER PRECIOUS BOUNTY.
"THE GIANTS ARE NOT THE DULLARDS YOU THINK.
THEY, AT LEAST, UNDERSTAND THE STAKES OF THIS GAME, AND HAVE AIMED AT YOUR HEARTS THROUGH FREIA'S GOLDEN FRUIT.
WITH FREIA SOLD, *EXCUSE* ME, I MEAN *STOLEN* FROM THE GAR-DEN, THE APPLES WILL SOON ROT ON THE BRANCH AND FALL DECAY-ING TO THE EARTH.
"SOON YOU WILL BE WEAK AND WITHERED AND HELD IN INFAMOUS CONTEMPT BY ALL THE WORLD.
"AND AT LONG LAST YOUR GOD-LIKE LIGHT WILL FADE AWAY..."
SUCH A PITY.
OH, UNHAPPY VOTON, SEE HOW YOUR THOUGHTLESS GREED HAS PLUNGED US INTO THIS DEEP DISGRACE.
UP, LOGE'! WE GO TO NIBELHEIM TO WIN THE GOLD!
AN *AMAZING* TURN OF EVENTS.

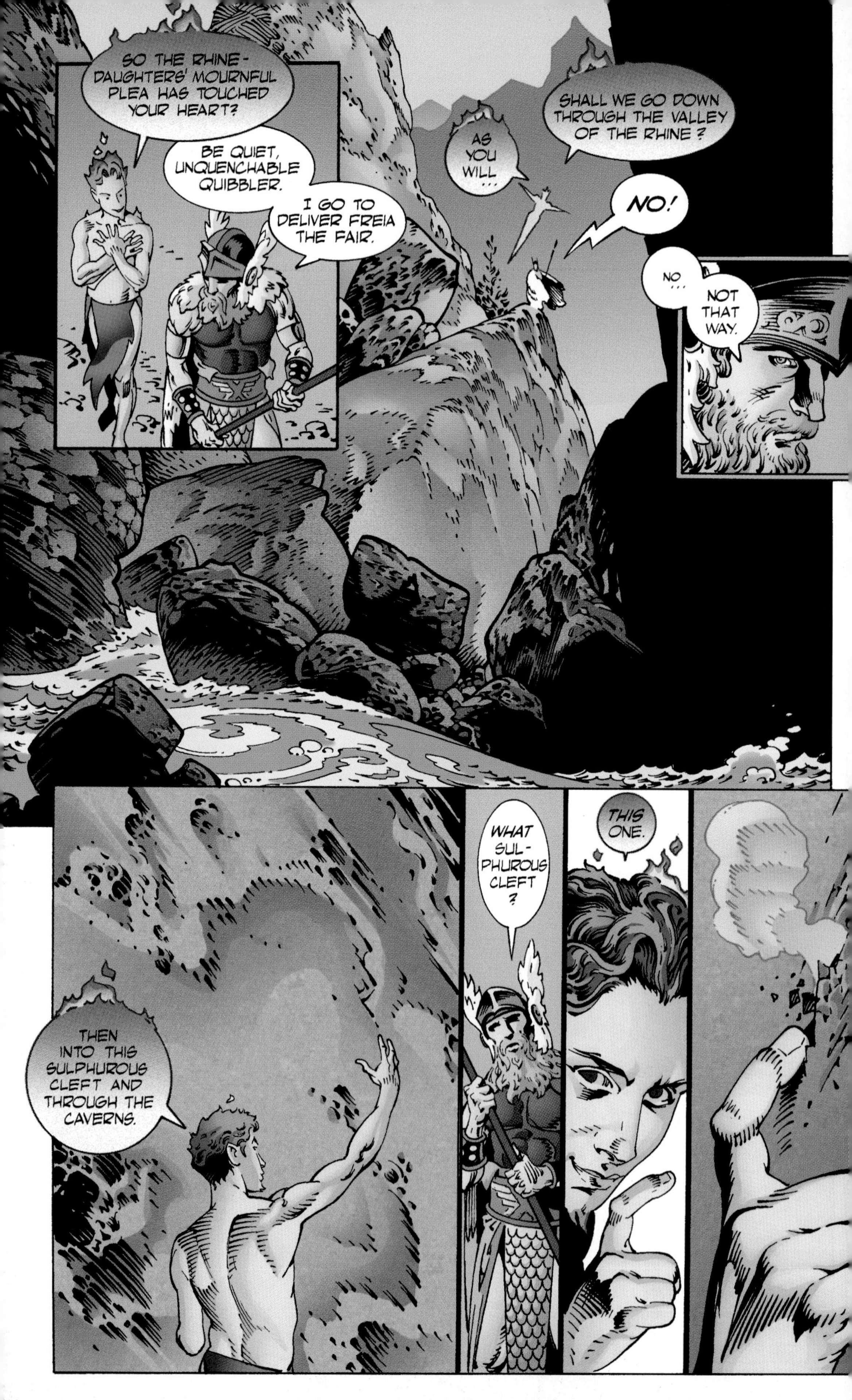

SO THE RHINE-DAUGHTERS' MOURNFUL PLEA HAS TOUCHED YOUR HEART?
BE QUIET, UNQUENCHABLE QUIBBLER.
I GO TO DELIVER FREIA THE FAIR.
AS YOU WILL . . .
SHALL WE GO DOWN THROUGH THE VALLEY OF THE RHINE?
NO!
NO . . .
NOT THAT WAY.
THEN INTO THIS SULPHUROUS CLEFT AND THROUGH THE CAVERNS.
WHAT SUL-PHUROUS CLEFT?
THIS ONE.

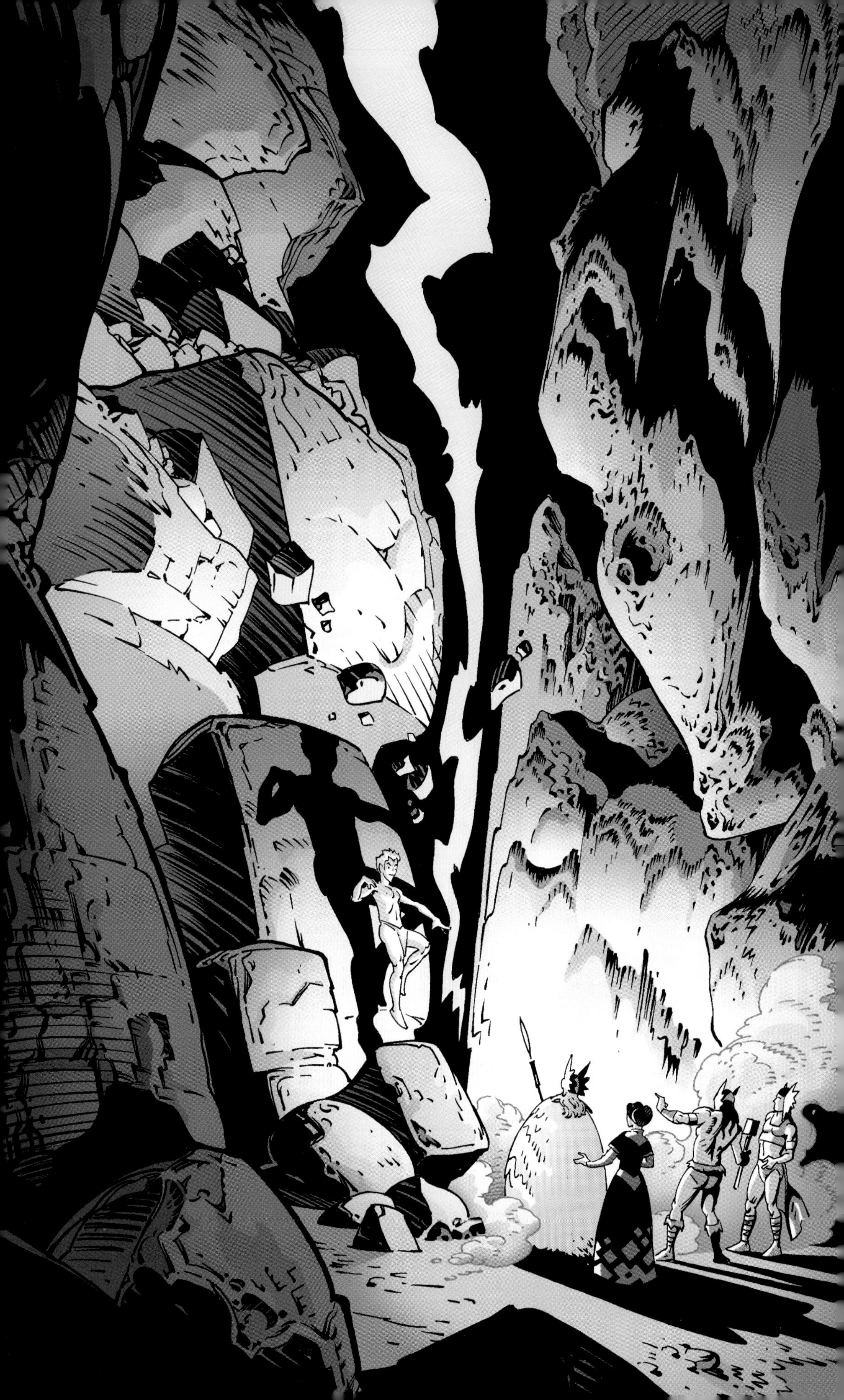

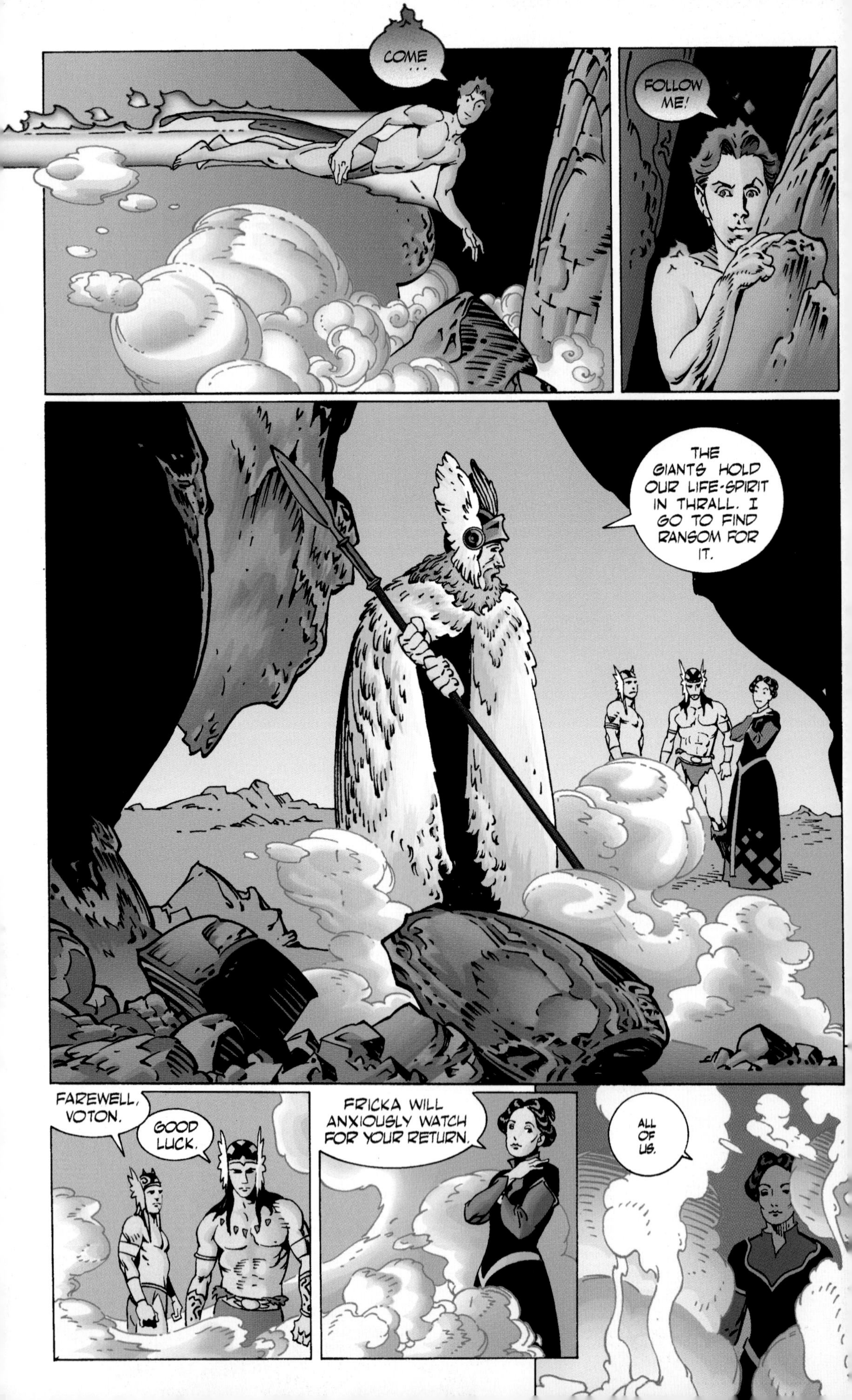
COME ...
FOLLOW ME!
THE GIANTS HOLD OUR LIFE-SPIRIT IN THRALL. I GO TO FIND RANSOM FOR IT.
FAREWELL, VOTON.
GOOD LUCK.
FRICKA WILL ANXIOUSLY WATCH FOR YOUR RETURN.
ALL OF US.

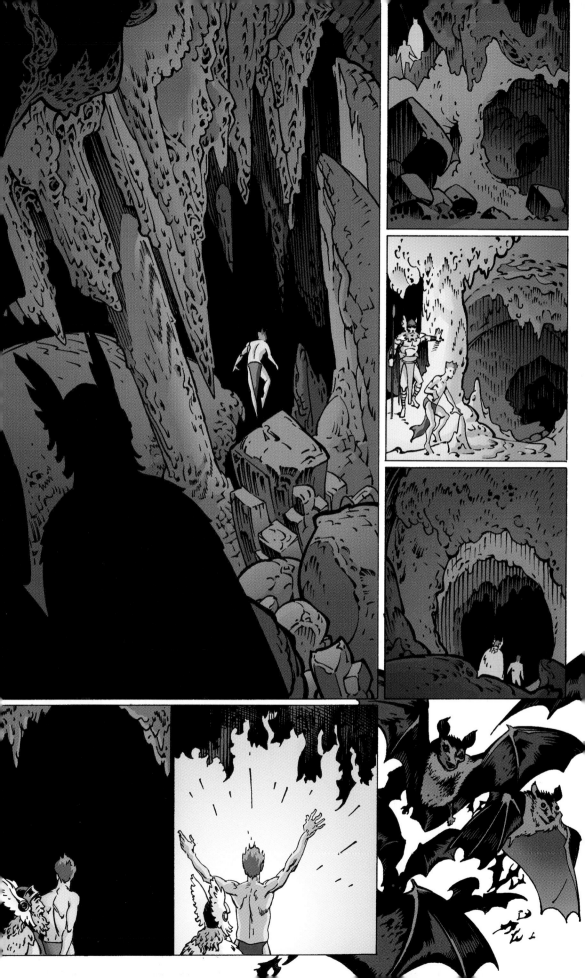

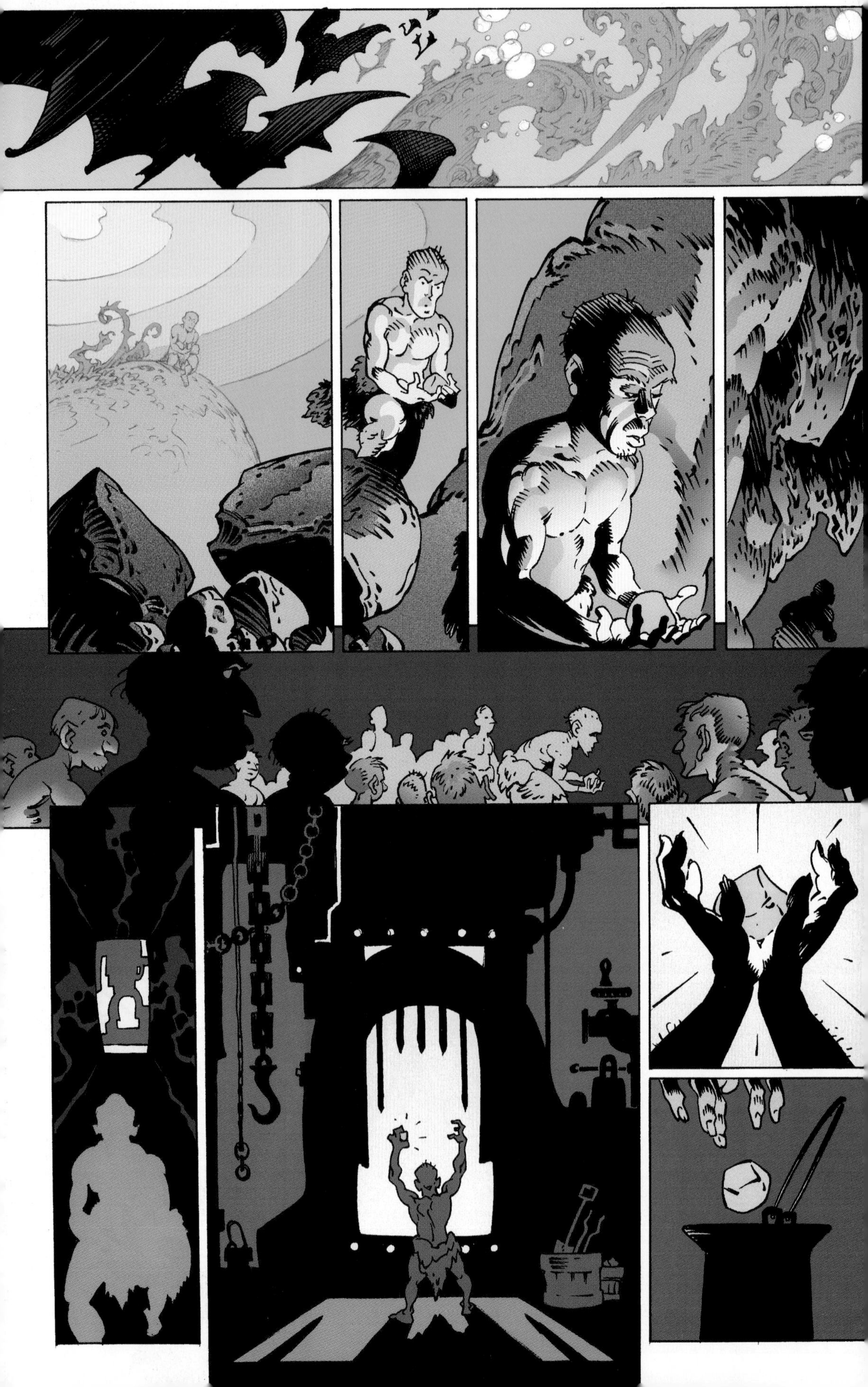

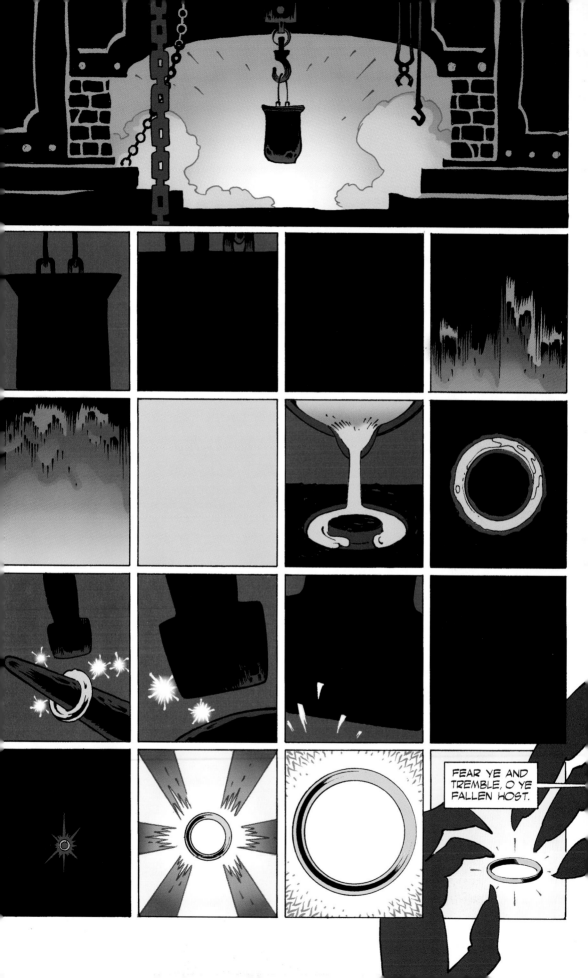

FEAR YE AND TREMBLE, O YE FALLEN HOST.

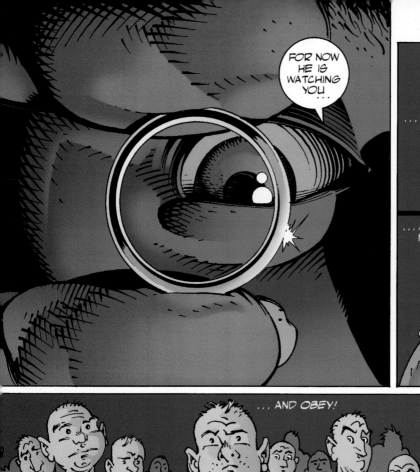

FOR NOW HE IS WATCHING YOU . . .

...FEAR YE...

...AND TREMBLE, NIBELUNGS...

... AND OBEY!

OBEY THE RING'S DREAD MASTER...

THE LORD OF THE NIBELUNGS

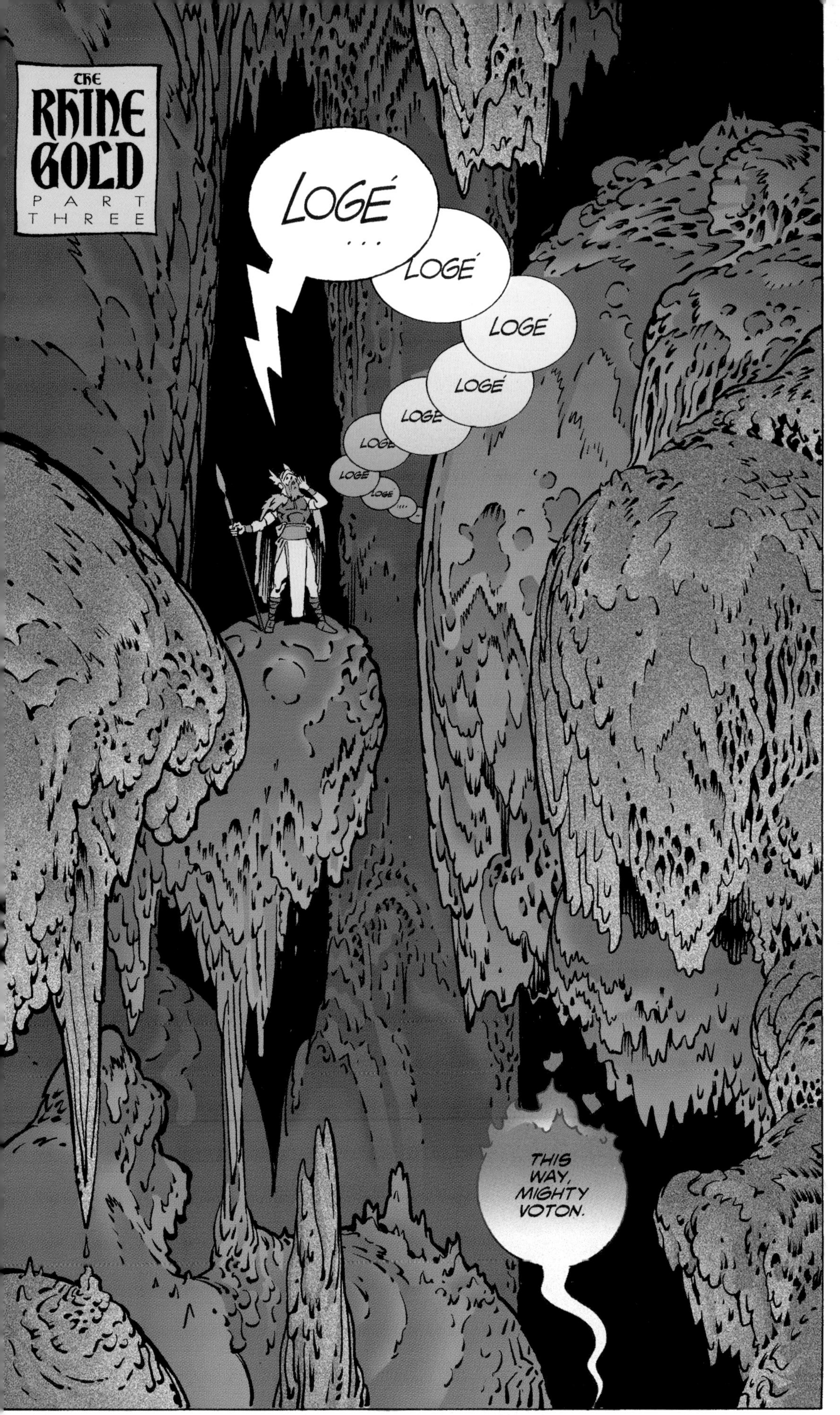
THE RHINE GOLD PART THREE
LOGÉ ...
LOGÉ
LOGÉ
LOGÉ
LOGÉ
LOGÉ
LOGÉ
LOGE ...
THIS WAY, MIGHTY VOTON.

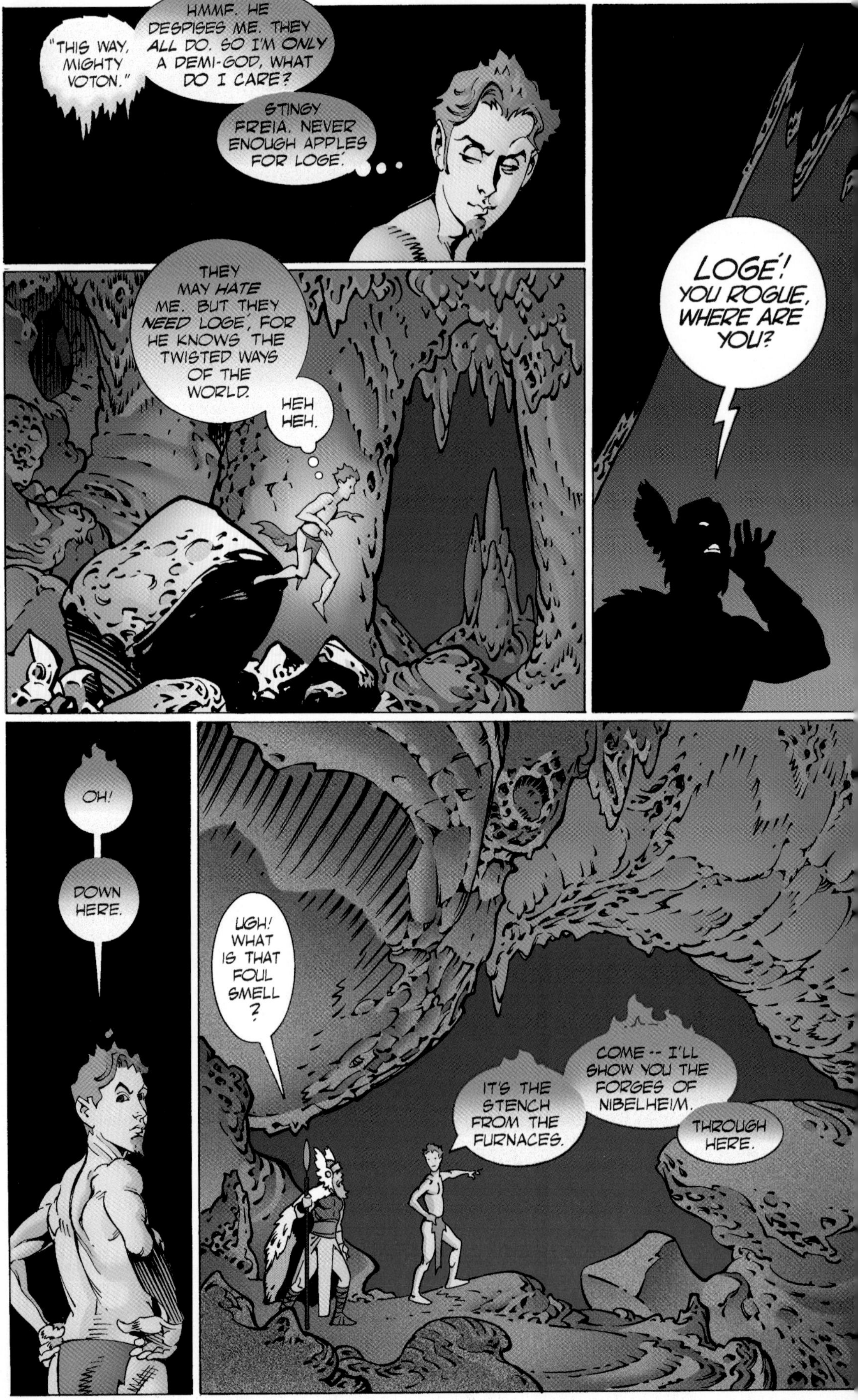
"THIS WAY, MIGHTY VOTON."
HMMF. HE DESPISES ME. THEY ALL DO. SO I'M ONLY A DEMI-GOD, WHAT DO I CARE?
STINGY FREIA. NEVER ENOUGH APPLES FOR LOGE.
THEY MAY HATE ME. BUT THEY NEED LOGE, FOR HE KNOWS THE TWISTED WAYS OF THE WORLD.
HEH HEH.
LOGE! YOU ROGUE, WHERE ARE YOU?
OH!
DOWN HERE.
UGH! WHAT IS THAT FOUL SMELL?
IT'S THE STENCH FROM THE FURNACES.
COME -- I'LL SHOW YOU THE FORGES OF NIBELHEIM.
THROUGH HERE.

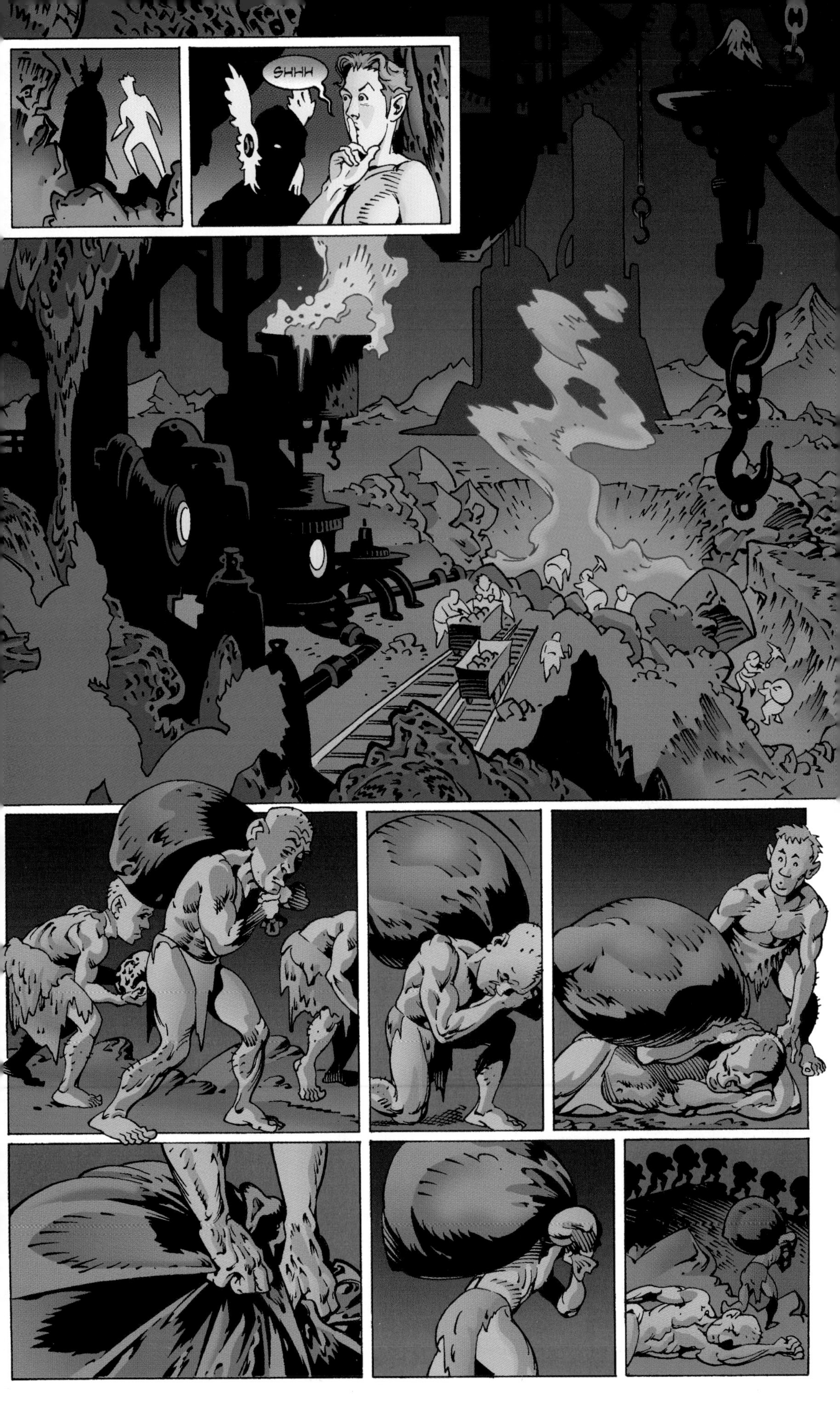
SHHH

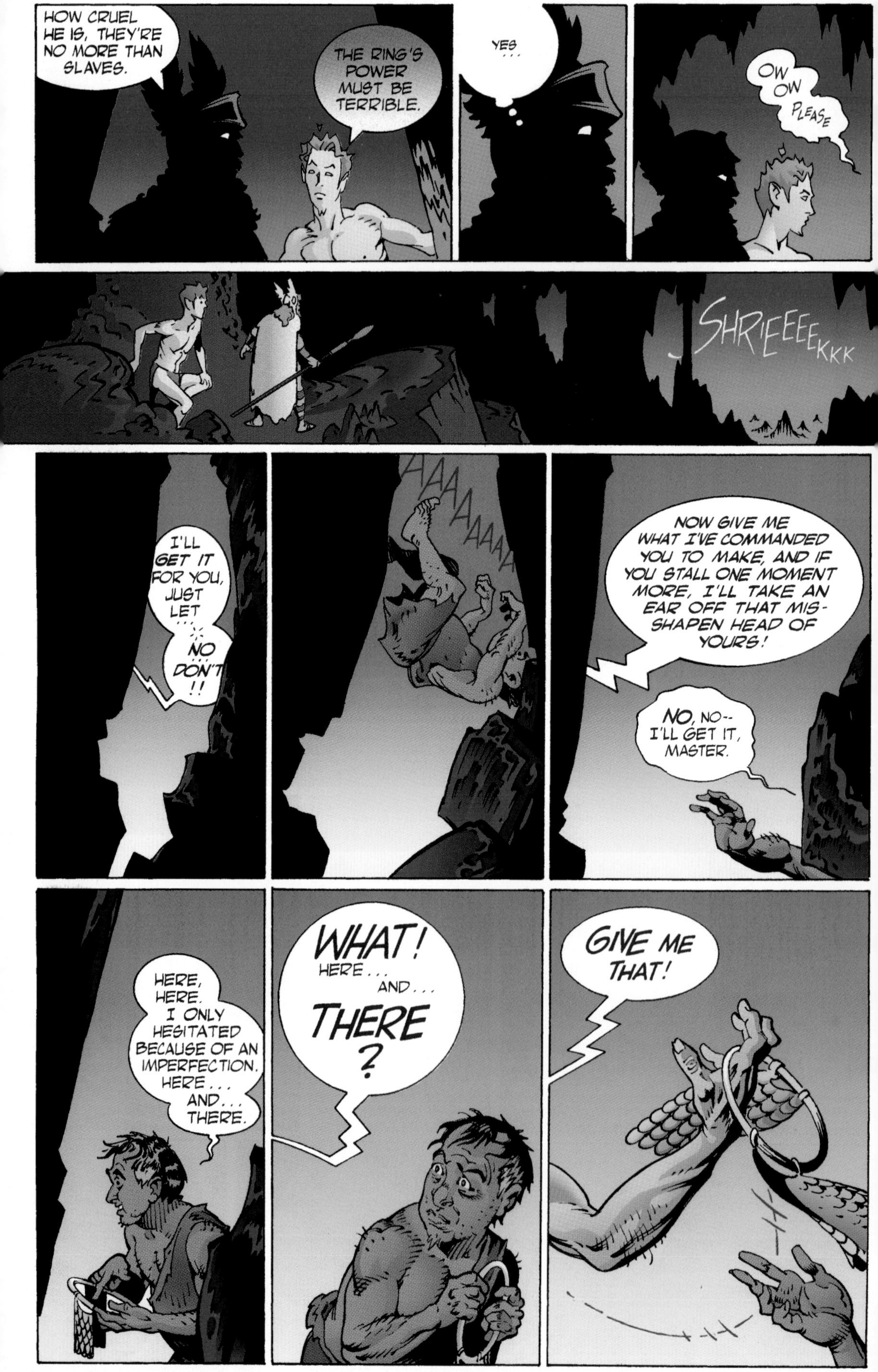
HOW CRUEL HE IS, THEY'RE NO MORE THAN SLAVES.
THE RING'S POWER MUST BE TERRIBLE.
YES . . .
OW OW PLEASE
SHRIEEEEEKKK
I'LL GET IT FOR YOU, JUST LET . . .
NO . . . DON'T !!
AAAAAAAA
NOW GIVE ME WHAT I'VE COMMANDED YOU TO MAKE, AND IF YOU STALL ONE MOMENT MORE, I'LL TAKE AN EAR OFF THAT MIS-SHAPEN HEAD OF YOURS!
NO, NO-- I'LL GET IT, MASTER.
HERE, HERE. I ONLY HESITATED BECAUSE OF AN IMPERFECTION. HERE . . . AND . . . THERE.
WHAT! HERE . . . AND . . . THERE ?
GIVE ME THAT!

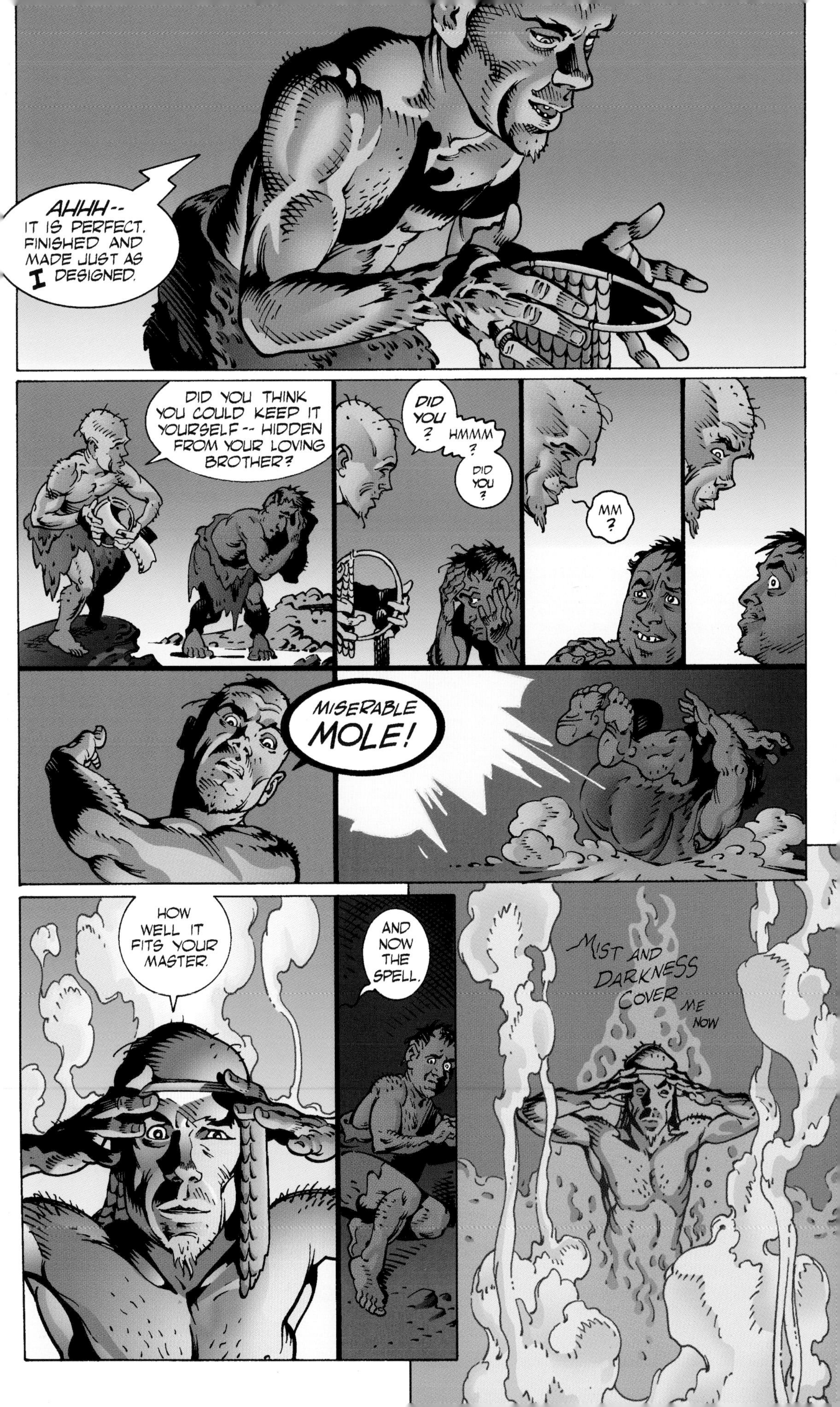
AHHH-- IT IS PERFECT. FINISHED AND MADE JUST AS I DESIGNED.
DID YOU THINK YOU COULD KEEP IT YOURSELF -- HIDDEN FROM YOUR LOVING BROTHER?
DID YOU?
HMMM?
DID YOU?
MM?
MISERABLE MOLE!
HOW WELL IT FITS YOUR MASTER.
AND NOW THE SPELL.
MIST AND DARKNESS COVER ME NOW

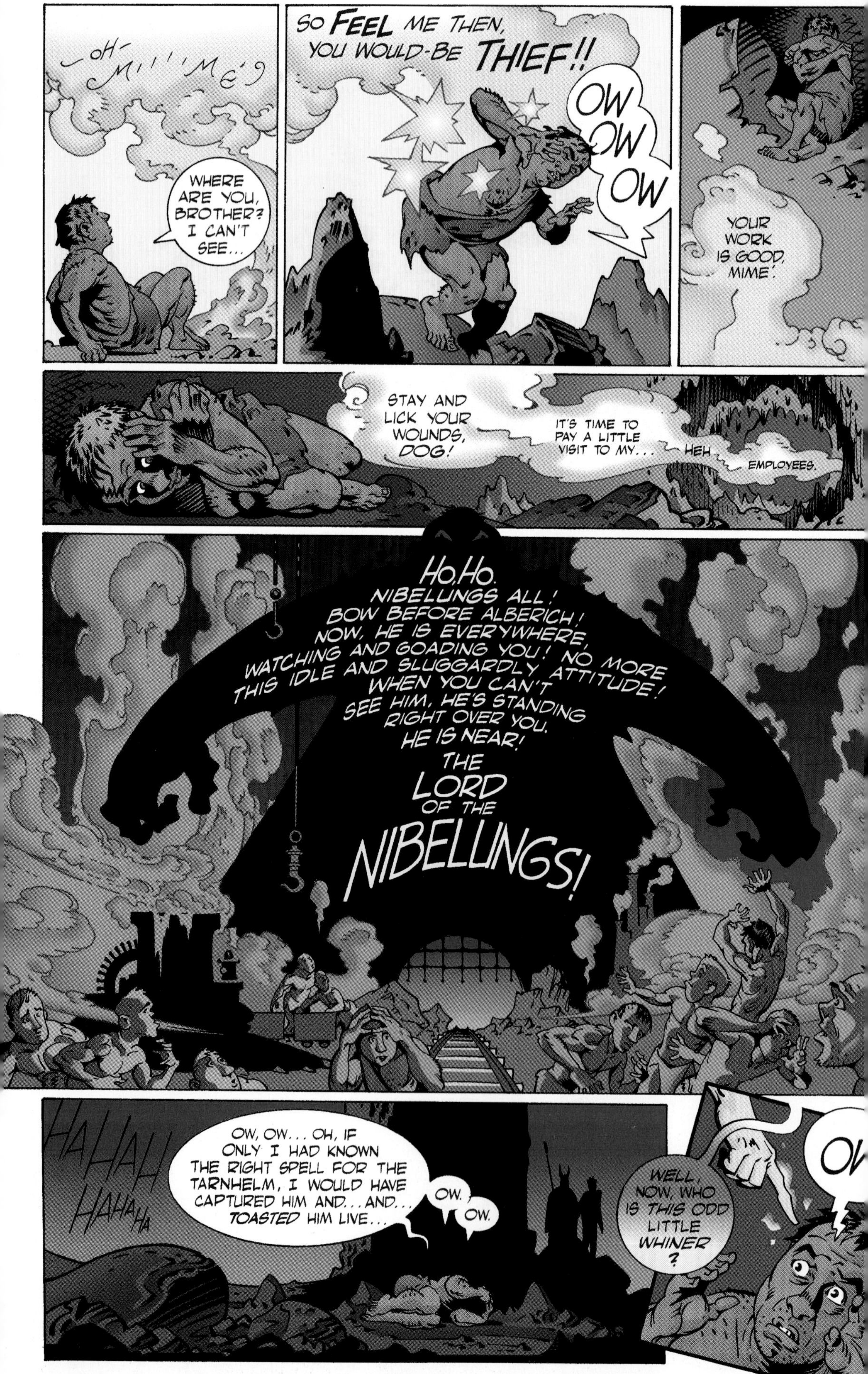

OH- MI'''ME'9
WHERE ARE YOU, BROTHER? I CAN'T SEE...
SO FEEL ME THEN, YOU WOULD-BE THIEF!!
OW OW OW
YOUR WORK IS GOOD, MIME'.
STAY AND LICK YOUR WOUNDS, DOG!
IT'S TIME TO PAY A LITTLE VISIT TO MY... HEH EMPLOYEES.
Ho,Ho. NIBELUNGS ALL! BOW BEFORE ALBERICH! NOW, HE IS EVERYWHERE, WATCHING AND GOADING YOU! NO MORE THIS IDLE AND SLUGGARDLY ATTITUDE! WHEN YOU CAN'T SEE HIM, HE'S STANDING RIGHT OVER YOU. HE IS NEAR! THE LORD OF THE NIBELUNGS!
HAHAH HAHAHA
OW, OW... OH, IF ONLY I HAD KNOWN THE RIGHT SPELL FOR THE TARNHELM, I WOULD HAVE CAPTURED HIM AND...AND... TOASTED HIM LIVE...
OW.
OW.
WELL, NOW, WHO IS THIS ODD LITTLE WHINER?

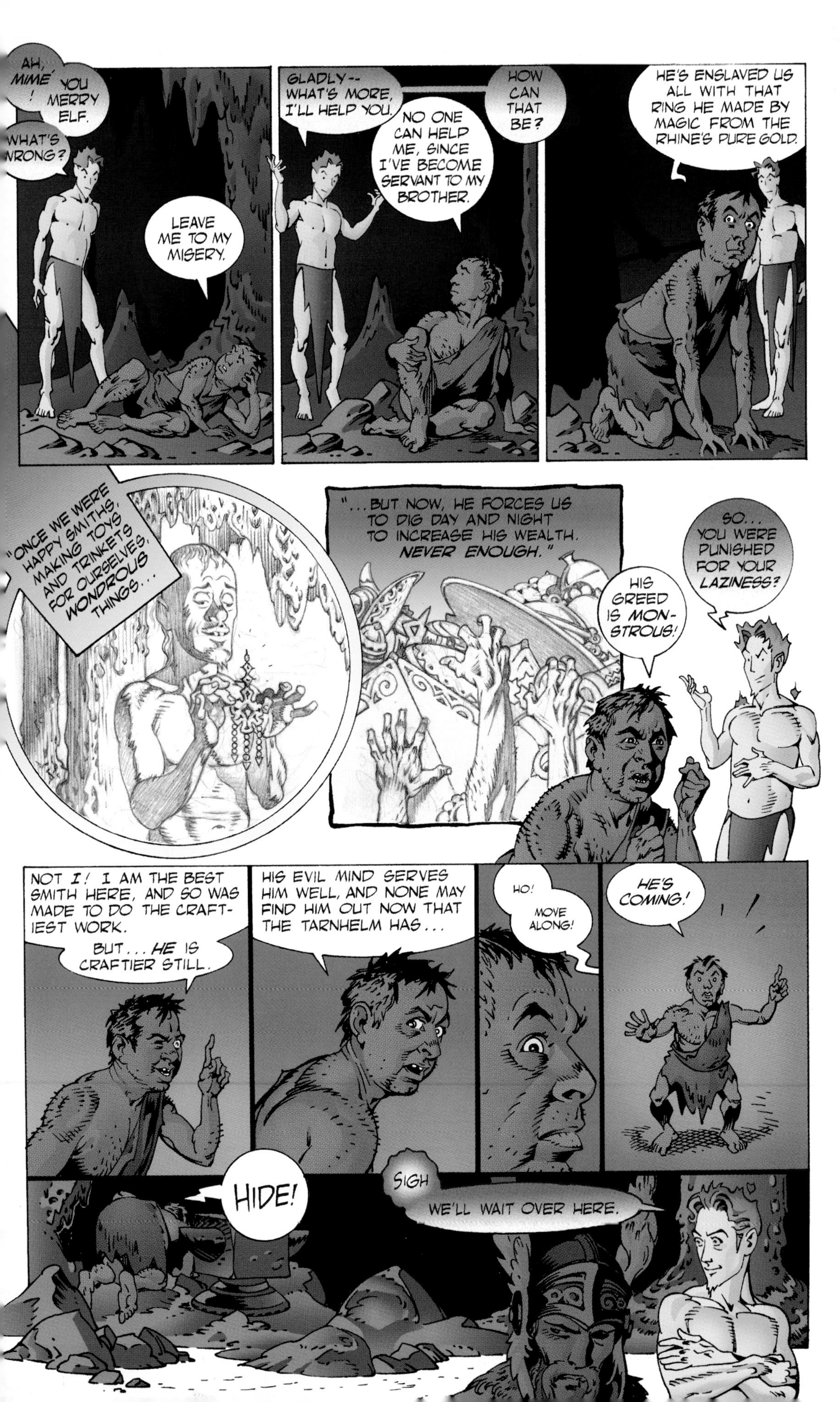

AH, MIME!
YOU MERRY ELF.
WHAT'S WRONG?
LEAVE ME TO MY MISERY.
GLADLY-- WHAT'S MORE, I'LL HELP YOU.
NO ONE CAN HELP ME, SINCE I'VE BECOME SERVANT TO MY BROTHER.
HOW CAN THAT BE?
HE'S ENSLAVED US ALL WITH THAT RING HE MADE BY MAGIC FROM THE RHINE'S PURE GOLD.
"ONCE WE WERE HAPPY SMITHS, MAKING TOYS AND TRINKETS FOR OURSELVES, WONDROUS THINGS...
"...BUT NOW, HE FORCES US TO DIG DAY AND NIGHT TO INCREASE HIS WEALTH. NEVER ENOUGH."
HIS GREED IS MON-STROUS!
SO... YOU WERE PUNISHED FOR YOUR LAZINESS?
NOT I! I AM THE BEST SMITH HERE, AND SO WAS MADE TO DO THE CRAFT-IEST WORK.
BUT... HE IS CRAFTIER STILL.
HIS EVIL MIND SERVES HIM WELL, AND NONE MAY FIND HIM OUT NOW THAT THE TARNHELM HAS...
HO!
MOVE ALONG!
HE'S COMING!
HIDE!
SIGH
WE'LL WAIT OVER HERE.

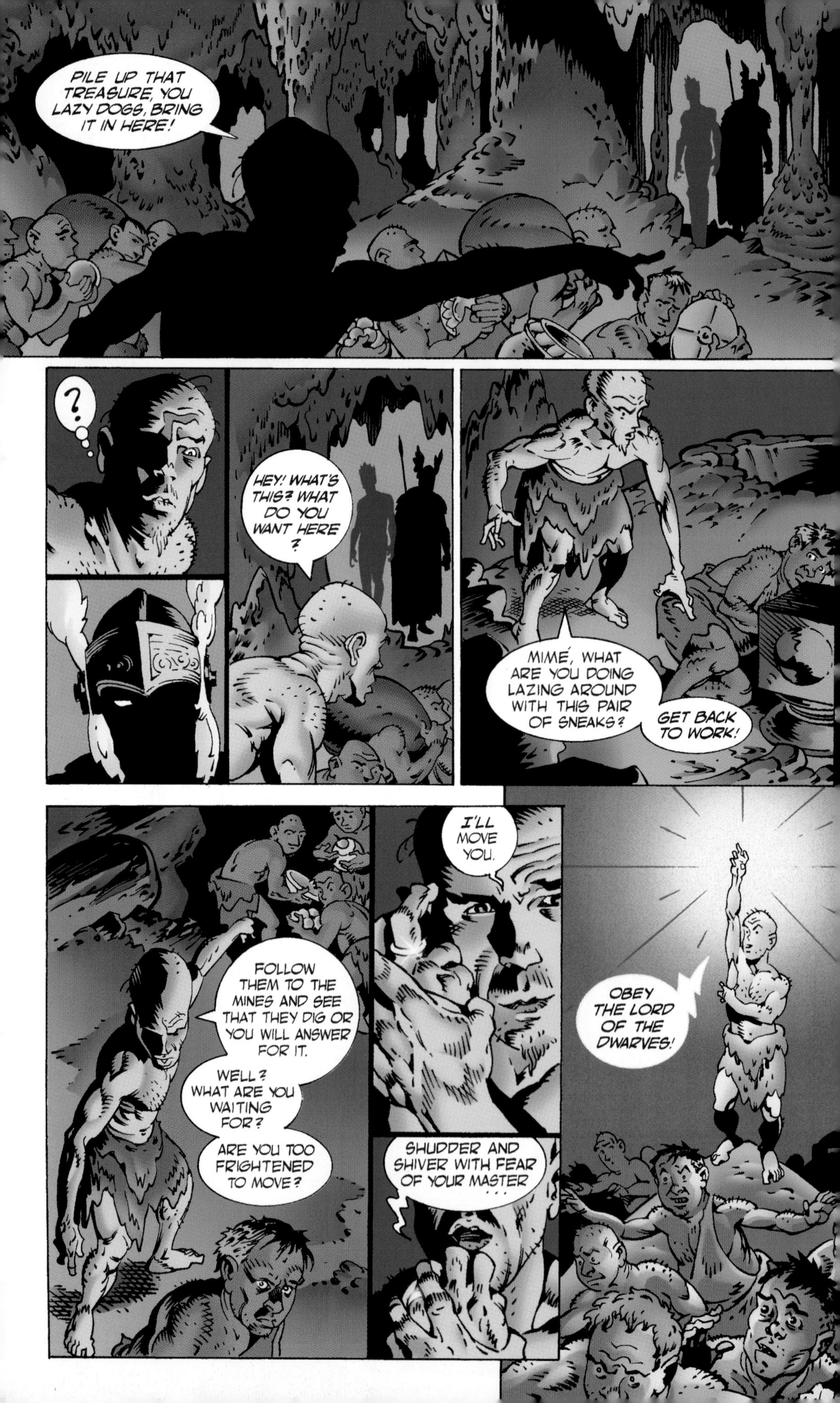
PILE UP THAT TREASURE, YOU LAZY DOGS, BRING IT IN HERE!
?
HEY! WHAT'S THIS? WHAT DO YOU WANT HERE ?
MIMÉ, WHAT ARE YOU DOING LAZING AROUND WITH THIS PAIR OF SNEAKS?
GET BACK TO WORK!
FOLLOW THEM TO THE MINES AND SEE THAT THEY DIG OR YOU WILL ANSWER FOR IT.
WELL? WHAT ARE YOU WAITING FOR?
ARE YOU TOO FRIGHTENED TO MOVE?
I'LL MOVE YOU.
SHUDDER AND SHIVER WITH FEAR OF YOUR MASTER . . .
OBEY THE LORD OF THE DWARVES!

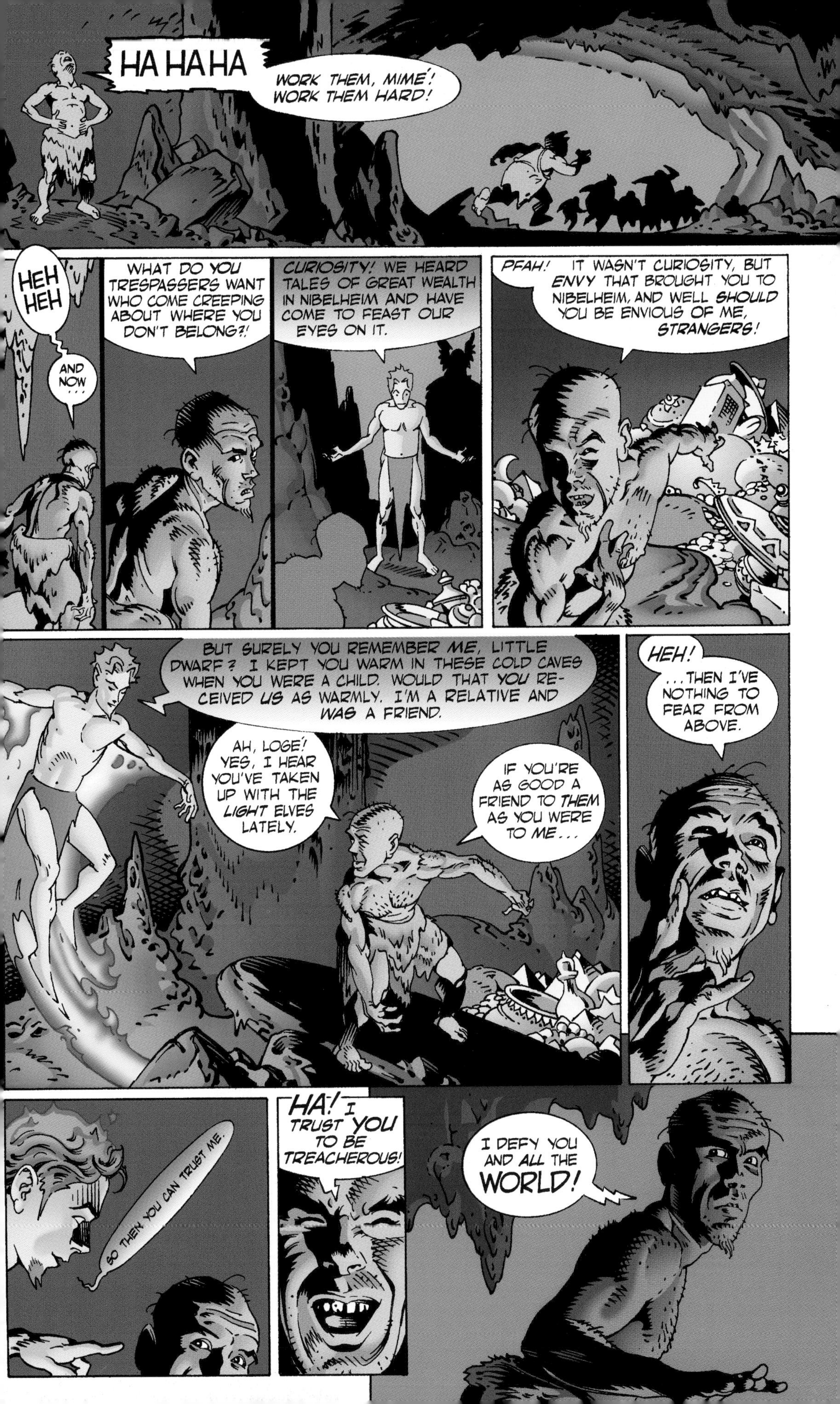
HA HA HA
WORK THEM, MIME! WORK THEM HARD!
HEH HEH
AND NOW . . .
WHAT DO YOU TRESPASSERS WANT WHO COME CREEPING ABOUT WHERE YOU DON'T BELONG?!
CURIOSITY! WE HEARD TALES OF GREAT WEALTH IN NIBELHEIM AND HAVE COME TO FEAST OUR EYES ON IT.
PFAH! IT WASN'T CURIOSITY, BUT ENVY THAT BROUGHT YOU TO NIBELHEIM, AND WELL SHOULD YOU BE ENVIOUS OF ME, STRANGERS!
BUT SURELY YOU REMEMBER ME, LITTLE DWARF? I KEPT YOU WARM IN THESE COLD CAVES WHEN YOU WERE A CHILD. WOULD THAT YOU RECEIVED US AS WARMLY. I'M A RELATIVE AND WAS A FRIEND.
AH, LOGE! YES, I HEAR YOU'VE TAKEN UP WITH THE LIGHT ELVES LATELY.
IF YOU'RE AS GOOD A FRIEND TO THEM AS YOU WERE TO ME . . .
HEH! . . . THEN I'VE NOTHING TO FEAR FROM ABOVE.
SO THEN YOU CAN TRUST ME.
HA! I TRUST YOU TO BE TREACHEROUS!
I DEFY YOU AND ALL THE WORLD!

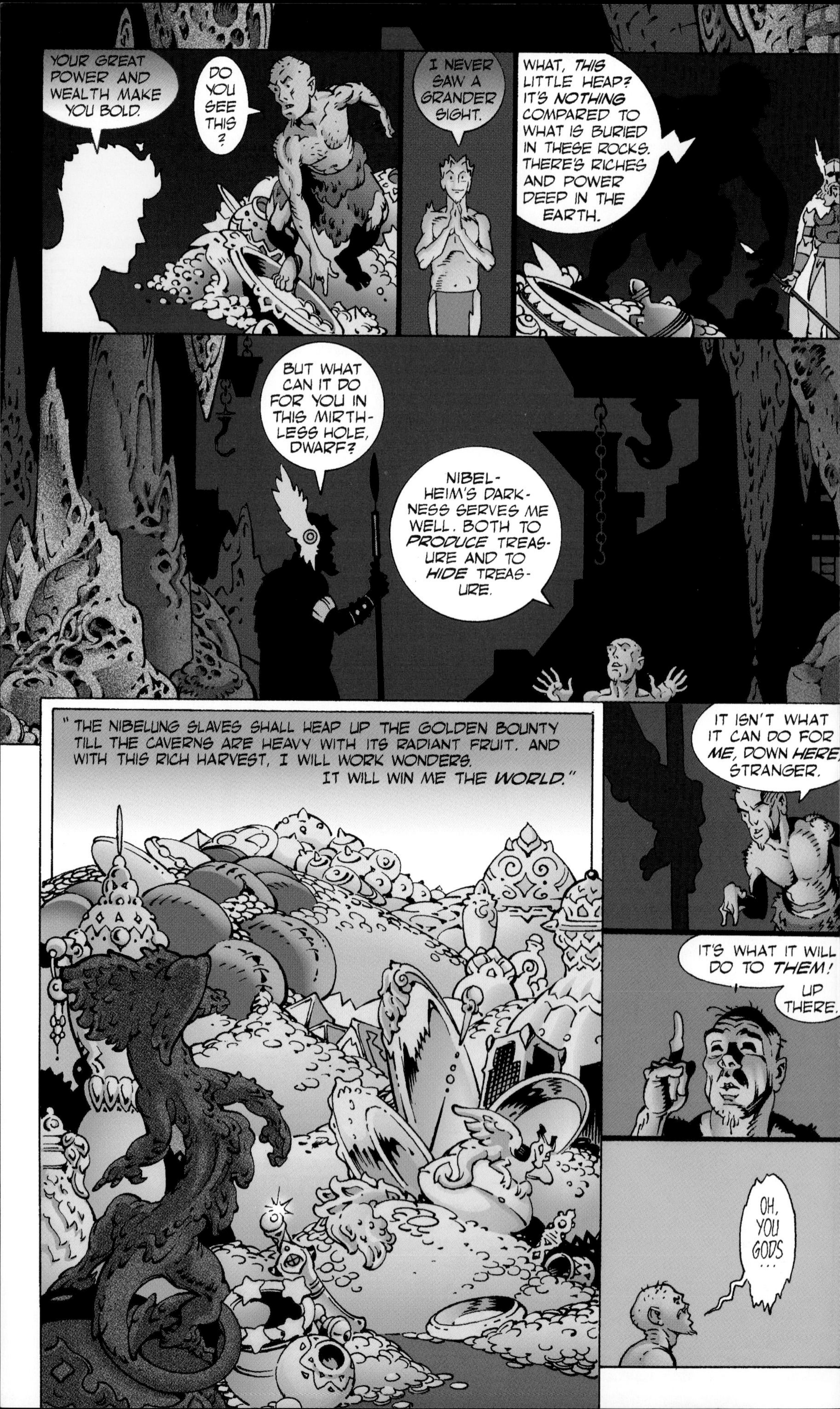
YOUR GREAT POWER AND WEALTH MAKE YOU BOLD.
DO YOU SEE THIS?
I NEVER SAW A GRANDER SIGHT.
WHAT, THIS LITTLE HEAP? IT'S NOTHING COMPARED TO WHAT IS BURIED IN THESE ROCKS. THERE'S RICHES AND POWER DEEP IN THE EARTH.
BUT WHAT CAN IT DO FOR YOU IN THIS MIRTHLESS HOLE, DWARF?
NIBELHEIM'S DARKNESS SERVES ME WELL. BOTH TO PRODUCE TREASURE AND TO HIDE TREASURE.
"THE NIBELUNG SLAVES SHALL HEAP UP THE GOLDEN BOUNTY TILL THE CAVERNS ARE HEAVY WITH ITS RADIANT FRUIT. AND WITH THIS RICH HARVEST, I WILL WORK WONDERS. IT WILL WIN ME THE WORLD."
IT ISN'T WHAT IT CAN DO FOR ME, DOWN HERE, STRANGER.
IT'S WHAT IT WILL DO TO THEM!
UP THERE.
OH, YOU GODS...

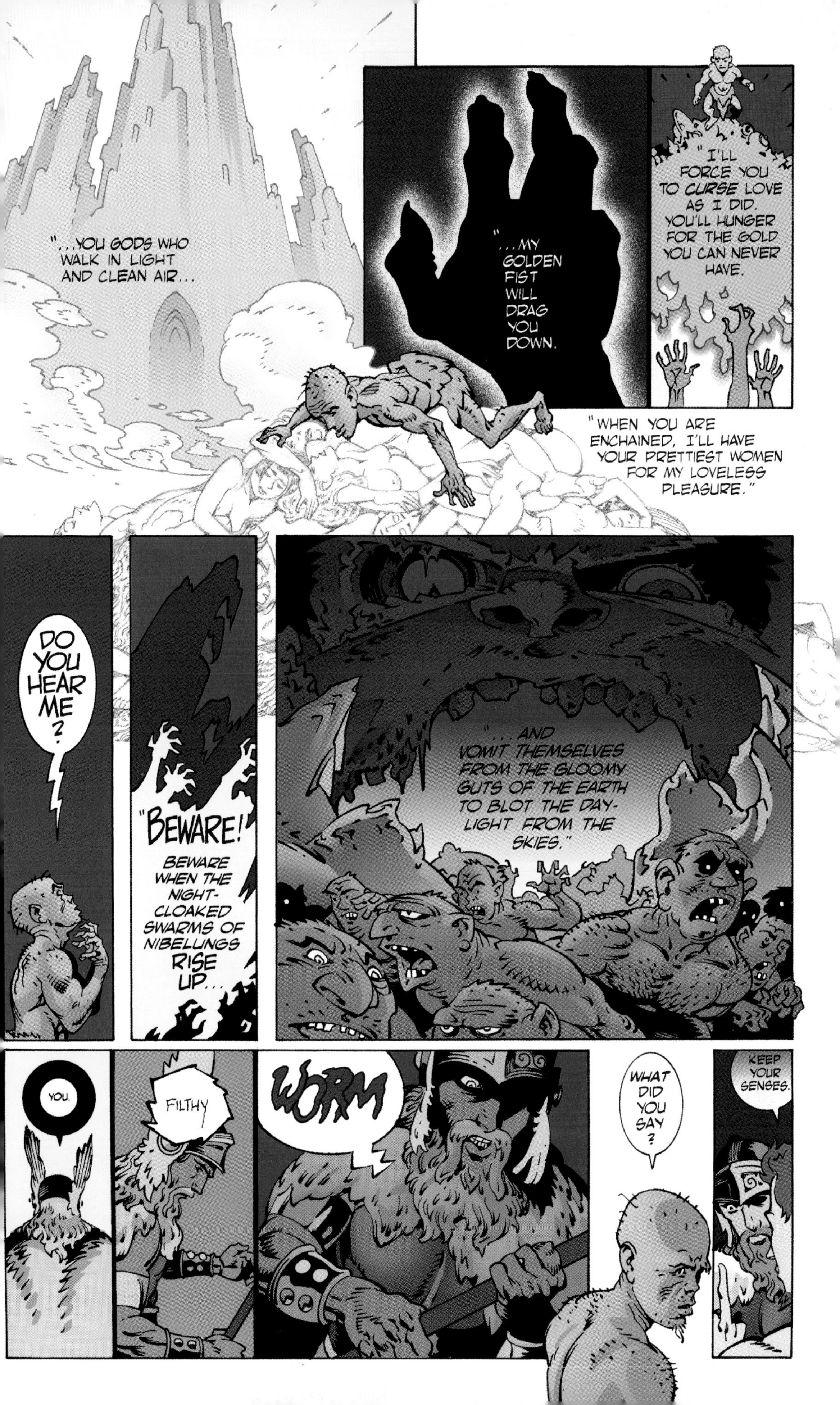
"...YOU GODS WHO WALK IN LIGHT AND CLEAN AIR...
"...MY GOLDEN FIST WILL DRAG YOU DOWN.
"I'LL FORCE YOU TO CURSE LOVE AS I DID. YOU'LL HUNGER FOR THE GOLD YOU CAN NEVER HAVE.
"WHEN YOU ARE ENCHAINED, I'LL HAVE YOUR PRETTIEST WOMEN FOR MY LOVELESS PLEASURE."
DO YOU HEAR ME?
"BEWARE!
BEWARE WHEN THE NIGHT-CLOAKED SWARMS OF NIBELUNGS RISE UP...
"...AND VOMIT THEMSELVES FROM THE GLOOMY GUTS OF THE EARTH TO BLOT THE DAYLIGHT FROM THE SKIES."
YOU.
FILTHY
WORM
WHAT DID YOU SAY?
KEEP YOUR SENSES.

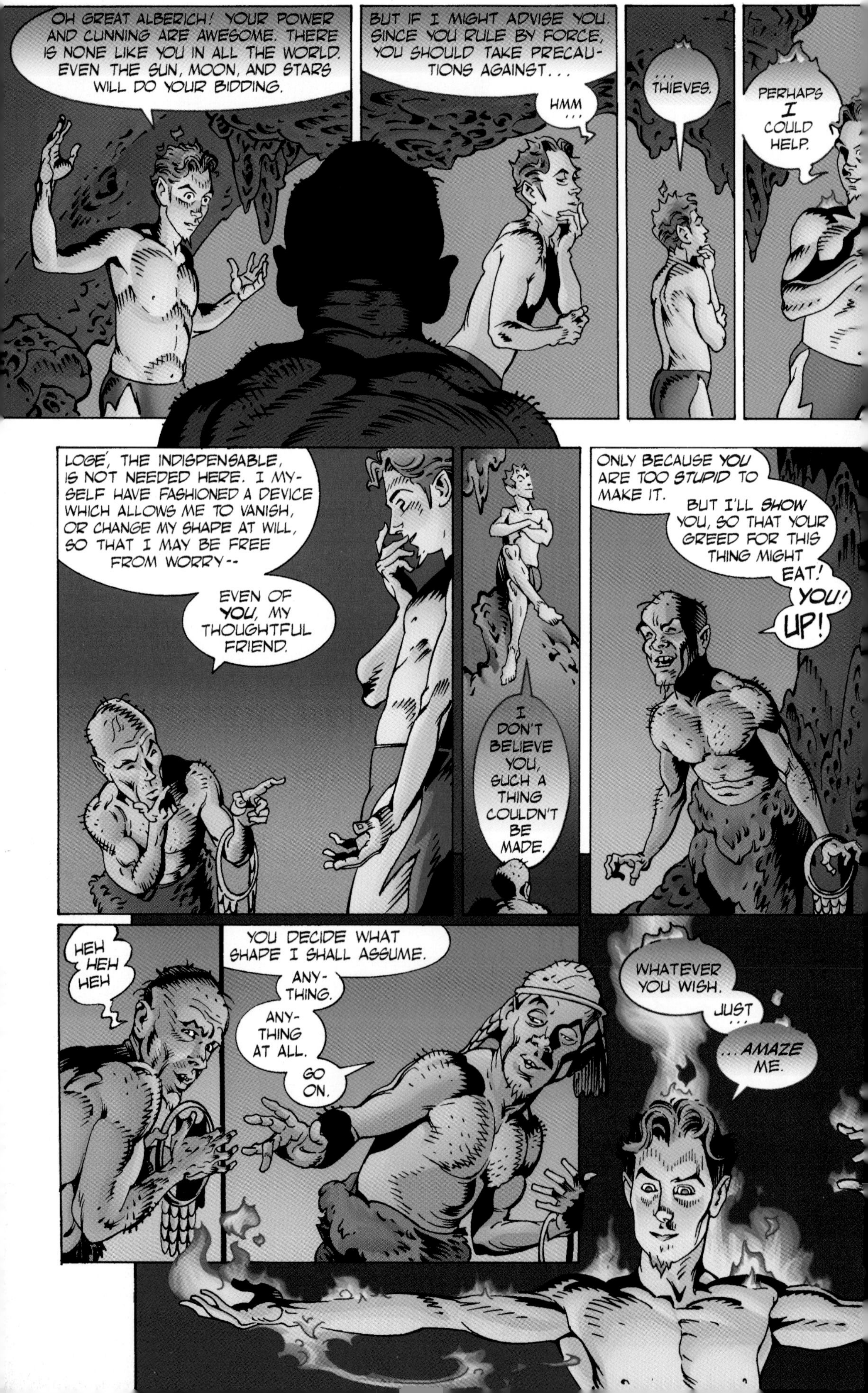
OH GREAT ALBERICH! YOUR POWER AND CUNNING ARE AWESOME. THERE IS NONE LIKE YOU IN ALL THE WORLD. EVEN THE SUN, MOON, AND STARS WILL DO YOUR BIDDING.
BUT IF I MIGHT ADVISE YOU. SINCE YOU RULE BY FORCE, YOU SHOULD TAKE PRECAUTIONS AGAINST . . .
HMM . . .
. . . THIEVES.
PERHAPS I COULD HELP.
LOGE, THE INDISPENSABLE, IS NOT NEEDED HERE. I MYSELF HAVE FASHIONED A DEVICE WHICH ALLOWS ME TO VANISH, OR CHANGE MY SHAPE AT WILL, SO THAT I MAY BE FREE FROM WORRY--
EVEN OF YOU, MY THOUGHTFUL FRIEND.
I DON'T BELIEVE YOU, SUCH A THING COULDN'T BE MADE.
ONLY BECAUSE YOU ARE TOO STUPID TO MAKE IT.
BUT I'LL SHOW YOU, SO THAT YOUR GREED FOR THIS THING MIGHT EAT! YOU! UP!
HEH HEH HEH
YOU DECIDE WHAT SHAPE I SHALL ASSUME.
ANYTHING.
ANYTHING AT ALL.
GO ON.
WHATEVER YOU WISH.
JUST . . .
. . . AMAZE ME.

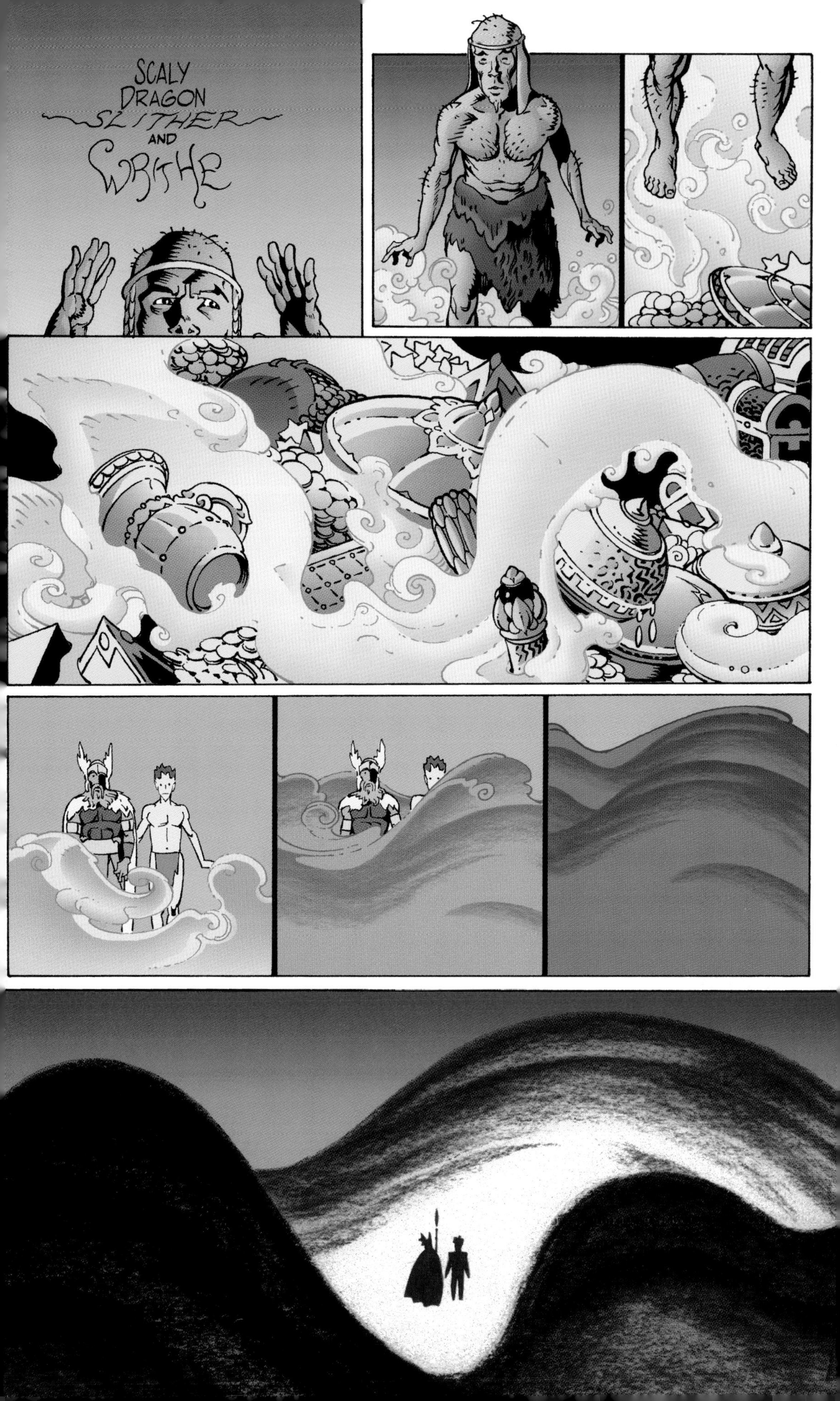
SCALY DRAGON SLITHER AND WRITHE

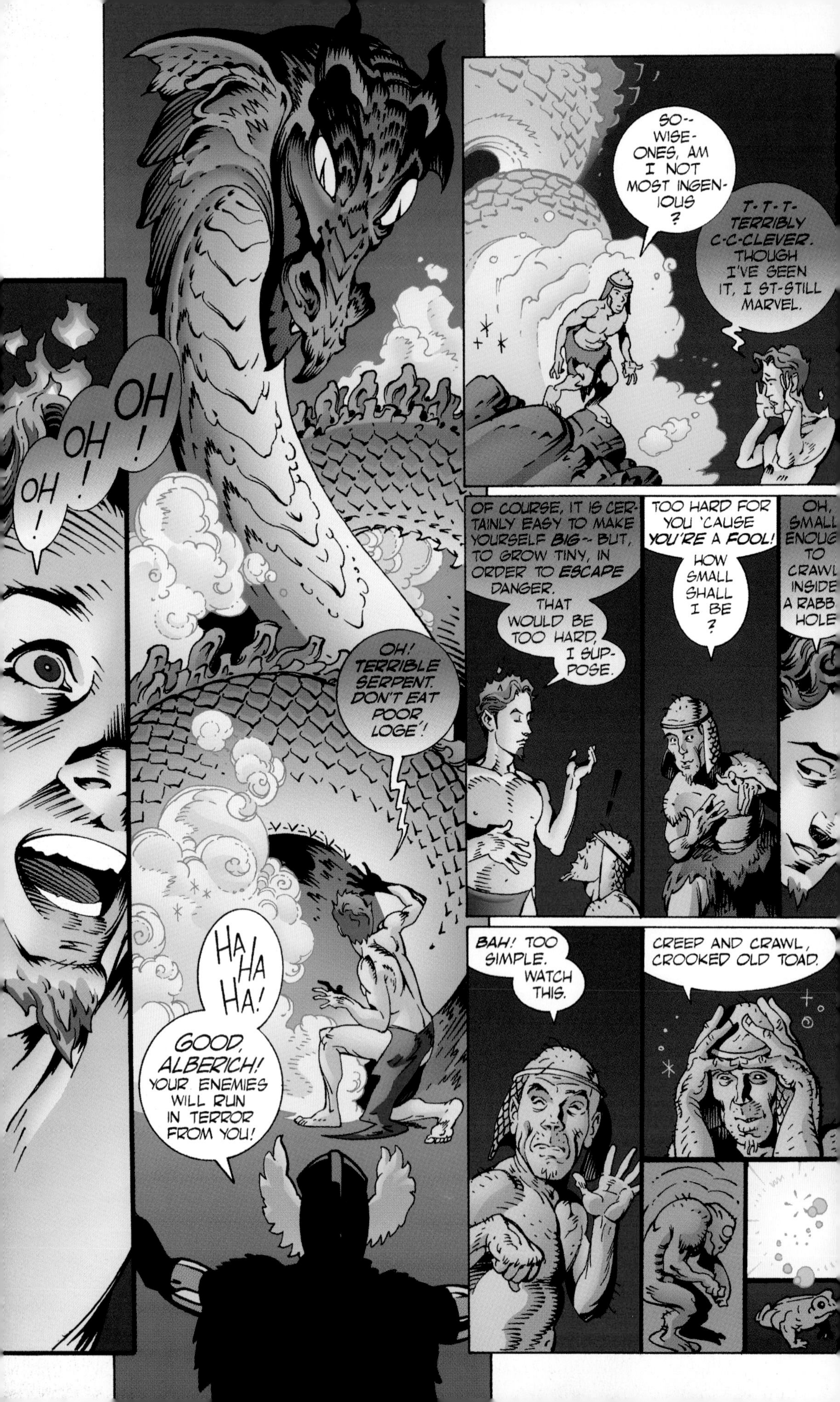

OH! OH! OH!
OH! TERRIBLE SERPENT. DON'T EAT POOR LOGE!
HA HA HA!
GOOD, ALBERICH! YOUR ENEMIES WILL RUN IN TERROR FROM YOU!
SO-- WISE-ONES, AM I NOT MOST INGENIOUS?
T-T-T-TERRIBLY C-C-CLEVER. THOUGH I'VE SEEN IT, I ST-STILL MARVEL.
OF COURSE, IT IS CERTAINLY EASY TO MAKE YOURSELF BIG-- BUT, TO GROW TINY, IN ORDER TO ESCAPE DANGER.
THAT WOULD BE TOO HARD, I SUPPOSE.
TOO HARD FOR YOU 'CAUSE YOU'RE A FOOL!
HOW SMALL SHALL I BE?
BAH! TOO SIMPLE. WATCH THIS.
CREEP AND CRAWL, CROOKED OLD TOAD.

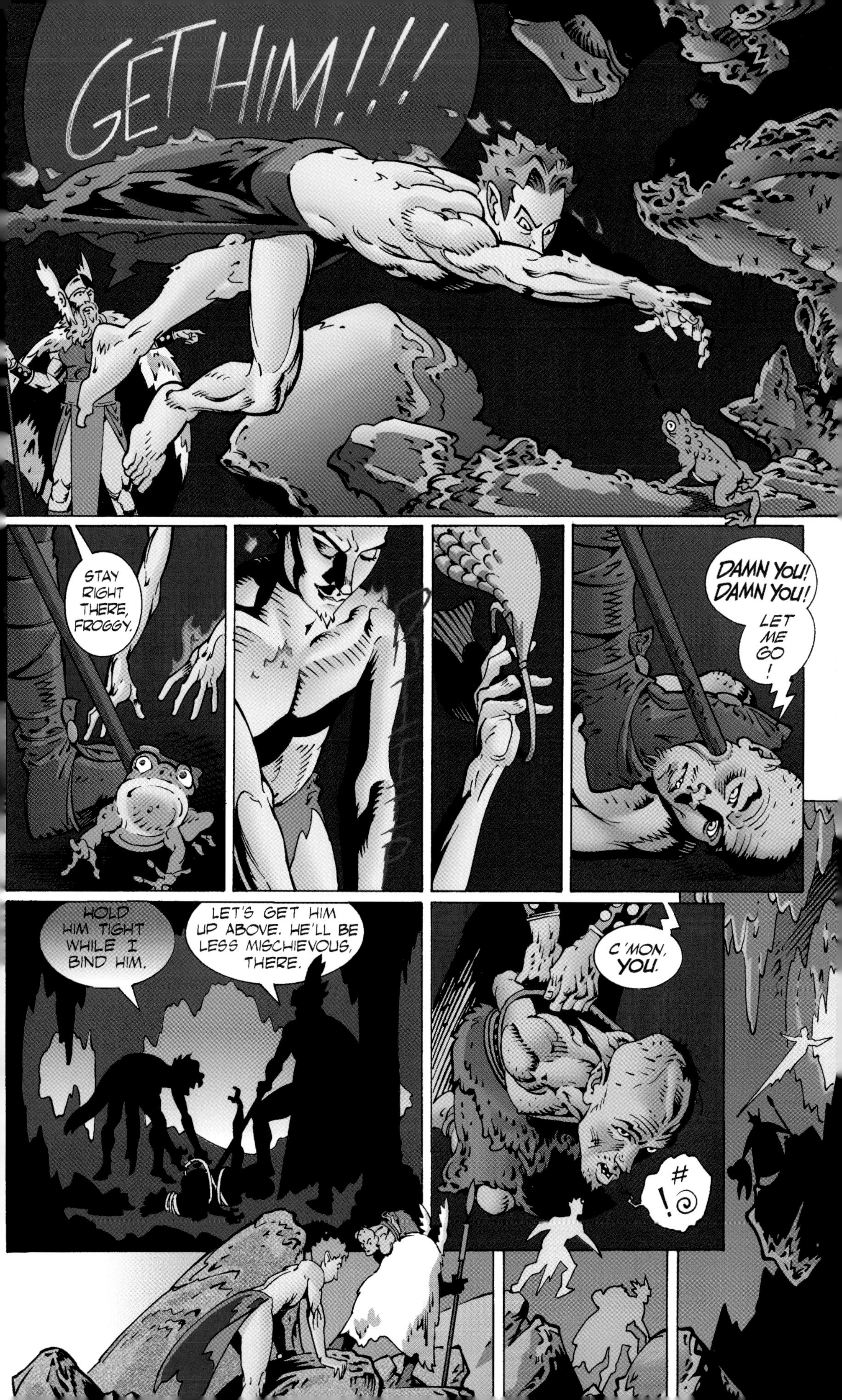
GET HIM!!!
STAY RIGHT THERE, FROGGY.
DAMN YOU! DAMN YOU!
LET ME GO!
HOLD HIM TIGHT WHILE I BIND HIM.
LET'S GET HIM UP ABOVE. HE'LL BE LESS MISCHIEVOUS, THERE.
C'MON, YOU.
#!

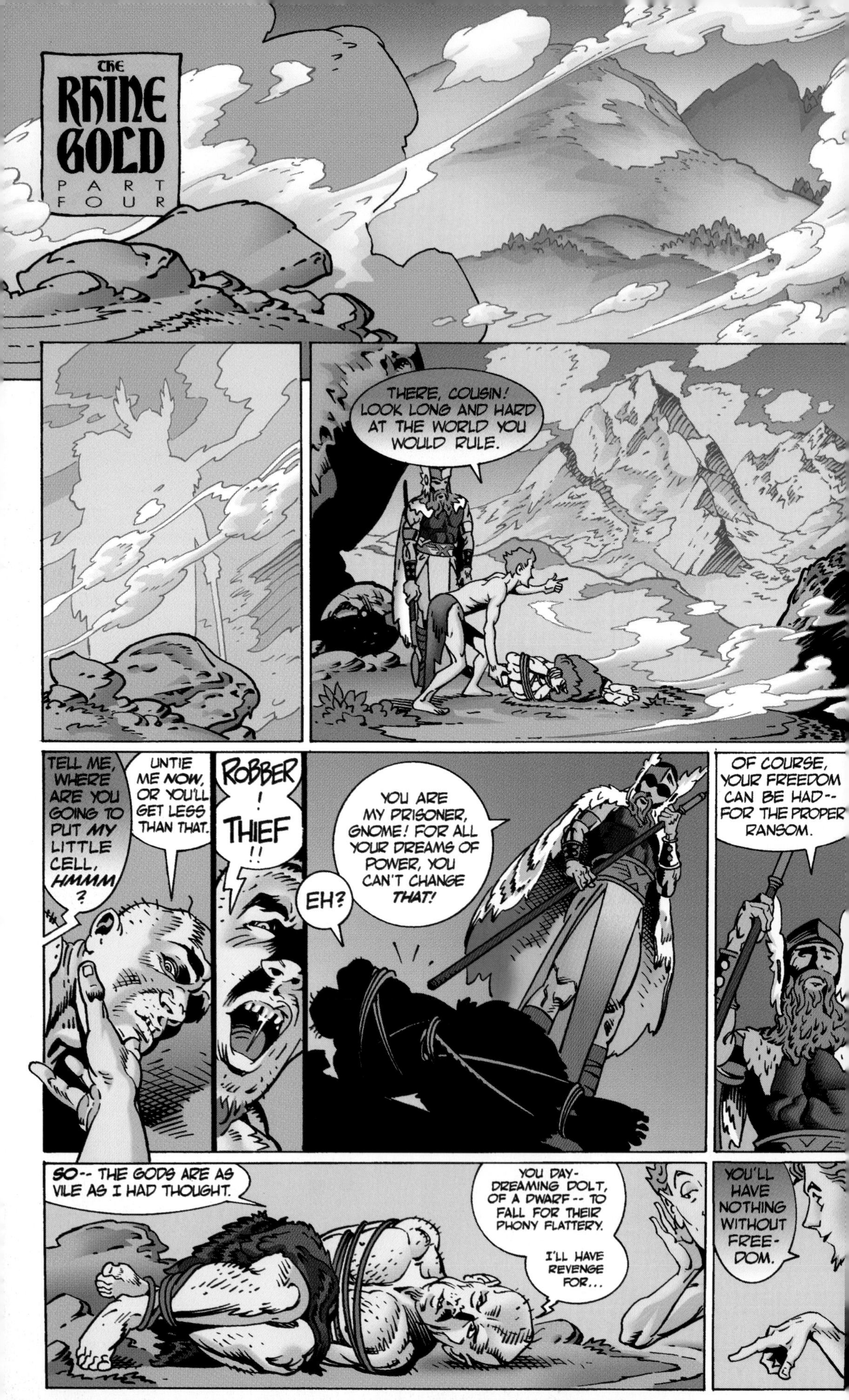

THE RHINE GOLD
PART FOUR
THERE, COUSIN! LOOK LONG AND HARD AT THE WORLD YOU WOULD RULE.
TELL ME, WHERE ARE YOU GOING TO PUT MY LITTLE CELL, HMMM?
UNTIE ME NOW, OR YOU'LL GET LESS THAN THAT.
ROBBER! THIEF!!
EH?
YOU ARE MY PRISONER, GNOME! FOR ALL YOUR DREAMS OF POWER, YOU CAN'T CHANGE THAT!
OF COURSE, YOUR FREEDOM CAN BE HAD-- FOR THE PROPER RANSOM.
SO-- THE GODS ARE AS VILE AS I HAD THOUGHT.
YOU DAY-DREAMING DOLT, OF A DWARF-- TO FALL FOR THEIR PHONY FLATTERY.
I'LL HAVE REVENGE FOR...
YOU'LL HAVE NOTHING WITHOUT FREE-DOM.

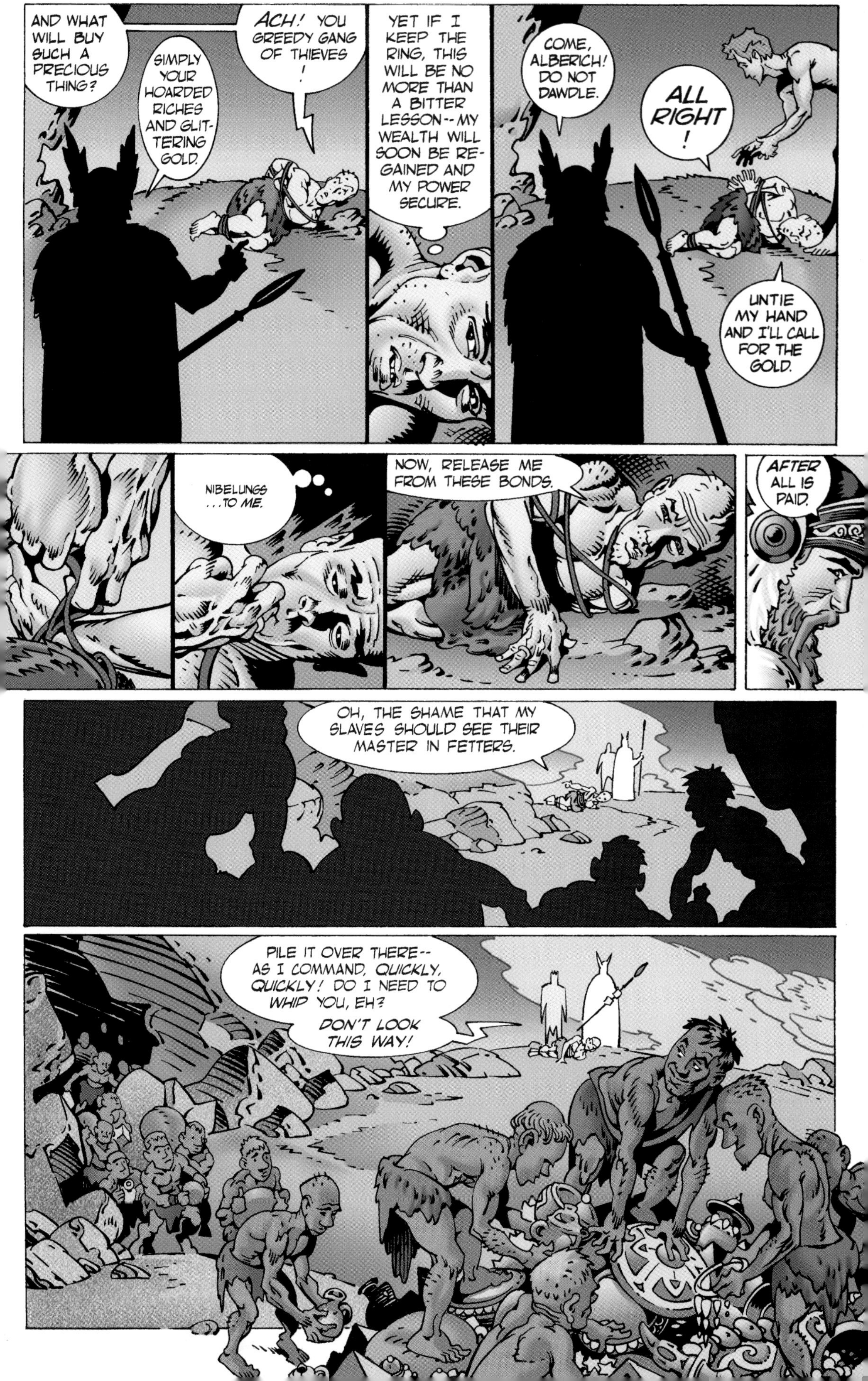
AND WHAT WILL BUY SUCH A PRECIOUS THING?
SIMPLY YOUR HOARDED RICHES AND GLITTERING GOLD.
ACH! YOU GREEDY GANG OF THIEVES!
YET IF I KEEP THE RING, THIS WILL BE NO MORE THAN A BITTER LESSON--MY WEALTH WILL SOON BE REGAINED AND MY POWER SECURE.
COME, ALBERICH! DO NOT DAWDLE.
ALL RIGHT!
UNTIE MY HAND AND I'LL CALL FOR THE GOLD.
NIBELUNGS ...TO ME.
NOW, RELEASE ME FROM THESE BONDS.
AFTER ALL IS PAID.
OH, THE SHAME THAT MY SLAVES SHOULD SEE THEIR MASTER IN FETTERS.
PILE IT OVER THERE-- AS I COMMAND, QUICKLY, QUICKLY! DO I NEED TO WHIP YOU, EH?
DON'T LOOK THIS WAY!

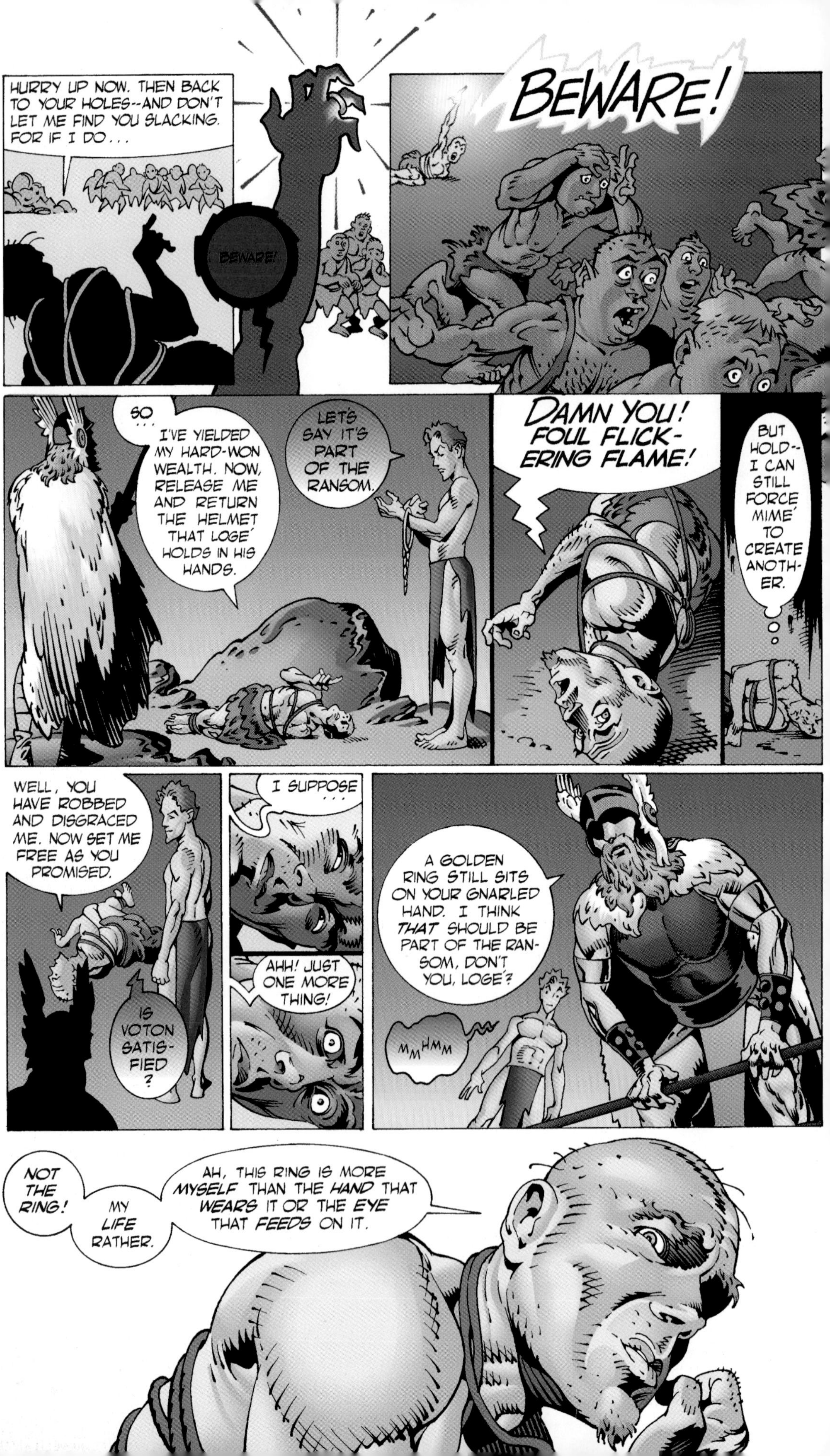
HURRY UP NOW. THEN BACK TO YOUR HOLES--AND DON'T LET ME FIND YOU SLACKING. FOR IF I DO . . .
BEWARE!
BEWARE!
SO . . . I'VE YIELDED MY HARD-WON WEALTH. NOW, RELEASE ME AND RETURN THE HELMET THAT LOGE' HOLDS IN HIS HANDS.
LET'S SAY IT'S PART OF THE RANSOM.
DAMN YOU! FOUL FLICK-ERING FLAME!
BUT HOLD-- I CAN STILL FORCE MIME' TO CREATE ANOTH-ER.
WELL, YOU HAVE ROBBED AND DISGRACED ME. NOW SET ME FREE AS YOU PROMISED.
IS VOTON SATIS-FIED ?
I SUPPOSE . . .
AHH! JUST ONE MORE THING!
A GOLDEN RING STILL SITS ON YOUR GNARLED HAND. I THINK THAT SHOULD BE PART OF THE RAN-SOM, DON'T YOU, LOGE'?
MMHMM
NOT THE RING!
MY LIFE RATHER.
AH, THIS RING IS MORE MYSELF THAN THE HAND THAT WEARS IT OR THE EYE THAT FEEDS ON IT.

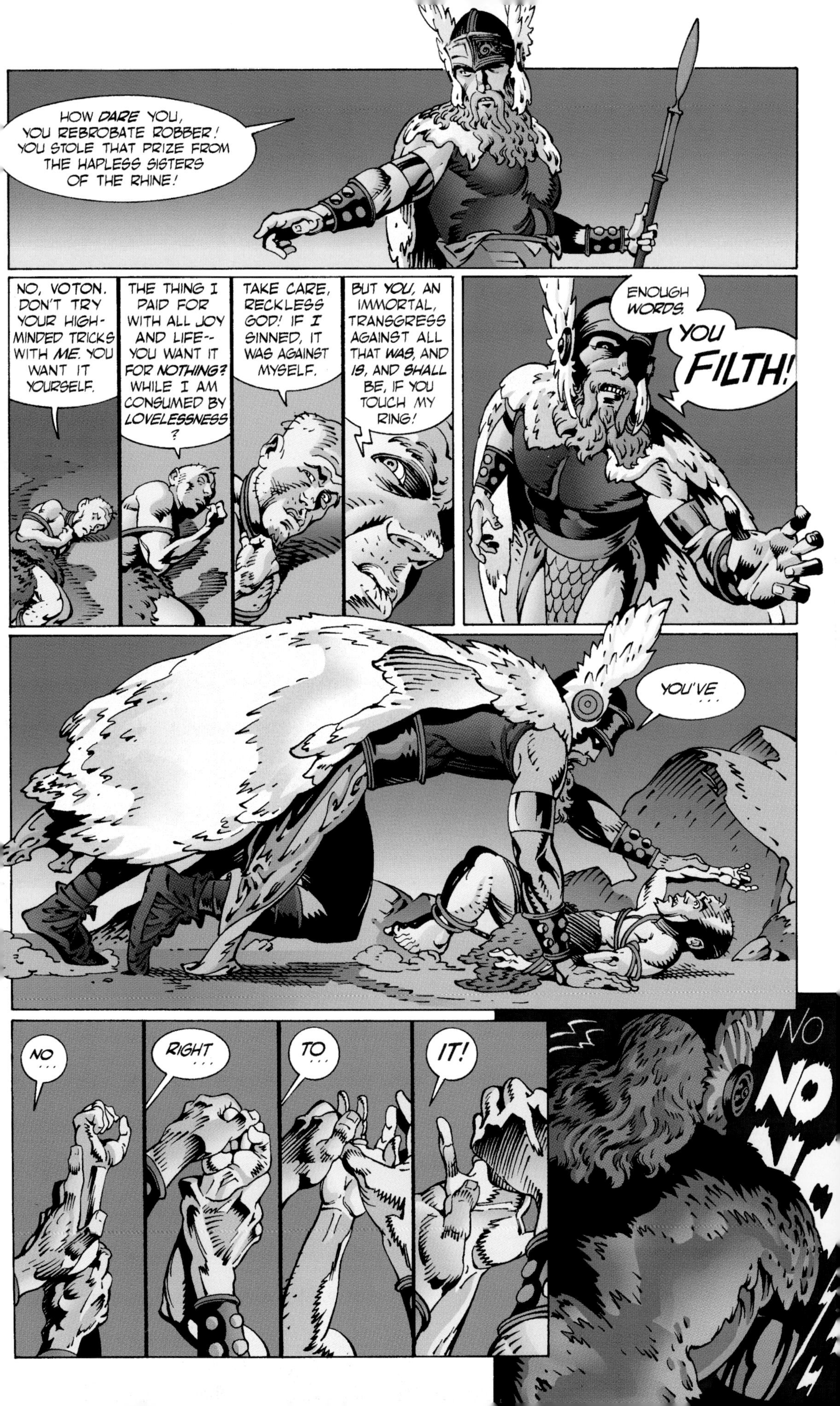
HOW DARE YOU, YOU REBROBATE ROBBER! YOU STOLE THAT PRIZE FROM THE HAPLESS SISTERS OF THE RHINE!
NO, VOTON. DON'T TRY YOUR HIGH-MINDED TRICKS WITH ME. YOU WANT IT YOURSELF.
THE THING I PAID FOR WITH ALL JOY AND LIFE-- YOU WANT IT FOR NOTHING? WHILE I AM CONSUMED BY LOVELESSNESS?
TAKE CARE, RECKLESS GOD! IF I SINNED, IT WAS AGAINST MYSELF.
BUT YOU, AN IMMORTAL, TRANSGRESS AGAINST ALL THAT WAS, AND IS, AND SHALL BE, IF YOU TOUCH MY RING!
ENOUGH WORDS.
YOU FILTH!
YOU'VE . . .
NO . . .
RIGHT . . .
TO . . .
IT!
NO
NO

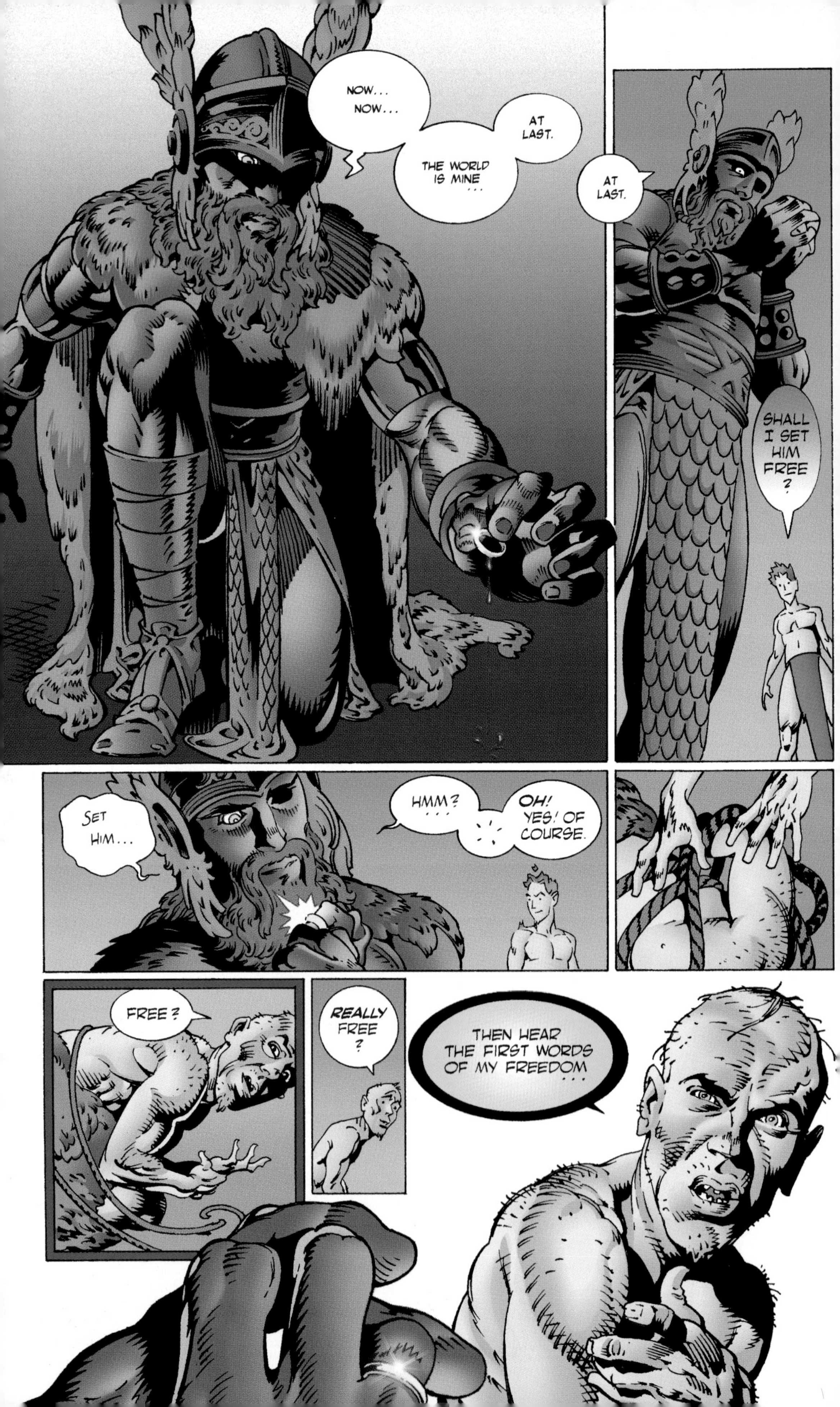
NOW... NOW...
AT LAST.
THE WORLD IS MINE...
AT LAST.
SHALL I SET HIM FREE?
SET HIM...
HMM?...
OH! YES! OF COURSE.
FREE?
REALLY FREE?
THEN HEAR THE FIRST WORDS OF MY FREEDOM...

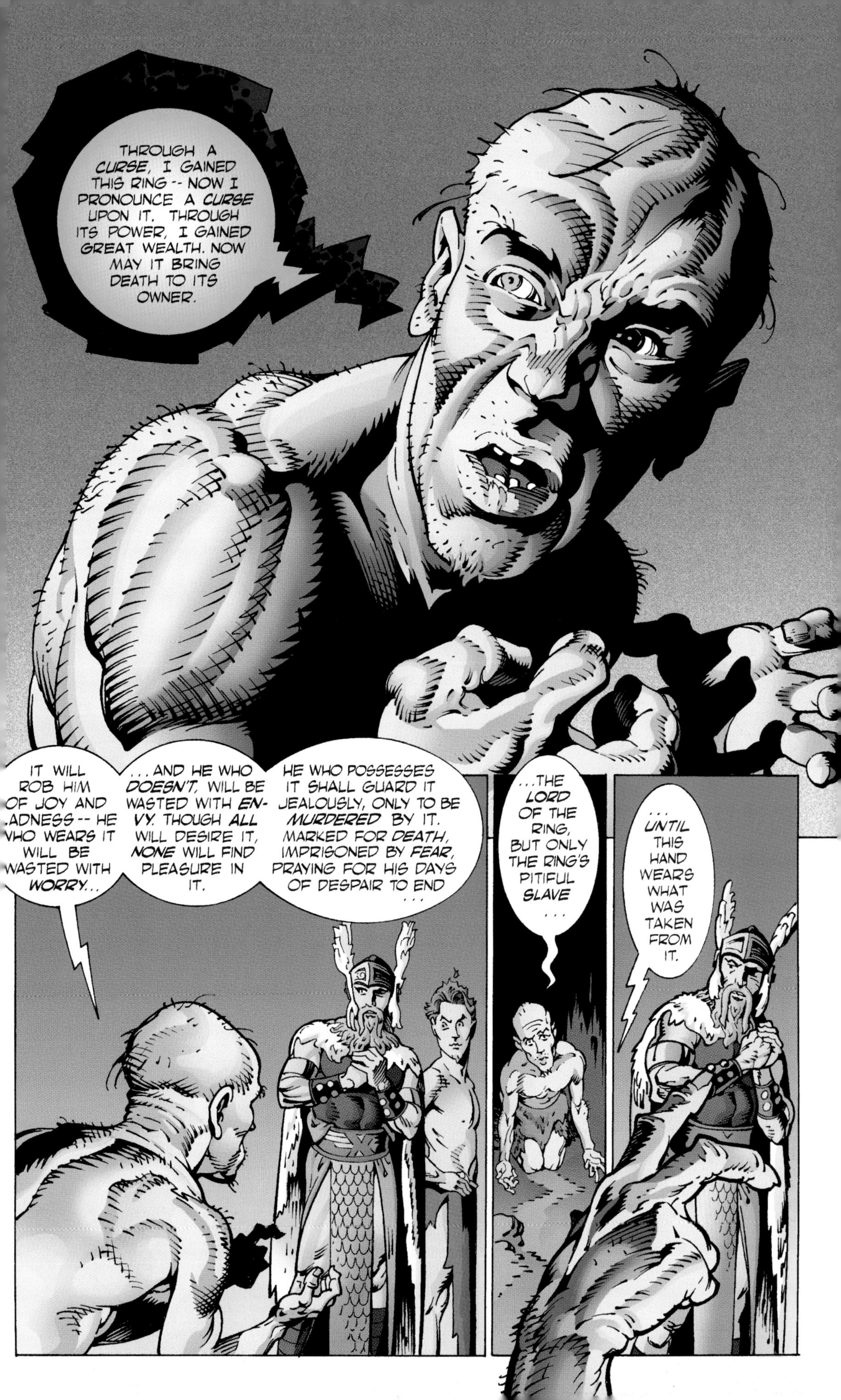
THROUGH A CURSE, I GAINED THIS RING -- NOW I PRONOUNCE A CURSE UPON IT. THROUGH ITS POWER, I GAINED GREAT WEALTH. NOW MAY IT BRING DEATH TO ITS OWNER.
IT WILL ROB HIM OF JOY AND ADNESS -- HE VHO WEARS IT WILL BE WASTED WITH WORRY...
...AND HE WHO DOESN'T, WILL BE WASTED WITH EN-VY. THOUGH ALL WILL DESIRE IT, NONE WILL FIND PLEASURE IN IT.
HE WHO POSSESSES IT SHALL GUARD IT JEALOUSLY, ONLY TO BE MURDERED BY IT. MARKED FOR DEATH, IMPRISONED BY FEAR, PRAYING FOR HIS DAYS OF DESPAIR TO END ...
...THE LORD OF THE RING, BUT ONLY THE RING'S PITIFUL SLAVE ...
... UNTIL THIS HAND WEARS WHAT WAS TAKEN FROM IT.

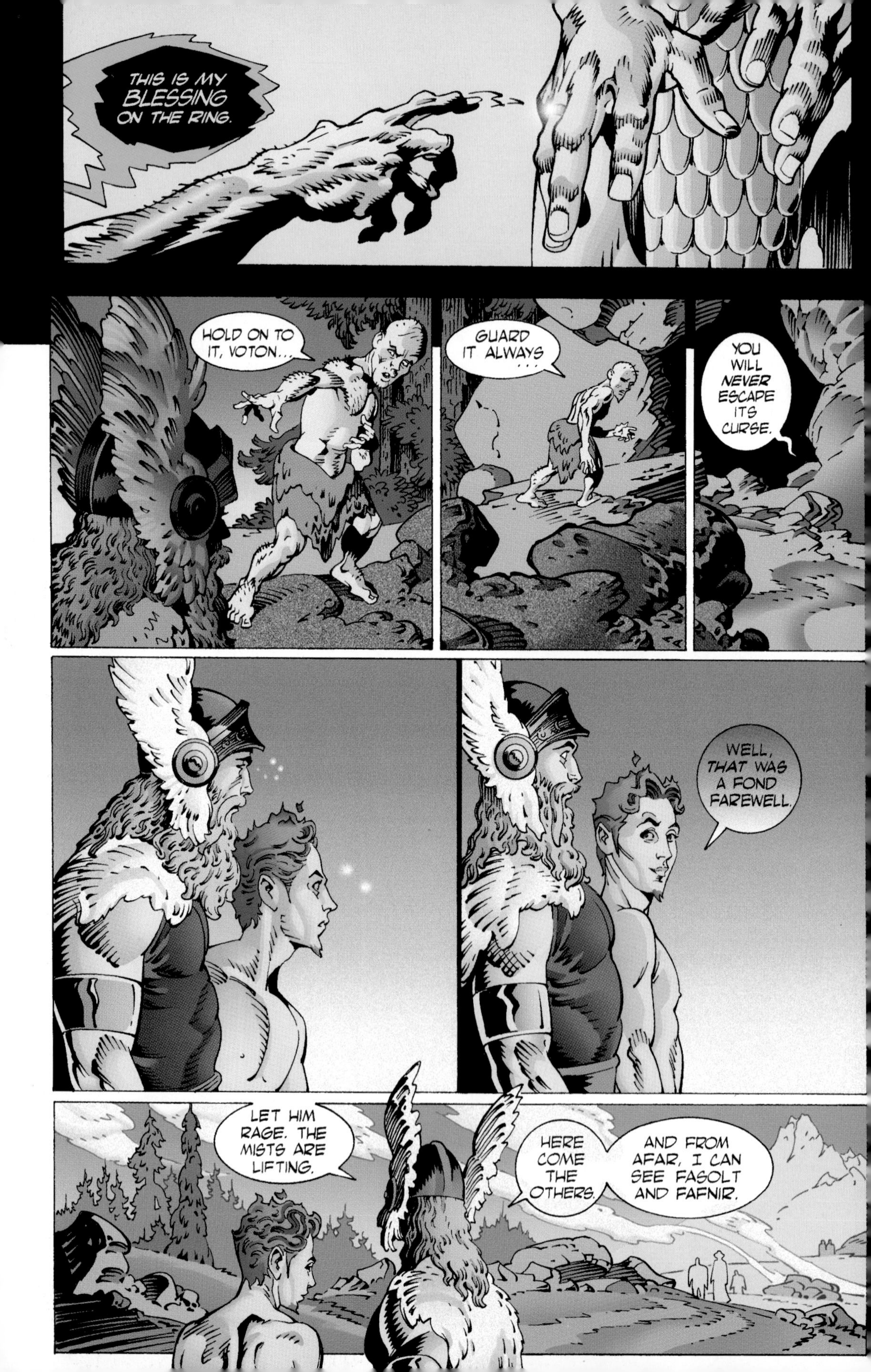
THIS IS MY BLESSING ON THE RING.
HOLD ON TO IT, VOTON...
GUARD IT ALWAYS ...
YOU WILL NEVER ESCAPE ITS CURSE.
WELL, THAT WAS A FOND FAREWELL.
LET HIM RAGE. THE MISTS ARE LIFTING.
HERE COME THE OTHERS.
AND FROM AFAR, I CAN SEE FASOLT AND FAFNIR.

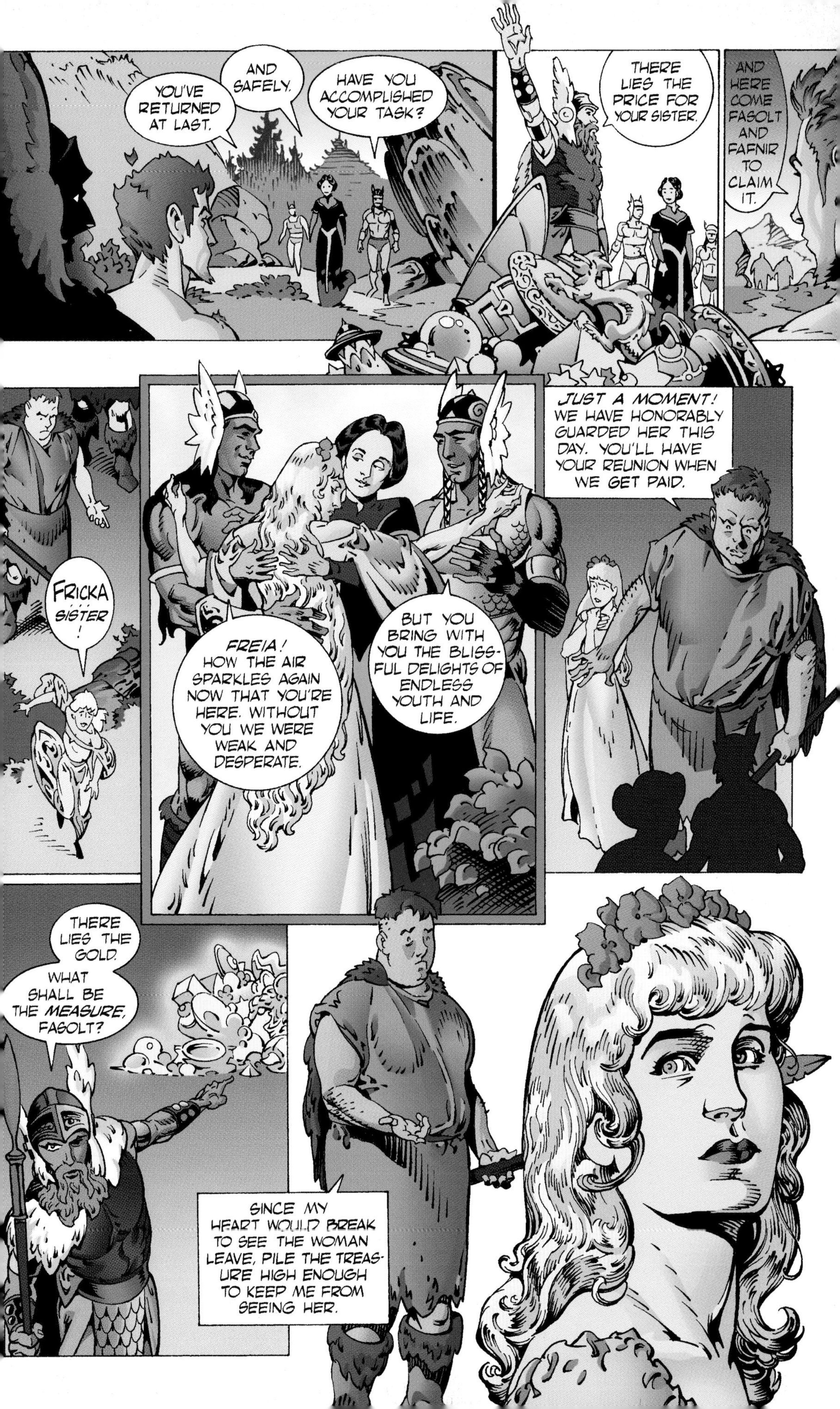
YOU'VE RETURNED AT LAST.
AND SAFELY.
HAVE YOU ACCOMPLISHED YOUR TASK?
THERE LIES THE PRICE FOR YOUR SISTER.
AND HERE COME FASOLT AND FAFNIR TO CLAIM IT.
FRICKA . . . SISTER!
FREIA! HOW THE AIR SPARKLES AGAIN NOW THAT YOU'RE HERE. WITHOUT YOU WE WERE WEAK AND DESPERATE.
BUT YOU BRING WITH YOU THE BLISSFUL DELIGHTS OF ENDLESS YOUTH AND LIFE.
JUST A MOMENT! WE HAVE HONORABLY GUARDED HER THIS DAY. YOU'LL HAVE YOUR REUNION WHEN WE GET PAID.
THERE LIES THE GOLD.
WHAT SHALL BE THE MEASURE, FASOLT?
SINCE MY HEART WOULD BREAK TO SEE THE WOMAN LEAVE, PILE THE TREASURE HIGH ENOUGH TO KEEP ME FROM SEEING HER.

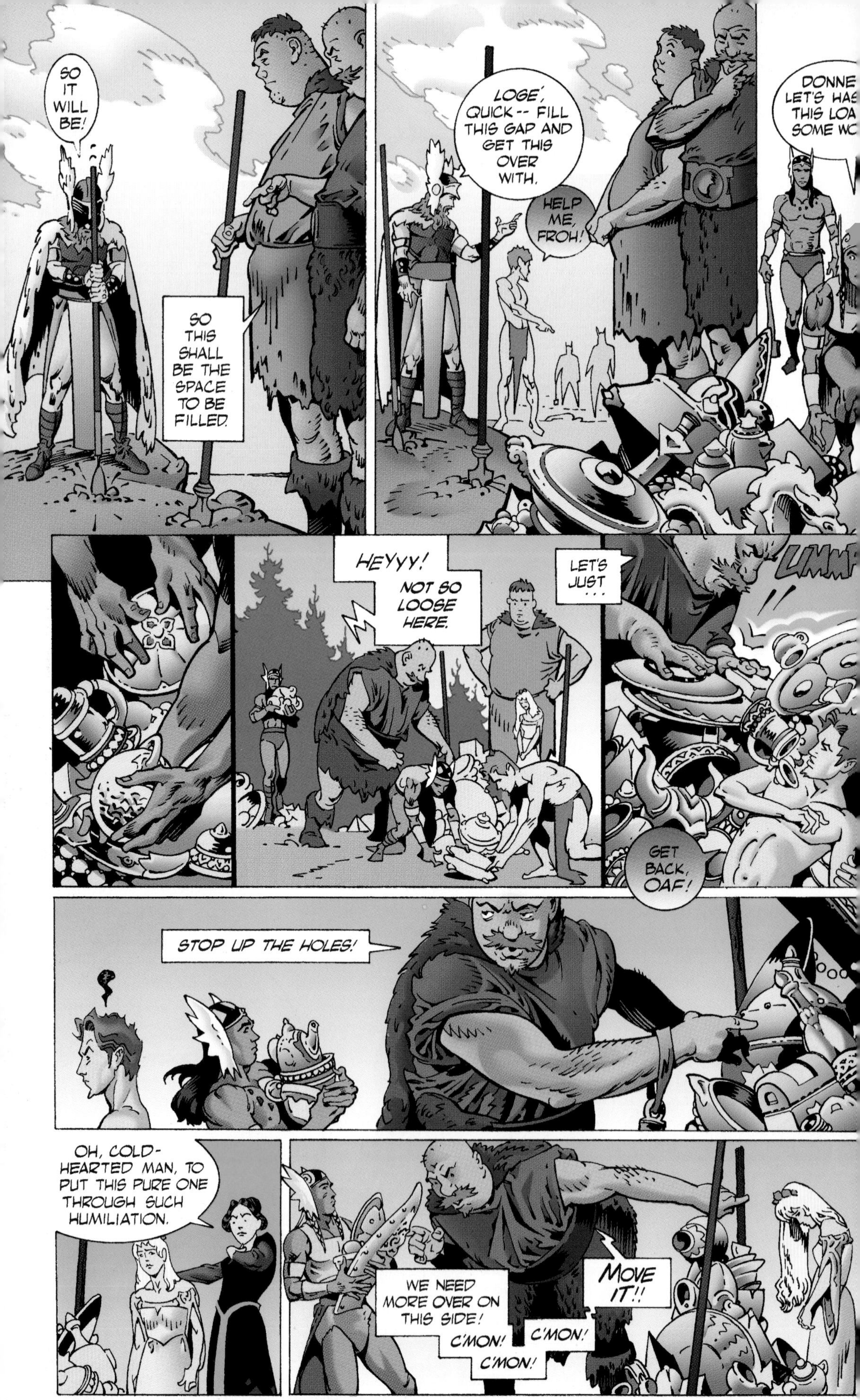
SO IT WILL BE!
SO THIS SHALL BE THE SPACE TO BE FILLED.
LOGE, QUICK -- FILL THIS GAP AND GET THIS OVER WITH.
HELP ME, FROH!
DONNE LET'S HAS THIS LOA SOME WO
HEYYY! NOT SO LOOSE HERE.
LET'S JUST . . .
GET BACK, OAF!
STOP UP THE HOLES!
OH, COLD-HEARTED MAN, TO PUT THIS PURE ONE THROUGH SUCH HUMILIATION.
WE NEED MORE OVER ON THIS SIDE! C'MON! C'MON!
C'MON!
MOVE IT!!

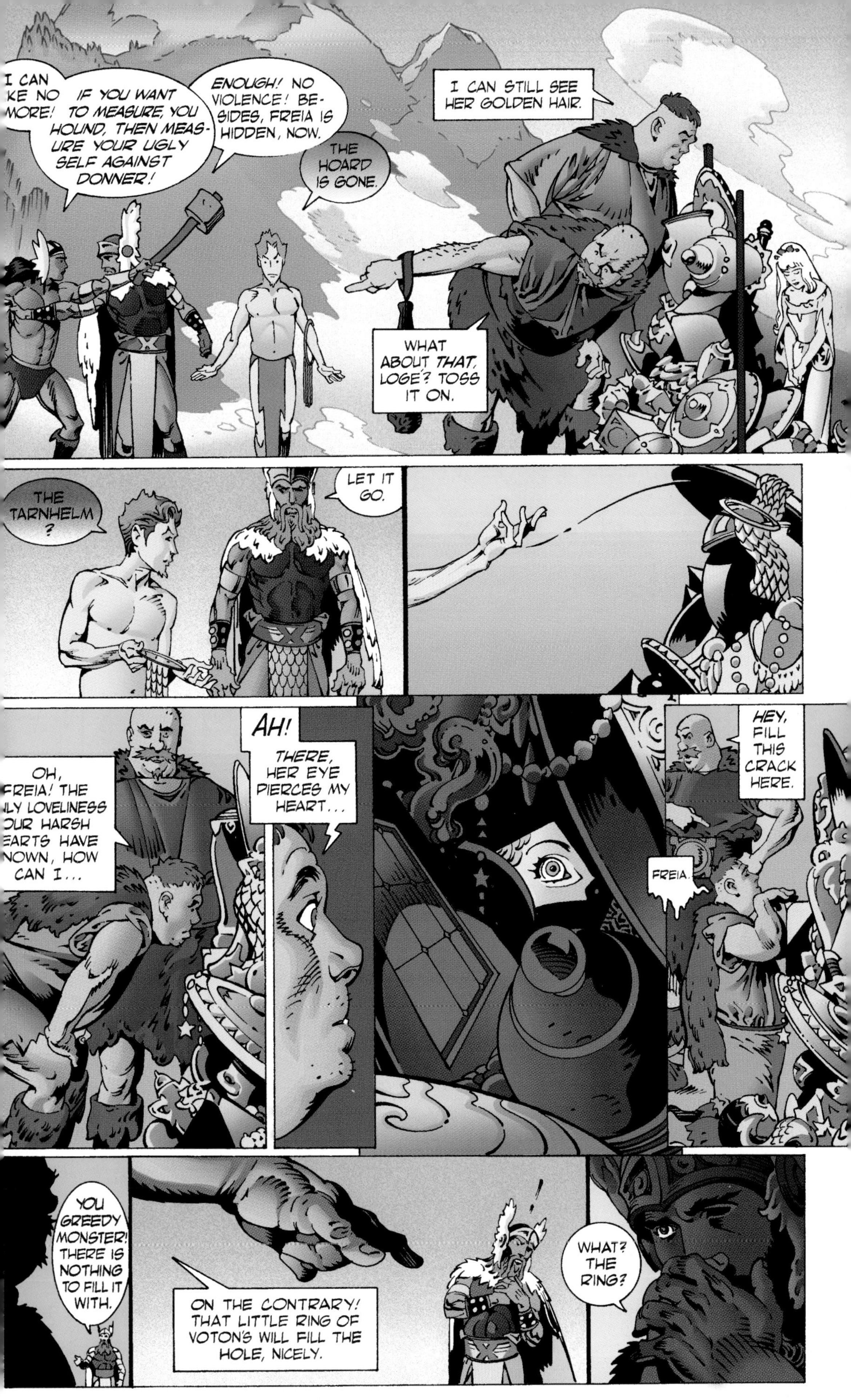

I CAN KE NO MORE!
IF YOU WANT TO MEASURE, YOU HOUND, THEN MEAS-URE YOUR UGLY SELF AGAINST DONNER!
ENOUGH! NO VIOLENCE! BE-SIDES, FREIA IS HIDDEN, NOW.
THE HOARD IS GONE.
I CAN STILL SEE HER GOLDEN HAIR.
WHAT ABOUT THAT, LOGE? TOSS IT ON.
THE TARNHELM?
LET IT GO.
OH, FREIA! THE LY LOVELINESS OUR HARSH EARTS HAVE NOWN, HOW CAN I...
AH!
THERE, HER EYE PIERCES MY HEART...
HEY, FILL THIS CRACK HERE.
FREIA.
YOU GREEDY MONSTER! THERE IS NOTHING TO FILL IT WITH.
ON THE CONTRARY! THAT LITTLE RING OF VOTON'S WILL FILL THE HOLE, NICELY.
!
WHAT? THE RING?

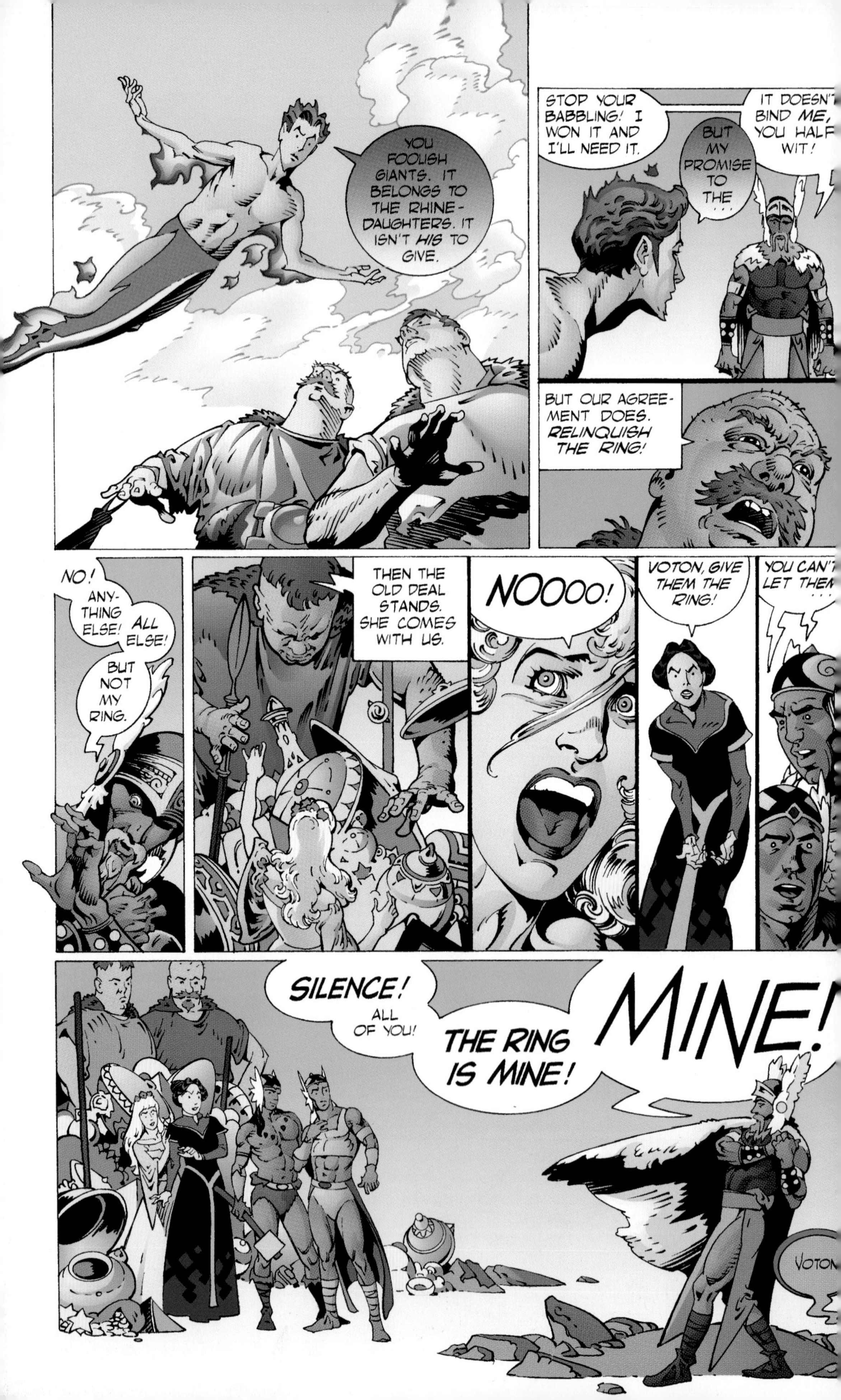

YOU FOOLISH GIANTS. IT BELONGS TO THE RHINE-DAUGHTERS. IT ISN'T HIS TO GIVE.
STOP YOUR BABBLING! I WON IT AND I'LL NEED IT.
BUT MY PROMISE TO THE . . .
IT DOESN'T BIND ME, YOU HALF WIT!
BUT OUR AGREEMENT DOES. RELINQUISH THE RING!
NO! ANYTHING ELSE! ALL ELSE!
BUT NOT MY RING.
THEN THE OLD DEAL STANDS. SHE COMES WITH US.
NOOOO!
VOTON, GIVE THEM THE RING!
YOU CAN'T LET THEM . . .
SILENCE! ALL OF YOU!
THE RING IS MINE!
MINE!
VOTON

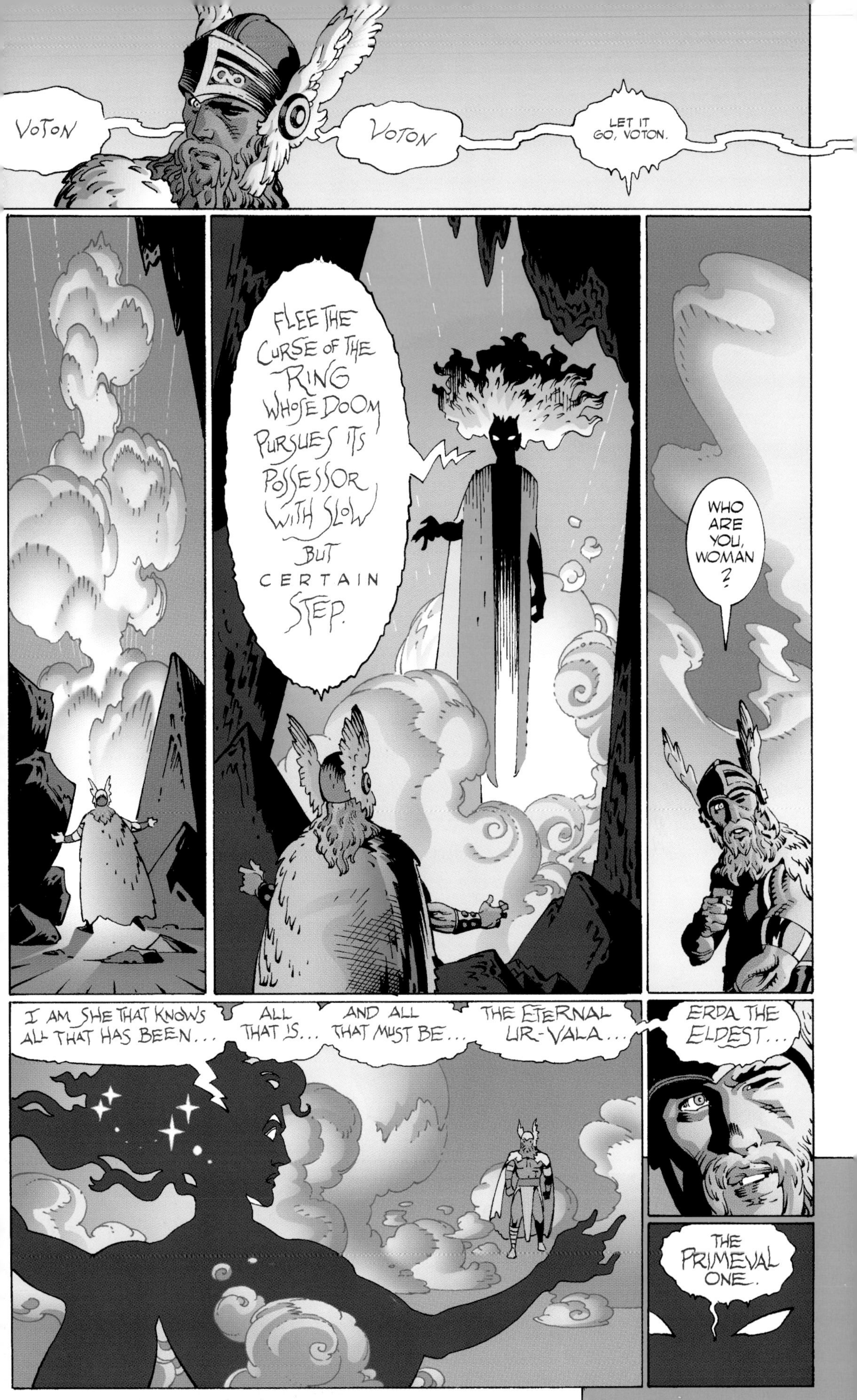
VOTON
VOTON
LET IT GO, VOTON.
FLEE THE CURSE OF THE RING WHOSE DOOM PURSUES ITS POSSESSOR WITH SLOW BUT CERTAIN STEP.
WHO ARE YOU, WOMAN?
I AM SHE THAT KNOWS ALL THAT HAS BEEN...
ALL THAT IS...
AND ALL THAT MUST BE...
THE ETERNAL UR-VALA...
ERDA THE ELDEST...
THE PRIMEVAL ONE.

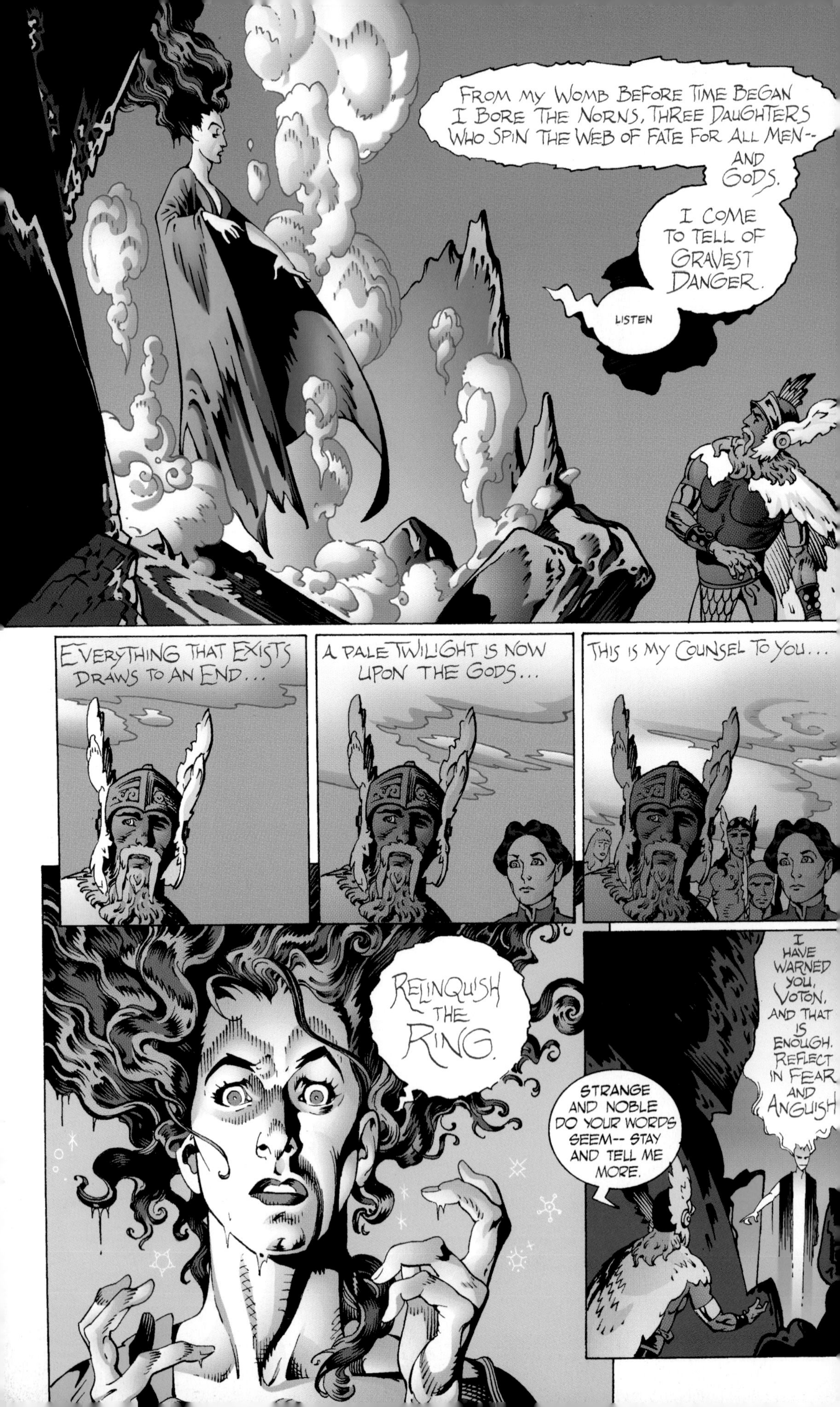

FROM MY WOMB BEFORE TIME BEGAN I BORE THE NORNS, THREE DAUGHTERS WHO SPIN THE WEB OF FATE FOR ALL MEN-- AND GODS.
I COME TO TELL OF GRAVEST DANGER.
LISTEN
EVERYTHING THAT EXISTS DRAWS TO AN END...
A PALE TWILIGHT IS NOW UPON THE GODS...
THIS IS MY COUNSEL TO YOU...
RELINQUISH THE RING.
STRANGE AND NOBLE DO YOUR WORDS SEEM-- STAY AND TELL ME MORE.
I HAVE WARNED YOU, VOTON, AND THAT IS ENOUGH. REFLECT IN FEAR AND ANGUISH

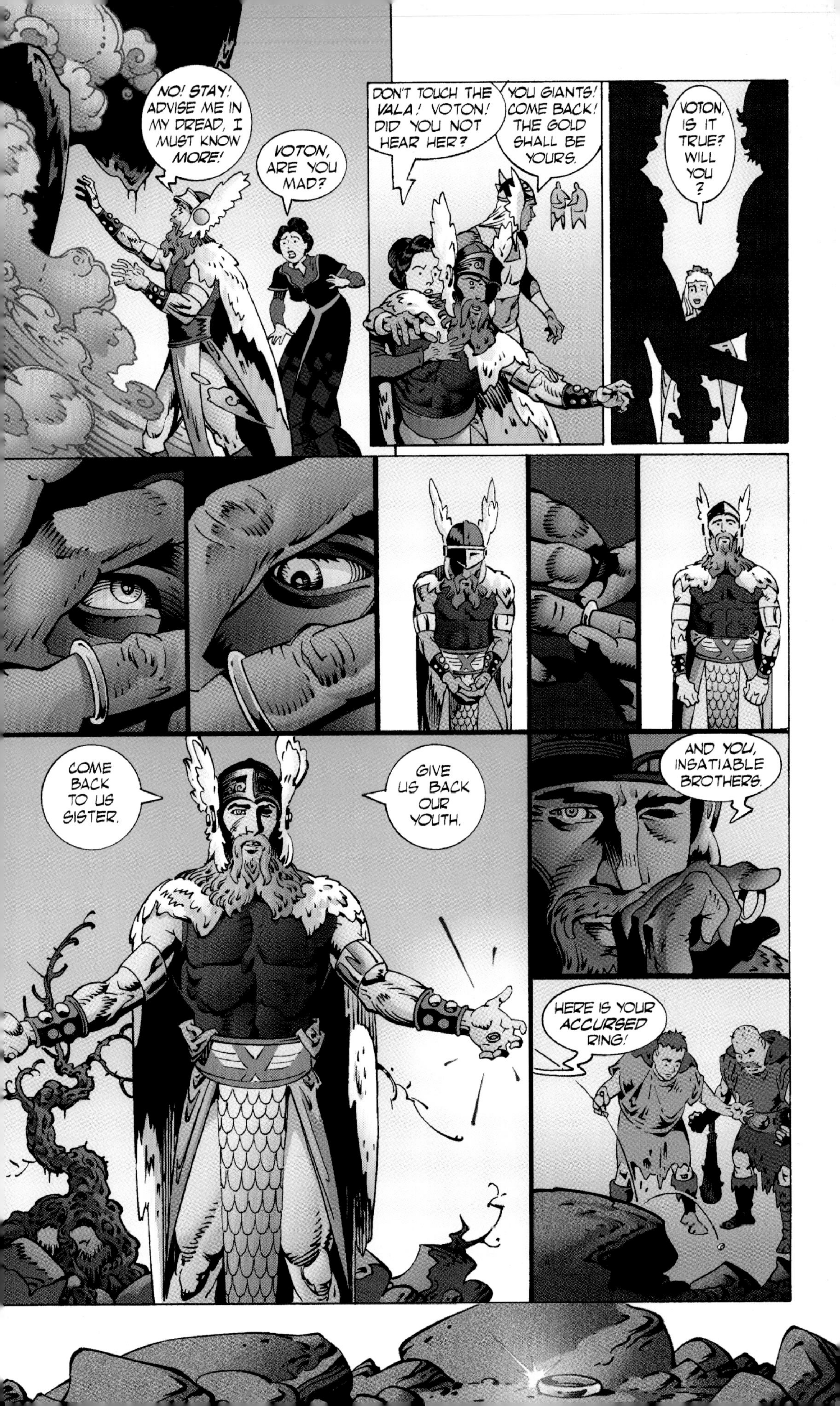
NO! STAY! ADVISE ME IN MY DREAD, I MUST KNOW MORE!
VOTON, ARE YOU MAD?
DON'T TOUCH THE VALA! VOTON! DID YOU NOT HEAR HER?
YOU GIANTS! COME BACK! THE GOLD SHALL BE YOURS.
VOTON, IS IT TRUE? WILL YOU ?
COME BACK TO US SISTER.
GIVE US BACK OUR YOUTH.
AND YOU, INSATIABLE BROTHERS.
HERE IS YOUR ACCURSED RING!

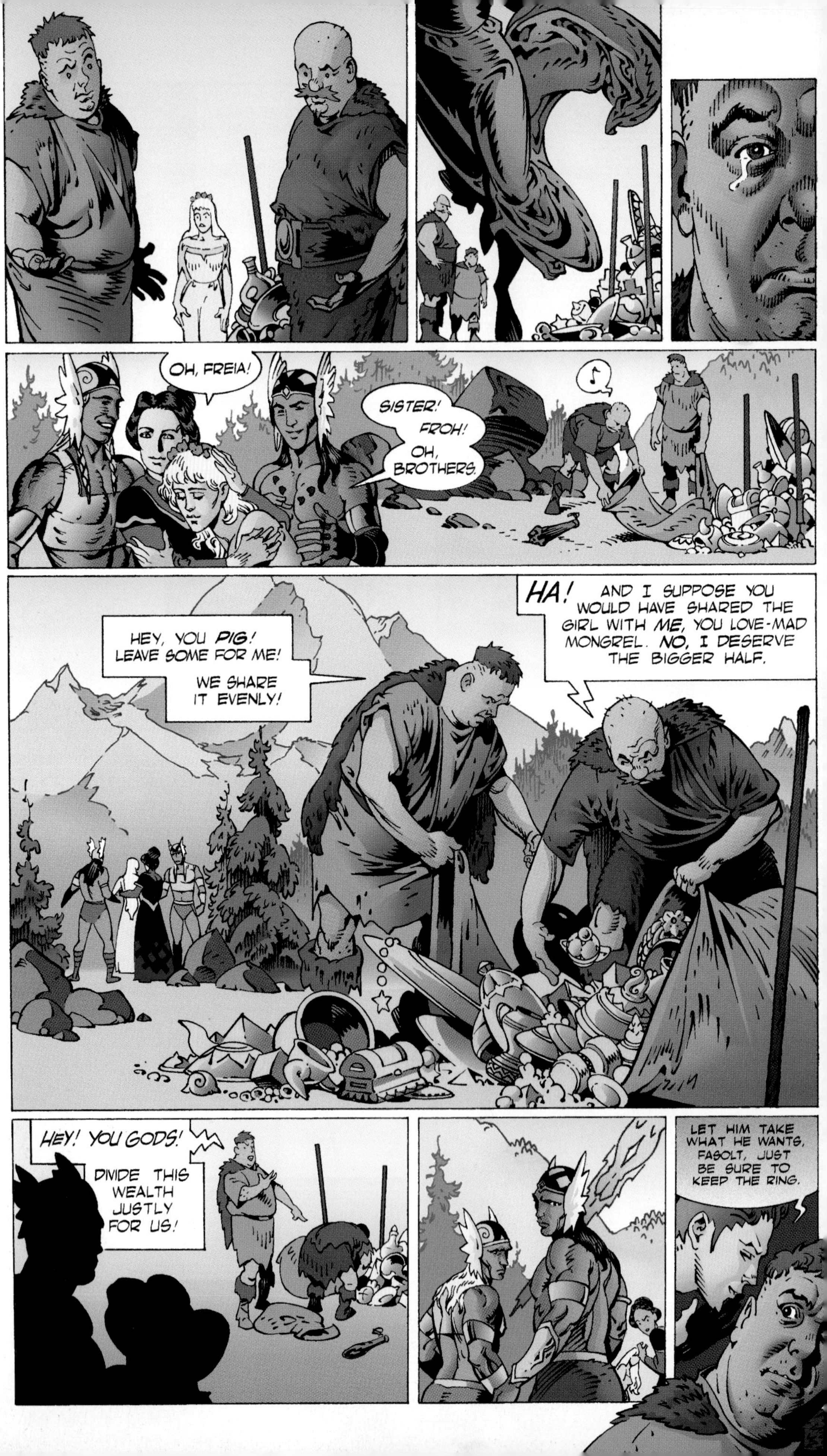
OH, FREIA!
SISTER!
FROH!
OH, BROTHERS.
HEY, YOU PIG! LEAVE SOME FOR ME!
WE SHARE IT EVENLY!
HA! AND I SUPPOSE YOU WOULD HAVE SHARED THE GIRL WITH ME, YOU LOVE-MAD MONGREL. NO, I DESERVE THE BIGGER HALF.
HEY! YOU GODS!
DIVIDE THIS WEALTH JUSTLY FOR US!
LET HIM TAKE WHAT HE WANTS, FASOLT, JUST BE SURE TO KEEP THE RING.

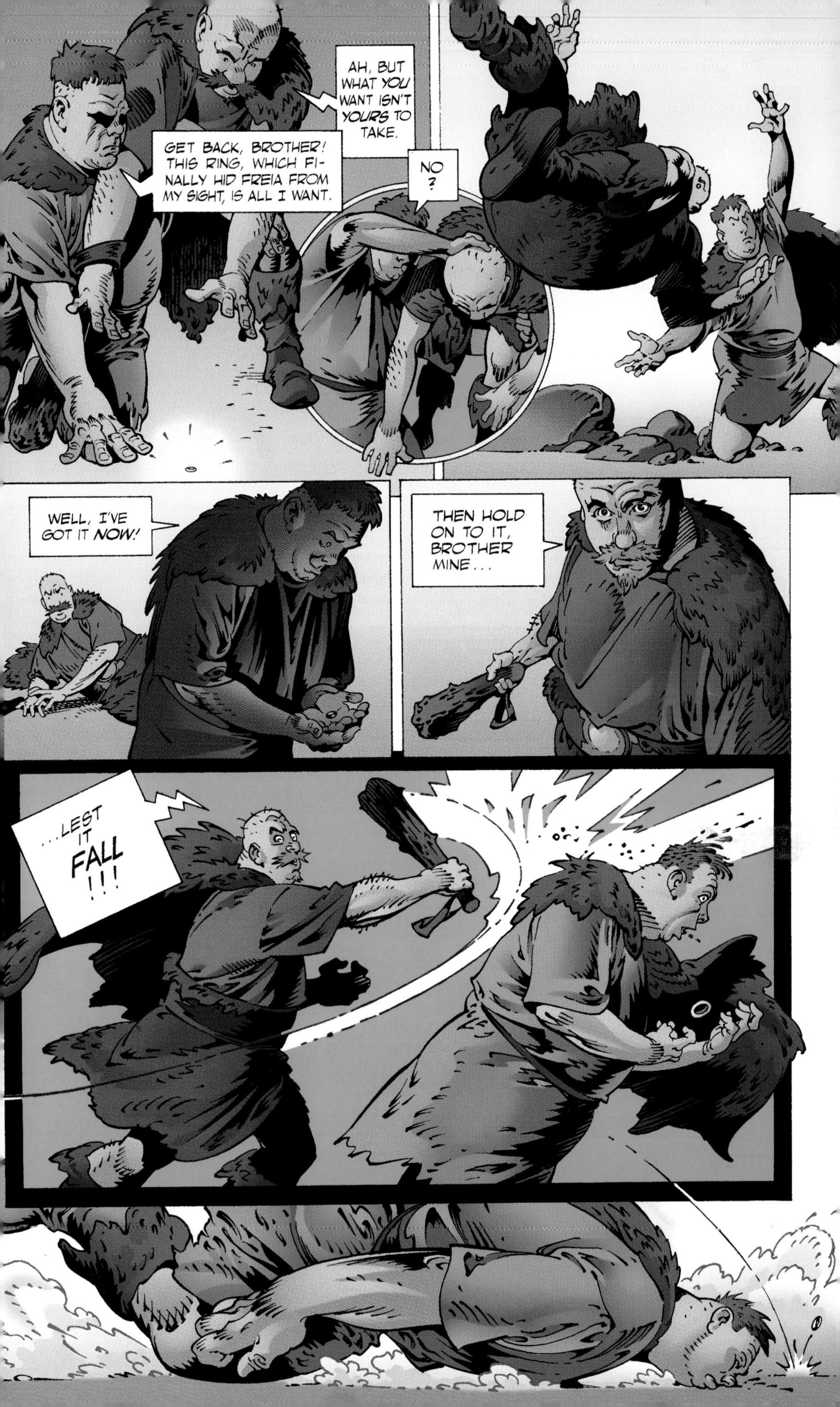
GET BACK, BROTHER! THIS RING, WHICH FI-NALLY HID FREIA FROM MY SIGHT, IS ALL I WANT.
AH, BUT WHAT YOU WANT ISN'T YOURS TO TAKE.
NO ?
WELL, I'VE GOT IT NOW!
THEN HOLD ON TO IT, BROTHER MINE . . .
. . . LEST IT FALL !!!

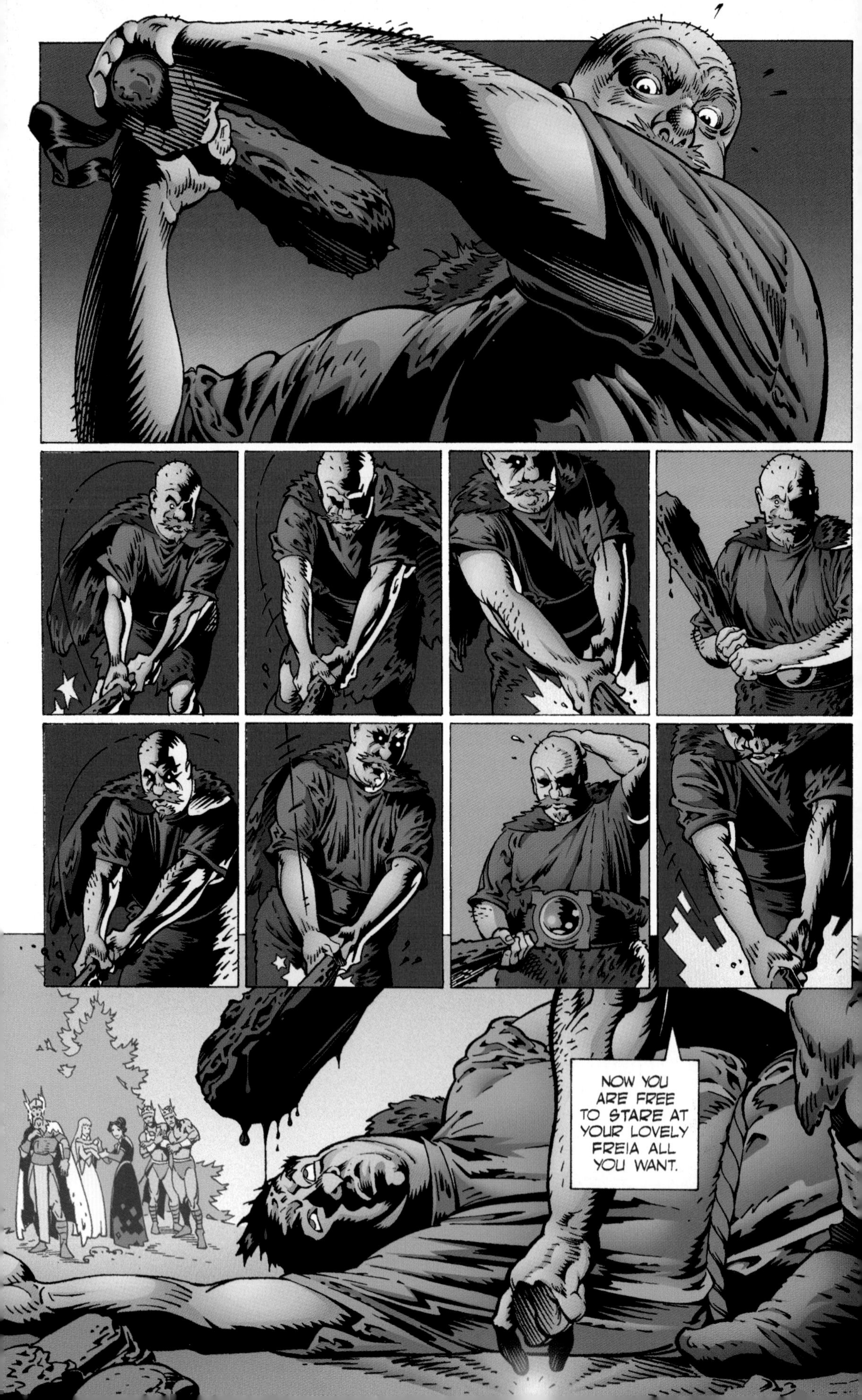
NOW YOU ARE FREE TO STARE AT YOUR LOVELY FREIA ALL YOU WANT.

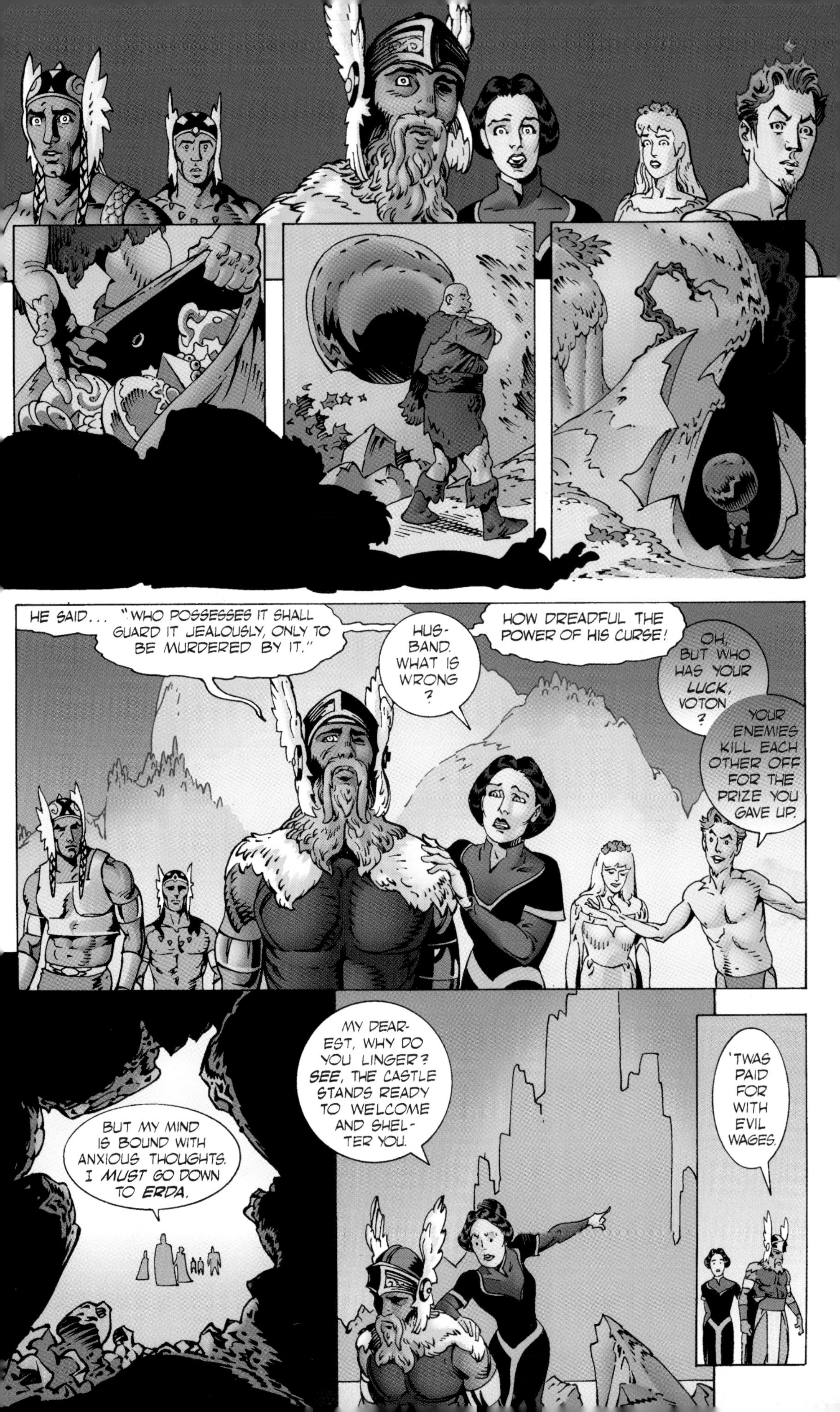

HE SAID... "WHO POSSESSES IT SHALL GUARD IT JEALOUSLY, ONLY TO BE MURDERED BY IT."
HUS-BAND. WHAT IS WRONG?
HOW DREADFUL THE POWER OF HIS CURSE!
OH, BUT WHO HAS YOUR LUCK, VOTON?
YOUR ENEMIES KILL EACH OTHER OFF FOR THE PRIZE YOU GAVE UP.
BUT MY MIND IS BOUND WITH ANXIOUS THOUGHTS. I MUST GO DOWN TO ERDA.
MY DEAR-EST, WHY DO YOU LINGER? SEE, THE CASTLE STANDS READY TO WELCOME AND SHEL-TER YOU.
'TWAS PAID FOR WITH EVIL WAGES.

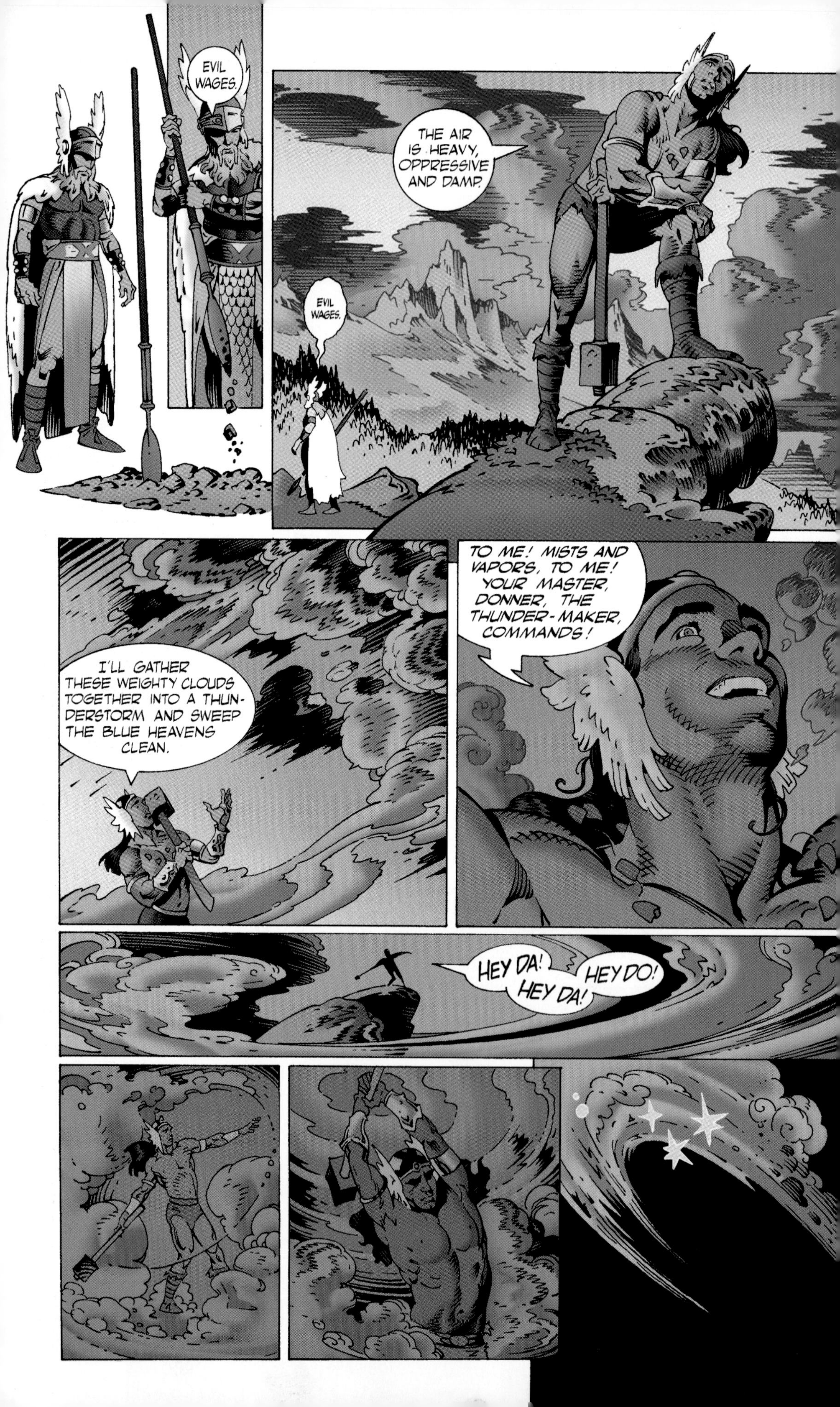
EVIL WAGES.
THE AIR IS HEAVY, OPPRESSIVE AND DAMP.
EVIL WAGES.
I'LL GATHER THESE WEIGHTY CLOUDS TOGETHER INTO A THUNDERSTORM AND SWEEP THE BLUE HEAVENS CLEAN.
TO ME! MISTS AND VAPORS, TO ME! YOUR MASTER, DONNER, THE THUNDER-MAKER, COMMANDS!
HEY DA!
HEY DA!
HEY DO!

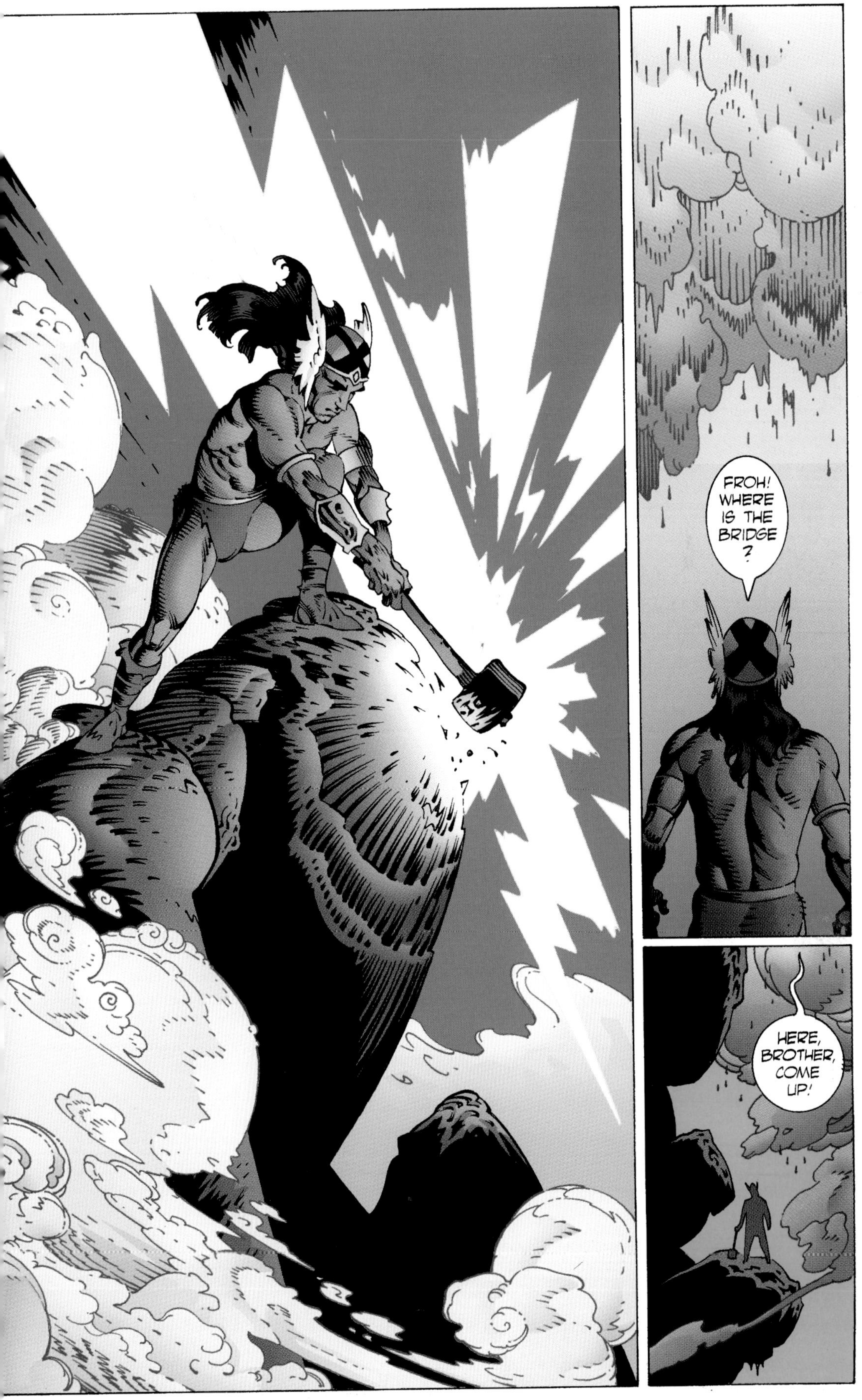
FROH! WHERE IS THE BRIDGE ?
HERE, BROTHER, COME UP!

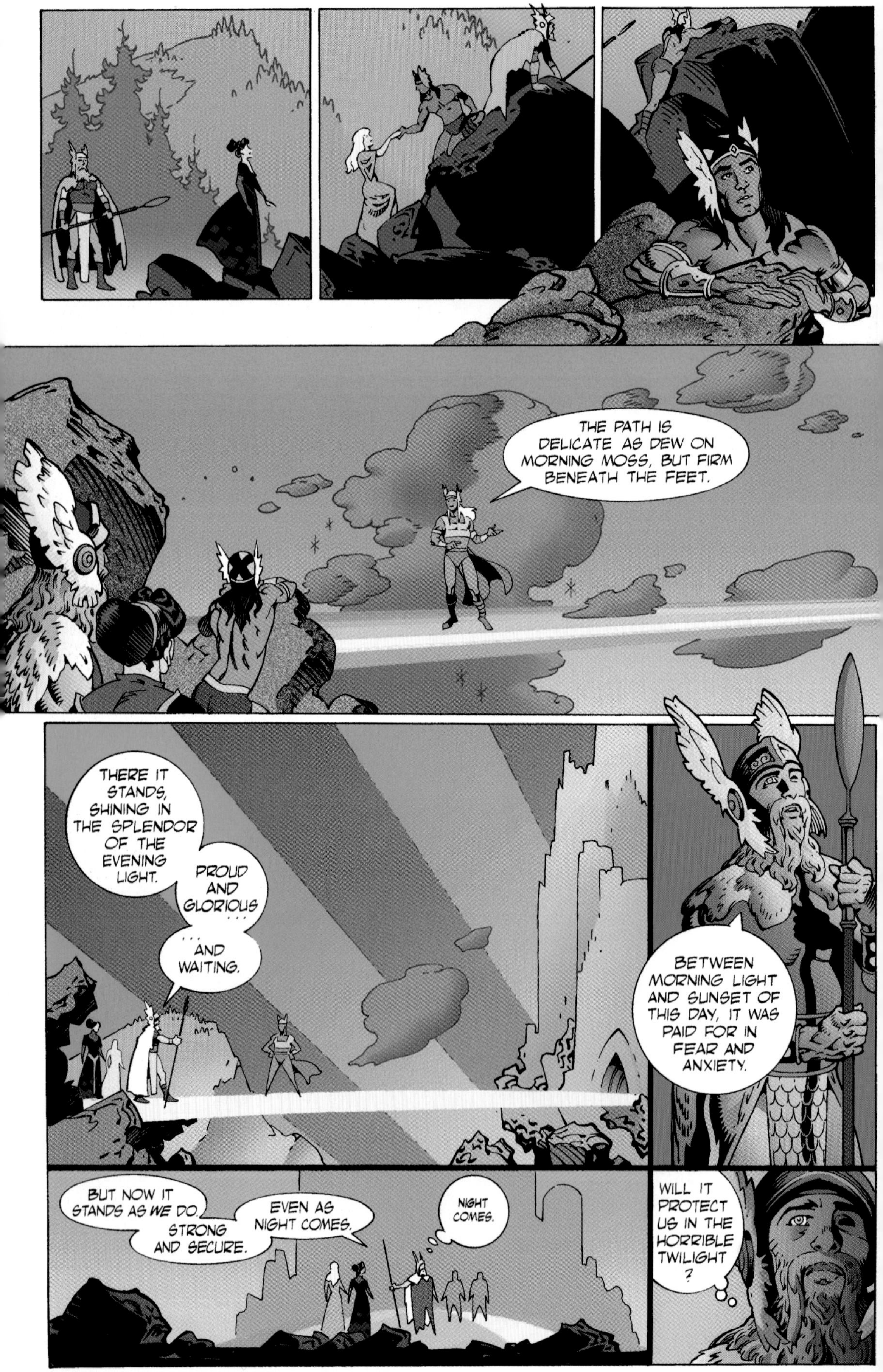
THE PATH IS DELICATE AS DEW ON MORNING MOSS, BUT FIRM BENEATH THE FEET.
THERE IT STANDS, SHINING IN THE SPLENDOR OF THE EVENING LIGHT.
PROUD AND GLORIOUS . . .
. . . AND WAITING.
BETWEEN MORNING LIGHT AND SUNSET OF THIS DAY, IT WAS PAID FOR IN FEAR AND ANXIETY.
BUT NOW IT STANDS AS WE DO.
STRONG AND SECURE.
EVEN AS NIGHT COMES.
NIGHT COMES.
WILL IT PROTECT US IN THE HORRIBLE TWILIGHT ?

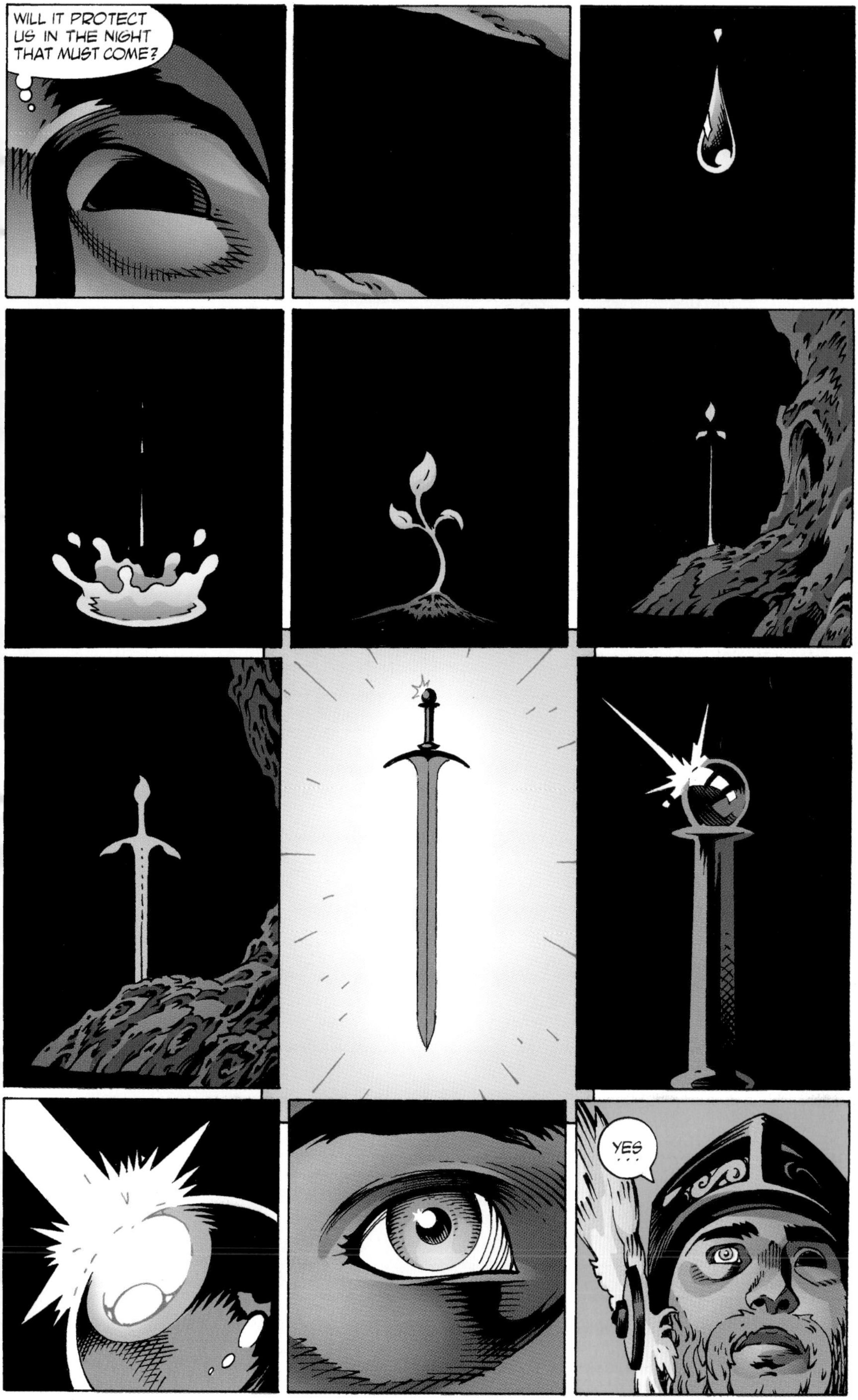
WILL IT PROTECT US IN THE NIGHT THAT MUST COME?
YES...

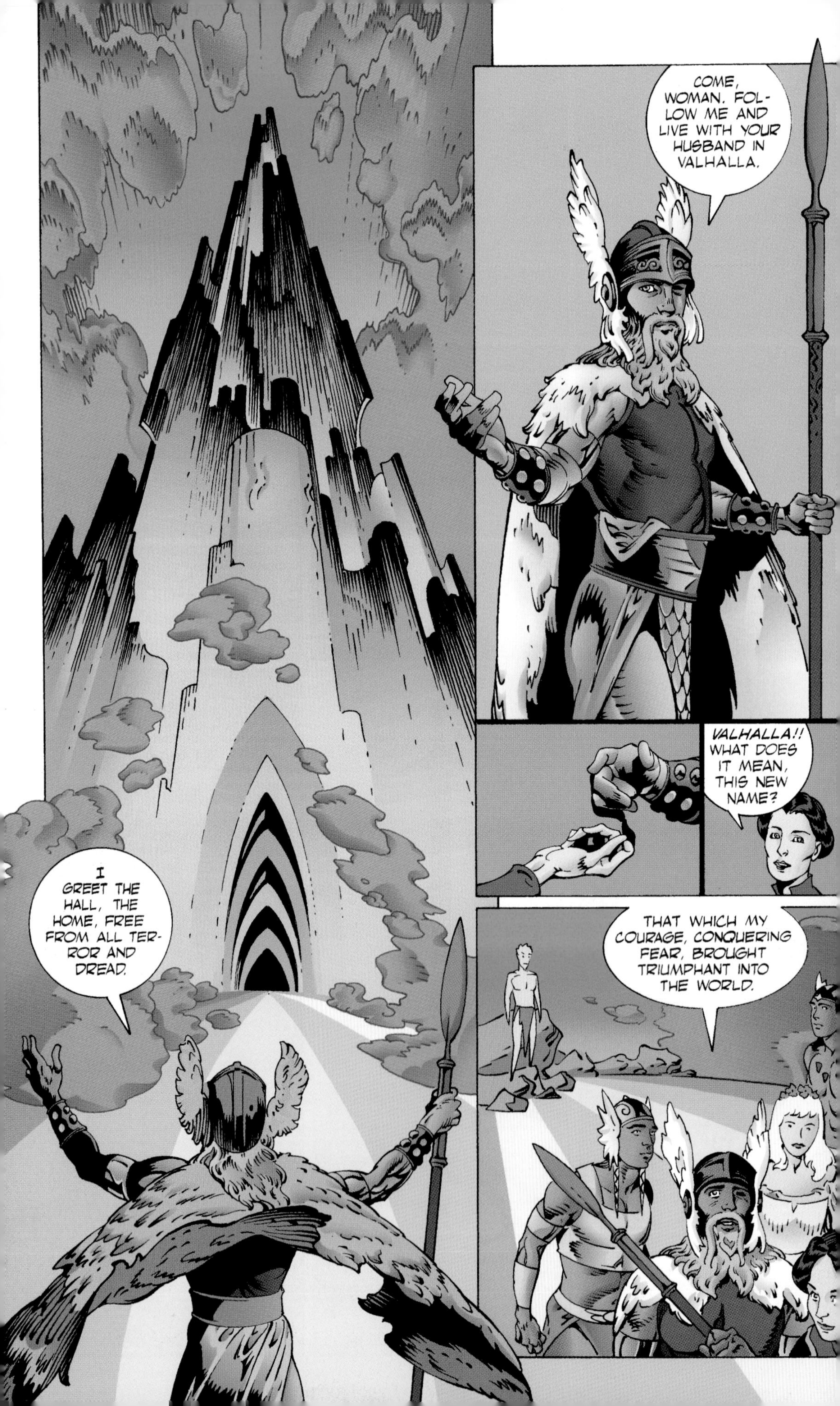
COME, WOMAN. FOL-LOW ME AND LIVE WITH YOUR HUSBAND IN VALHALLA.
VALHALLA!! WHAT DOES IT MEAN, THIS NEW NAME?
I GREET THE HALL, THE HOME, FREE FROM ALL TER-ROR AND DREAD.
THAT WHICH MY COURAGE, CONQUERING FEAR, BROUGHT TRIUMPHANT INTO THE WORLD.

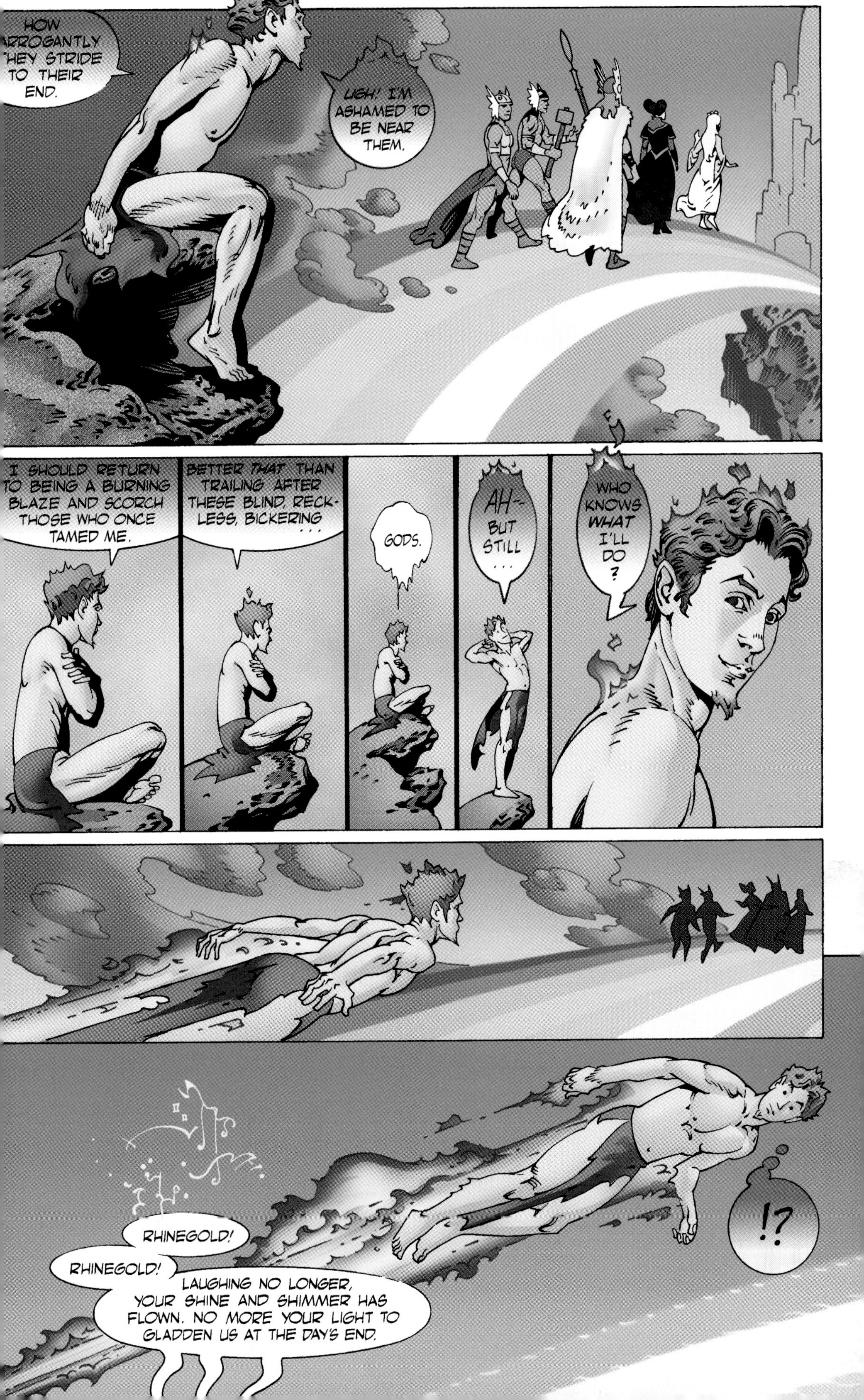
HOW ARROGANTLY THEY STRIDE TO THEIR END.
UGH! I'M ASHAMED TO BE NEAR THEM.
I SHOULD RETURN TO BEING A BURNING BLAZE AND SCORCH THOSE WHO ONCE TAMED ME.
BETTER THAT THAN TRAILING AFTER THESE BLIND, RECKLESS, BICKERING . . .
GODS.
AH-- BUT STILL . . .
WHO KNOWS WHAT I'LL DO ?
RHINEGOLD!
RHINEGOLD!
LAUGHING NO LONGER, YOUR SHINE AND SHIMMER HAS FLOWN. NO MORE YOUR LIGHT TO GLADDEN US AT THE DAY'S END.
!?

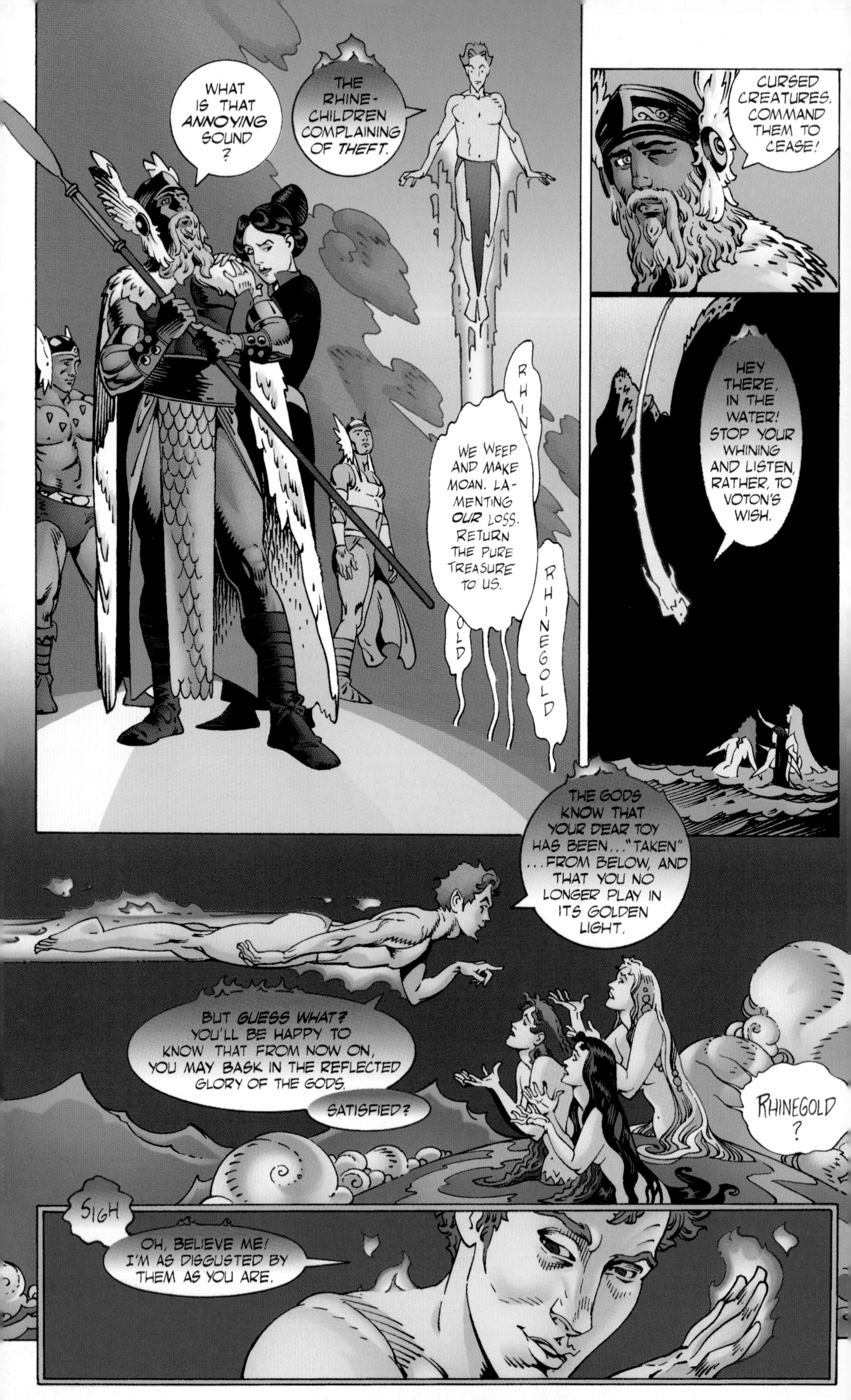
WHAT IS THAT *ANNOYING* SOUND?
THE RHINE-CHILDREN COMPLAINING OF *THEFT*.
RHINEGOLD
WE WEEP AND MAKE MOAN. LAMENTING *OUR* LOSS. RETURN THE PURE TREASURE TO US.
RHINEGOLD
CURSED CREATURES. COMMAND THEM TO CEASE!
HEY THERE, IN THE WATER! STOP YOUR WHINING AND LISTEN, RATHER, TO VOTON'S WISH.
THE GODS KNOW THAT YOUR DEAR TOY HAS BEEN..."TAKEN"...FROM BELOW, AND THAT YOU NO LONGER PLAY IN ITS GOLDEN LIGHT.
BUT *GUESS WHAT?* YOU'LL BE HAPPY TO KNOW THAT FROM NOW ON, YOU MAY *BASK* IN THE REFLECTED GLORY OF THE GODS.
SATISFIED?
RHINEGOLD?
SIGH
OH, BELIEVE ME! I'M AS DISGUSTED BY THEM AS YOU ARE.

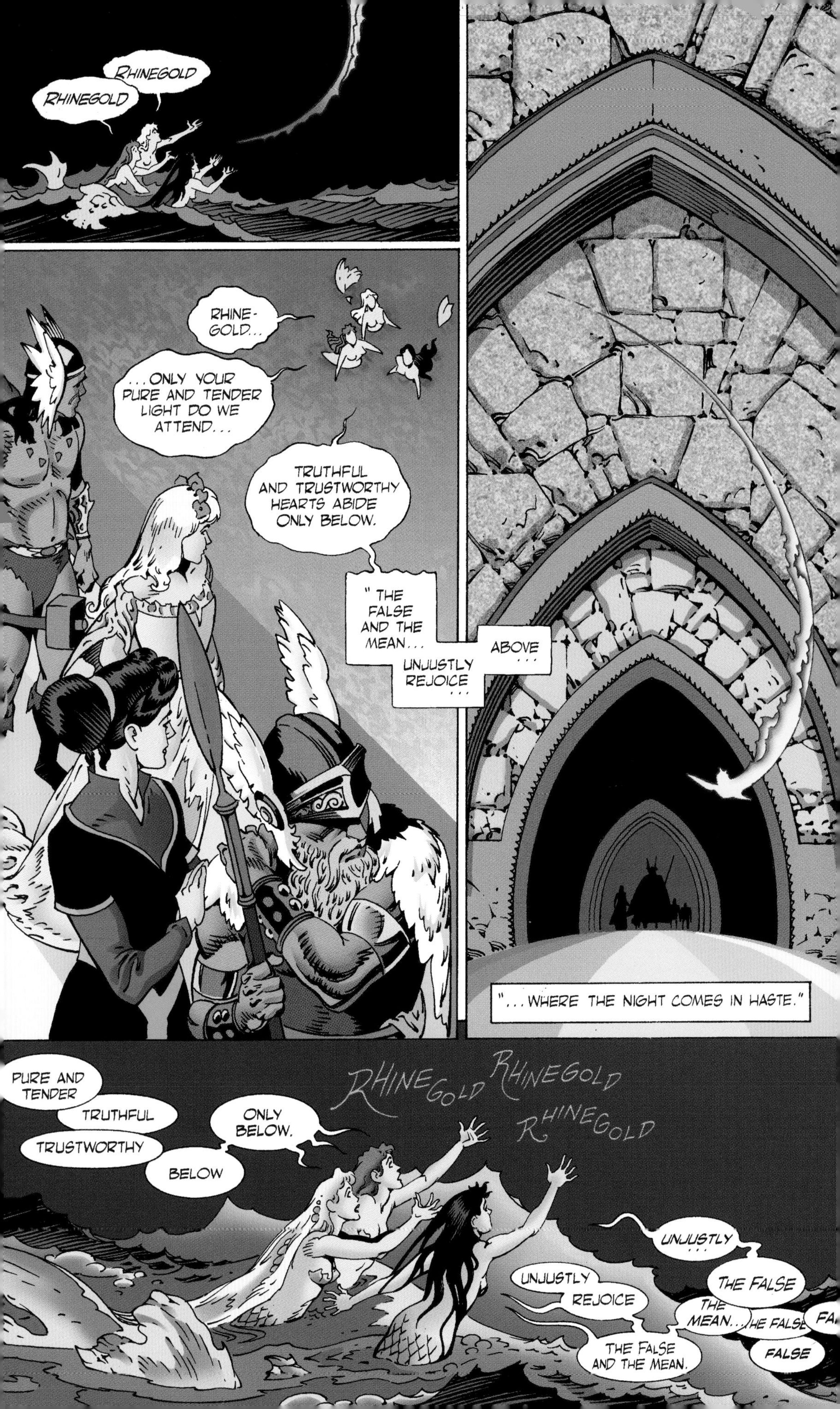

RHINEGOLD
RHINEGOLD
RHINE-GOLD...
...ONLY YOUR PURE AND TENDER LIGHT DO WE ATTEND...
TRUTHFUL AND TRUSTWORTHY HEARTS ABIDE ONLY BELOW.
" THE FALSE AND THE MEAN...
UNJUSTLY REJOICE...
ABOVE...
"...WHERE THE NIGHT COMES IN HASTE."
RHINEGOLD RHINEGOLD
RHINEGOLD
PURE AND TENDER
TRUTHFUL
TRUSTWORTHY
BELOW
ONLY BELOW.
UNJUSTLY...
UNJUSTLY
REJOICE
THE FALSE
THE MEAN...
THE FALSE AND THE MEAN.
FALSE

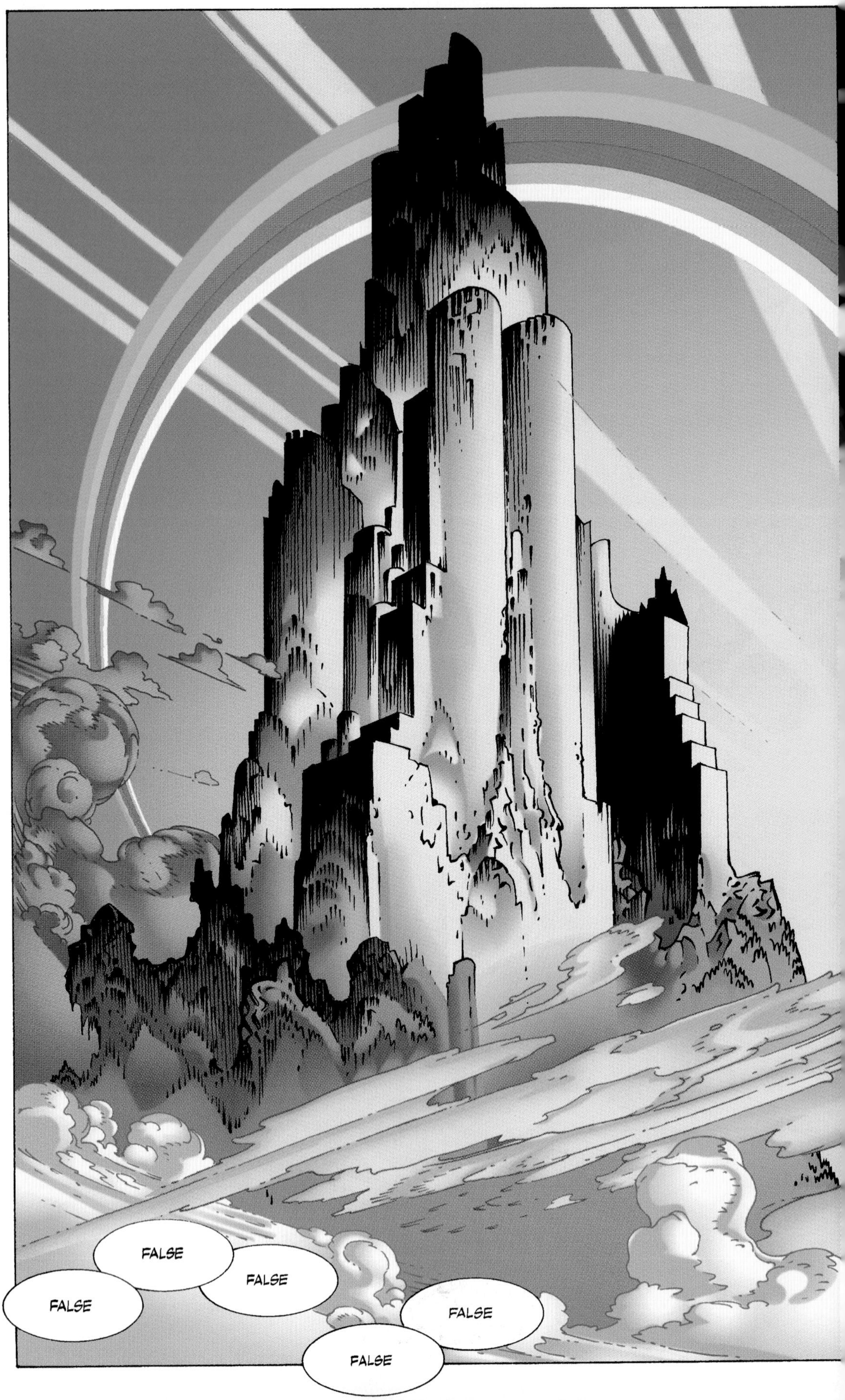
FALSE
FALSE
FALSE
FALSE
FALSE

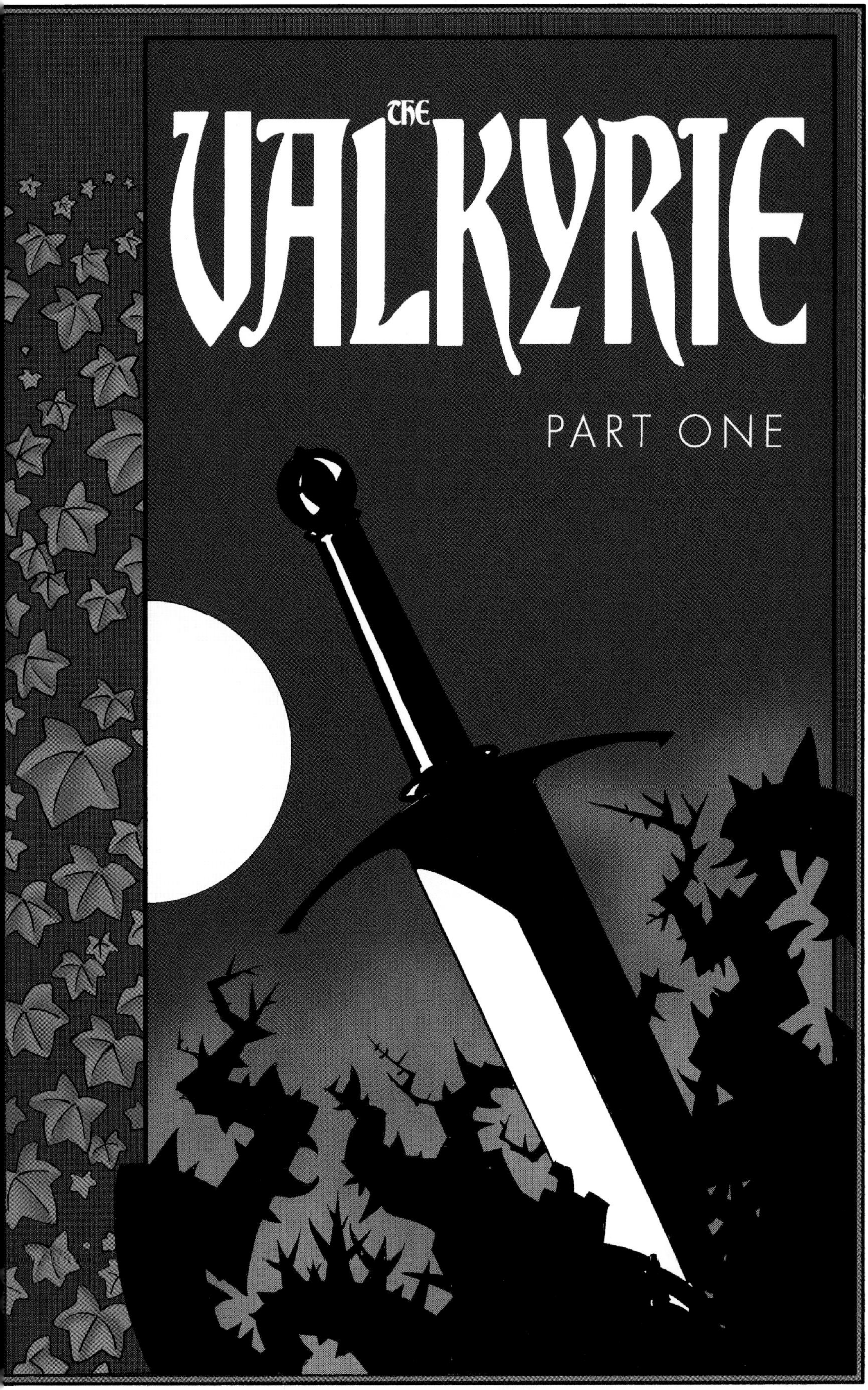
THE VALKYRIE
PART ONE

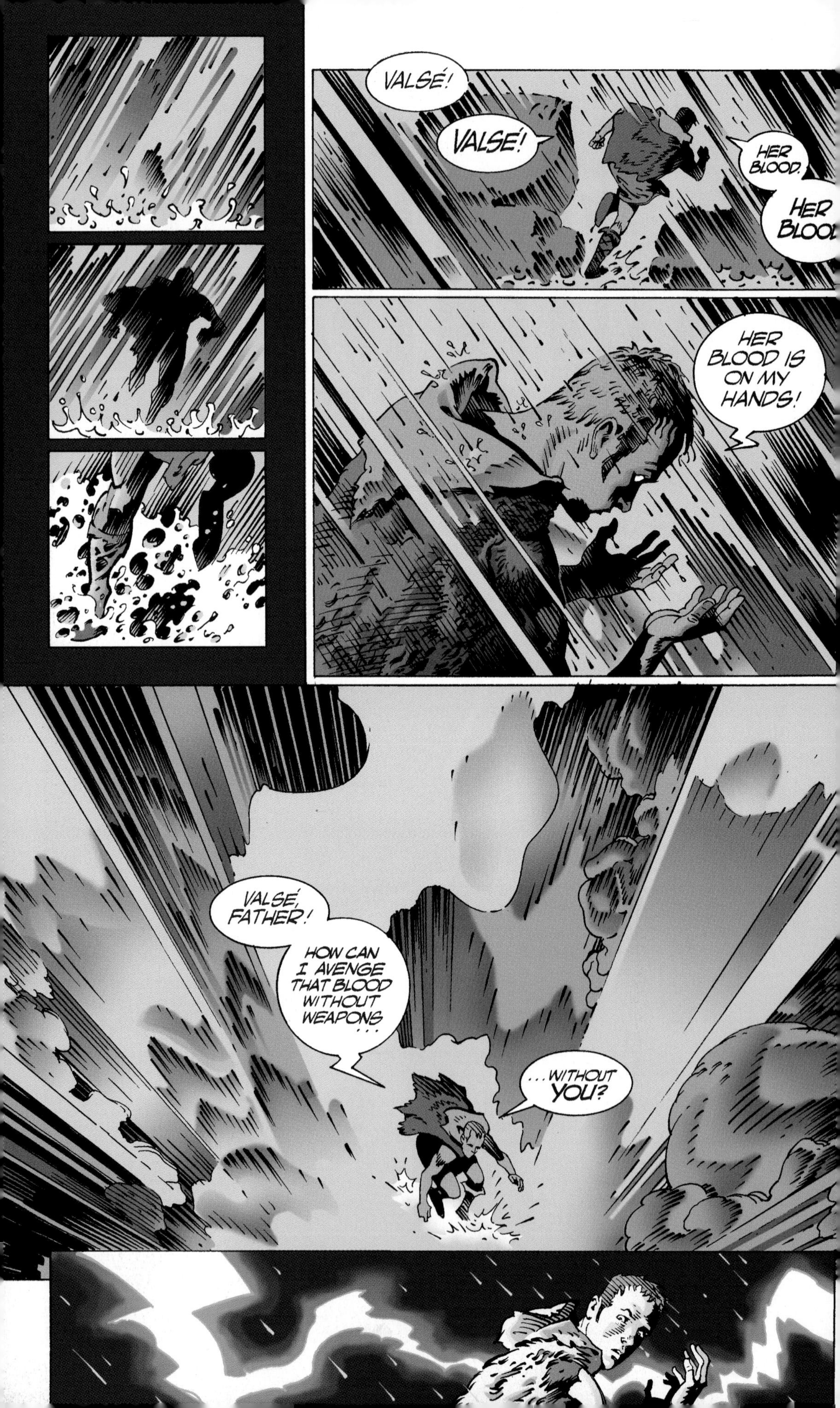

VALSÉ!
VALSÉ!
HER BLOOD,
HER BLOOD
HER BLOOD IS ON MY HANDS!
VALSÉ, FATHER!
HOW CAN I AVENGE THAT BLOOD WITHOUT WEAPONS . . .
. . . WITHOUT YOU?

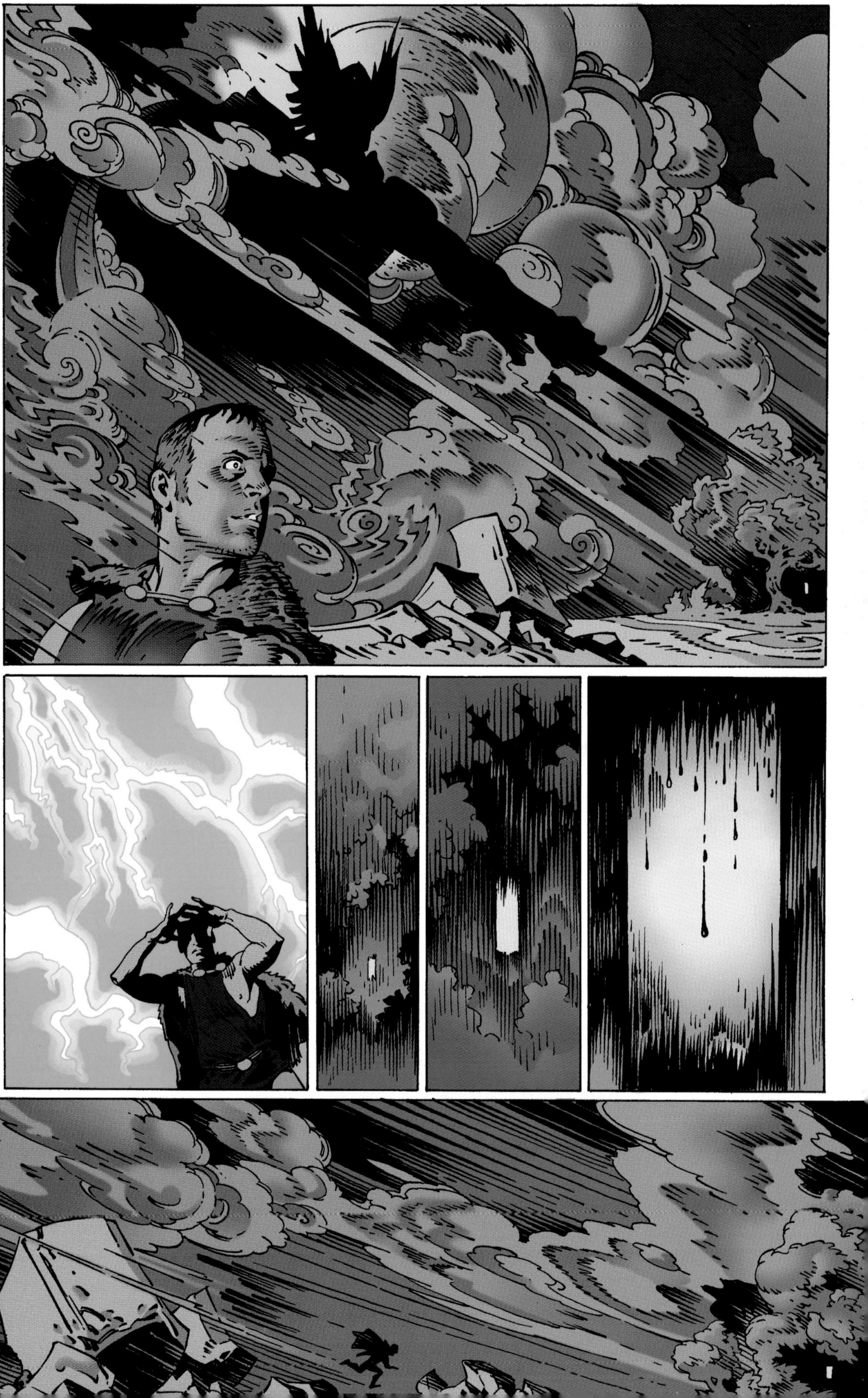

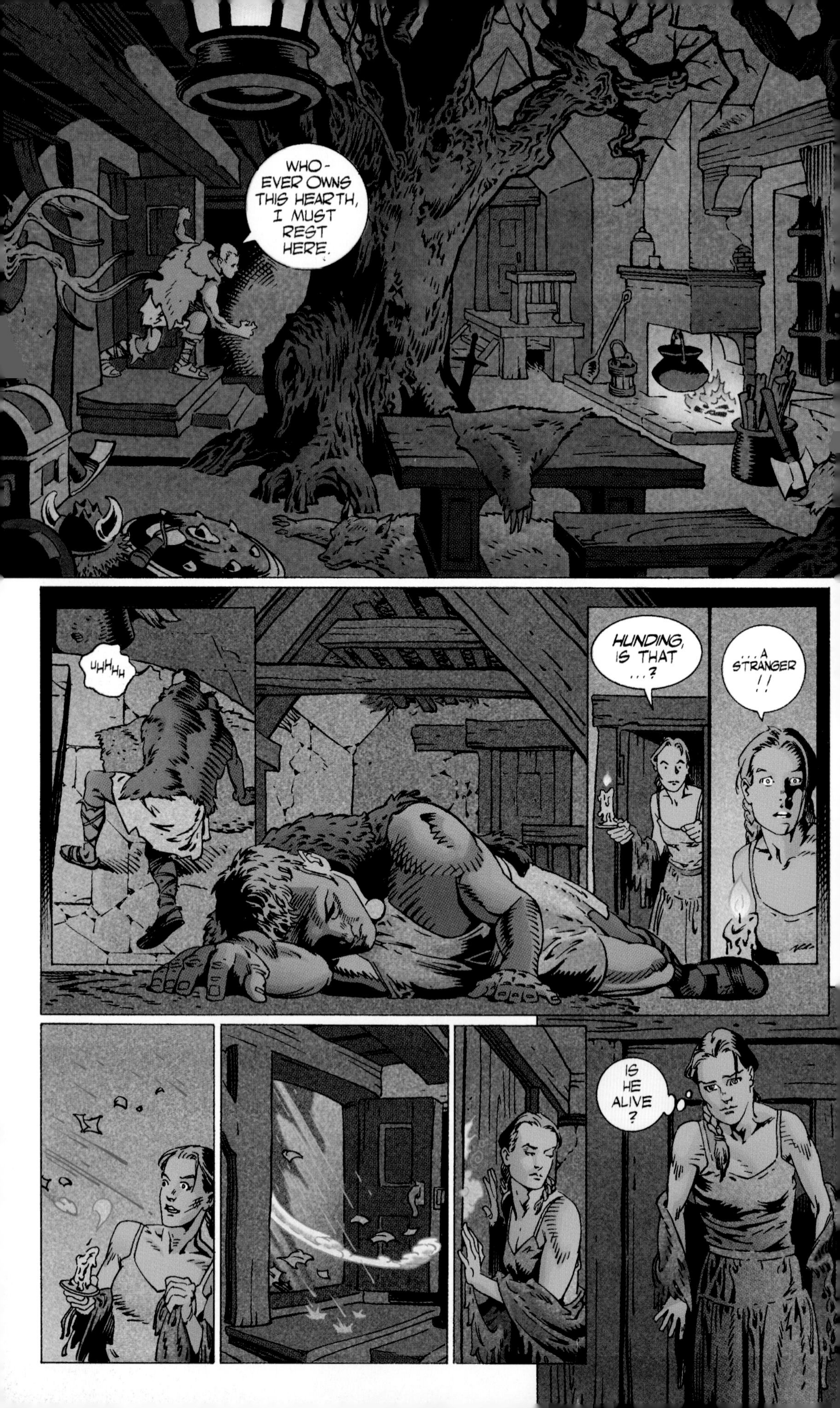
WHO-EVER OWNS THIS HEARTH, I MUST REST HERE.
UHHHH
HUNDING, IS THAT ...?
...A STRANGER !!
IS HE ALIVE ?

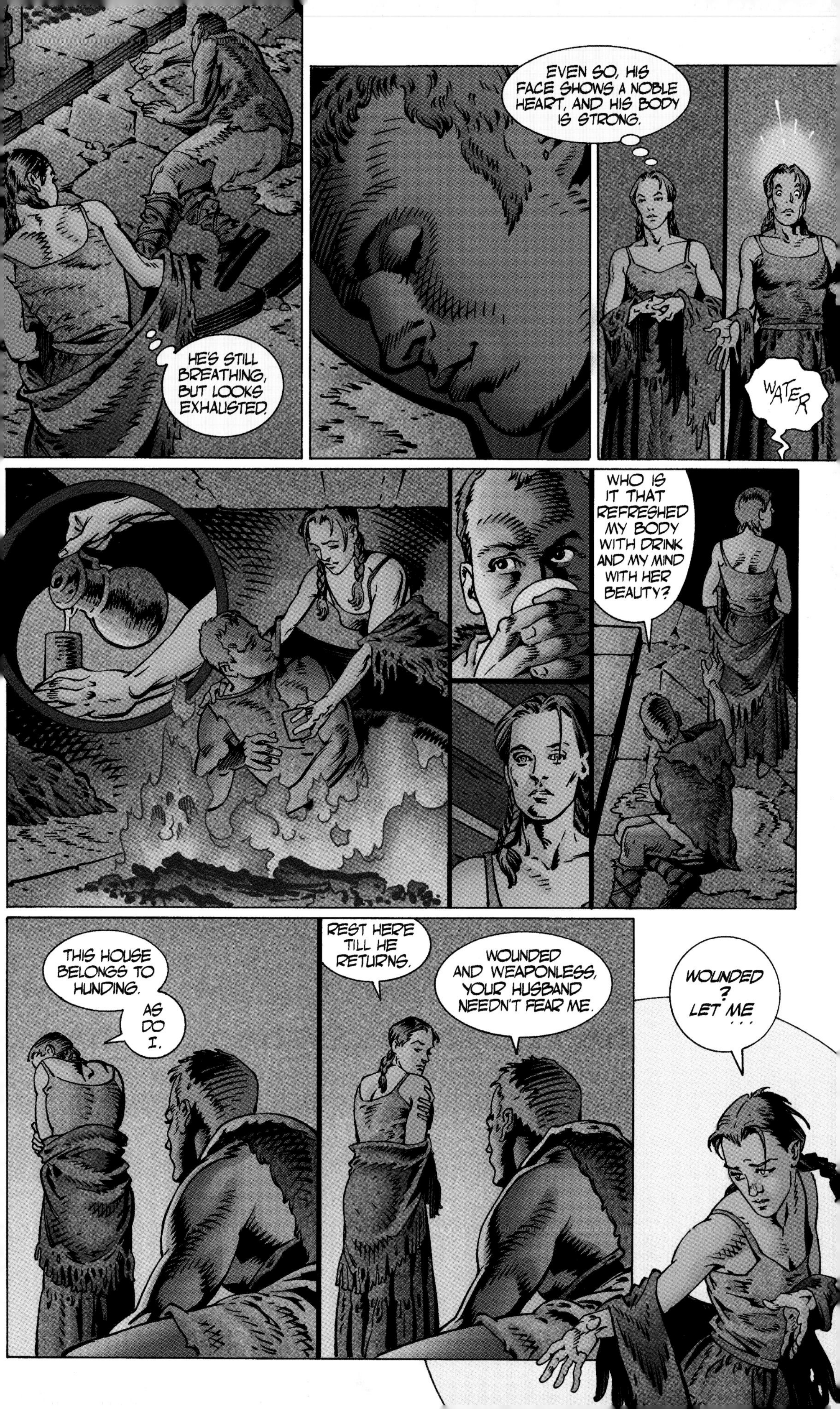
HE'S STILL BREATHING, BUT LOOKS EXHAUSTED.
EVEN SO, HIS FACE SHOWS A NOBLE HEART, AND HIS BODY IS STRONG.
WATER
WHO IS IT THAT REFRESHED MY BODY WITH DRINK AND MY MIND WITH HER BEAUTY?
THIS HOUSE BELONGS TO HUNDING.
AS DO I.
REST HERE TILL HE RETURNS.
WOUNDED AND WEAPONLESS, YOUR HUSBAND NEEDN'T FEAR ME.
WOUNDED ? LET ME . . .

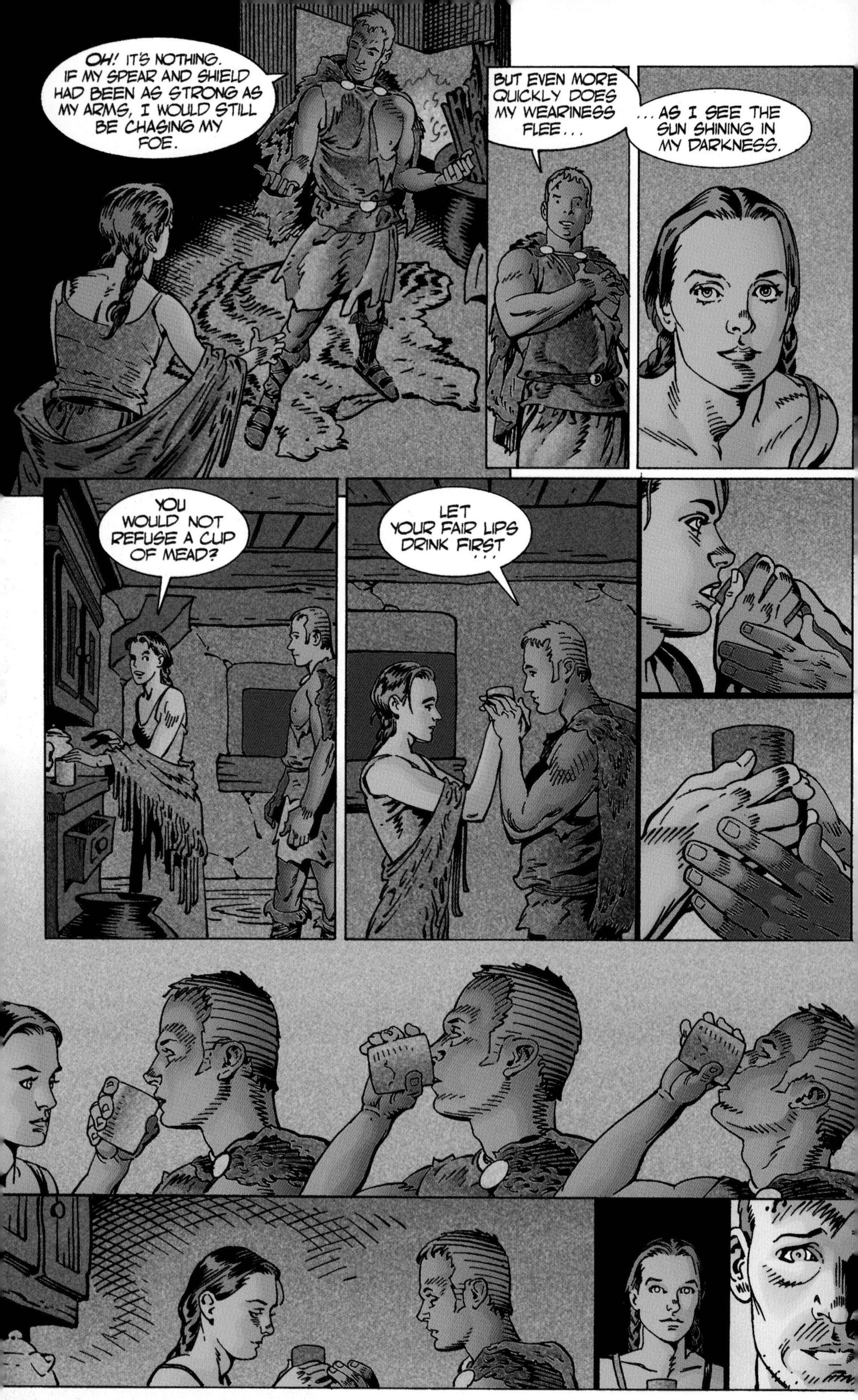
OH! IT'S NOTHING. IF MY SPEAR AND SHIELD HAD BEEN AS STRONG AS MY ARMS, I WOULD STILL BE CHASING MY FOE.
BUT EVEN MORE QUICKLY DOES MY WEARINESS FLEE...
...AS I SEE THE SUN SHINING IN MY DARKNESS.
YOU WOULD NOT REFUSE A CUP OF MEAD?
LET YOUR FAIR LIPS DRINK FIRST...

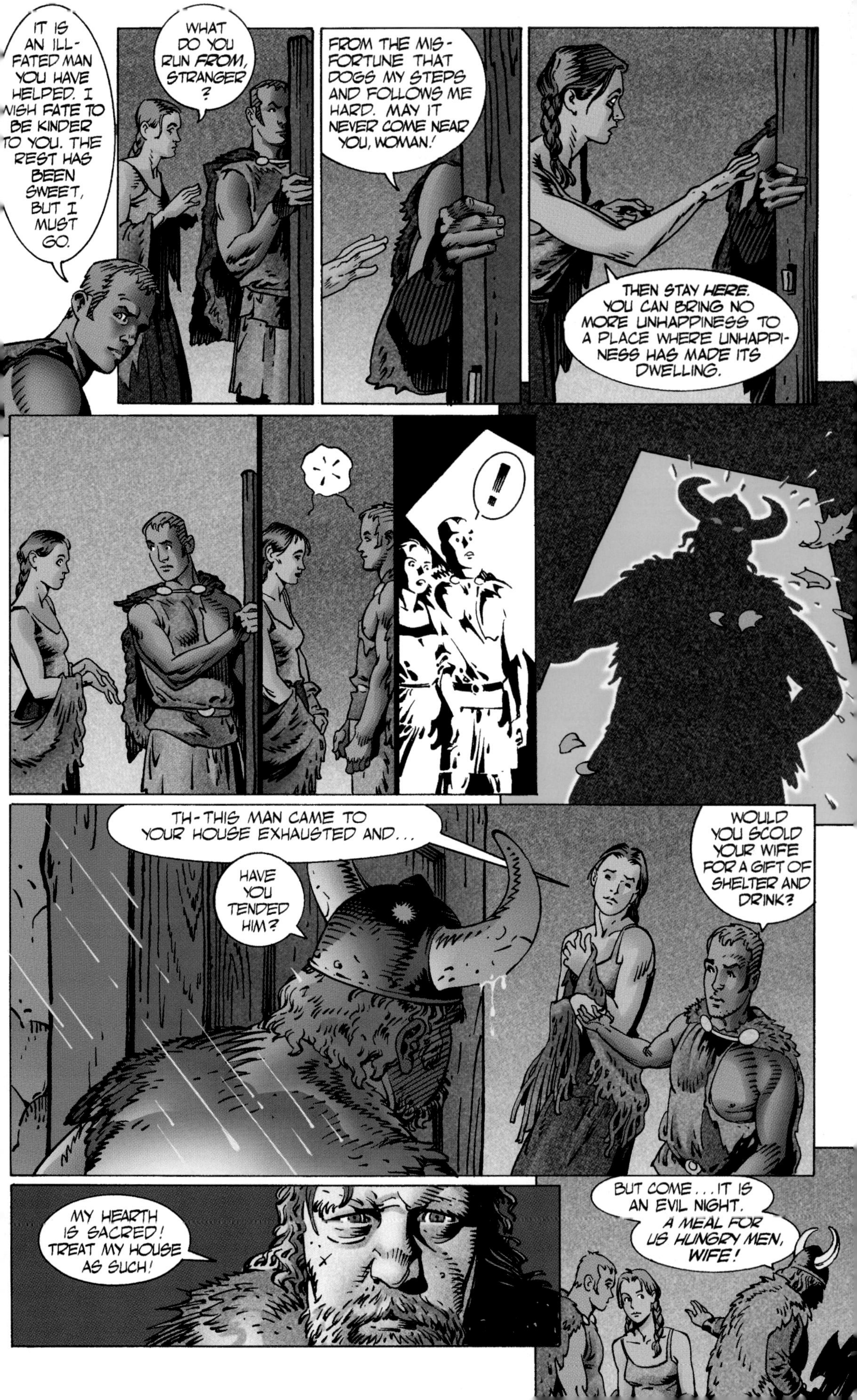

IT IS AN ILL-FATED MAN YOU HAVE HELPED. I WISH FATE TO BE KINDER TO YOU. THE REST HAS BEEN SWEET, BUT I MUST GO.
WHAT DO YOU RUN *FROM*, STRANGER?
FROM THE MISFORTUNE THAT DOGS MY STEPS AND FOLLOWS ME HARD. MAY IT NEVER COME NEAR YOU, WOMAN!
THEN STAY *HERE*. YOU CAN BRING NO MORE UNHAPPINESS TO A PLACE WHERE UNHAPPINESS HAS MADE ITS DWELLING.
!
TH-THIS MAN CAME TO YOUR HOUSE EXHAUSTED AND...
HAVE YOU TENDED HIM?
WOULD YOU SCOLD YOUR WIFE FOR A GIFT OF SHELTER AND DRINK?
MY HEARTH IS SACRED! TREAT MY HOUSE AS SUCH!
BUT COME... IT IS AN EVIL NIGHT. *A MEAL FOR US HUNGRY MEN, WIFE!*

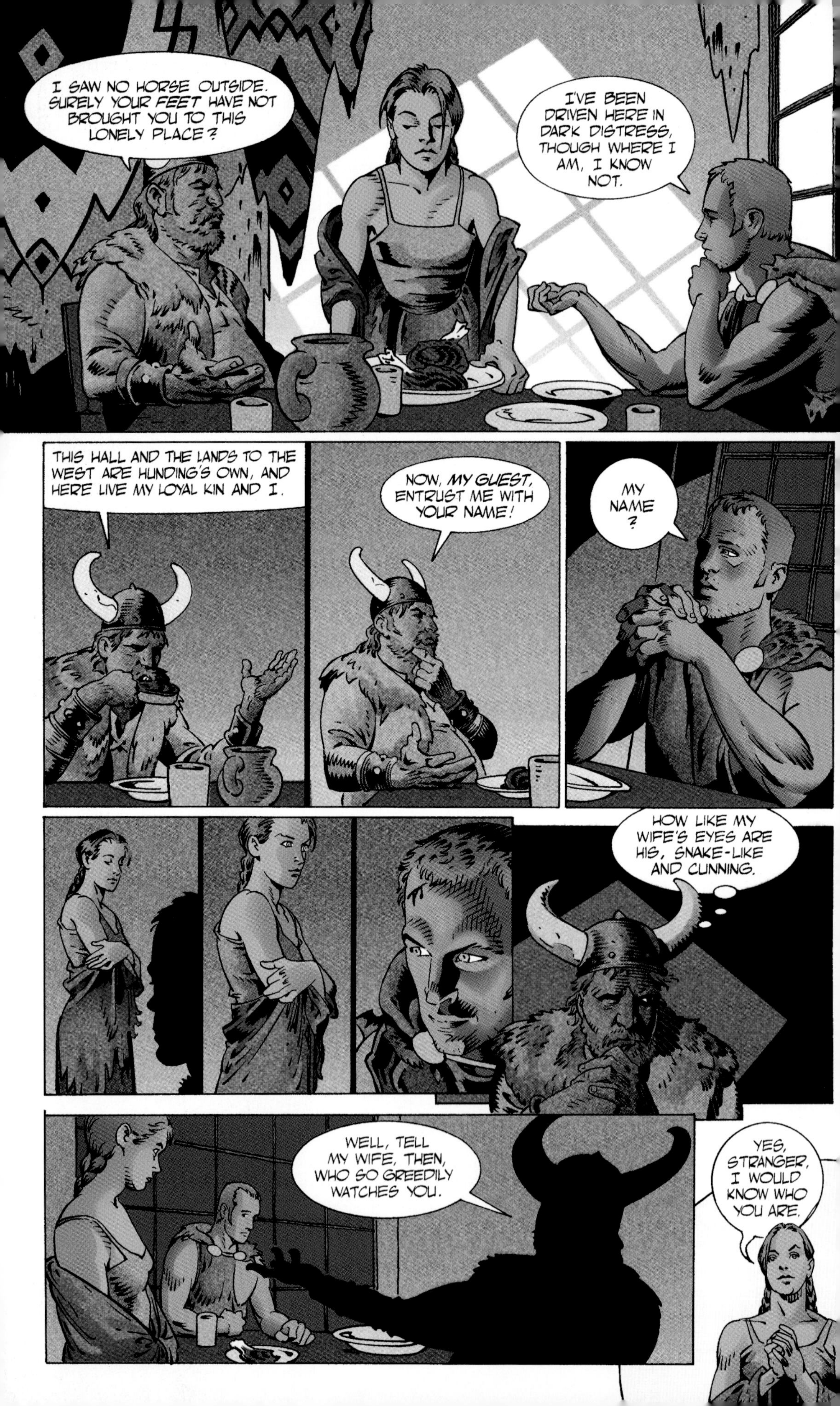
I SAW NO HORSE OUTSIDE. SURELY YOUR *FEET* HAVE NOT BROUGHT YOU TO THIS LONELY PLACE?
I'VE BEEN DRIVEN HERE IN DARK DISTRESS, THOUGH WHERE I AM, I KNOW NOT.
THIS HALL AND THE LANDS TO THE WEST ARE HUNDING'S OWN, AND HERE LIVE MY LOYAL KIN AND I.
NOW, *MY GUEST*, ENTRUST ME WITH YOUR NAME!
MY NAME?
HOW LIKE MY WIFE'S EYES ARE HIS, SNAKE-LIKE AND CUNNING.
WELL, TELL MY WIFE, THEN, WHO SO GREEDILY WATCHES YOU.
YES, STRANGER, I WOULD KNOW WHO YOU ARE.

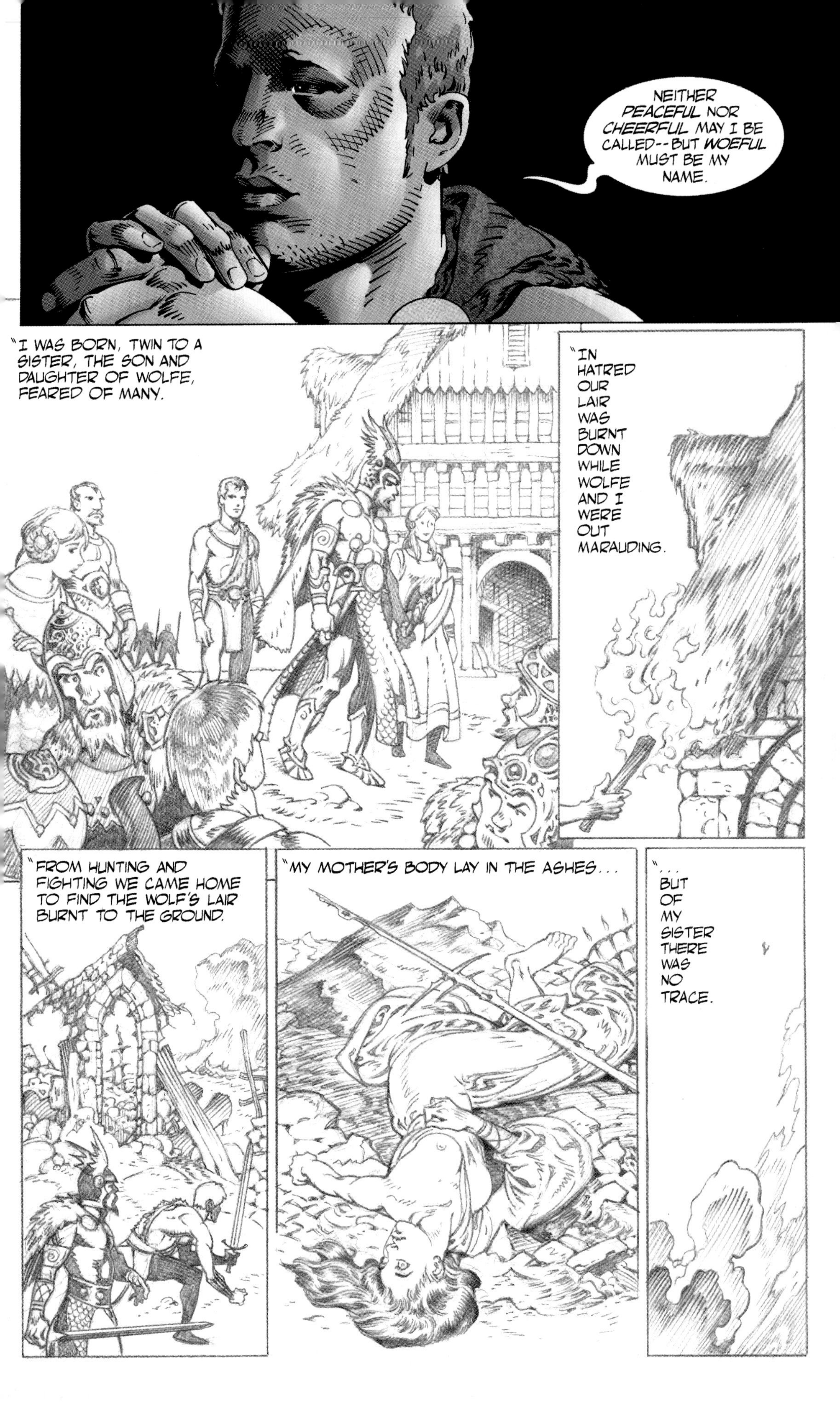
NEITHER PEACEFUL NOR CHEERFUL MAY I BE CALLED--BUT WOEFUL MUST BE MY NAME.
"I WAS BORN, TWIN TO A SISTER, THE SON AND DAUGHTER OF WOLFE, FEARED OF MANY.
"IN HATRED OUR LAIR WAS BURNT DOWN WHILE WOLFE AND I WERE OUT MARAUDING.
"FROM HUNTING AND FIGHTING WE CAME HOME TO FIND THE WOLF'S LAIR BURNT TO THE GROUND.
"MY MOTHER'S BODY LAY IN THE ASHES...
"...BUT OF MY SISTER THERE WAS NO TRACE.

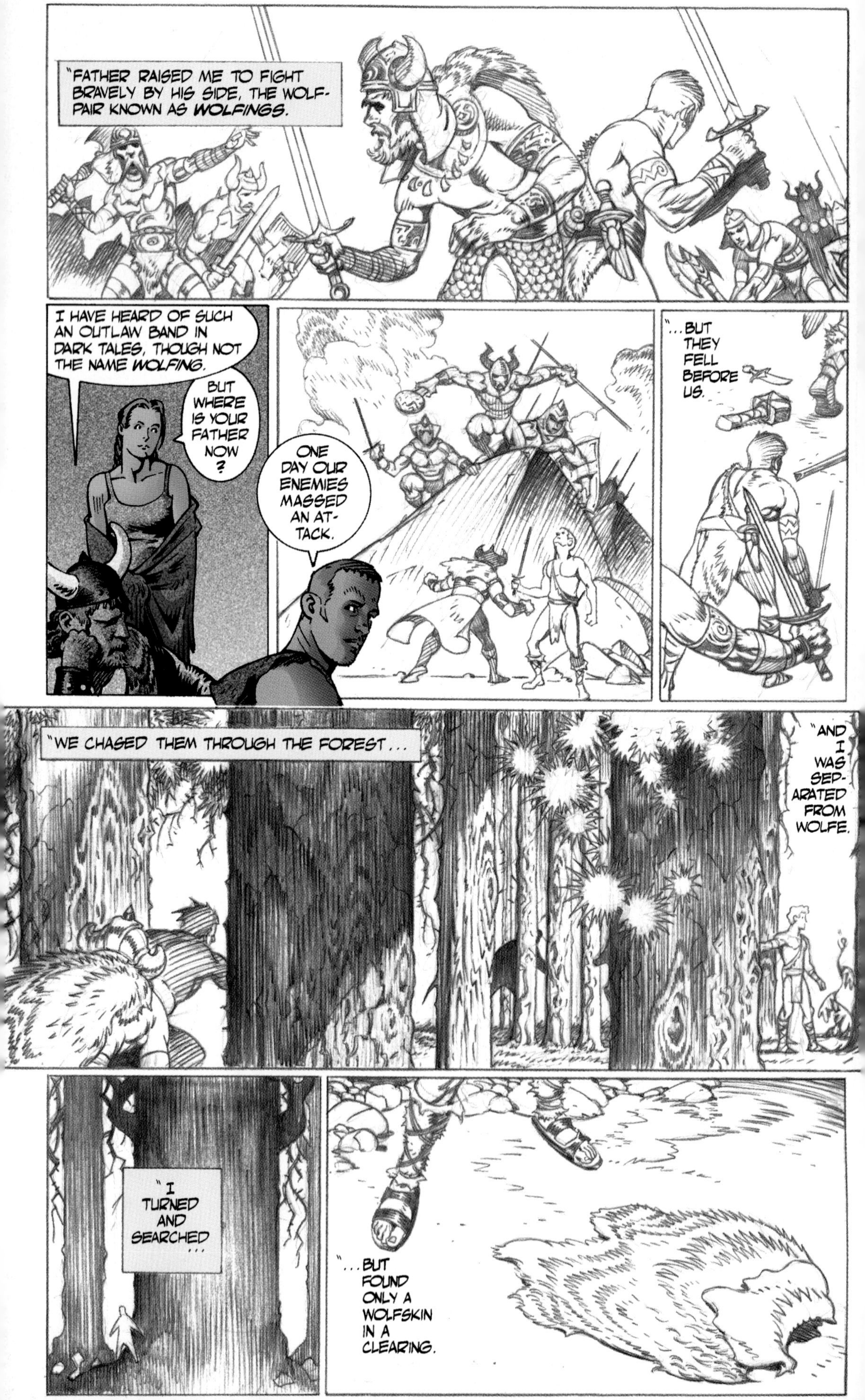
"FATHER RAISED ME TO FIGHT BRAVELY BY HIS SIDE, THE WOLF-PAIR KNOWN AS WOLFINGS.
I HAVE HEARD OF SUCH AN OUTLAW BAND IN DARK TALES, THOUGH NOT THE NAME WOLFING.
BUT WHERE IS YOUR FATHER NOW ?
ONE DAY OUR ENEMIES MASSED AN AT-TACK.
"...BUT THEY FELL BEFORE US.
"WE CHASED THEM THROUGH THE FOREST...
"AND I WAS SEP-ARATED FROM WOLFE.
"I TURNED AND SEARCHED ...
"...BUT FOUND ONLY A WOLFSKIN IN A CLEARING.

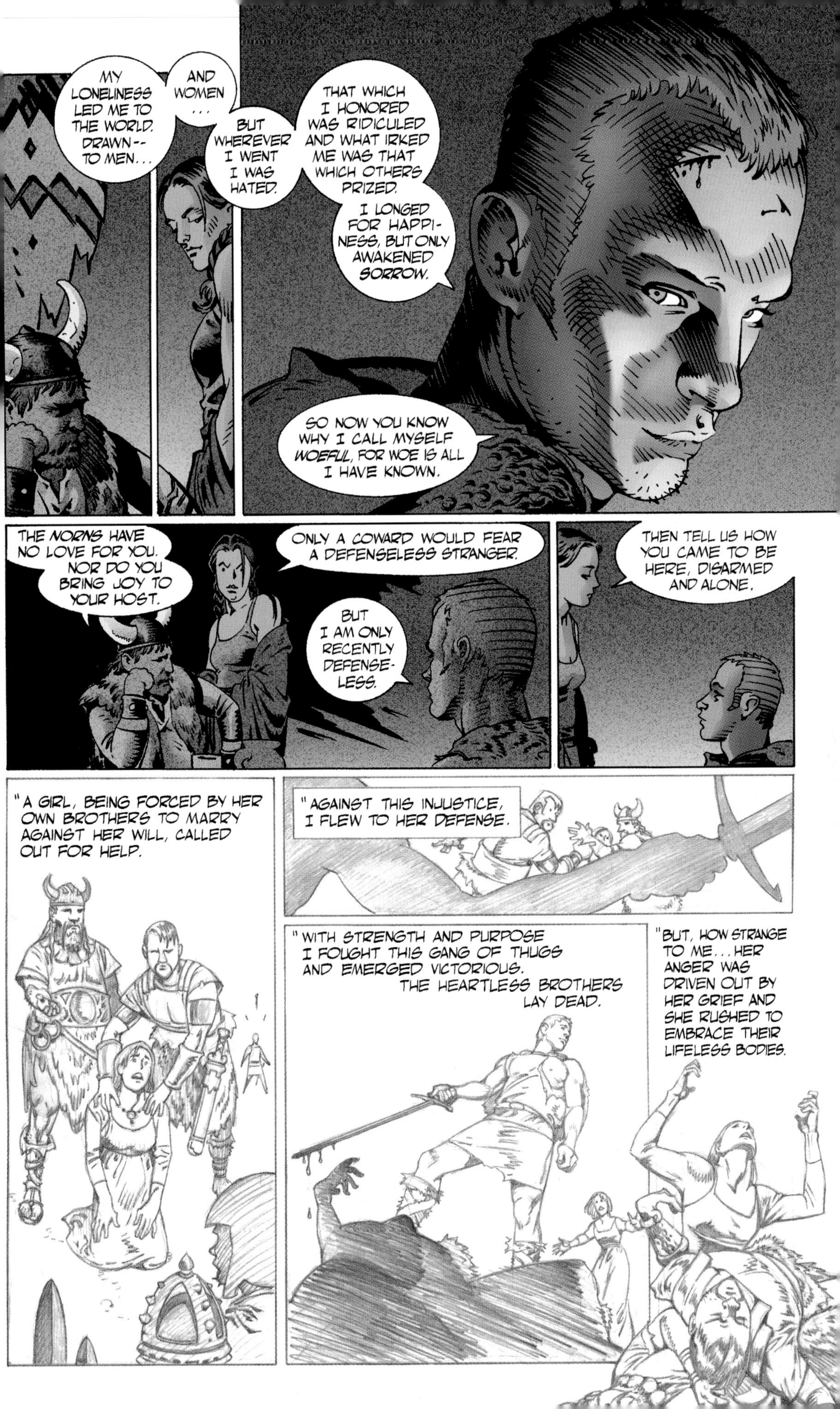
MY LONELINESS LED ME TO THE WORLD. DRAWN-- TO MEN...
AND WOMEN ...
BUT WHEREVER I WENT I WAS HATED.
THAT WHICH I HONORED WAS RIDICULED AND WHAT IRKED ME WAS THAT WHICH OTHERS PRIZED.
I LONGED FOR HAPPINESS, BUT ONLY AWAKENED SORROW.
SO NOW YOU KNOW WHY I CALL MYSELF WOEFUL, FOR WOE IS ALL I HAVE KNOWN.
THE NORNS HAVE NO LOVE FOR YOU.
NOR DO YOU BRING JOY TO YOUR HOST.
ONLY A COWARD WOULD FEAR A DEFENSELESS STRANGER.
BUT I AM ONLY RECENTLY DEFENSELESS.
THEN TELL US HOW YOU CAME TO BE HERE, DISARMED AND ALONE.
"A GIRL, BEING FORCED BY HER OWN BROTHERS TO MARRY AGAINST HER WILL, CALLED OUT FOR HELP.
"AGAINST THIS INJUSTICE, I FLEW TO HER DEFENSE.
"WITH STRENGTH AND PURPOSE I FOUGHT THIS GANG OF THUGS AND EMERGED VICTORIOUS.
THE HEARTLESS BROTHERS LAY DEAD.
"BUT, HOW STRANGE TO ME...HER ANGER WAS DRIVEN OUT BY HER GRIEF AND SHE RUSHED TO EMBRACE THEIR LIFELESS BODIES.

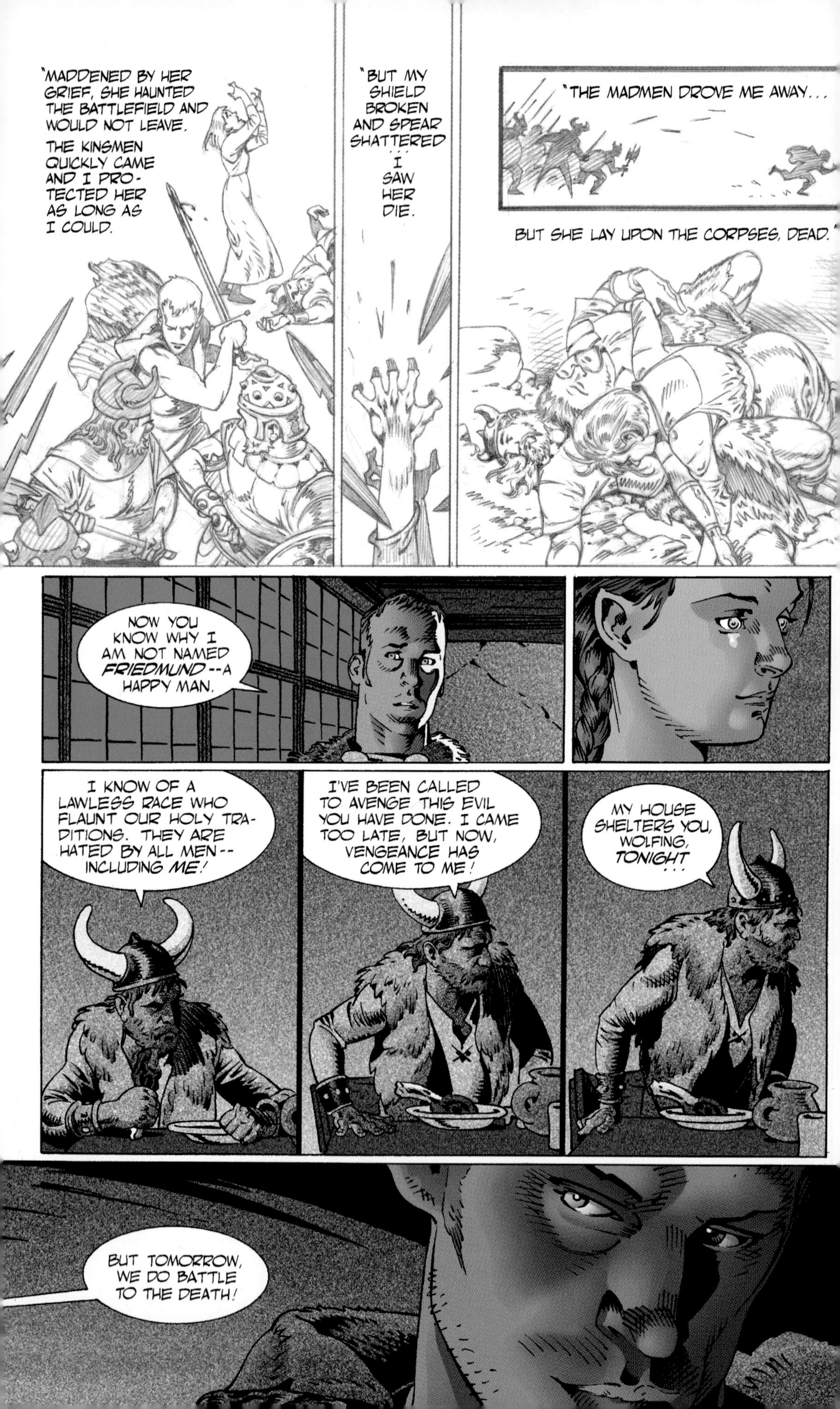
"MADDENED BY HER GRIEF, SHE HAUNTED THE BATTLEFIELD AND WOULD NOT LEAVE.
THE KINSMEN QUICKLY CAME AND I PROTECTED HER AS LONG AS I COULD.
"BUT MY SHIELD BROKEN AND SPEAR SHATTERED . . . I SAW HER DIE.
"THE MADMEN DROVE ME AWAY . . .
BUT SHE LAY UPON THE CORPSES, DEAD."
NOW YOU KNOW WHY I AM NOT NAMED *FRIEDMUND* -- A HAPPY MAN.
I KNOW OF A LAWLESS RACE WHO FLAUNT OUR HOLY TRADITIONS. THEY ARE HATED BY ALL MEN -- INCLUDING *ME*!
I'VE BEEN CALLED TO AVENGE THIS EVIL YOU HAVE DONE. I CAME TOO LATE, BUT NOW, VENGEANCE HAS COME TO ME!
MY HOUSE SHELTERS YOU, WOLFING, *TONIGHT* . . .
BUT TOMORROW, WE DO BATTLE TO THE DEATH!

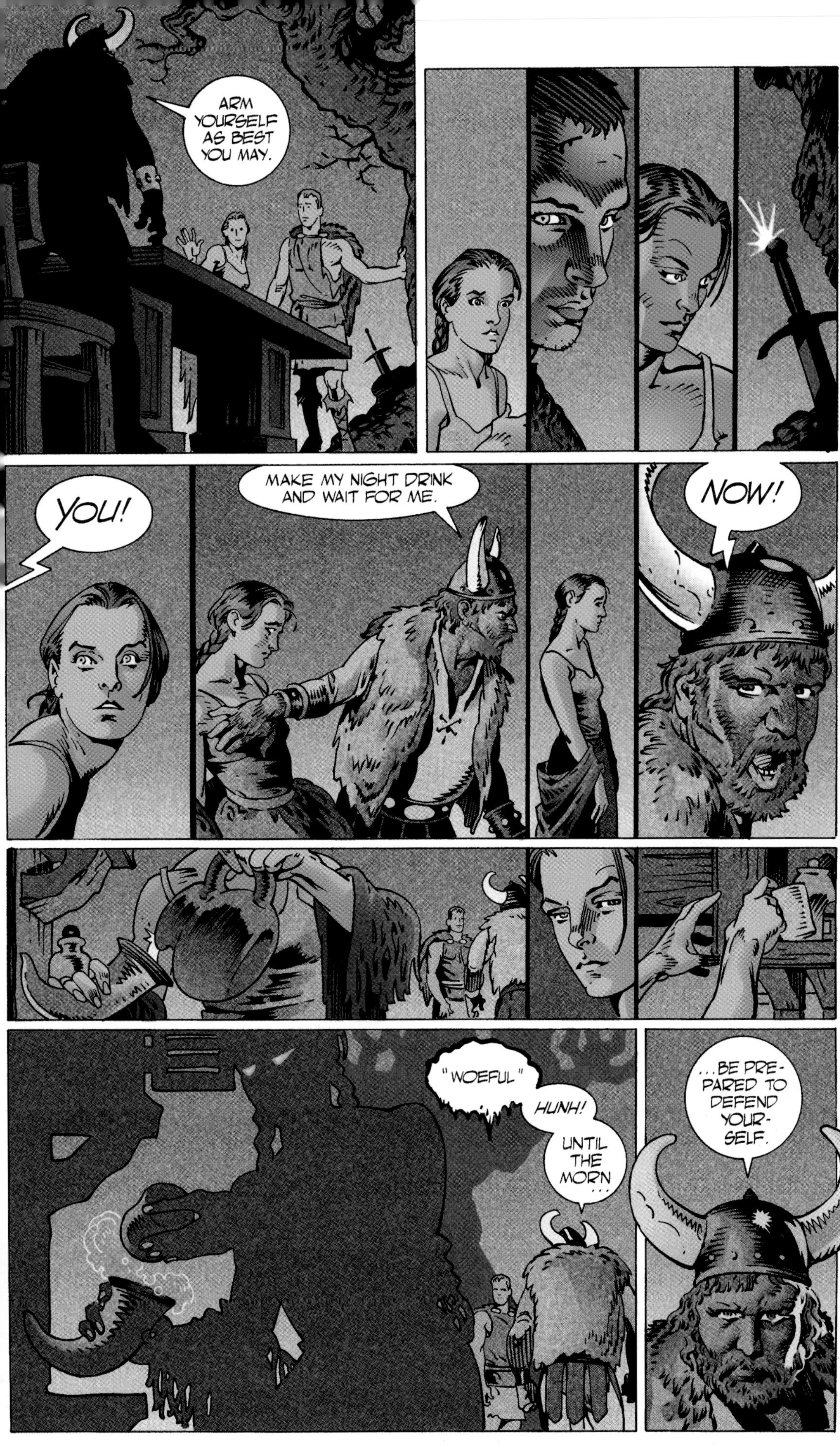
ARM YOURSELF AS BEST YOU MAY.
YOU!
MAKE MY NIGHT DRINK AND WAIT FOR ME.
NOW!
"WOEFUL"
HUNH!
UNTIL THE MORN . . .
. . . BE PREPARED TO DEFEND YOURSELF.

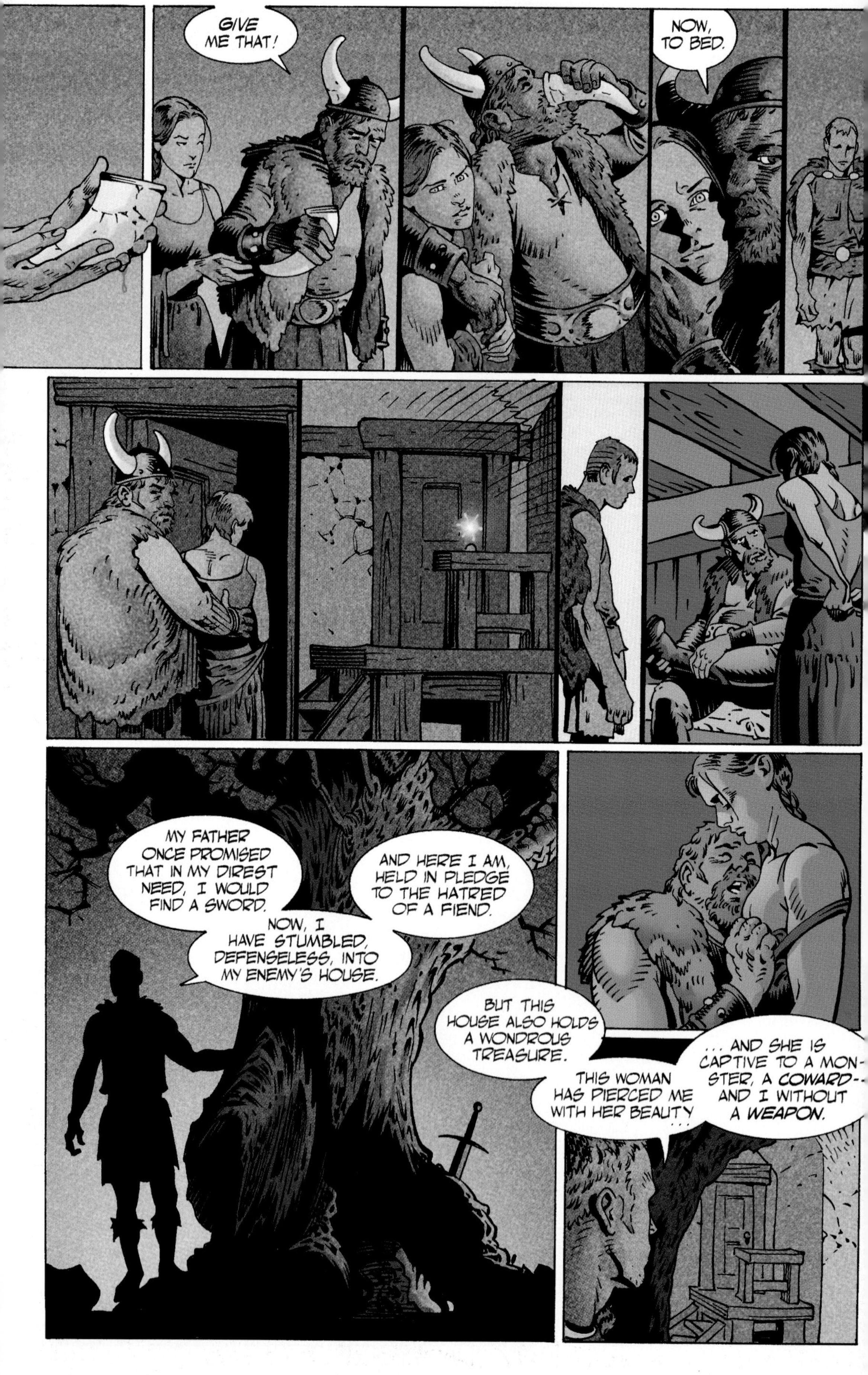
GIVE ME THAT!
NOW, TO BED.
MY FATHER ONCE PROMISED THAT IN MY DIREST NEED, I WOULD FIND A SWORD.
AND HERE I AM, HELD IN PLEDGE TO THE HATRED OF A FIEND.
NOW, I HAVE STUMBLED, DEFENSELESS, INTO MY ENEMY'S HOUSE.
BUT THIS HOUSE ALSO HOLDS A WONDROUS TREASURE.
THIS WOMAN HAS PIERCED ME WITH HER BEAUTY . . .
. . . AND SHE IS CAPTIVE TO A MONSTER, A COWARD-- AND I WITHOUT A WEAPON.

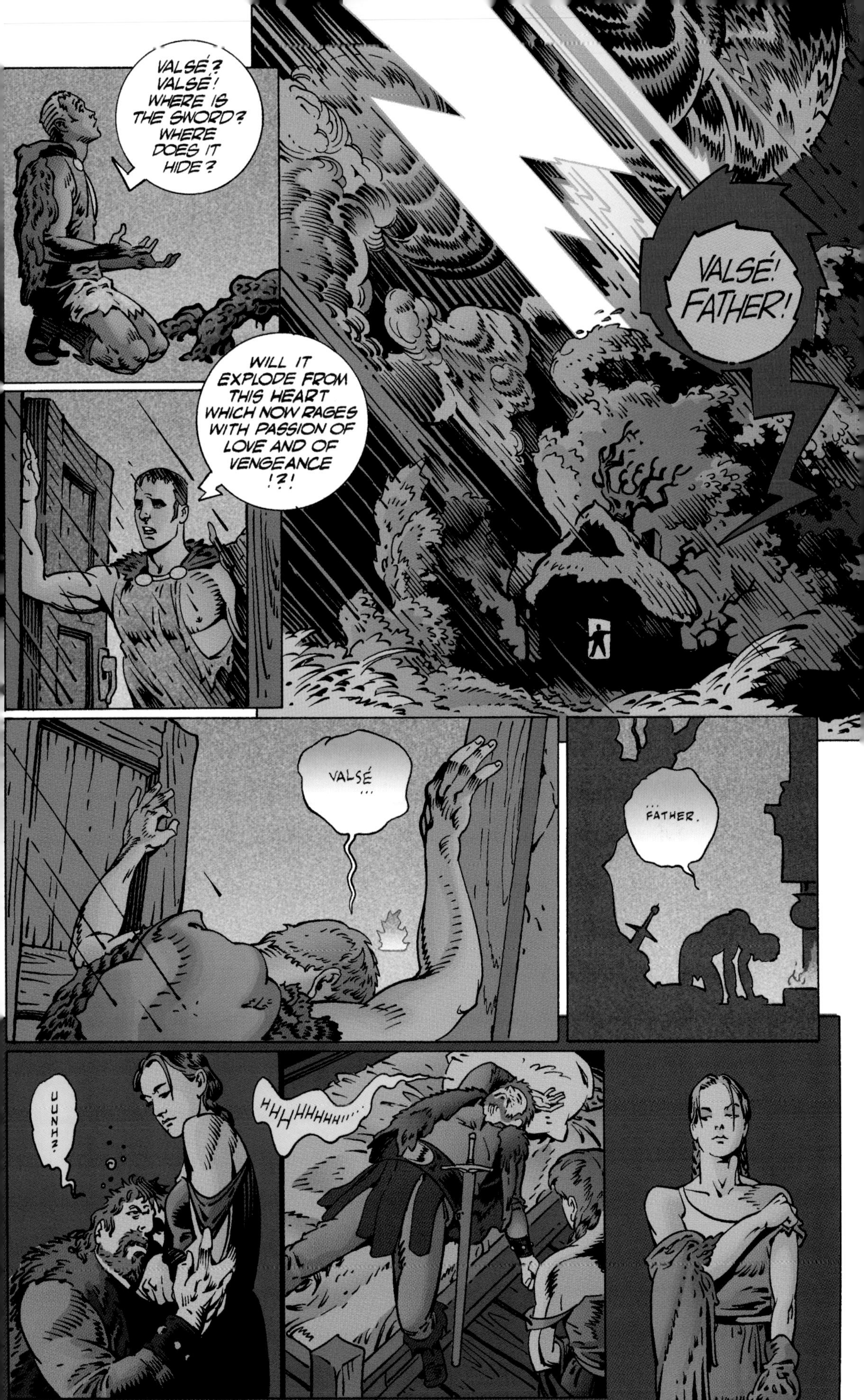
VALSÉ? VALSÉ! WHERE IS THE SWORD? WHERE DOES IT HIDE?
WILL IT EXPLODE FROM THIS HEART WHICH NOW RAGES WITH PASSION OF LOVE AND OF VENGEANCE !?!
VALSÉ! FATHER!
VALSÉ ...
... FATHER.
UUNHZ.
HHHHHHHHH...

?

AH— SO YOU HAVEN'T SLEPT?

I'VE BEEN THINKING OF HOW TO SAVE MYSELF... AND YOU.

LISTEN! I'VE DRUGGED HUNDING.

I NEED TO SHOW YOU SOMETHING.

LISTEN CLOSELY TO WHAT I TELL YOU.

IN THIS HALL SAT ALL THE KINSMEN OF HUNDING, INVITED BY HIM TO HIS MARRIAGE.

"THE 'MARRIAGE' WAS NO CHOICE OF MINE. I HAD BEEN SOLD TO HIM BY BRIGANDS WHO SAT DRINKING WITH HIM...

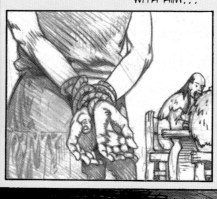

"I SAT ALONE AND DEFENSELESS AMONG THEM.

"THEN, WHILE THEY DRANK, A STRANGER ENTERED: AN OLD MAN WITH A HAT PULLED LOW OVER ONE EYE. THE MEN ROSE UP AS ONE AT THIS UNEXPECTED INTRUSION.

"BUT THE LIGHT FROM HIS OTHER EYE COWED THE OTHERS WITH ITS FLASHING GLANCE.

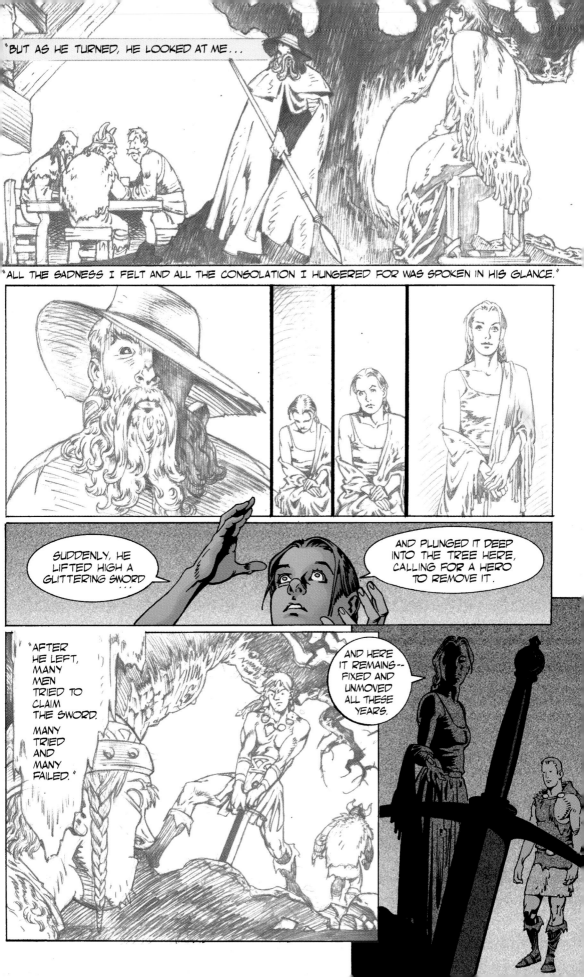

"BUT AS HE TURNED, HE LOOKED AT ME..."

"ALL THE SADNESS I FELT AND ALL THE CONSOLATION I HUNGERED FOR WAS SPOKEN IN HIS GLANCE."

SUDDENLY, HE LIFTED HIGH A GLITTERING SWORD...

AND PLUNGED IT DEEP INTO THE TREE HERE, CALLING FOR A HERO TO REMOVE IT.

"AFTER HE LEFT, MANY MEN TRIED TO CLAIM THE SWORD.

MANY TRIED AND MANY FAILED."

AND HERE IT REMAINS -- FIXED AND UNMOVED ALL THESE YEARS.

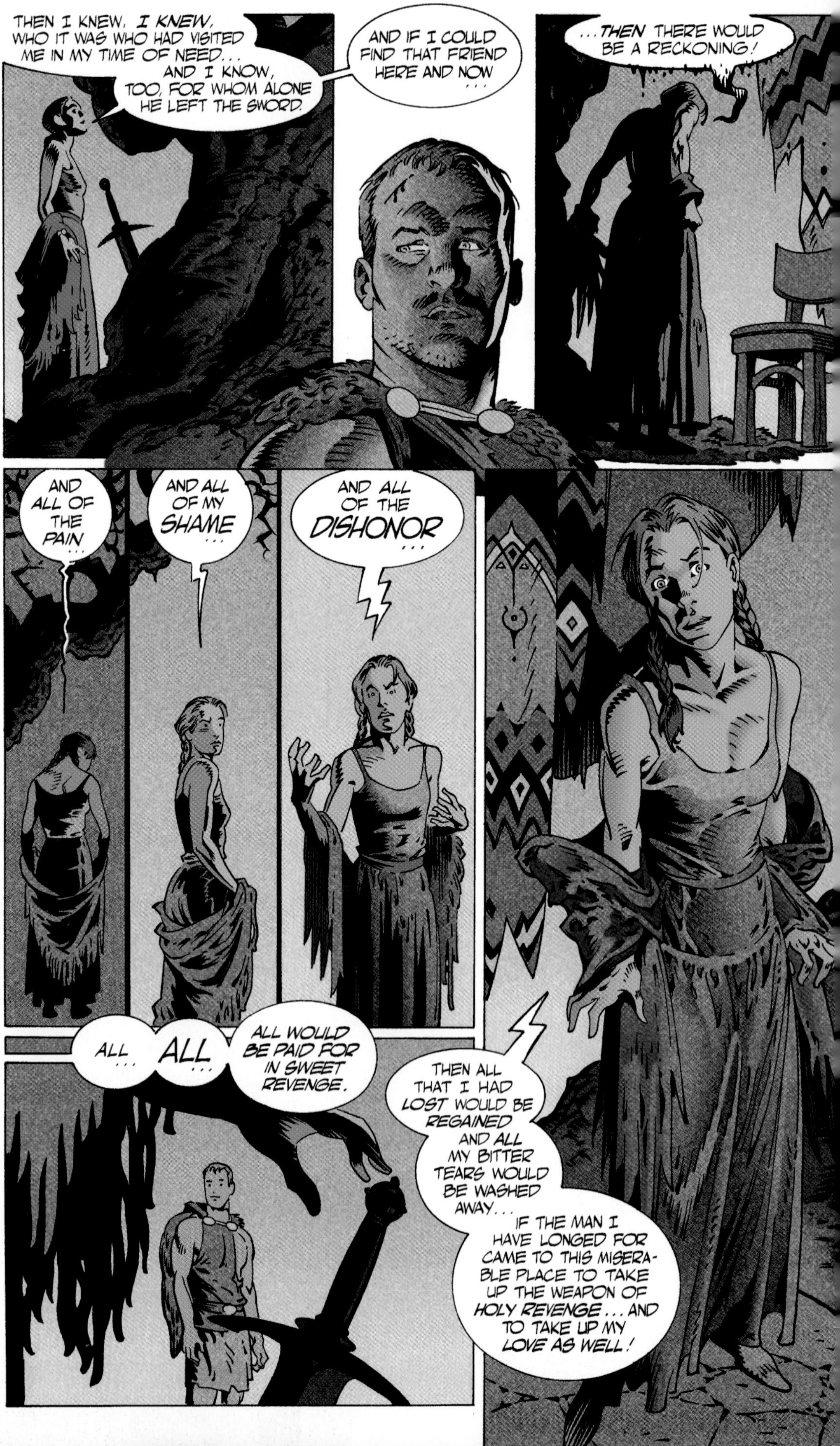
THEN I KNEW, I KNEW, WHO IT WAS WHO HAD VISITED ME IN MY TIME OF NEED... AND I KNOW, TOO, FOR WHOM ALONE HE LEFT THE SWORD.
AND IF I COULD FIND THAT FRIEND HERE AND NOW ...
...THEN THERE WOULD BE A RECKONING!
AND ALL OF THE PAIN ...
AND ALL OF MY SHAME ...
AND ALL OF THE DISHONOR ...
ALL ...
ALL ...
ALL WOULD BE PAID FOR IN SWEET REVENGE.
THEN ALL THAT I HAD LOST WOULD BE REGAINED AND ALL MY BITTER TEARS WOULD BE WASHED AWAY...
IF THE MAN I HAVE LONGED FOR CAME TO THIS MISERABLE PLACE TO TAKE UP THE WEAPON OF HOLY REVENGE... AND TO TAKE UP MY LOVE AS WELL!

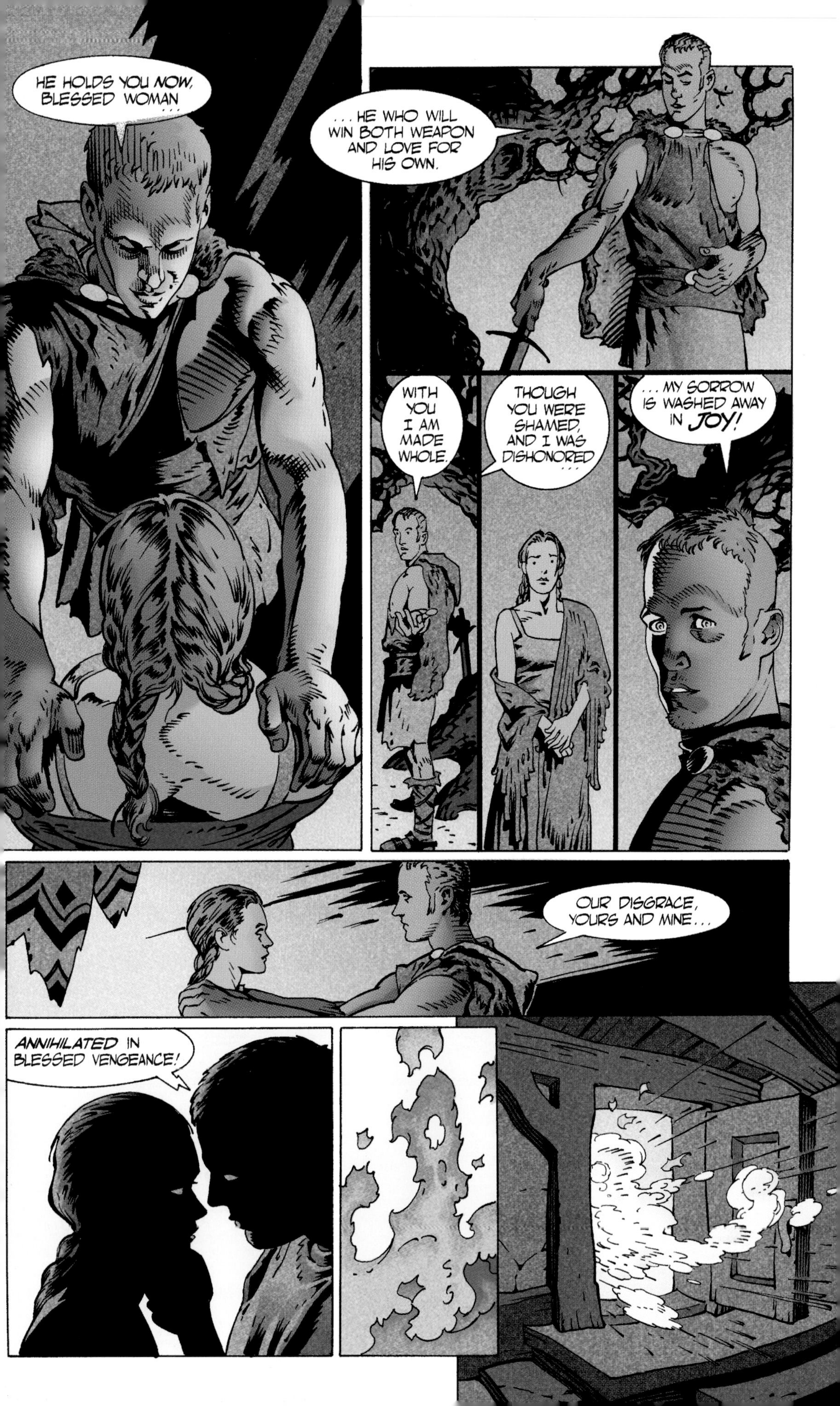
HE HOLDS YOU NOW, BLESSED WOMAN . . .
. . . HE WHO WILL WIN BOTH WEAPON AND LOVE FOR HIS OWN.
WITH YOU I AM MADE WHOLE.
THOUGH YOU WERE SHAMED, AND I WAS DISHONORED . . .
. . . MY SORROW IS WASHED AWAY IN JOY!
OUR DISGRACE, YOURS AND MINE . . .
ANNIHILATED IN BLESSED VENGEANCE!

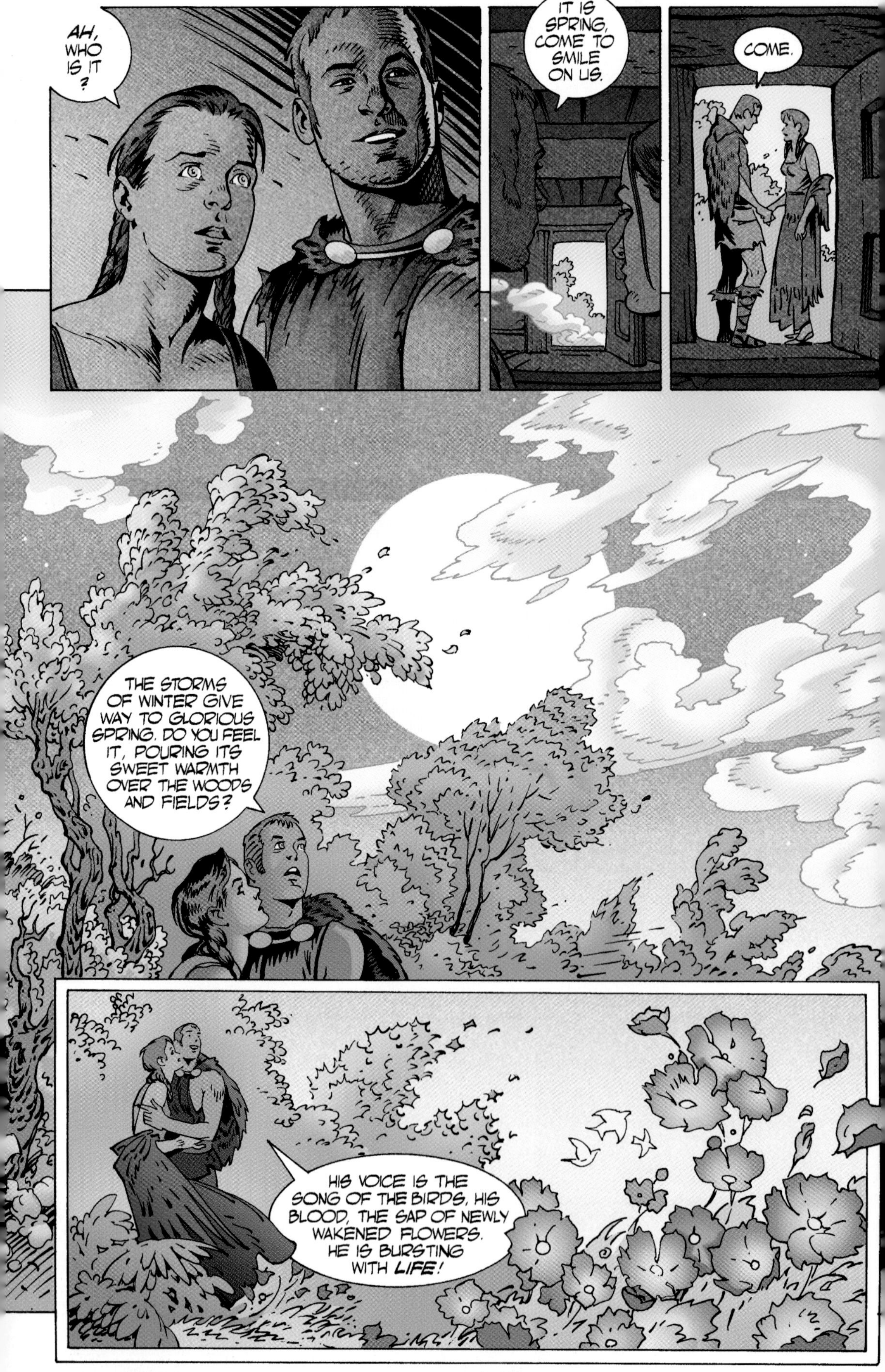
AH, WHO IS IT ?
IT IS SPRING, COME TO SMILE ON US.
COME.
THE STORMS OF WINTER GIVE WAY TO GLORIOUS SPRING. DO YOU FEEL IT, POURING ITS SWEET WARMTH OVER THE WOODS AND FIELDS?
HIS VOICE IS THE SONG OF THE BIRDS, HIS BLOOD, THE SAP OF NEWLY WAKENED FLOWERS. HE IS BURSTING WITH LIFE!

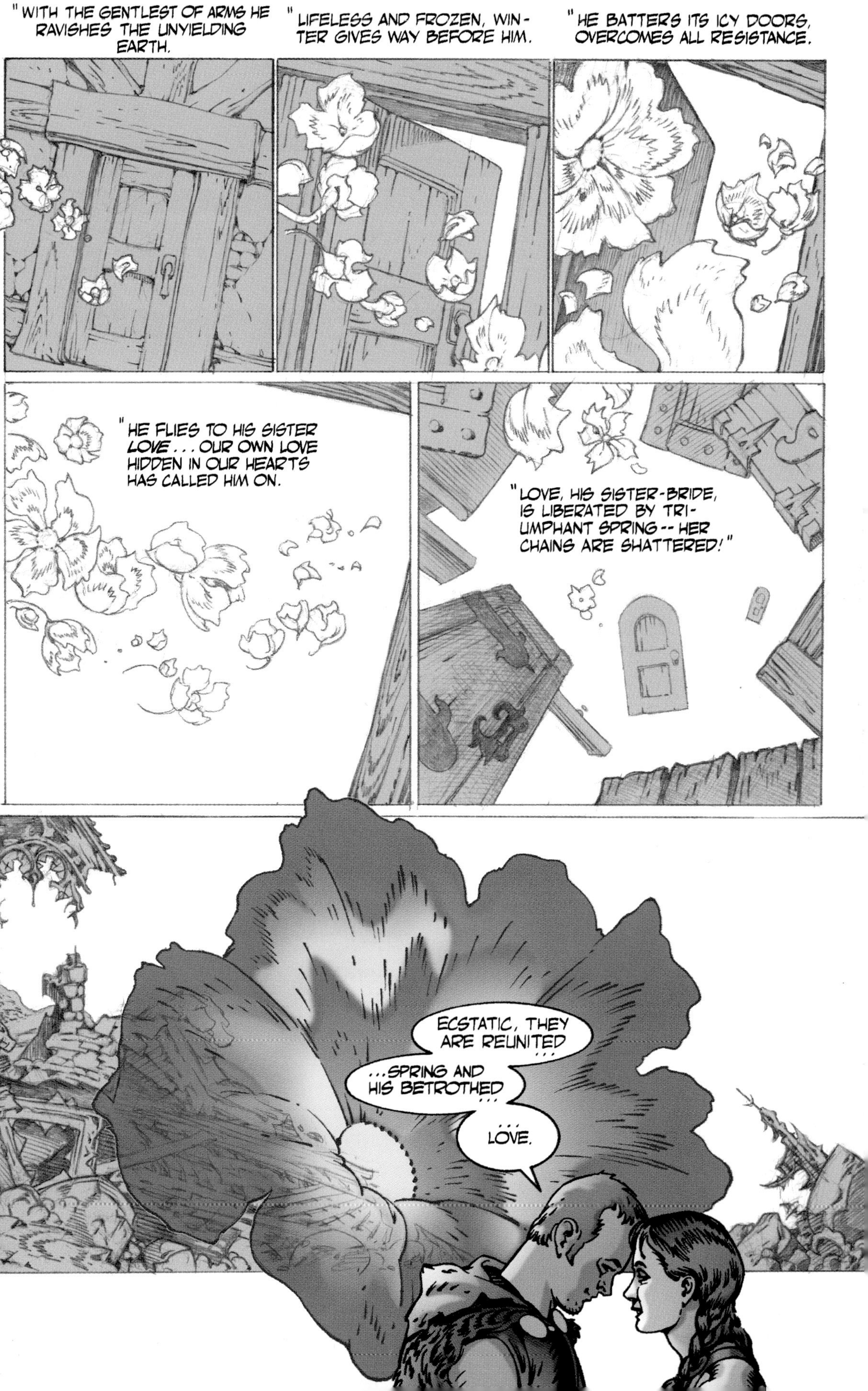
"WITH THE GENTLEST OF ARMS HE RAVISHES THE UNYIELDING EARTH.
"LIFELESS AND FROZEN, WINTER GIVES WAY BEFORE HIM.
"HE BATTERS ITS ICY DOORS, OVERCOMES ALL RESISTANCE.
"HE FLIES TO HIS SISTER *LOVE* . . . OUR OWN LOVE HIDDEN IN OUR HEARTS HAS CALLED HIM ON.
"LOVE, HIS SISTER-BRIDE, IS LIBERATED BY TRIUMPHANT SPRING -- HER CHAINS ARE SHATTERED!"
ECSTATIC, THEY ARE REUNITED . . .
. . .SPRING AND HIS BETROTHED . . .
. . . LOVE.

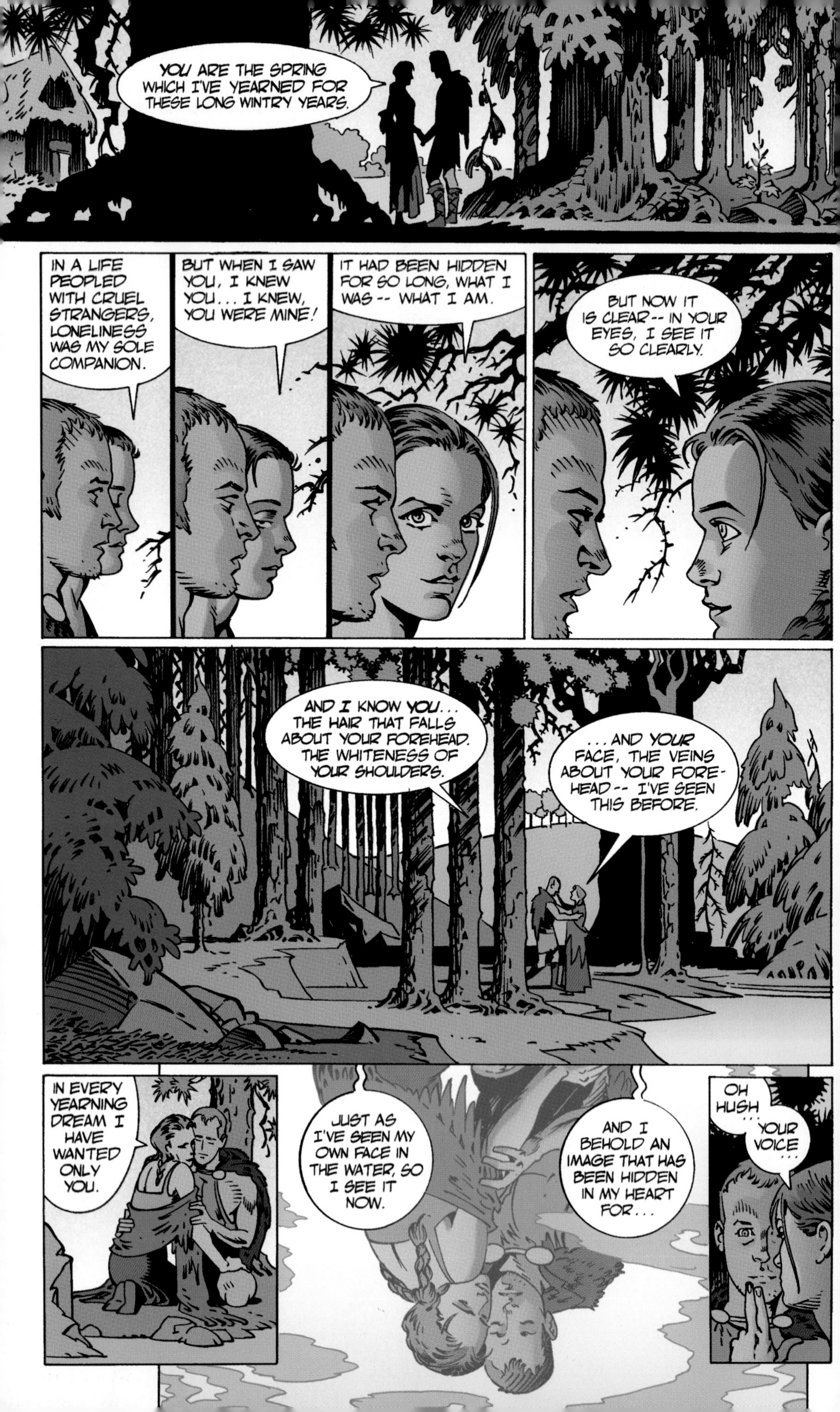
YOU ARE THE SPRING WHICH I'VE YEARNED FOR THESE LONG WINTRY YEARS.
IN A LIFE PEOPLED WITH CRUEL STRANGERS, LONELINESS WAS MY SOLE COMPANION.
BUT WHEN I SAW YOU, I KNEW YOU... I KNEW, YOU WERE MINE!
IT HAD BEEN HIDDEN FOR SO LONG, WHAT I WAS -- WHAT I AM.
BUT NOW IT IS CLEAR -- IN YOUR EYES, I SEE IT SO CLEARLY.
AND I KNOW YOU... THE HAIR THAT FALLS ABOUT YOUR FOREHEAD. THE WHITENESS OF YOUR SHOULDERS.
...AND YOUR FACE, THE VEINS ABOUT YOUR FORE-HEAD -- I'VE SEEN THIS BEFORE.
IN EVERY YEARNING DREAM I HAVE WANTED ONLY YOU.
JUST AS I'VE SEEN MY OWN FACE IN THE WATER, SO I SEE IT NOW.
AND I BEHOLD AN IMAGE THAT HAS BEEN HIDDEN IN MY HEART FOR...
OH HUSH... YOUR VOICE...

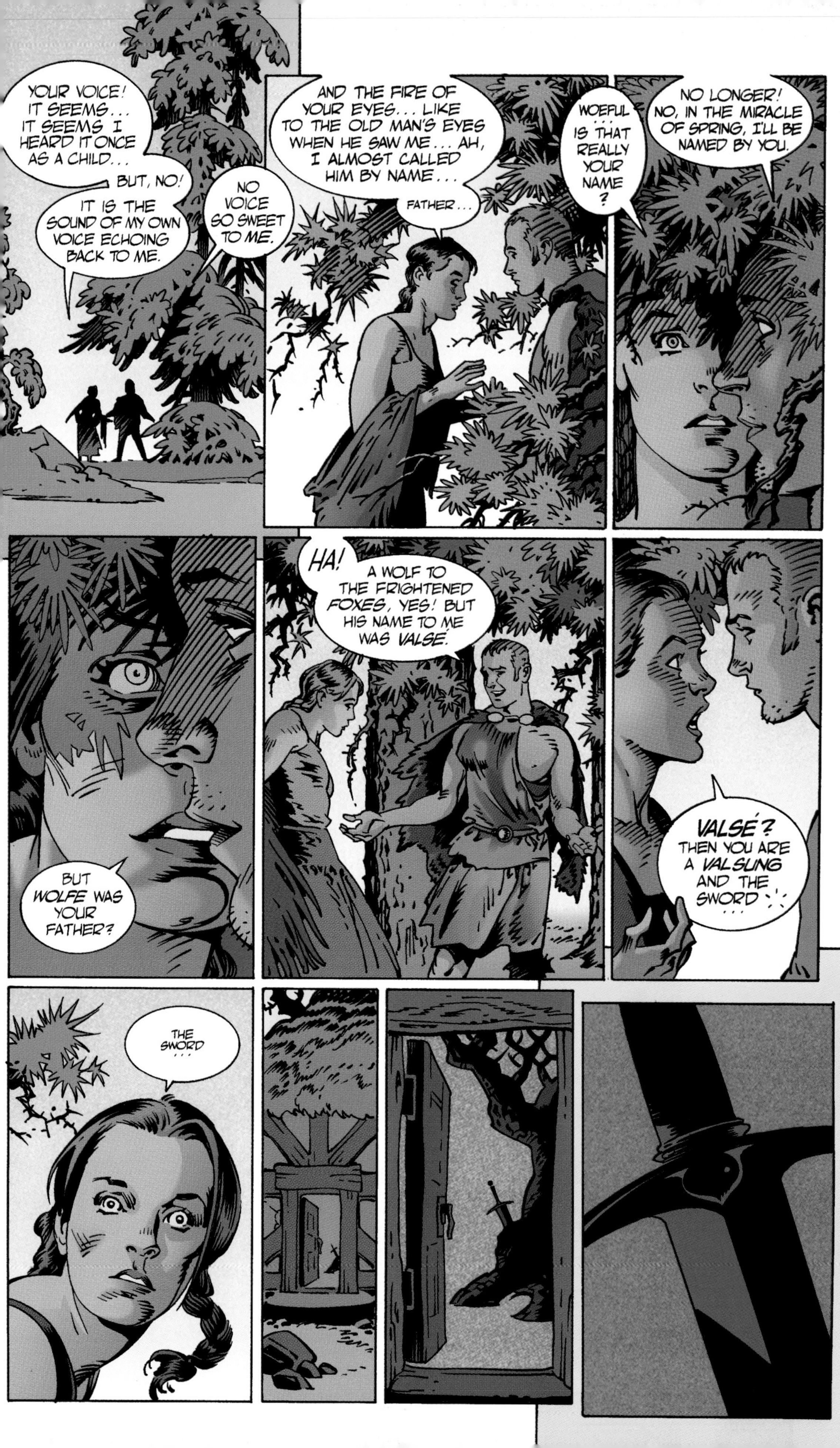
YOUR VOICE! IT SEEMS... IT SEEMS I HEARD IT ONCE AS A CHILD...
BUT, NO!
IT IS THE SOUND OF MY OWN VOICE ECHOING BACK TO ME.
NO VOICE SO SWEET TO ME.
AND THE FIRE OF YOUR EYES... LIKE TO THE OLD MAN'S EYES WHEN HE SAW ME... AH, I ALMOST CALLED HIM BY NAME...
FATHER...
WOEFUL... IS THAT REALLY YOUR NAME?
NO LONGER! NO, IN THE MIRACLE OF SPRING, I'LL BE NAMED BY YOU.
BUT WOLFE WAS YOUR FATHER?
HA!
A WOLF TO THE FRIGHTENED FOXES, YES! BUT HIS NAME TO ME WAS VALSÉ.
VALSÉ? THEN YOU ARE A VALSUNG AND THE SWORD...
THE SWORD...

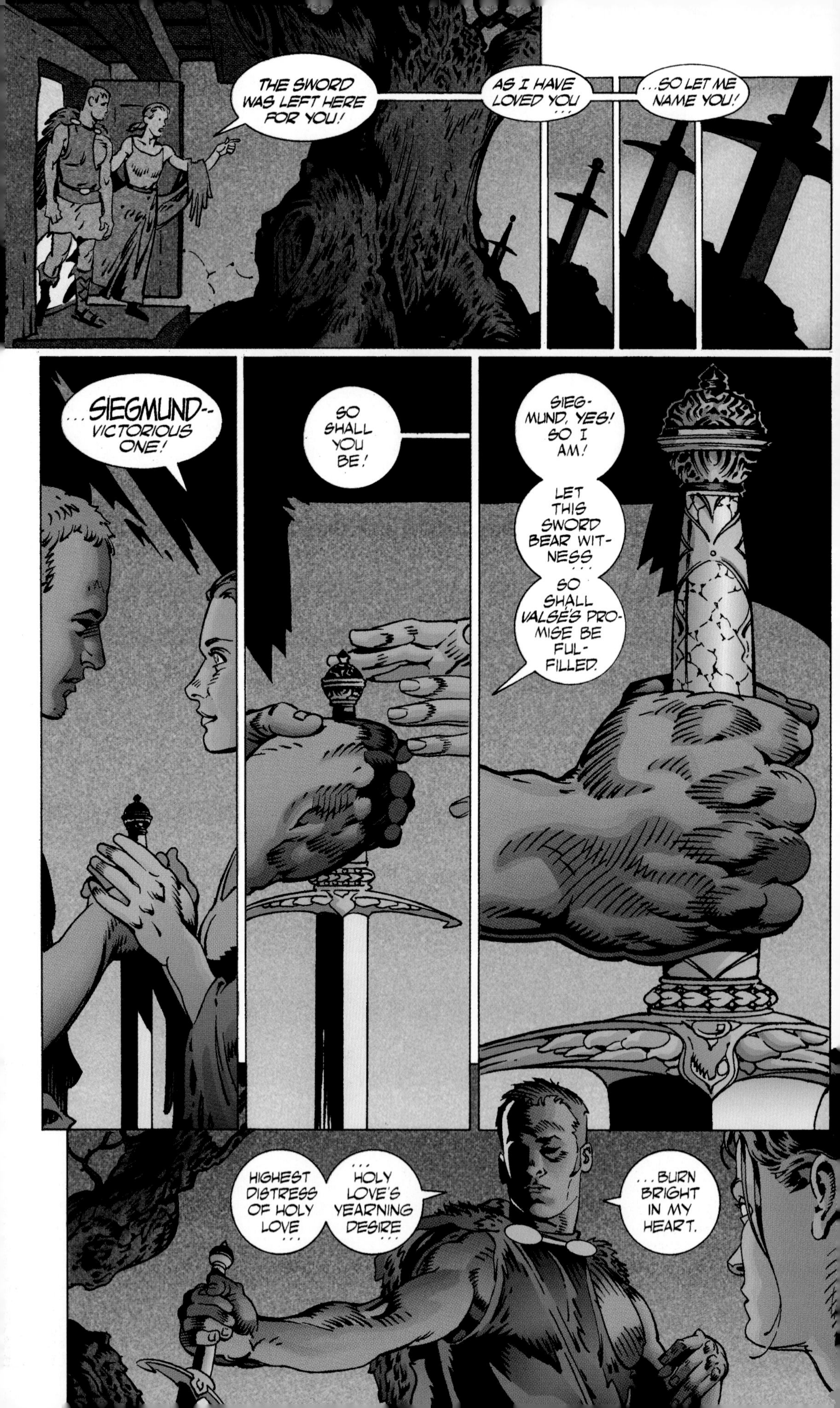
THE SWORD WAS LEFT HERE FOR YOU!
AS I HAVE LOVED YOU...
...SO LET ME NAME YOU!
...SIEGMUND--VICTORIOUS ONE!
SO SHALL YOU BE!
SIEG-MUND, YES! SO I AM!
LET THIS SWORD BEAR WIT-NESS...
SO SHALL VALSE'S PRO-MISE BE FUL-FILLED.
HIGHEST DISTRESS OF HOLY LOVE...
...HOLY LOVE'S YEARNING DESIRE...
...BURN BRIGHT IN MY HEART.

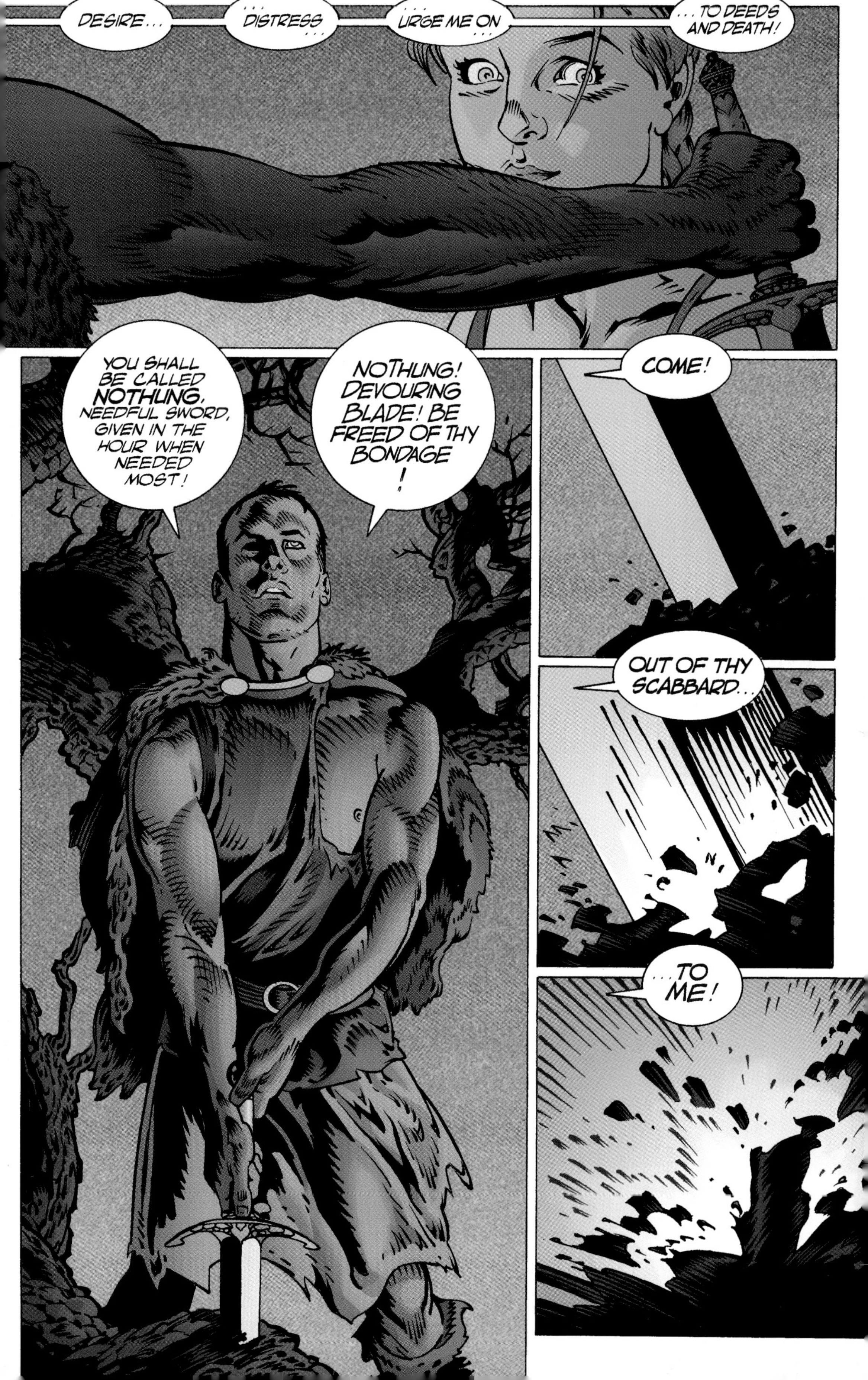
DESIRE...
...DISTRESS...
...URGE ME ON...
...TO DEEDS AND DEATH!
YOU SHALL BE CALLED **NOTHUNG**, NEEDFUL SWORD, GIVEN IN THE HOUR WHEN NEEDED MOST!
NOTHUNG! DEVOURING BLADE! BE FREED OF THY BONDAGE!
COME!
OUT OF THY SCABBARD...
...TO ME!

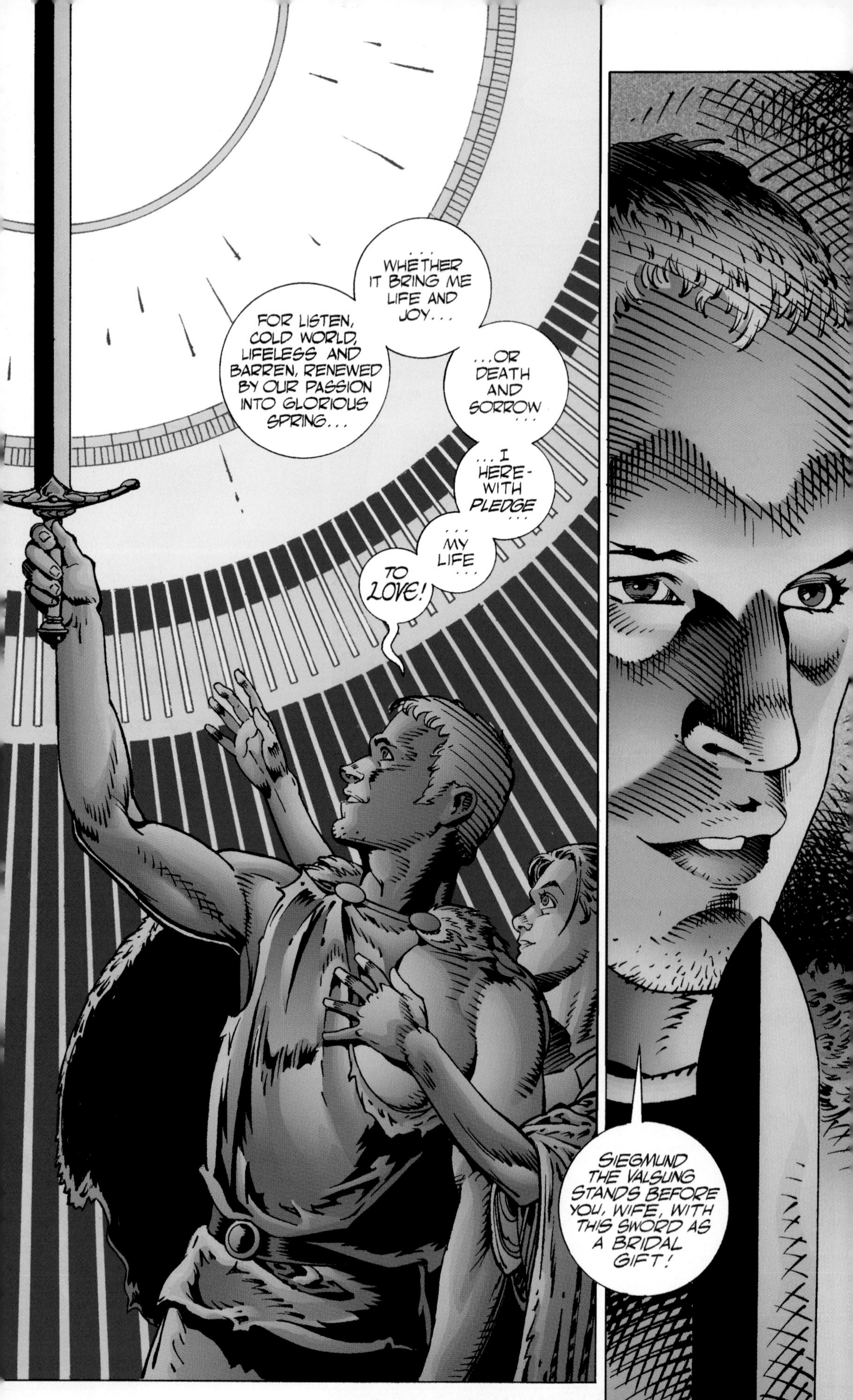
FOR LISTEN, COLD WORLD, LIFELESS AND BARREN, RENEWED BY OUR PASSION INTO GLORIOUS SPRING...
...WHETHER IT BRING ME LIFE AND JOY...
...OR DEATH AND SORROW...
...I HERE-WITH PLEDGE...
...MY LIFE...
TO LOVE!
SIEGMUND THE VALSUNG STANDS BEFORE YOU, WIFE, WITH THIS SWORD AS A BRIDAL GIFT!

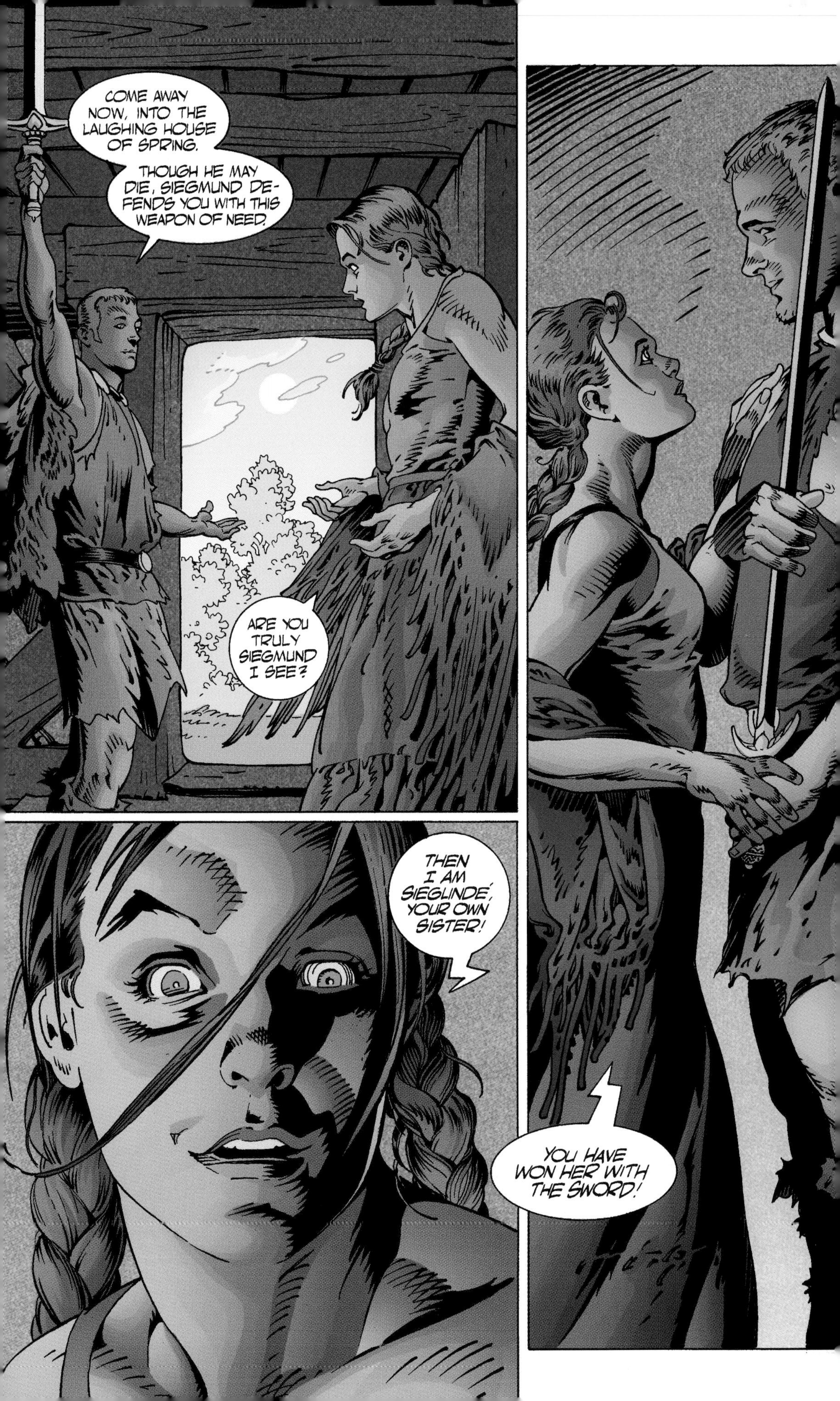
COME AWAY NOW, INTO THE LAUGHING HOUSE OF SPRING.
THOUGH HE MAY DIE, SIEGMUND DE- FENDS YOU WITH THIS WEAPON OF NEED.
ARE YOU TRULY SIEGMUND I SEE?
THEN I AM SIEGLINDE, YOUR OWN SISTER!
YOU HAVE WON HER WITH THE SWORD!

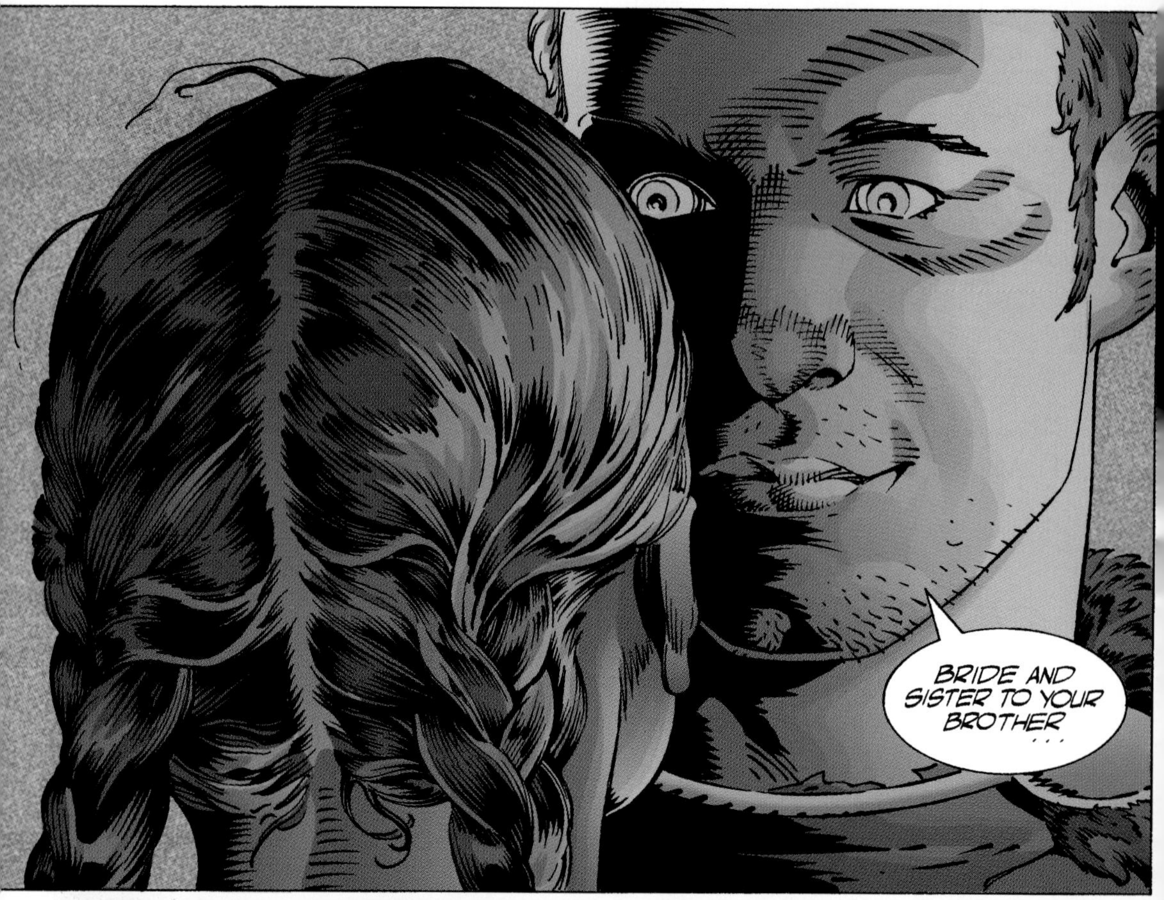
BRIDE AND SISTER TO YOUR BROTHER . . .
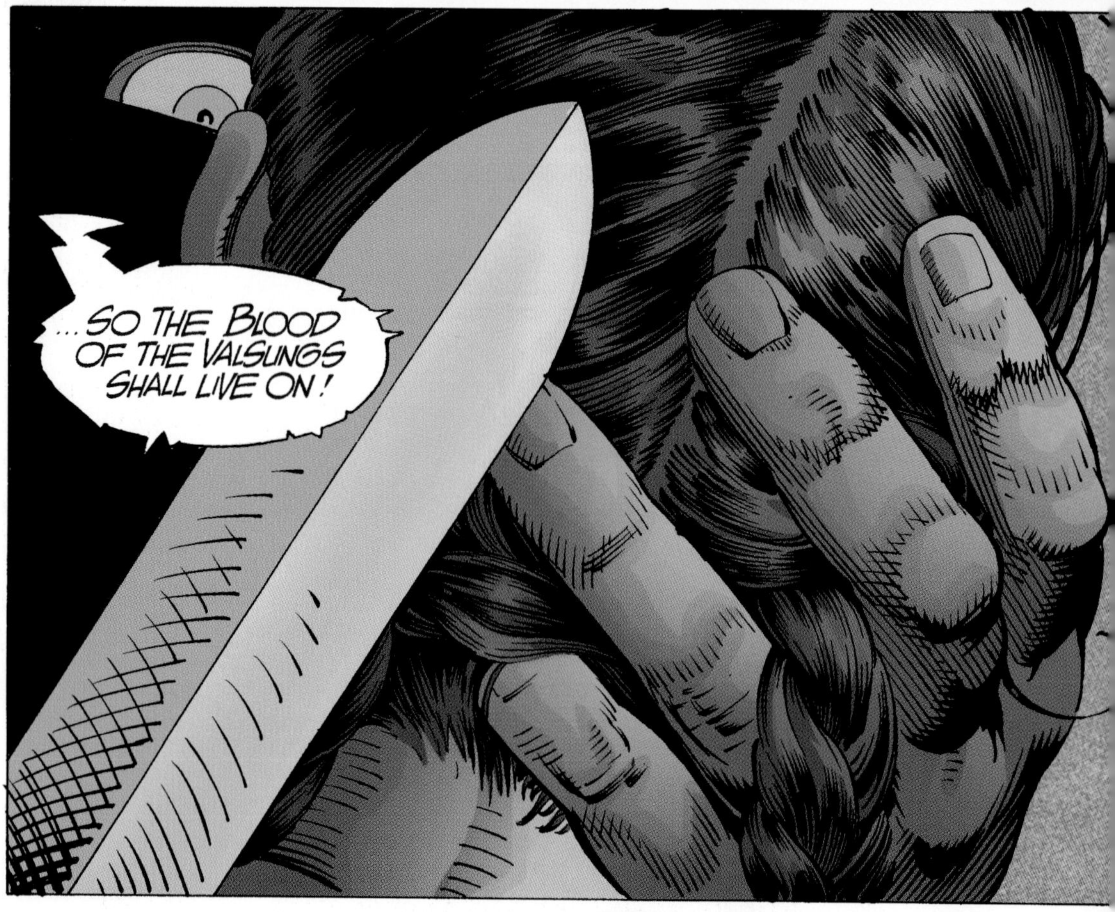
. . . SO THE BLOOD OF THE VALSUNGS SHALL LIVE ON!

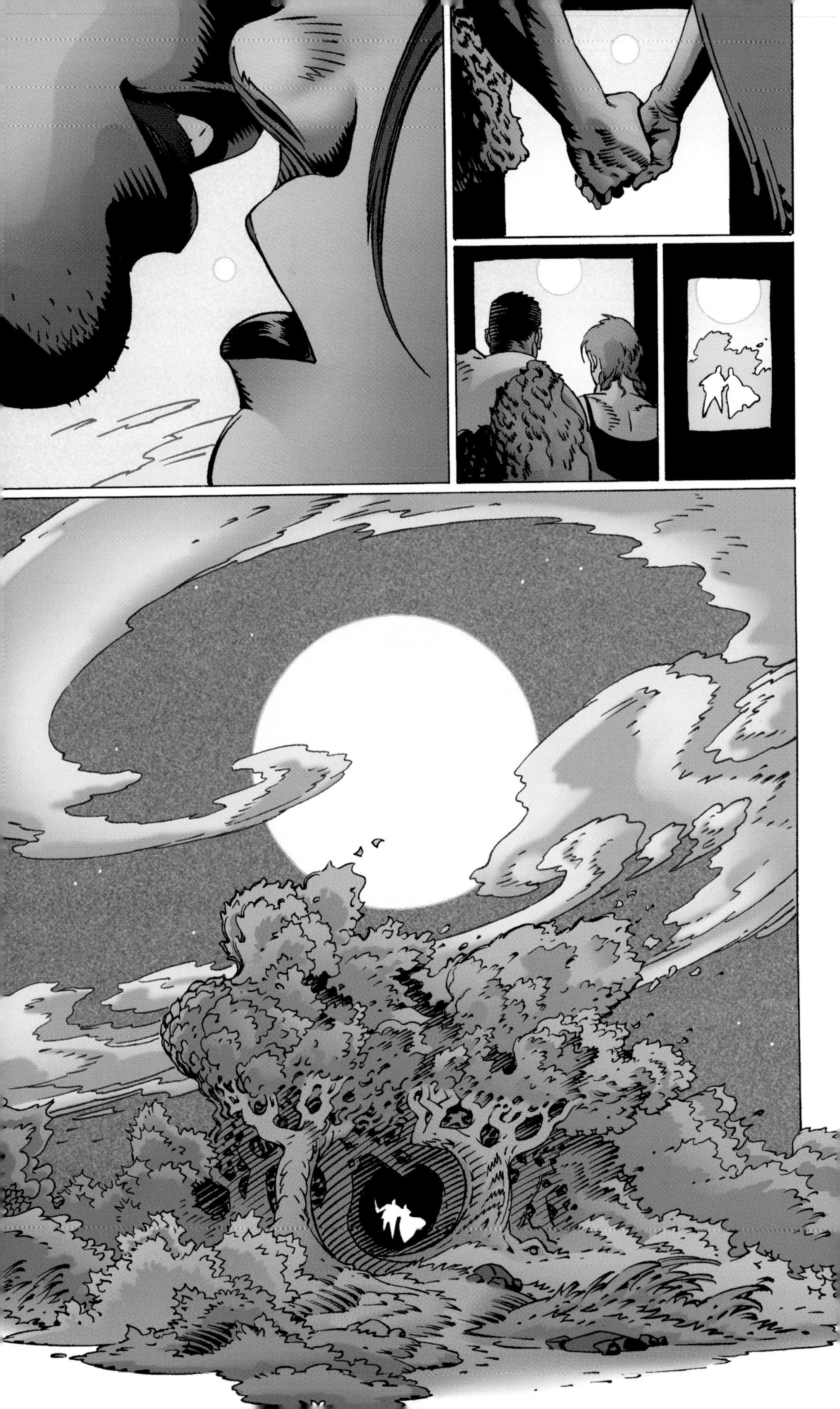

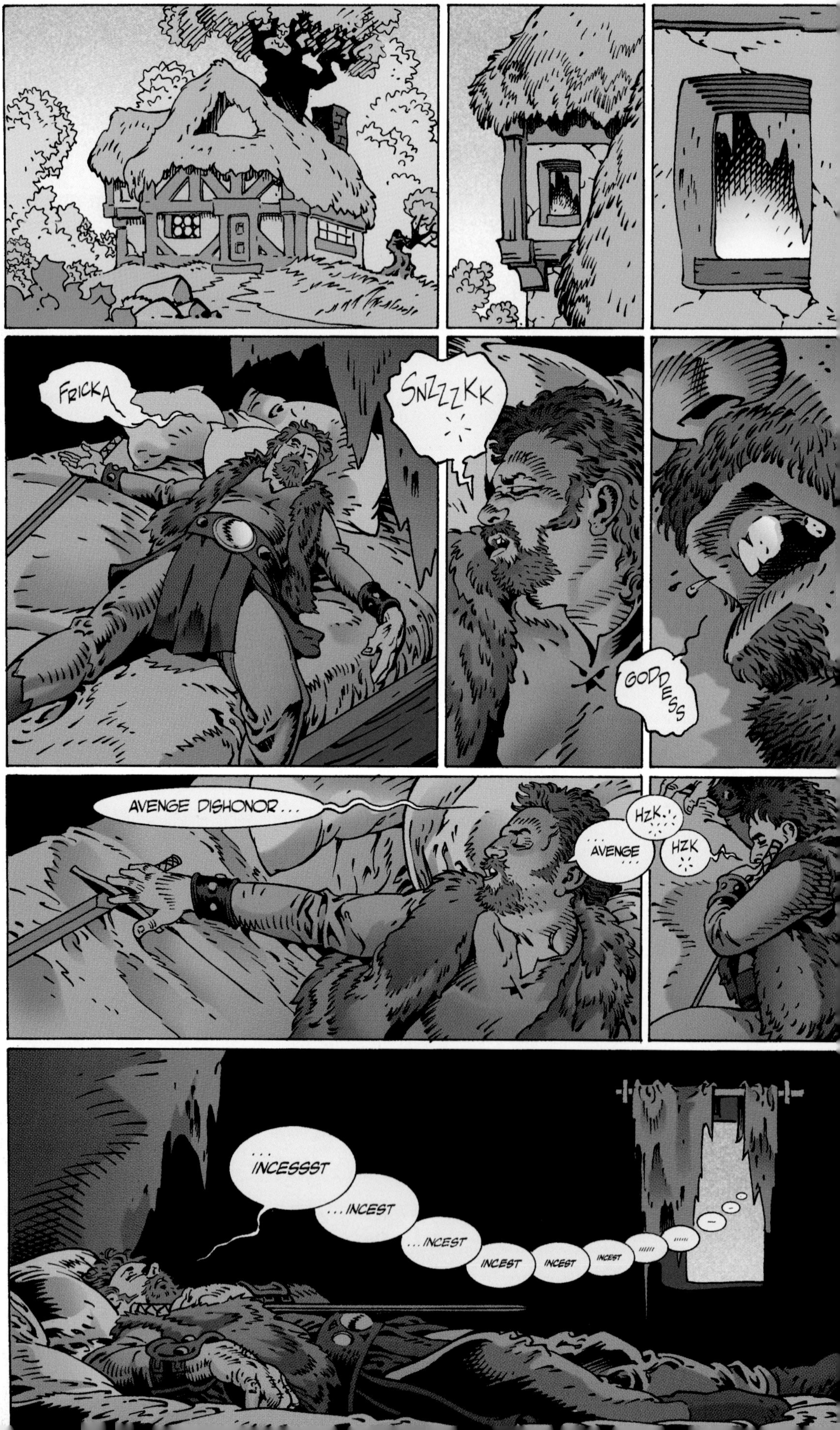

FRICKA
SNZZZKK
GODDESS
AVENGE DISHONOR...
...AVENGE
HZK.
HZK
...INCESSST
...INCEST
...INCEST
INCEST
INCEST
INCEST

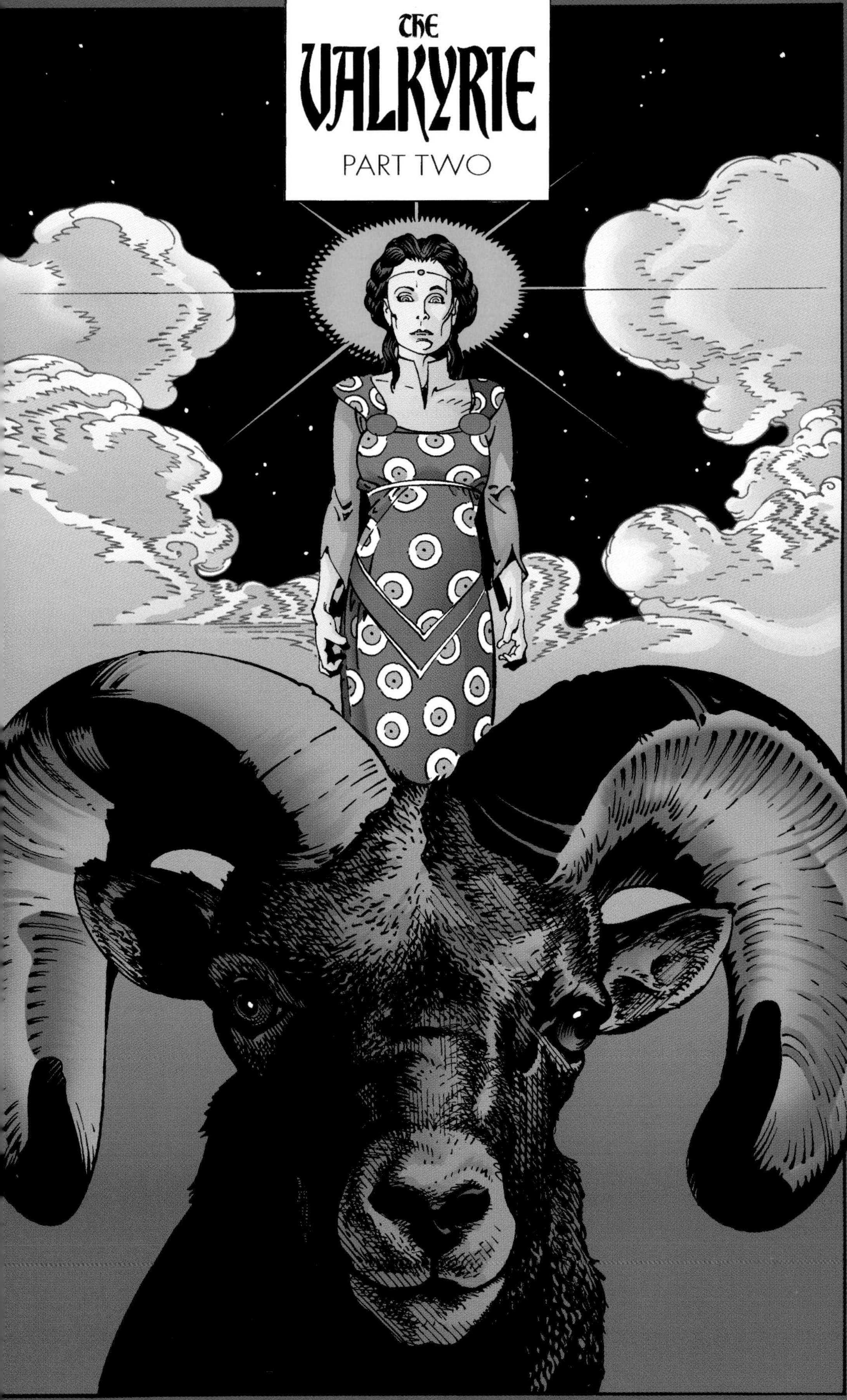
THE
VALKYRIE
PART TWO

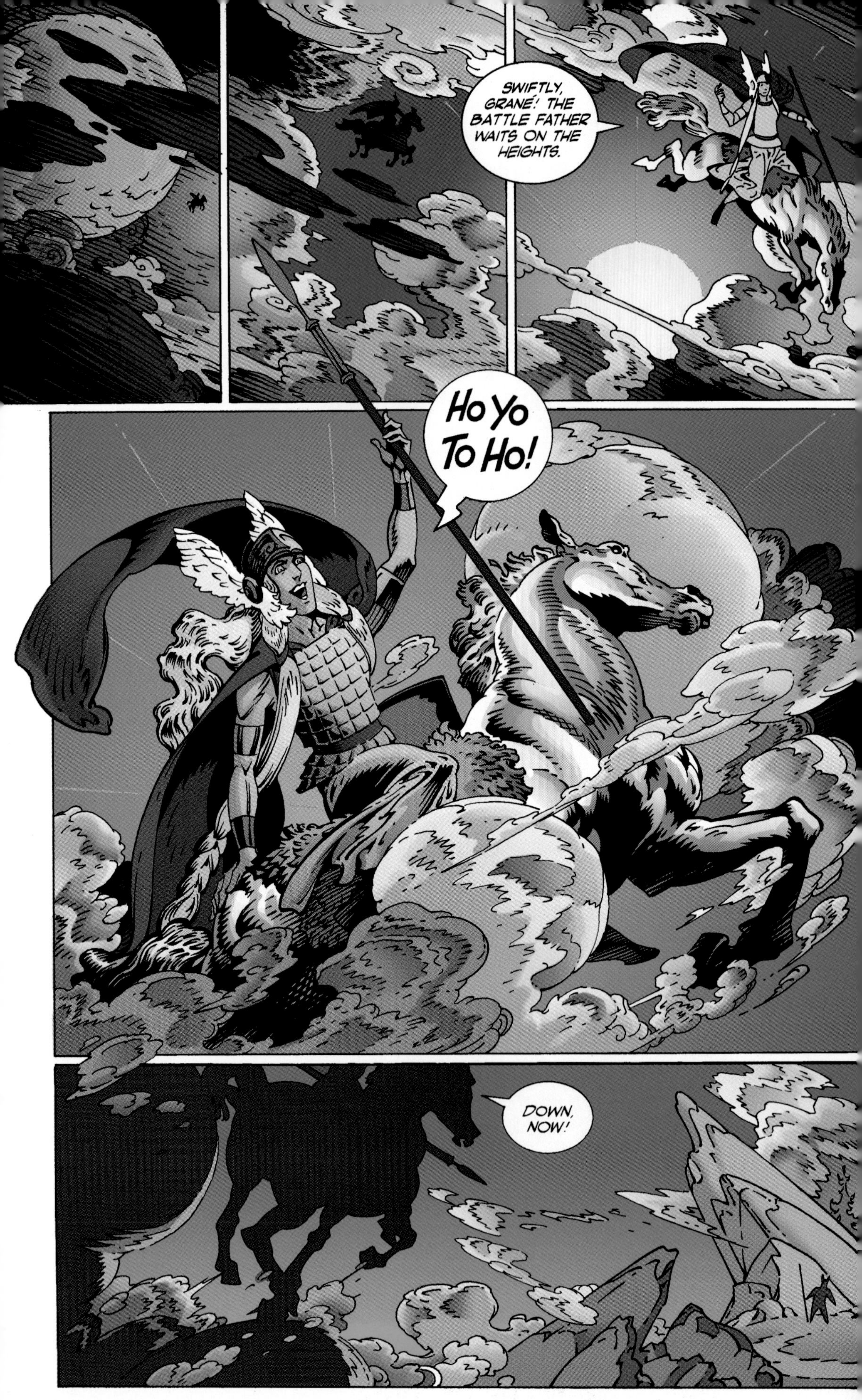
SWIFTLY, GRANÉ! THE BATTLE FATHER WAITS ON THE HEIGHTS.
Ho Yo To Ho!
DOWN, NOW!

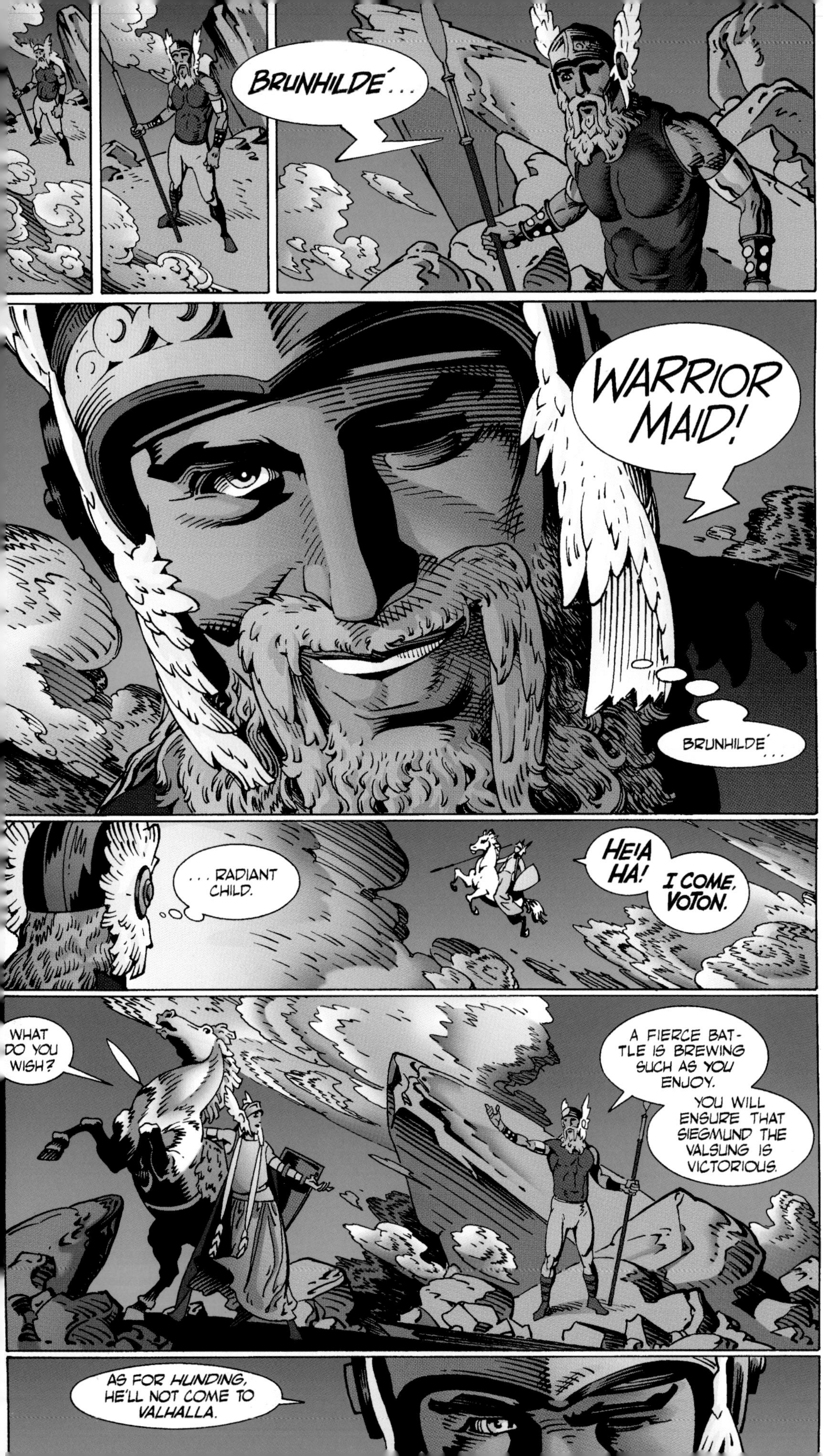
BRUNHILDÉ...
WARRIOR MAID!
BRUNHILDÉ...
...RADIANT CHILD.
HEIA HA!
I COME, VOTON.
WHAT DO YOU WISH?
A FIERCE BATTLE IS BREWING SUCH AS YOU ENJOY.
YOU WILL ENSURE THAT SIEGMUND THE VALSUNG IS VICTORIOUS.
AS FOR HUNDING, HE'LL NOT COME TO VALHALLA.

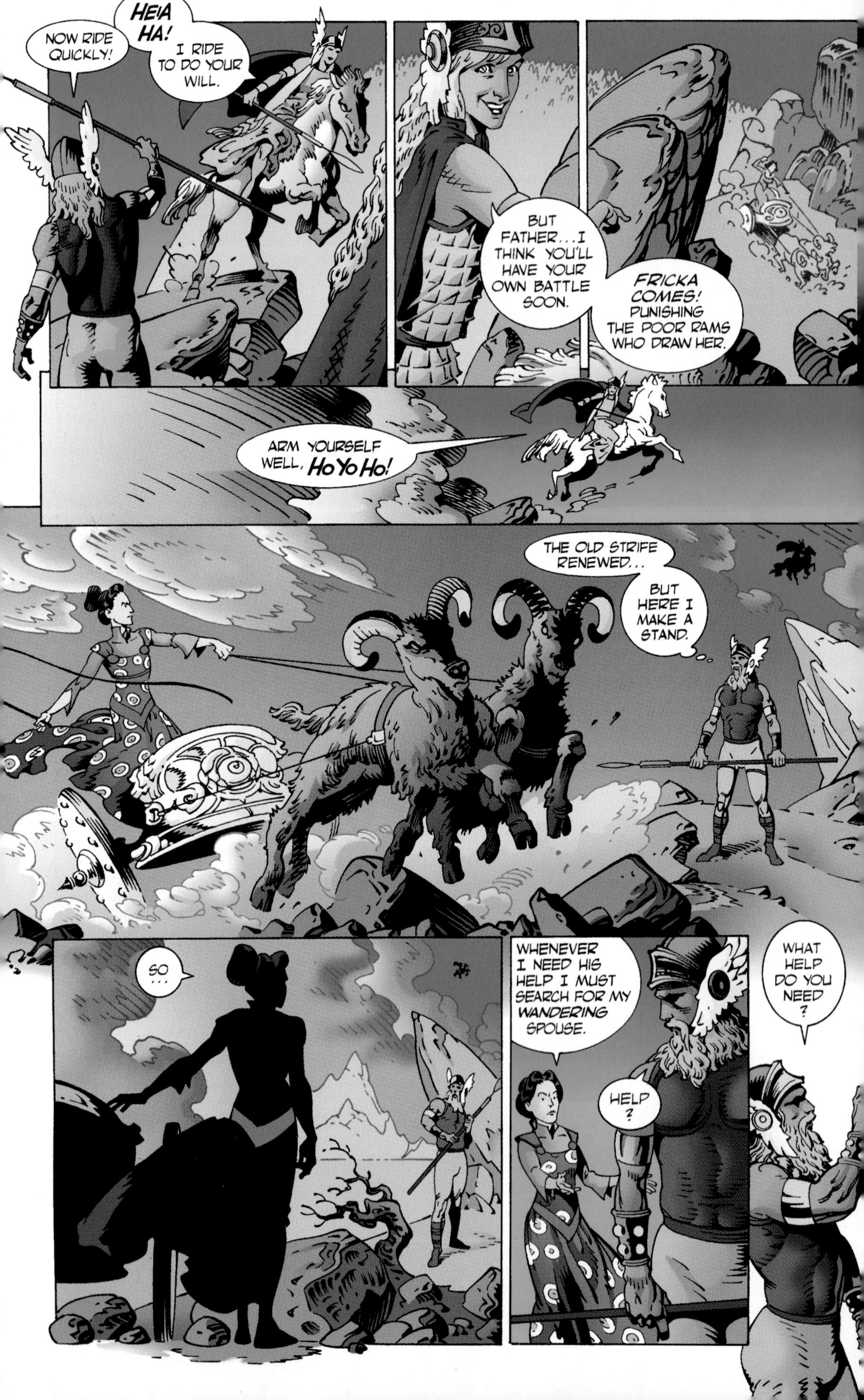
NOW RIDE QUICKLY!
HEIA HA!
I RIDE TO DO YOUR WILL.
BUT FATHER...I THINK YOU'LL HAVE YOUR OWN BATTLE SOON.
FRICKA COMES! PUNISHING THE POOR RAMS WHO DRAW HER.
ARM YOURSELF WELL, HOYOHO!
THE OLD STRIFE RENEWED...
BUT HERE I MAKE A STAND.
SO...
WHENEVER I NEED HIS HELP I MUST SEARCH FOR MY WANDERING SPOUSE.
HELP?
WHAT HELP DO YOU NEED?

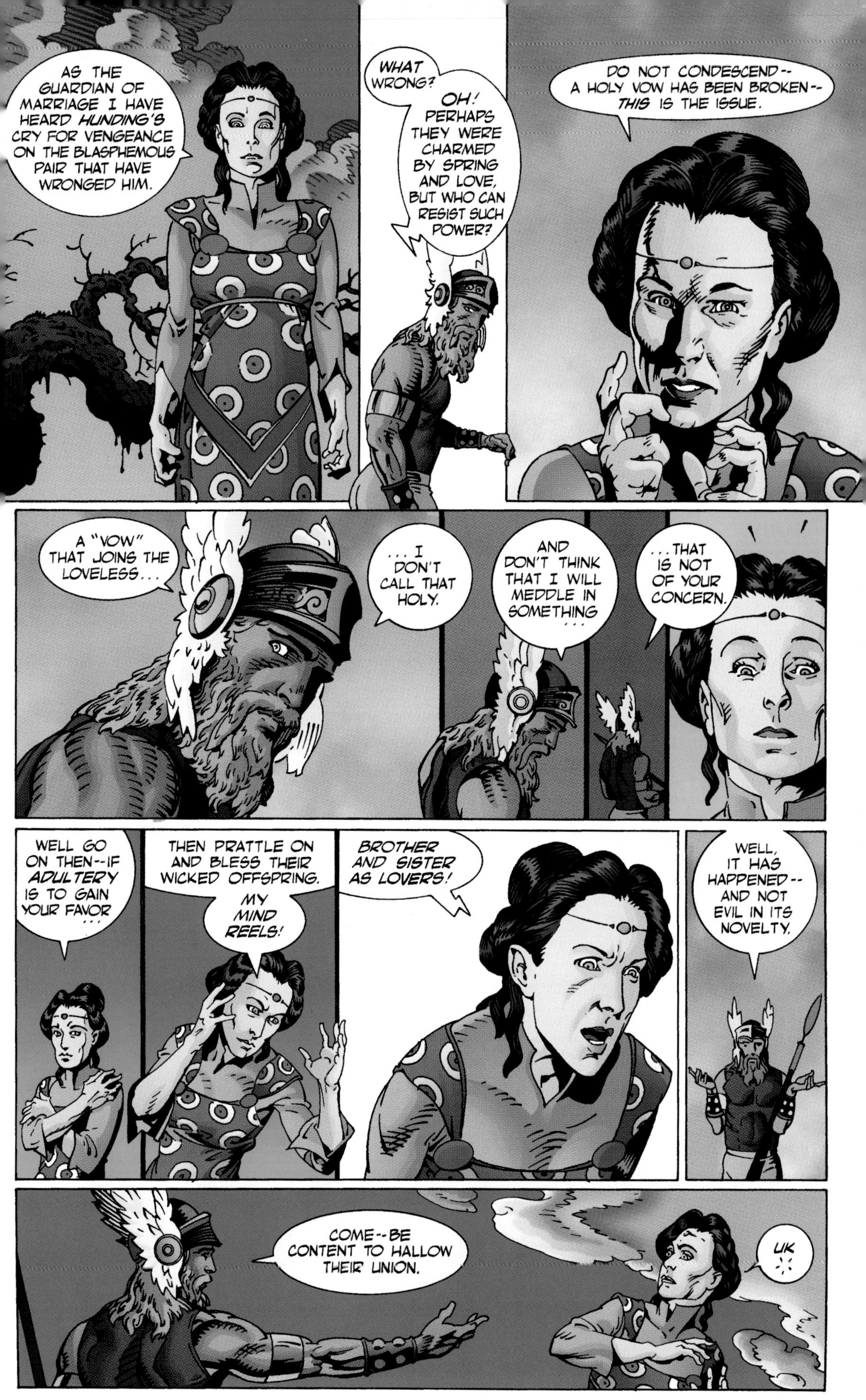
AS THE GUARDIAN OF MARRIAGE I HAVE HEARD HUNDING'S CRY FOR VENGEANCE ON THE BLASPHEMOUS PAIR THAT HAVE WRONGED HIM.
WHAT WRONG?
OH! PERHAPS THEY WERE CHARMED BY SPRING AND LOVE, BUT WHO CAN RESIST SUCH POWER?
DO NOT CONDESCEND-- A HOLY VOW HAS BEEN BROKEN-- THIS IS THE ISSUE.
A "VOW" THAT JOINS THE LOVELESS...
...I DON'T CALL THAT HOLY.
AND DON'T THINK THAT I WILL MEDDLE IN SOMETHING...
...THAT IS NOT OF YOUR CONCERN.
WELL GO ON THEN--IF ADULTERY IS TO GAIN YOUR FAVOR...
THEN PRATTLE ON AND BLESS THEIR WICKED OFFSPRING.
MY MIND REELS!
BROTHER AND SISTER AS LOVERS!
WELL, IT HAS HAPPENED-- AND NOT EVIL IN ITS NOVELTY.
COME--BE CONTENT TO HALLOW THEIR UNION.
UK

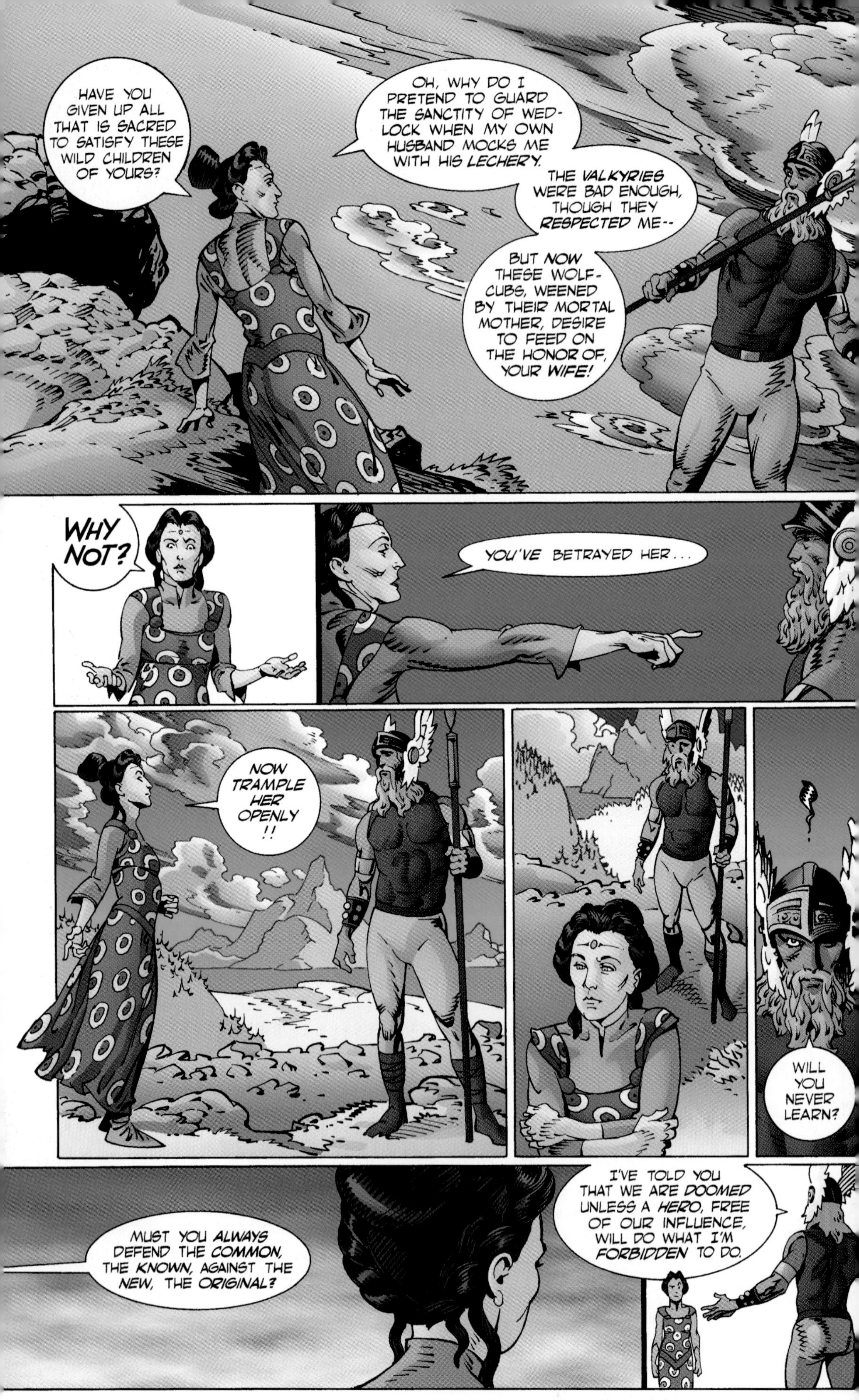
HAVE YOU GIVEN UP ALL THAT IS SACRED TO SATISFY THESE WILD CHILDREN OF YOURS?
OH, WHY DO I PRETEND TO GUARD THE SANCTITY OF WEDLOCK WHEN MY OWN HUSBAND MOCKS ME WITH HIS *LECHERY.*
THE *VALKYRIES* WERE BAD ENOUGH, THOUGH THEY *RESPECTED* ME--
BUT *NOW* THESE WOLF-CUBS, WEENED BY THEIR MORTAL MOTHER, DESIRE TO FEED ON THE HONOR OF, YOUR *WIFE!*
WHY NOT?
YOU'VE BETRAYED HER...
NOW TRAMPLE HER OPENLY !!
WILL YOU NEVER LEARN?
MUST YOU *ALWAYS* DEFEND THE *COMMON,* THE *KNOWN,* AGAINST THE *NEW,* THE *ORIGINAL?*
I'VE TOLD YOU THAT WE ARE *DOOMED* UNLESS A *HERO,* FREE OF OUR INFLUENCE, WILL DO WHAT I'M *FORBIDDEN* TO DO.

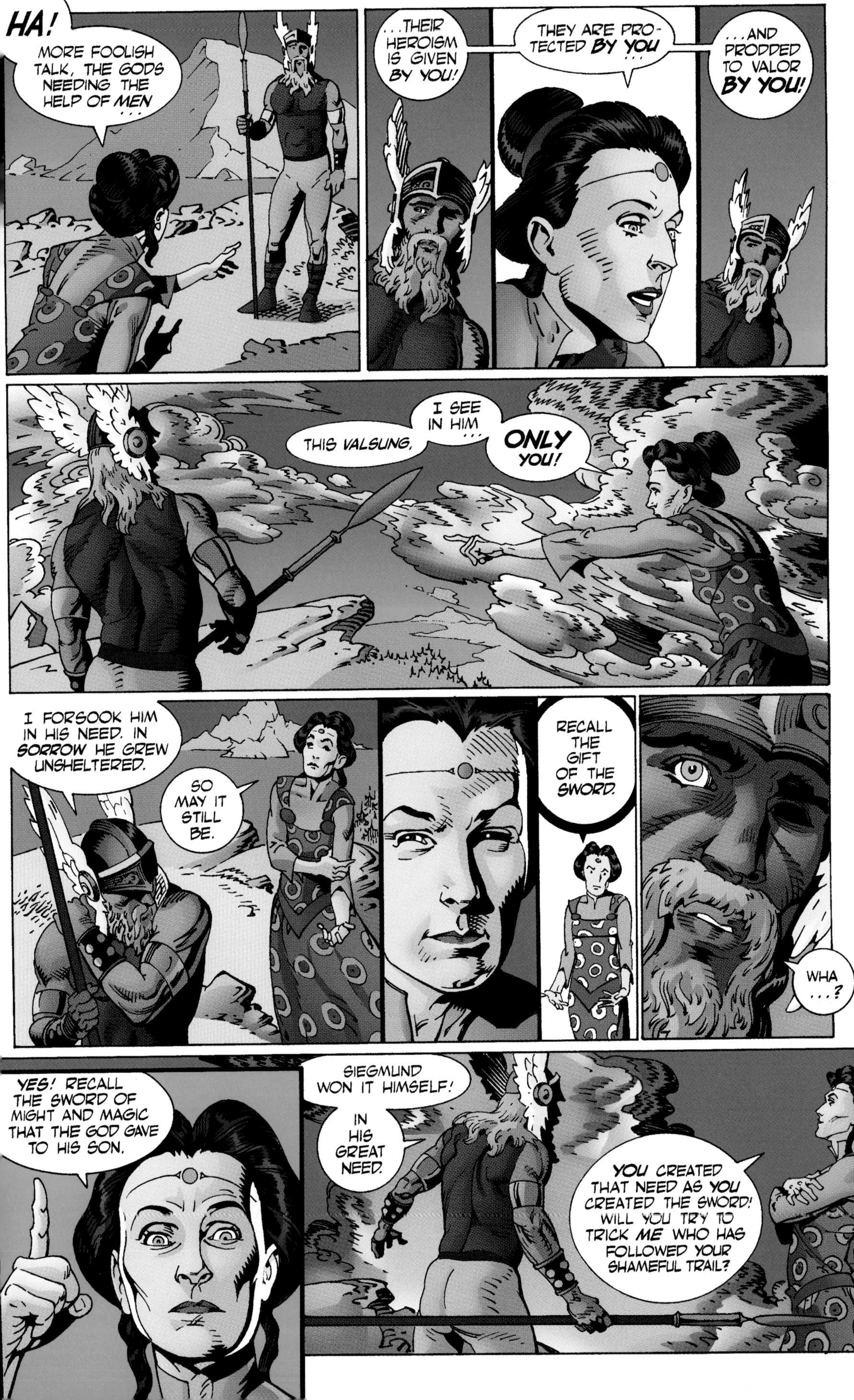
HA!
MORE FOOLISH TALK, THE GODS NEEDING THE HELP OF MEN...
...THEIR HEROISM IS GIVEN BY YOU!
THEY ARE PROTECTED BY YOU...
...AND PRODDED TO VALOR BY YOU!
THIS VALSUNG,
I SEE IN HIM...
ONLY YOU!
I FORSOOK HIM IN HIS NEED. IN SORROW HE GREW UNSHELTERED.
SO MAY IT STILL BE.
RECALL THE GIFT OF THE SWORD.
WHA...?
YES! RECALL THE SWORD OF MIGHT AND MAGIC THAT THE GOD GAVE TO HIS SON.
SIEGMUND WON IT HIMSELF!
IN HIS GREAT NEED.
YOU CREATED THAT NEED AS YOU CREATED THE SWORD! WILL YOU TRY TO TRICK ME WHO HAS FOLLOWED YOUR SHAMEFUL TRAIL?

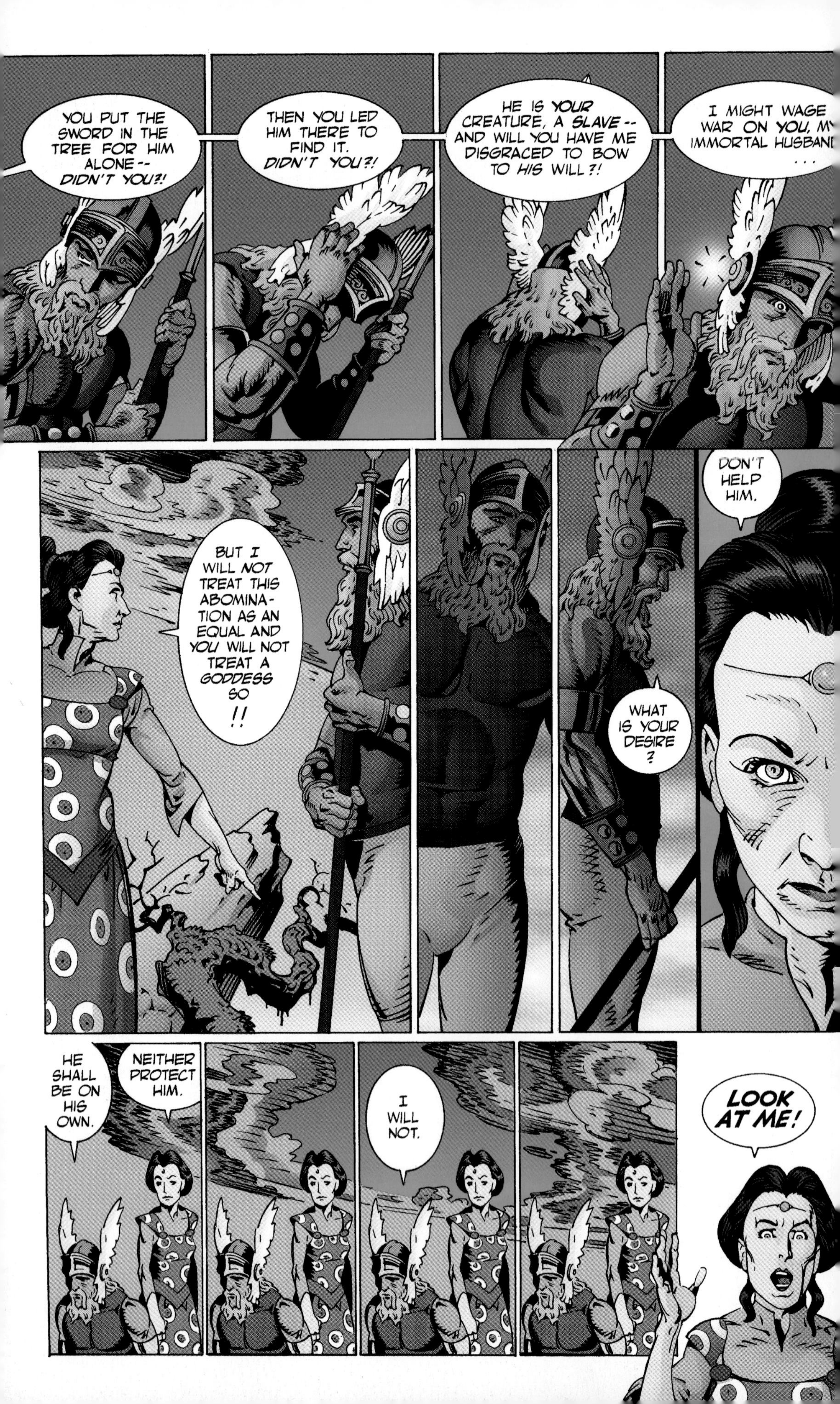
YOU PUT THE SWORD IN THE TREE FOR HIM ALONE -- DIDN'T YOU?!
THEN YOU LED HIM THERE TO FIND IT. DIDN'T YOU?!
HE IS YOUR CREATURE, A SLAVE -- AND WILL YOU HAVE ME DISGRACED TO BOW TO HIS WILL?!
I MIGHT WAGE WAR ON YOU, MY IMMORTAL HUSBAND . . .
BUT I WILL NOT TREAT THIS ABOMINATION AS AN EQUAL AND YOU WILL NOT TREAT A GODDESS SO !!
WHAT IS YOUR DESIRE ?
DON'T HELP HIM.
HE SHALL BE ON HIS OWN.
NEITHER PROTECT HIM.
I WILL NOT.
LOOK AT ME!

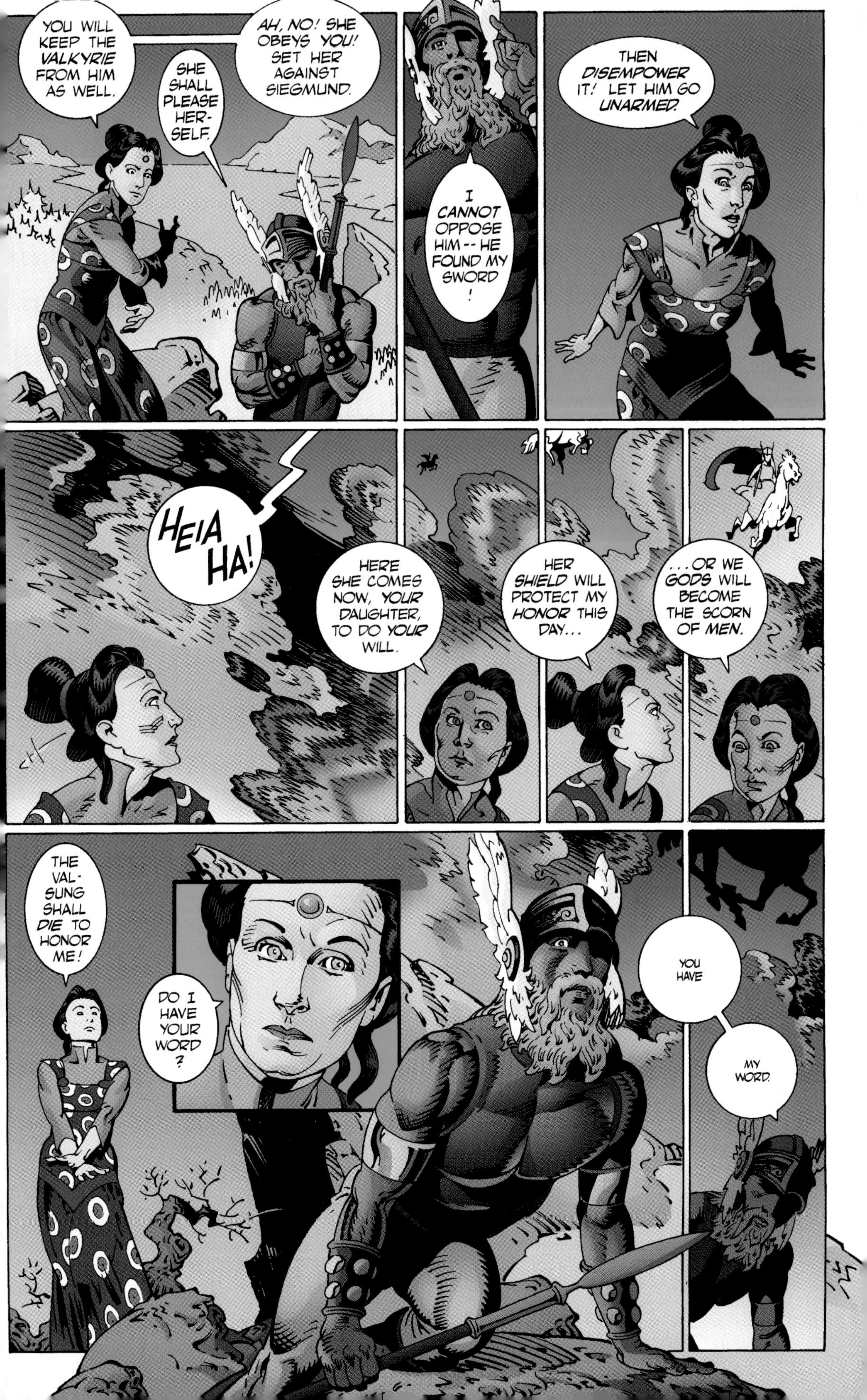
YOU WILL KEEP THE VALKYRIE FROM HIM AS WELL.
SHE SHALL PLEASE HER-SELF.
AH, NO! SHE OBEYS YOU! SET HER AGAINST SIEGMUND.
I CANNOT OPPOSE HIM -- HE FOUND MY SWORD!
THEN DISEMPOWER IT! LET HIM GO UNARMED.
HEIA HA!
HERE SHE COMES NOW, YOUR DAUGHTER, TO DO YOUR WILL.
HER SHIELD WILL PROTECT MY HONOR THIS DAY...
...OR WE GODS WILL BECOME THE SCORN OF MEN.
THE VAL-SUNG SHALL DIE TO HONOR ME!
DO I HAVE YOUR WORD?
YOU HAVE
MY WORD.

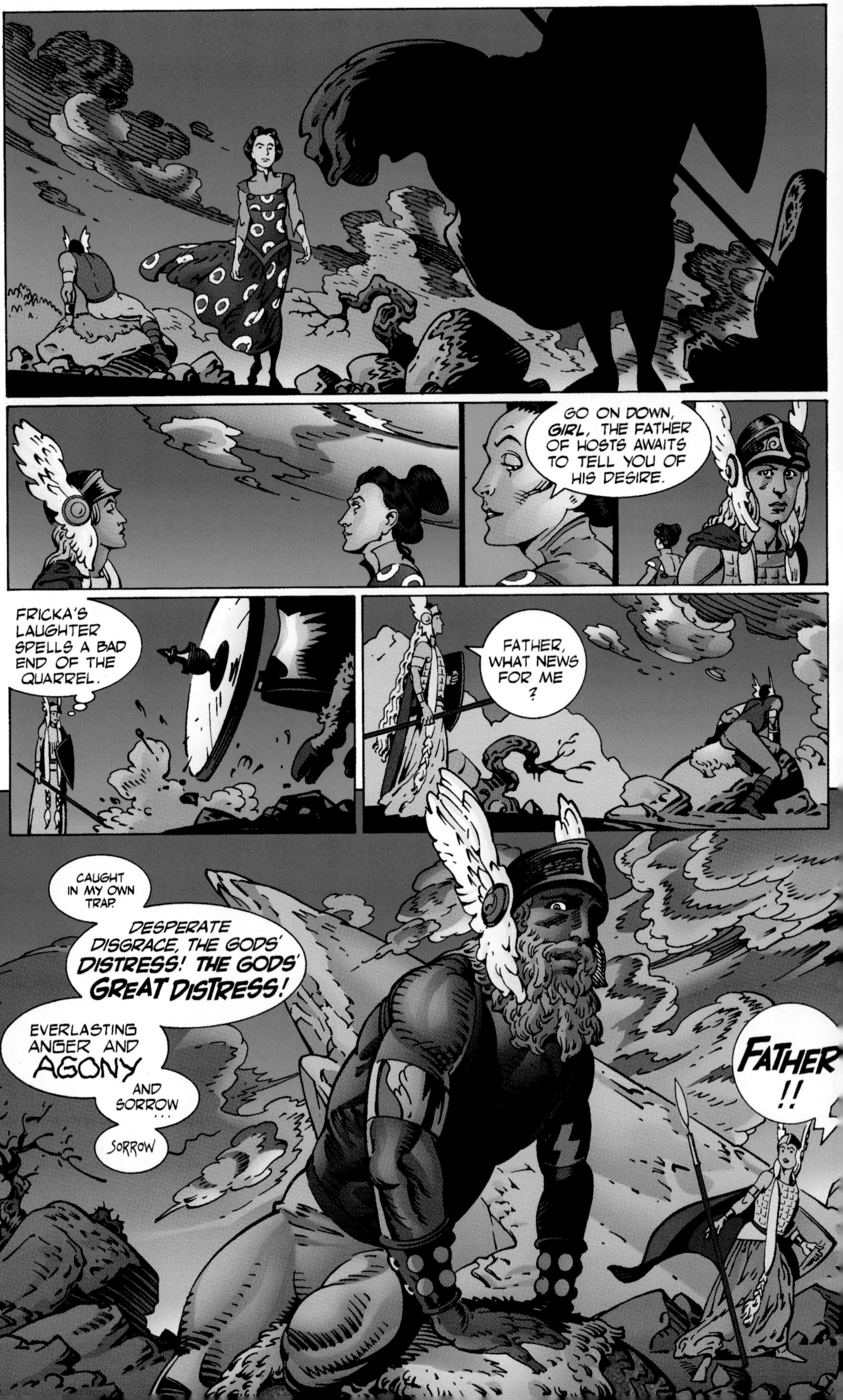
GO ON DOWN, GIRL, THE FATHER OF HOSTS AWAITS TO TELL YOU OF HIS DESIRE.
FRICKA'S LAUGHTER SPELLS A BAD END OF THE QUARREL.
FATHER, WHAT NEWS FOR ME ?
CAUGHT IN MY OWN TRAP.
DESPERATE DISGRACE, THE GODS' DISTRESS! THE GODS' GREAT DISTRESS!
EVERLASTING ANGER AND AGONY
AND SORROW ...
SORROW
FATHER !!

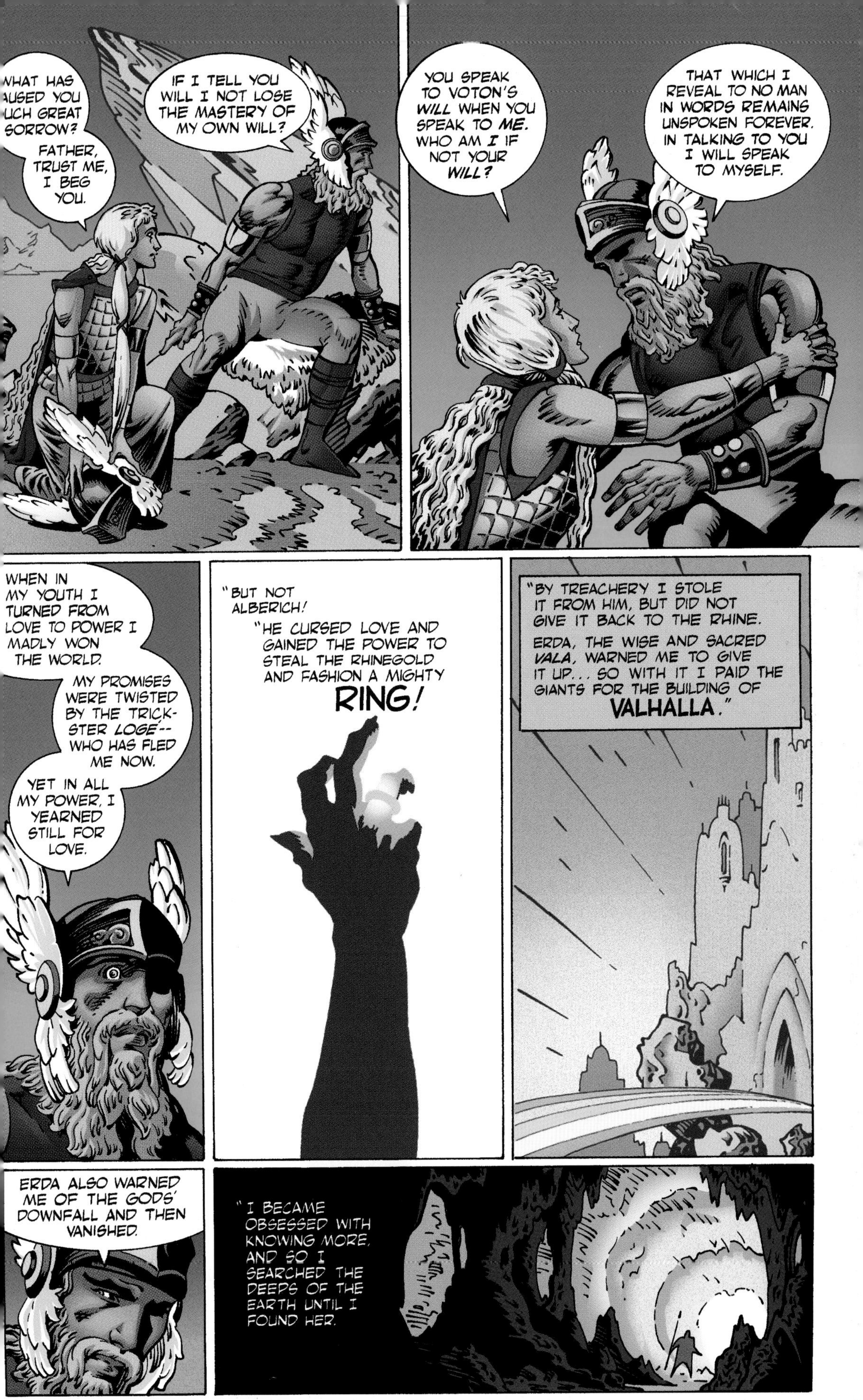
WHAT HAS AUSED YOU UCH GREAT SORROW?
FATHER, TRUST ME, I BEG YOU.
IF I TELL YOU WILL I NOT LOSE THE MASTERY OF MY OWN WILL?
YOU SPEAK TO VOTON'S WILL WHEN YOU SPEAK TO ME. WHO AM I IF NOT YOUR WILL?
THAT WHICH I REVEAL TO NO MAN IN WORDS REMAINS UNSPOKEN FOREVER. IN TALKING TO YOU I WILL SPEAK TO MYSELF.
WHEN IN MY YOUTH I TURNED FROM LOVE TO POWER I MADLY WON THE WORLD.
MY PROMISES WERE TWISTED BY THE TRICK-STER LOGE-- WHO HAS FLED ME NOW.
YET IN ALL MY POWER, I YEARNED STILL FOR LOVE.
"BUT NOT ALBERICH!
"HE CURSED LOVE AND GAINED THE POWER TO STEAL THE RHINEGOLD AND FASHION A MIGHTY RING!
"BY TREACHERY I STOLE IT FROM HIM, BUT DID NOT GIVE IT BACK TO THE RHINE.
ERDA, THE WISE AND SACRED VALA, WARNED ME TO GIVE IT UP... SO WITH IT I PAID THE GIANTS FOR THE BUILDING OF VALHALLA."
ERDA ALSO WARNED ME OF THE GODS' DOWNFALL AND THEN VANISHED.
"I BECAME OBSESSED WITH KNOWING MORE, AND SO I SEARCHED THE DEEPS OF THE EARTH UNTIL I FOUND HER.

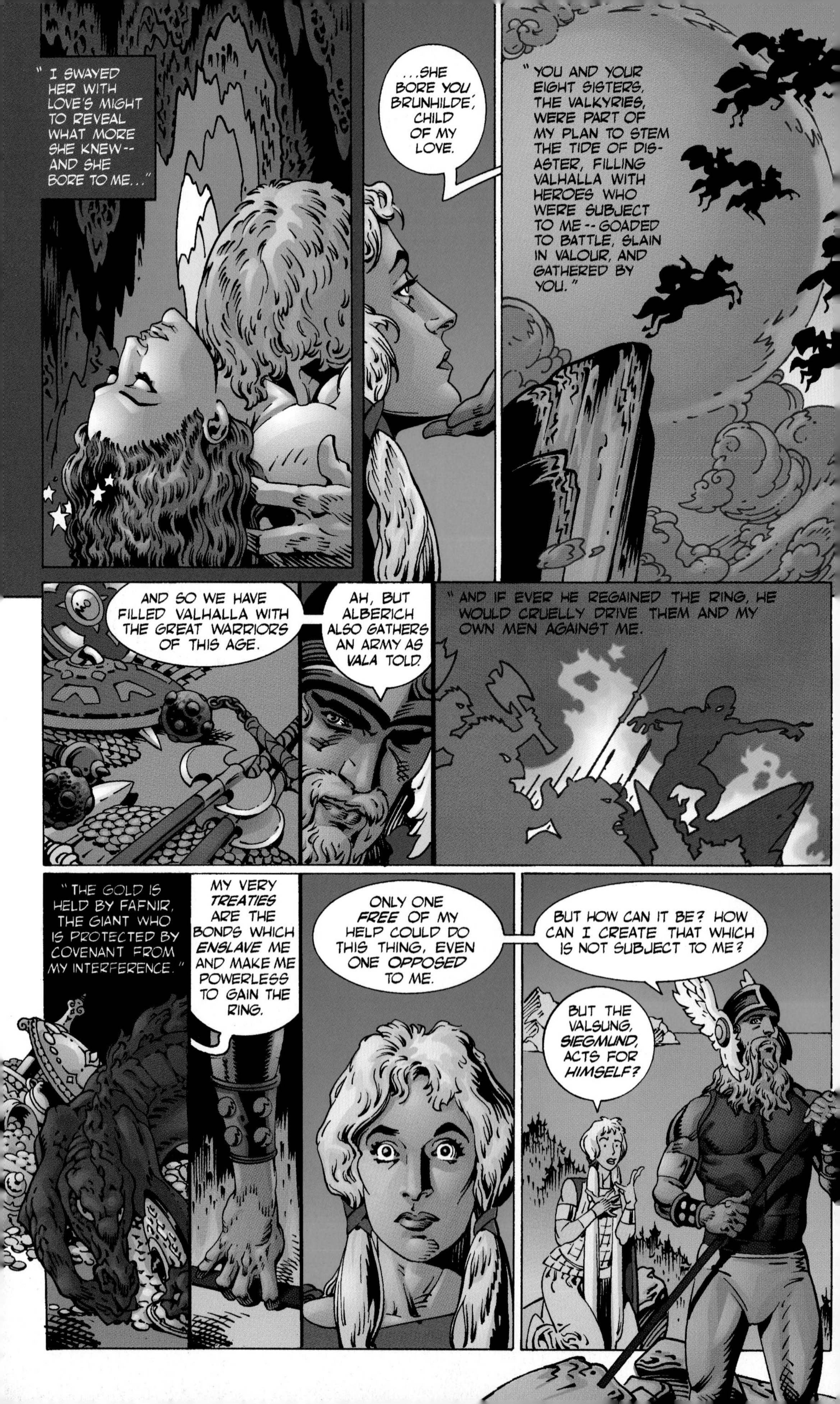
"I SWAYED HER WITH LOVE'S MIGHT TO REVEAL WHAT MORE SHE KNEW-- AND SHE BORE TO ME..."
...SHE BORE YOU BRUNHILDE, CHILD OF MY LOVE.
"YOU AND YOUR EIGHT SISTERS, THE VALKYRIES, WERE PART OF MY PLAN TO STEM THE TIDE OF DISASTER, FILLING VALHALLA WITH HEROES WHO WERE SUBJECT TO ME -- GOADED TO BATTLE, SLAIN IN VALOUR, AND GATHERED BY YOU."
AND SO WE HAVE FILLED VALHALLA WITH THE GREAT WARRIORS OF THIS AGE.
AH, BUT ALBERICH ALSO GATHERS AN ARMY AS VALA TOLD.
"AND IF EVER HE REGAINED THE RING, HE WOULD CRUELLY DRIVE THEM AND MY OWN MEN AGAINST ME.
"THE GOLD IS HELD BY FAFNIR, THE GIANT WHO IS PROTECTED BY COVENANT FROM MY INTERFERENCE."
MY VERY TREATIES ARE THE BONDS WHICH ENSLAVE ME AND MAKE ME POWERLESS TO GAIN THE RING.
ONLY ONE FREE OF MY HELP COULD DO THIS THING, EVEN ONE OPPOSED TO ME.
BUT HOW CAN IT BE? HOW CAN I CREATE THAT WHICH IS NOT SUBJECT TO ME?
BUT THE VALSUNG, SIEGMUND, ACTS FOR HIMSELF?

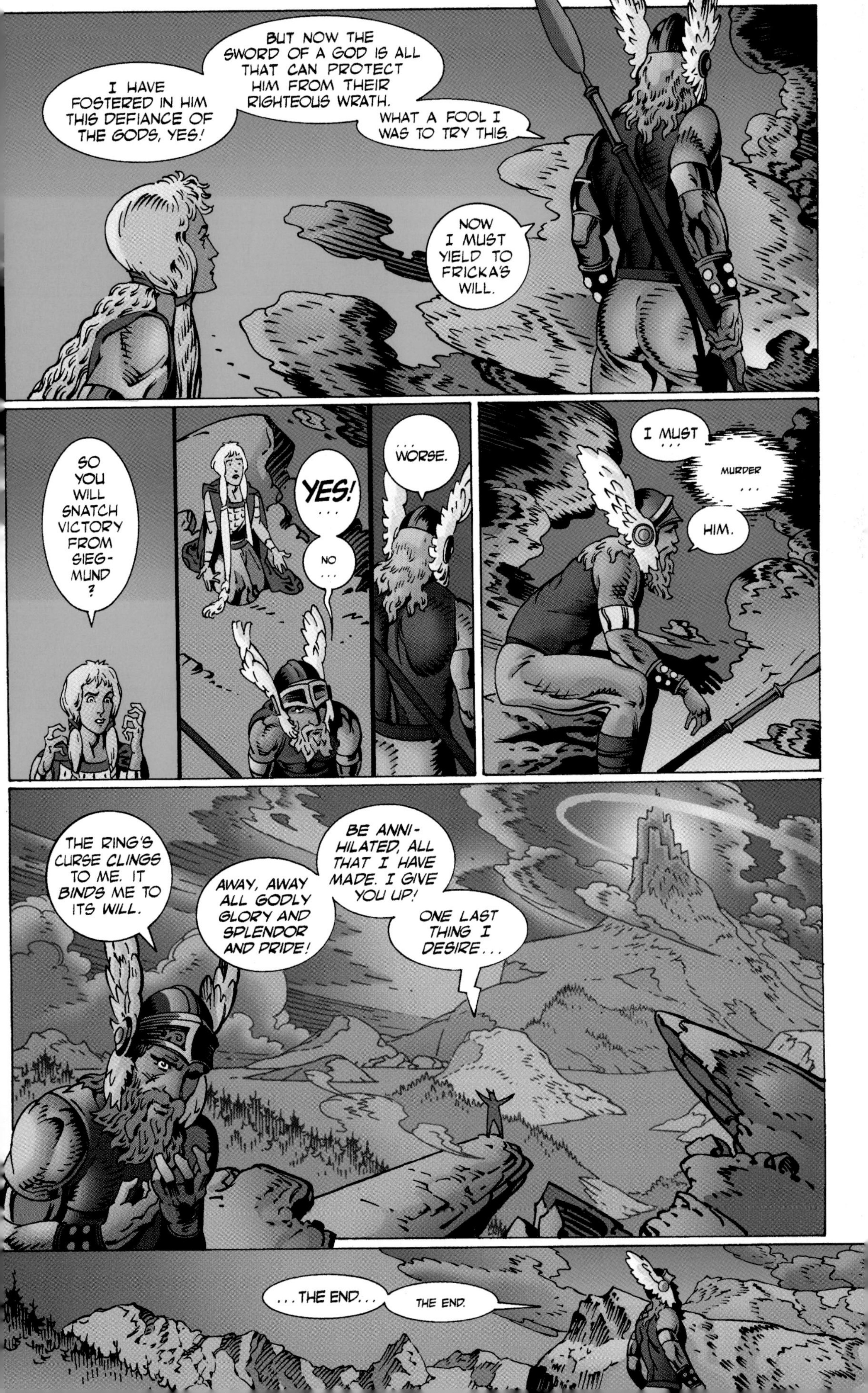

I HAVE FOSTERED IN HIM THIS DEFIANCE OF THE GODS, YES!
BUT NOW THE SWORD OF A GOD IS ALL THAT CAN PROTECT HIM FROM THEIR RIGHTEOUS WRATH.
WHAT A FOOL I WAS TO TRY THIS.
NOW I MUST YIELD TO FRICKA'S WILL.
SO YOU WILL SNATCH VICTORY FROM SIEG-MUND?
YES! ...
NO ...
... WORSE.
I MUST ...
MURDER ...
HIM.
THE RING'S CURSE CLINGS TO ME. IT BINDS ME TO ITS WILL.
AWAY, AWAY ALL GODLY GLORY AND SPLENDOR AND PRIDE!
BE ANNI-HILATED, ALL THAT I HAVE MADE. I GIVE YOU UP!
ONE LAST THING I DESIRE...
...THE END...
THE END.

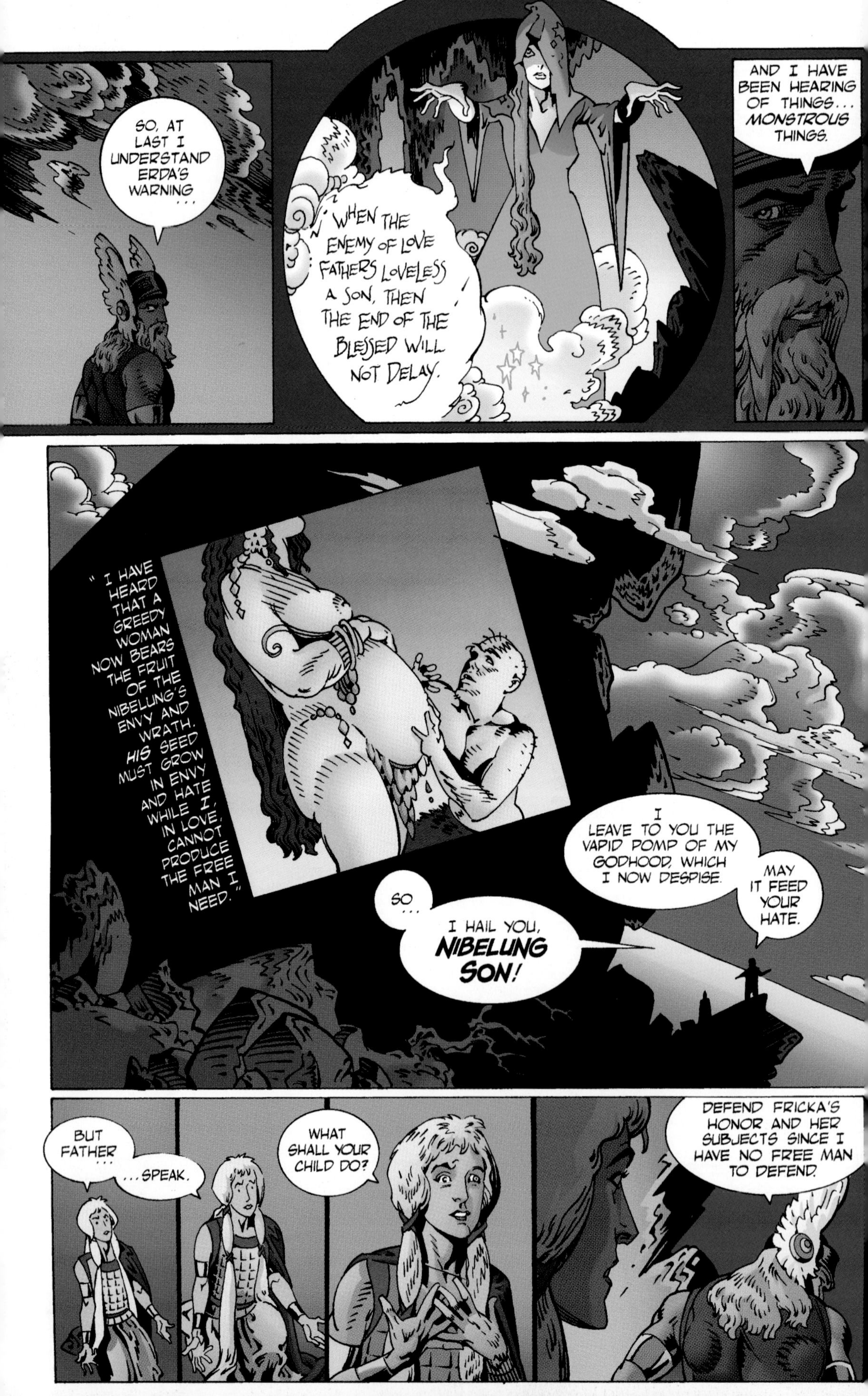

SO, AT LAST I UNDERSTAND ERDA'S WARNING . . .
"WHEN THE ENEMY OF LOVE FATHERS LOVELESS A SON, THEN THE END OF THE BLESSED WILL NOT DELAY.
AND I HAVE BEEN HEARING OF THINGS... MONSTROUS THINGS.
"I HAVE HEARD THAT A GREEDY WOMAN NOW BEARS THE FRUIT OF THE NIBELUNG'S ENVY AND WRATH. HIS SEED MUST GROW IN ENVY AND HATE WHILE I, IN LOVE, CANNOT PRODUCE THE FREE MAN I NEED."
I LEAVE TO YOU THE VAPID POMP OF MY GODHOOD, WHICH I NOW DESPISE.
MAY IT FEED YOUR HATE.
SO . . .
I HAIL YOU, NIBELUNG SON!
BUT FATHER . . .
. . . SPEAK.
WHAT SHALL YOUR CHILD DO?
DEFEND FRICKA'S HONOR AND HER SUBJECTS SINCE I HAVE NO FREE MAN TO DEFEND.

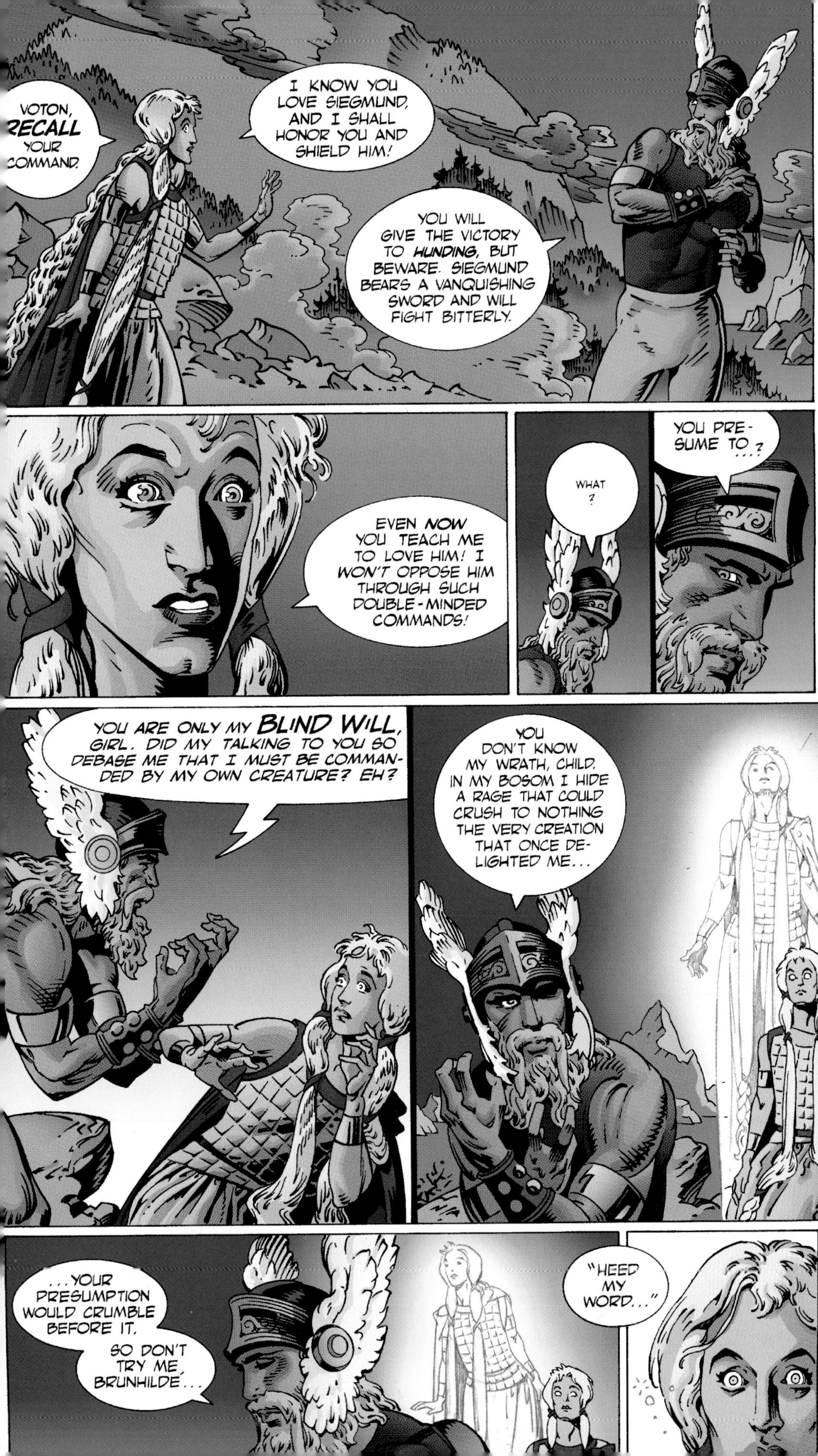
VOTON, RECALL YOUR COMMAND.
I KNOW YOU LOVE SIEGMUND, AND I SHALL HONOR YOU AND SHIELD HIM!
YOU WILL GIVE THE VICTORY TO HUNDING, BUT BEWARE. SIEGMUND BEARS A VANQUISHING SWORD AND WILL FIGHT BITTERLY.
EVEN NOW YOU TEACH ME TO LOVE HIM! I WON'T OPPOSE HIM THROUGH SUCH DOUBLE-MINDED COMMANDS!
WHAT?
YOU PRESUME TO...?
YOU ARE ONLY MY BLIND WILL, GIRL. DID MY TALKING TO YOU SO DEBASE ME THAT I MUST BE COMMANDED BY MY OWN CREATURE? EH?
YOU DON'T KNOW MY WRATH, CHILD. IN MY BOSOM I HIDE A RAGE THAT COULD CRUSH TO NOTHING THE VERY CREATION THAT ONCE DELIGHTED ME...
...YOUR PRESUMPTION WOULD CRUMBLE BEFORE IT.
SO DON'T TRY ME, BRUNHILDE...
"HEED MY WORD..."

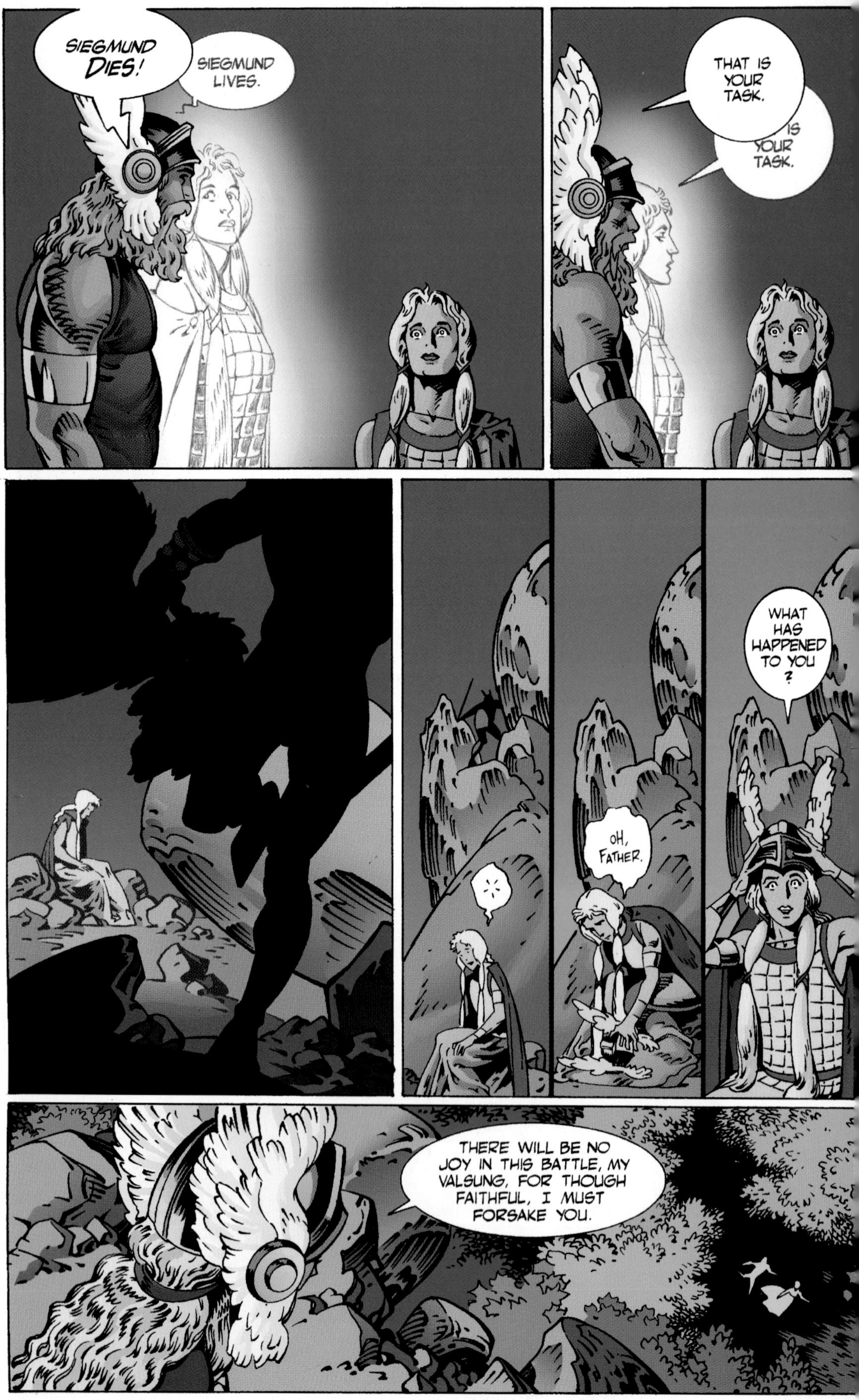
SIEGMUND DIES!
SIEGMUND LIVES.
THAT IS YOUR TASK.
IS YOUR TASK.
OH, FATHER.
WHAT HAS HAPPENED TO YOU ?
THERE WILL BE NO JOY IN THIS BATTLE, MY VALSUNG, FOR THOUGH FAITHFUL, I MUST FORSAKE YOU.

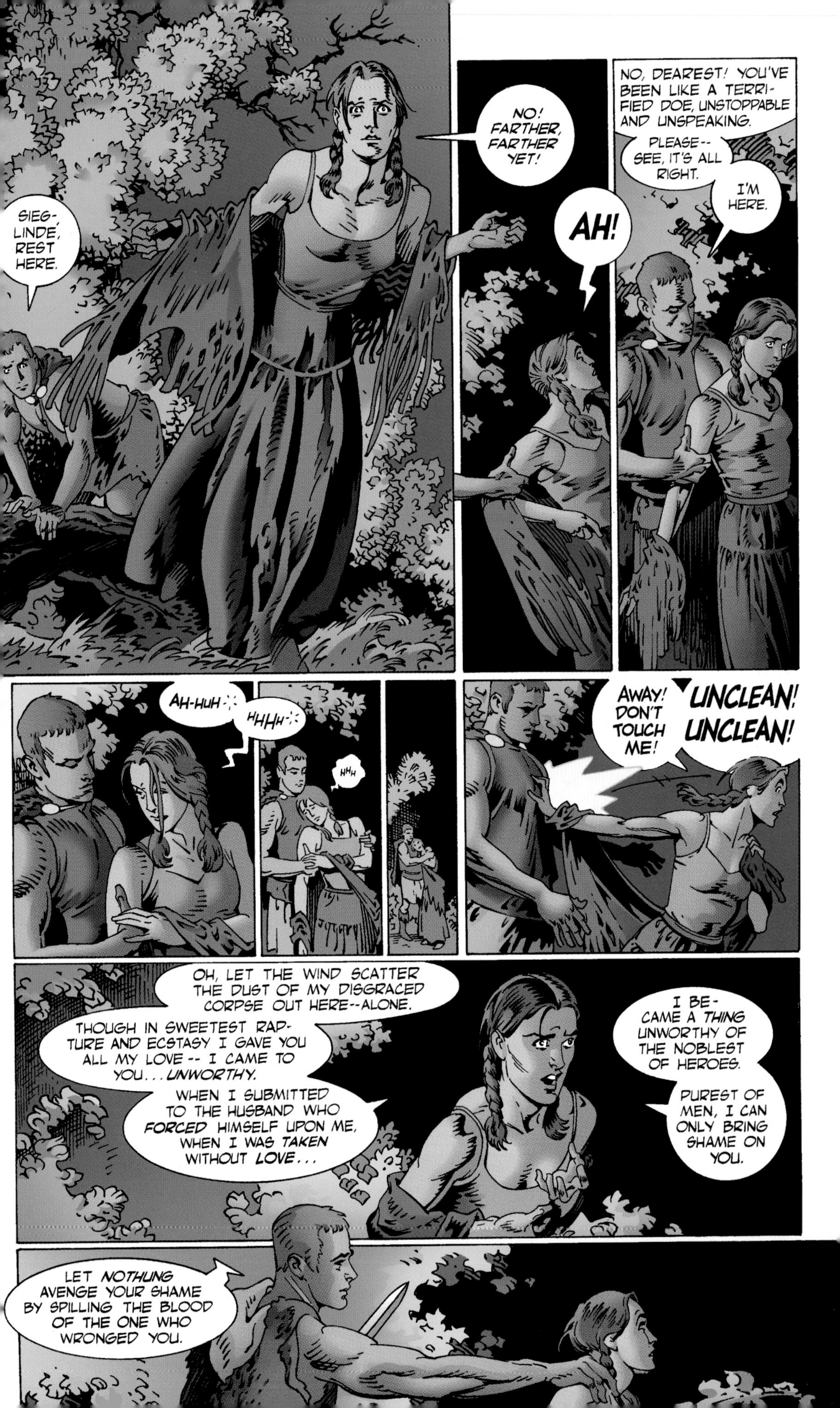

NO! FARTHER, FARTHER YET!
SIEG-LINDE, REST HERE.
AH!
NO, DEAREST! YOU'VE BEEN LIKE A TERRI-FIED DOE, UNSTOPPABLE AND UNSPEAKING.
PLEASE-- SEE, IT'S ALL RIGHT.
I'M HERE.
AH-HUH
HHHH
HHH
AWAY! DON'T TOUCH ME!
UNCLEAN! UNCLEAN!
OH, LET THE WIND SCATTER THE DUST OF MY DISGRACED CORPSE OUT HERE--ALONE.
THOUGH IN SWEETEST RAP-TURE AND ECSTASY I GAVE YOU ALL MY LOVE -- I CAME TO YOU... UNWORTHY.
WHEN I SUBMITTED TO THE HUSBAND WHO FORCED HIMSELF UPON ME, WHEN I WAS TAKEN WITHOUT LOVE...
I BE-CAME A THING UNWORTHY OF THE NOBLEST OF HEROES.
PUREST OF MEN, I CAN ONLY BRING SHAME ON YOU.
LET NOTHUNG AVENGE YOUR SHAME BY SPILLING THE BLOOD OF THE ONE WHO WRONGED YOU.

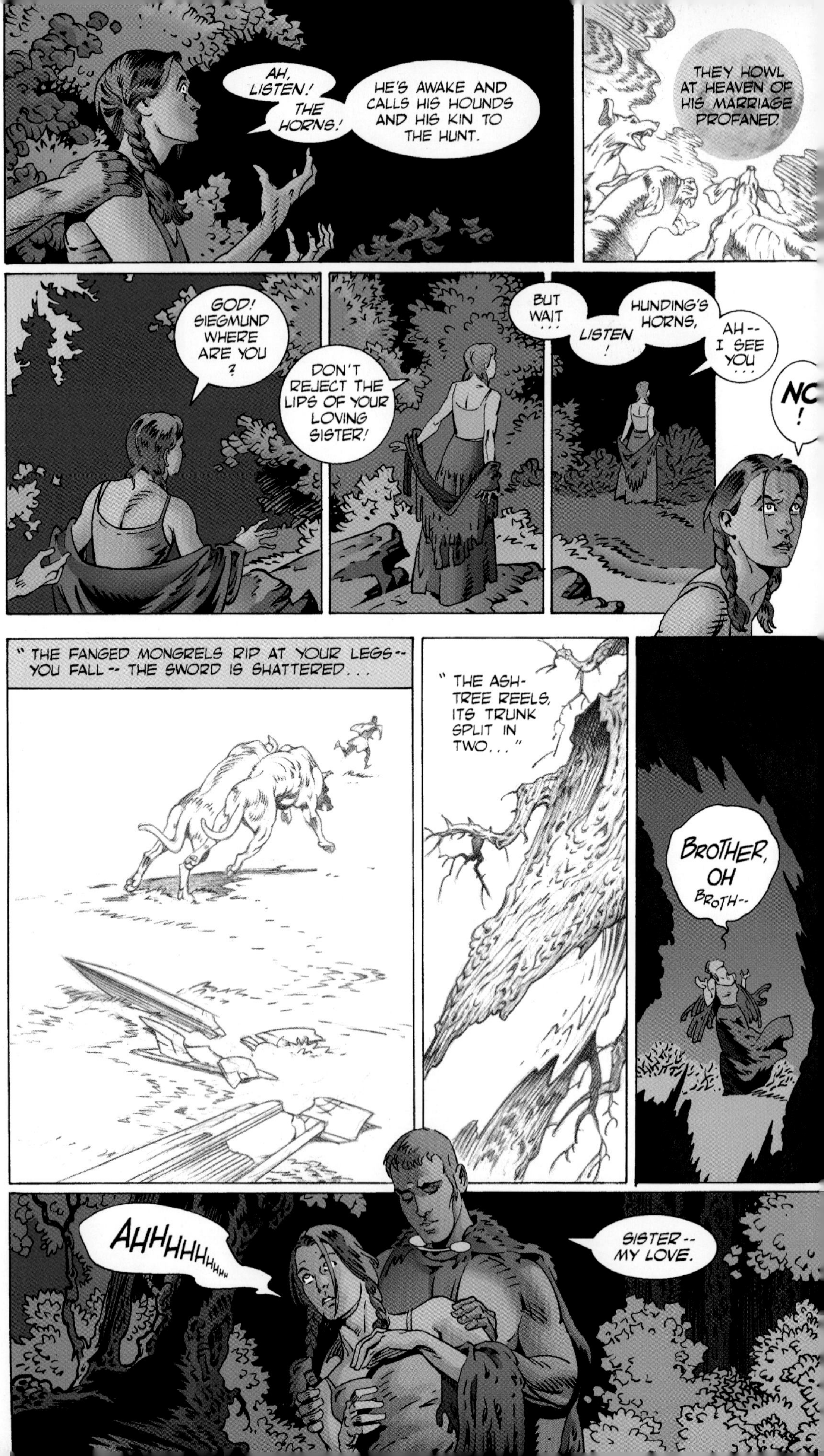
AH, LISTEN! THE HORNS!
HE'S AWAKE AND CALLS HIS HOUNDS AND HIS KIN TO THE HUNT.
THEY HOWL AT HEAVEN OF HIS MARRIAGE PROFANED.
GOD! SIEGMUND WHERE ARE YOU?
DON'T REJECT THE LIPS OF YOUR LOVING SISTER!
BUT WAIT...
LISTEN!
HUNDING'S HORNS,
AH -- I SEE YOU...
NO!
"THE FANGED MONGRELS RIP AT YOUR LEGS -- YOU FALL -- THE SWORD IS SHATTERED...
"THE ASH-TREE REELS, ITS TRUNK SPLIT IN TWO..."
BROTHER, OH BROTH--
AHHHHHHHH
SISTER -- MY LOVE.

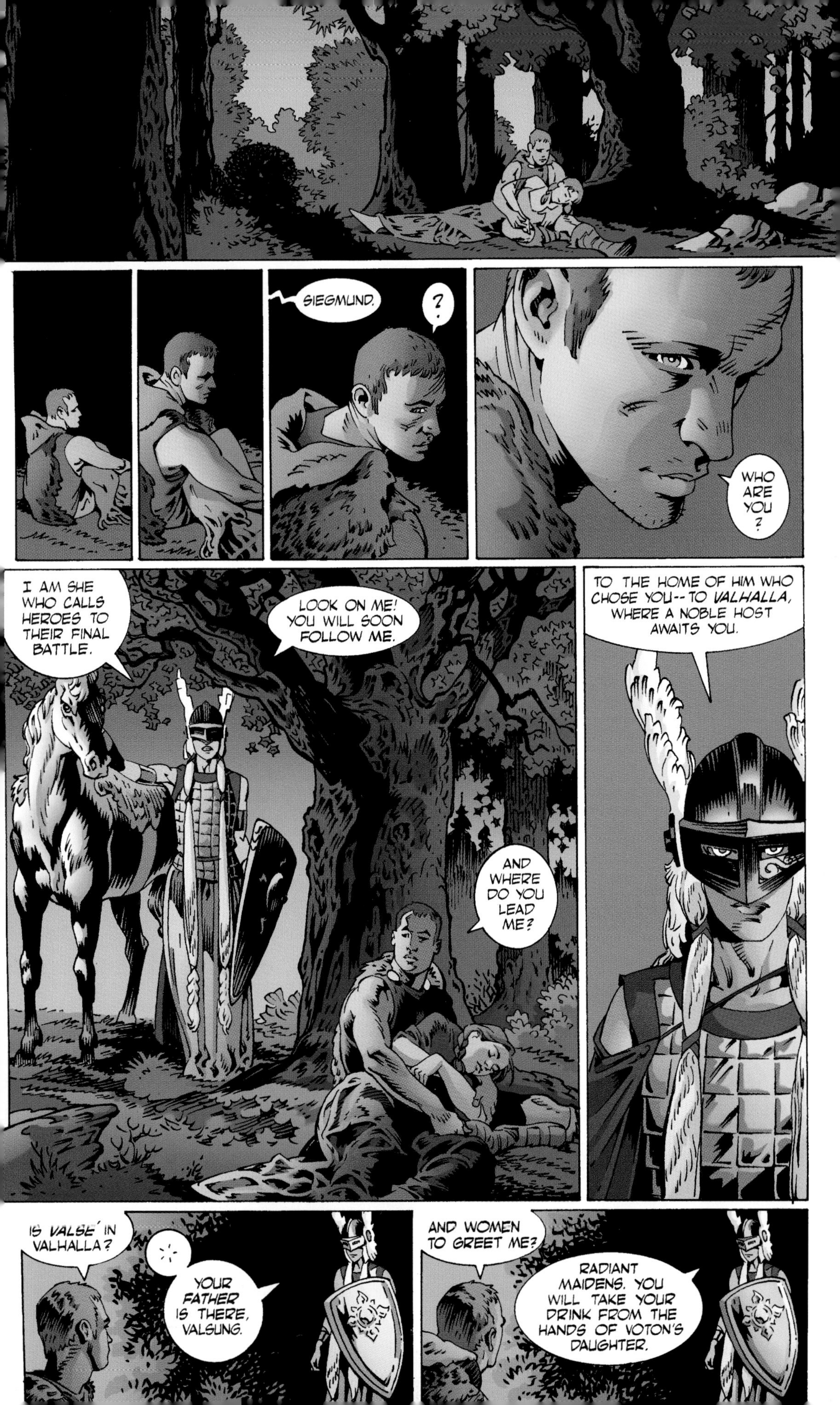
SIEGMUND.
?
WHO ARE YOU ?
I AM SHE WHO CALLS HEROES TO THEIR FINAL BATTLE.
LOOK ON ME! YOU WILL SOON FOLLOW ME.
AND WHERE DO YOU LEAD ME?
TO THE HOME OF HIM WHO CHOSE YOU--TO VALHALLA, WHERE A NOBLE HOST AWAITS YOU.
IS VALSE´ IN VALHALLA?
YOUR FATHER IS THERE, VALSUNG.
AND WOMEN TO GREET ME?
RADIANT MAIDENS. YOU WILL TAKE YOUR DRINK FROM THE HANDS OF VOTON'S DAUGHTER.

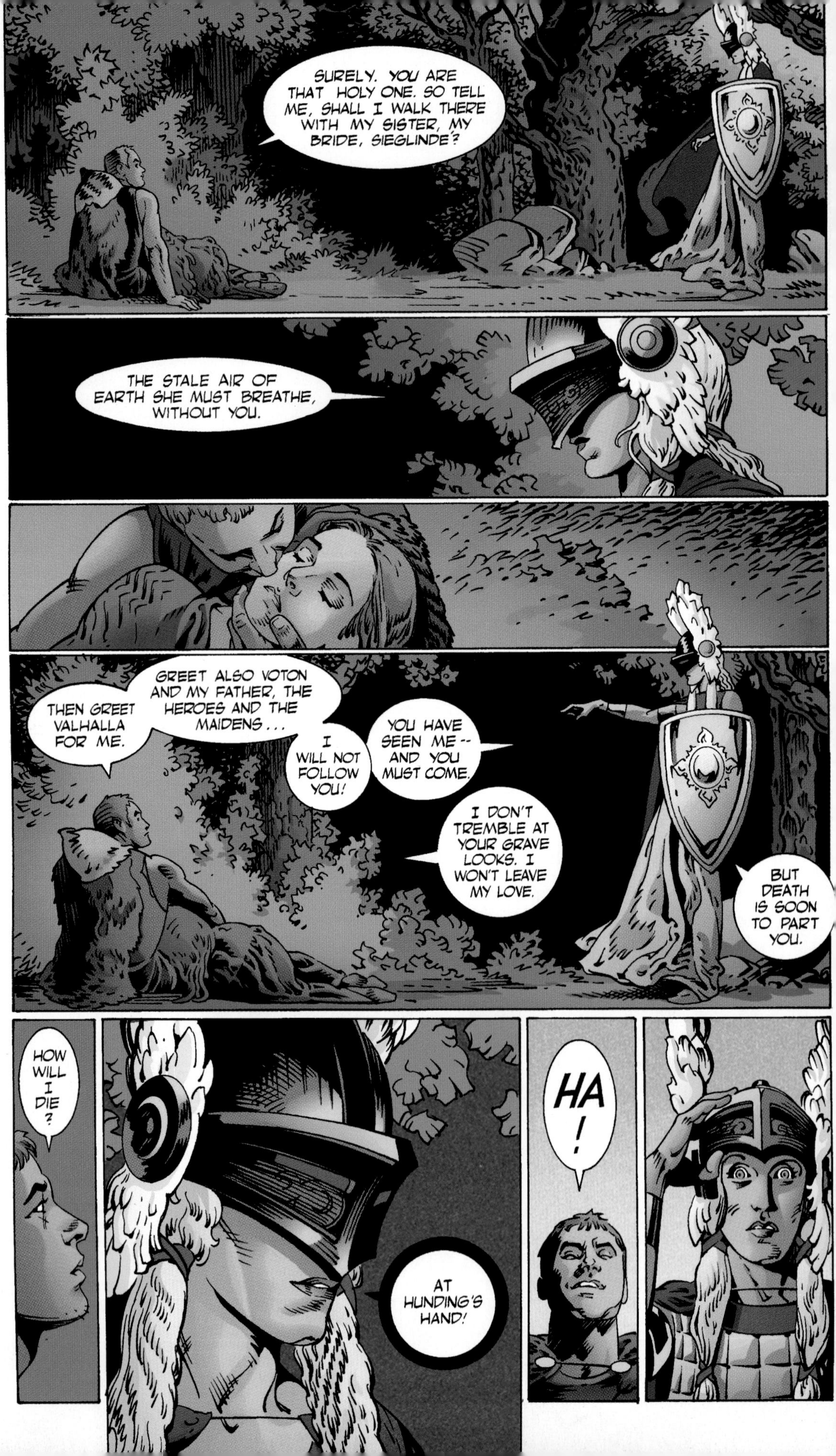
SURELY. YOU ARE THAT HOLY ONE. SO TELL ME, SHALL I WALK THERE WITH MY SISTER, MY BRIDE, SIEGLINDE?
THE STALE AIR OF EARTH SHE MUST BREATHE, WITHOUT YOU.
THEN GREET VALHALLA FOR ME.
GREET ALSO VOTON AND MY FATHER, THE HEROES AND THE MAIDENS...
YOU HAVE SEEN ME -- AND YOU MUST COME.
I WILL NOT FOLLOW YOU!
I DON'T TREMBLE AT YOUR GRAVE LOOKS. I WON'T LEAVE MY LOVE.
BUT DEATH IS SOON TO PART YOU.
HOW WILL I DIE?
AT HUNDING'S HAND!
HA!

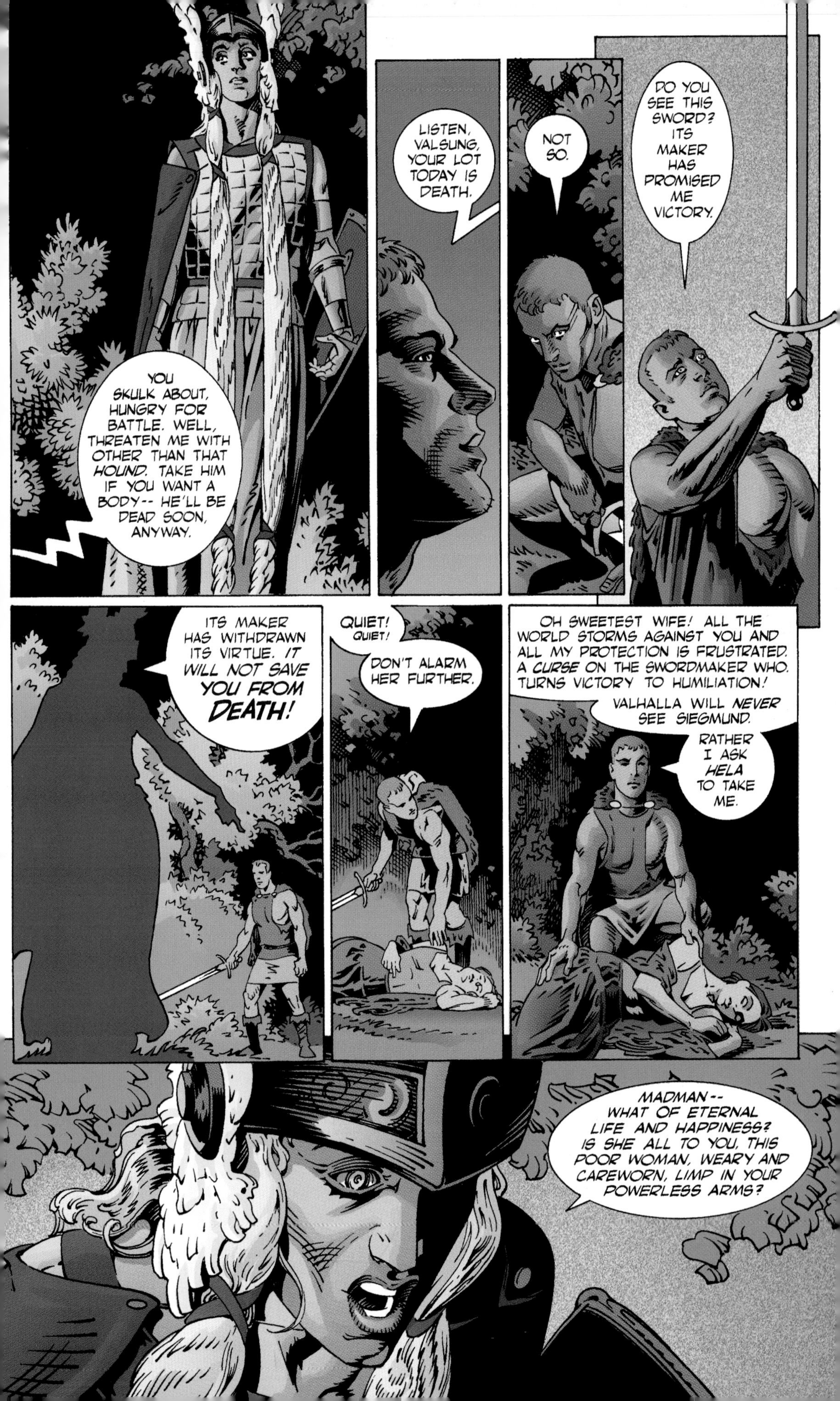

YOU SKULK ABOUT, HUNGRY FOR BATTLE. WELL, THREATEN ME WITH OTHER THAN THAT *HOUND*. TAKE HIM IF YOU WANT A BODY-- HE'LL BE DEAD SOON, ANYWAY.
LISTEN, VALSUNG, YOUR LOT TODAY IS DEATH.
NOT SO.
DO YOU SEE THIS SWORD? ITS MAKER HAS PROMISED ME VICTORY.
ITS MAKER HAS WITHDRAWN ITS VIRTUE. *IT WILL NOT SAVE* **YOU FROM DEATH!**
QUIET! QUIET!
DON'T ALARM HER FURTHER.
OH SWEETEST WIFE! ALL THE WORLD STORMS AGAINST YOU AND ALL MY PROTECTION IS FRUSTRATED. A *CURSE* ON THE SWORDMAKER WHO TURNS VICTORY TO HUMILIATION!
VALHALLA WILL *NEVER* SEE SIEGMUND.
RATHER I ASK *HELA* TO TAKE ME.
MADMAN-- WHAT OF ETERNAL LIFE AND HAPPINESS? IS SHE ALL TO YOU, THIS POOR WOMAN, WEARY AND CAREWORN, LIMP IN YOUR POWERLESS ARMS?

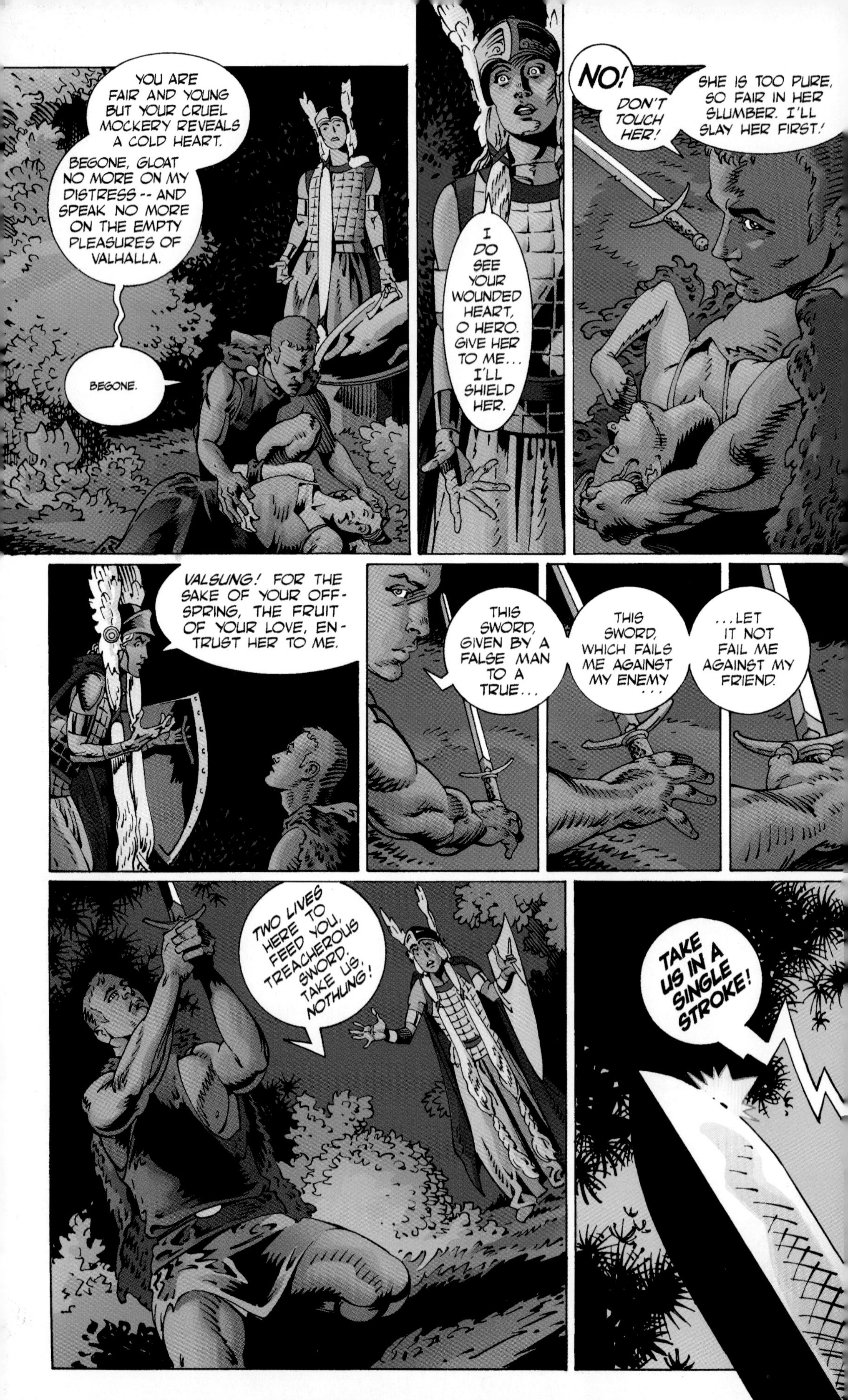
YOU ARE FAIR AND YOUNG BUT YOUR CRUEL MOCKERY REVEALS A COLD HEART.
BEGONE, GLOAT NO MORE ON MY DISTRESS -- AND SPEAK NO MORE ON THE EMPTY PLEASURES OF VALHALLA.
BEGONE.
I DO SEE YOUR WOUNDED HEART, O HERO. GIVE HER TO ME... I'LL SHIELD HER.
NO!
DON'T TOUCH HER!
SHE IS TOO PURE, SO FAIR IN HER SLUMBER. I'LL SLAY HER FIRST!
VALSUNG! FOR THE SAKE OF YOUR OFF-SPRING, THE FRUIT OF YOUR LOVE, EN-TRUST HER TO ME.
THIS SWORD, GIVEN BY A FALSE MAN TO A TRUE...
THIS SWORD, WHICH FAILS ME AGAINST MY ENEMY ...
...LET IT NOT FAIL ME AGAINST MY FRIEND.
TWO LIVES HERE TO FEED YOU, TREACHEROUS SWORD. TAKE US, NOTHUNG!
TAKE US IN A SINGLE STROKE!

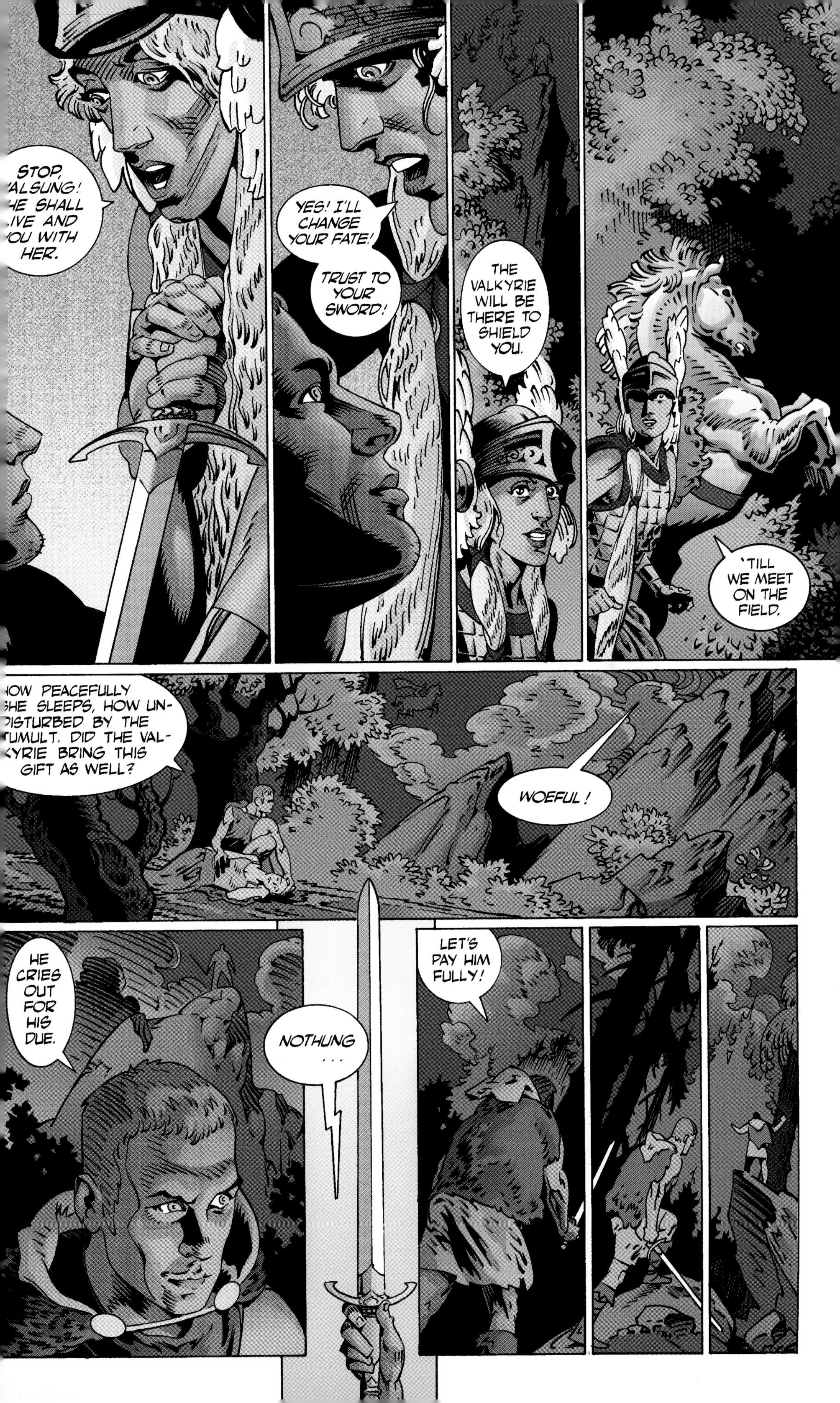
STOP, ALSUNG! HE SHALL LIVE AND YOU WITH HER.
YES! I'LL CHANGE YOUR FATE!
TRUST TO YOUR SWORD!
THE VALKYRIE WILL BE THERE TO SHIELD YOU.
'TILL WE MEET ON THE FIELD.
HOW PEACEFULLY SHE SLEEPS, HOW UNDISTURBED BY THE TUMULT. DID THE VALKYRIE BRING THIS GIFT AS WELL?
WOEFUL!
HE CRIES OUT FOR HIS DUE.
NOTHUNG . . .
LET'S PAY HIM FULLY!

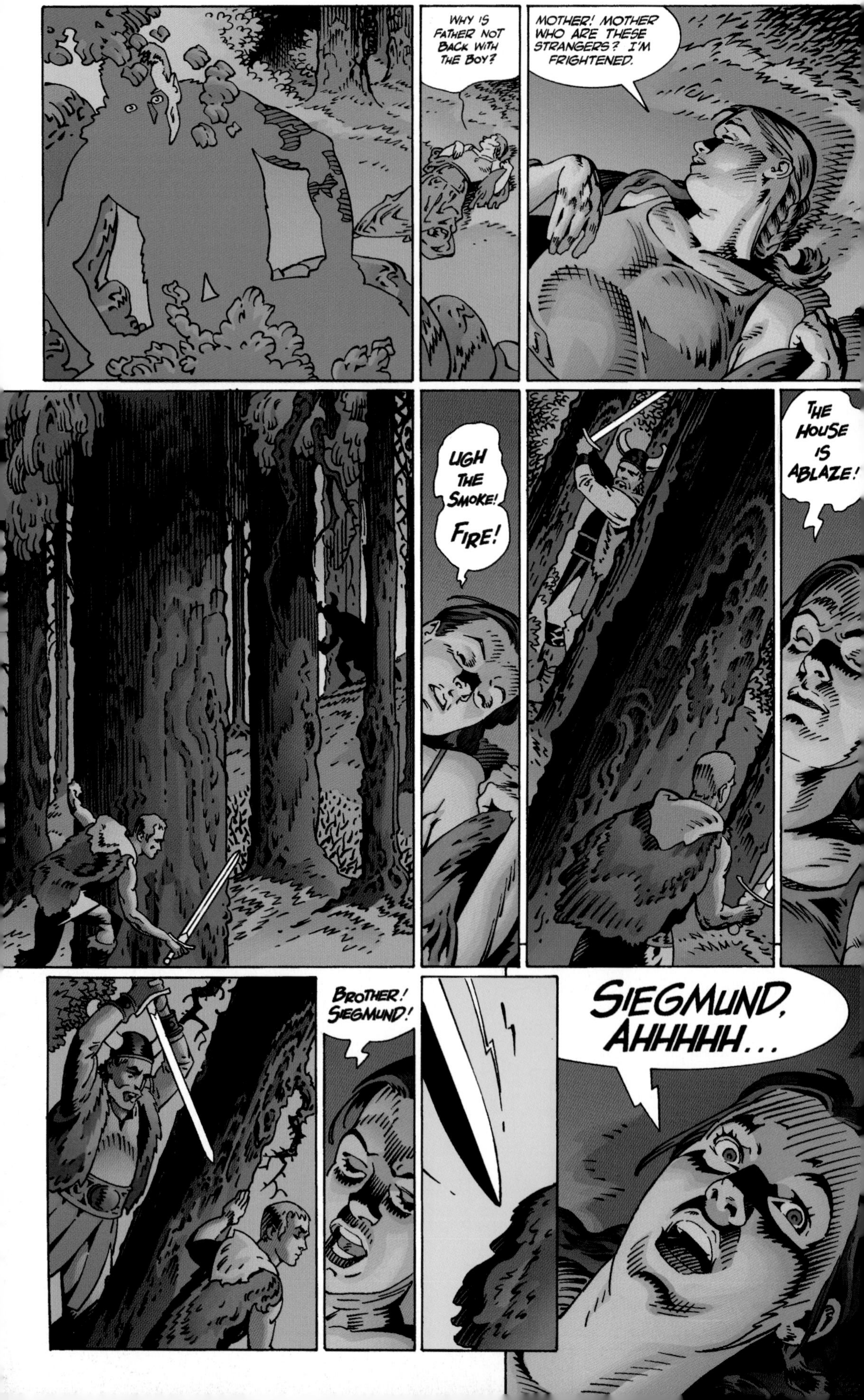
WHY IS FATHER NOT BACK WITH THE BOY?
MOTHER! MOTHER WHO ARE THESE STRANGERS? I'M FRIGHTENED.
UGH THE SMOKE!
FIRE!
THE HOUSE IS ABLAZE!
BROTHER! SIEGMUND!
SIEGMUND, AHHHHH...

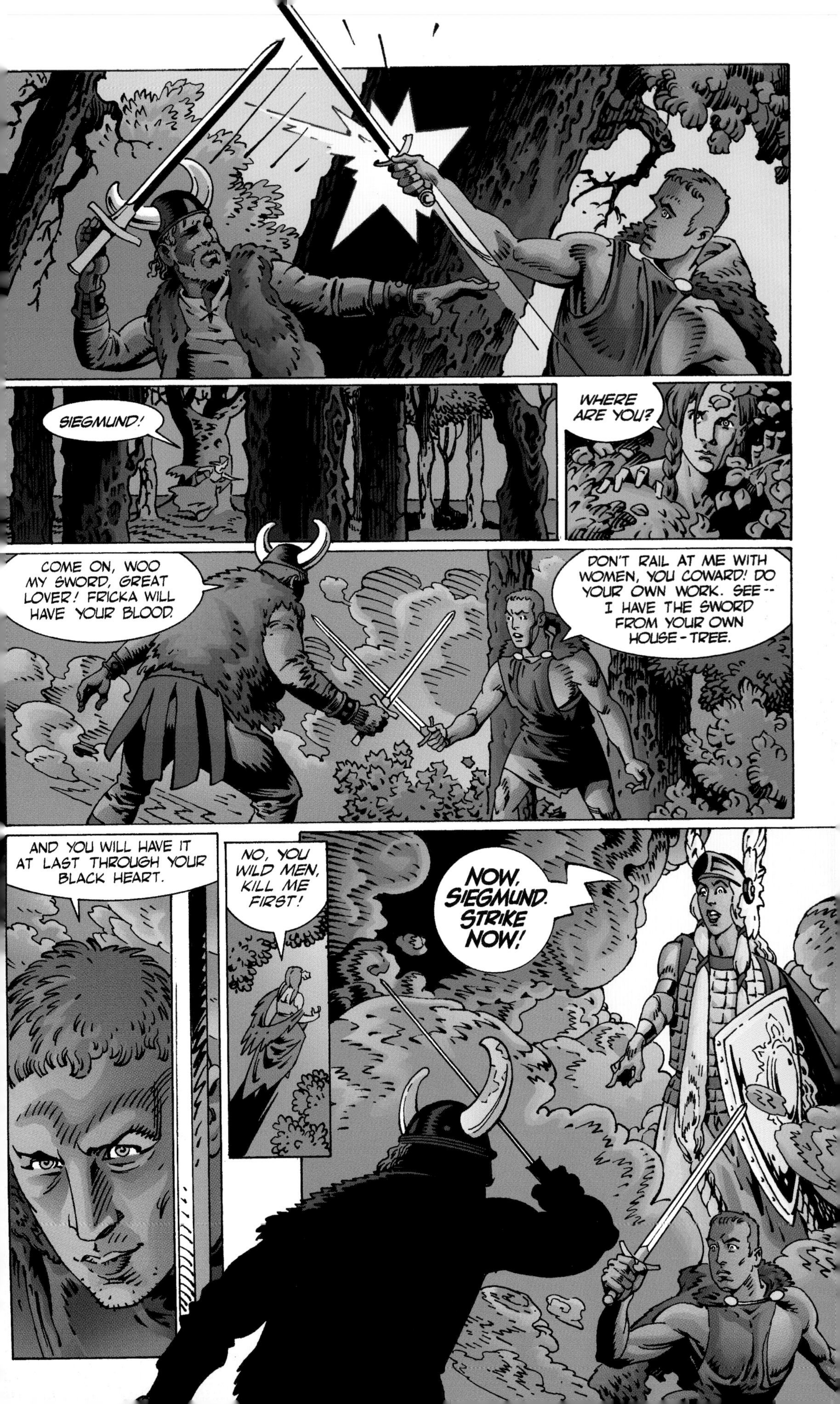
SIEGMUND!
WHERE ARE YOU?
COME ON, WOO MY SWORD, GREAT LOVER! FRICKA WILL HAVE YOUR BLOOD.
DON'T RAIL AT ME WITH WOMEN, YOU COWARD! DO YOUR OWN WORK. SEE-- I HAVE THE SWORD FROM YOUR OWN HOUSE-TREE.
AND YOU WILL HAVE IT AT LAST THROUGH YOUR BLACK HEART.
NO, YOU WILD MEN, KILL ME FIRST!
NOW, SIEGMUND. STRIKE NOW!

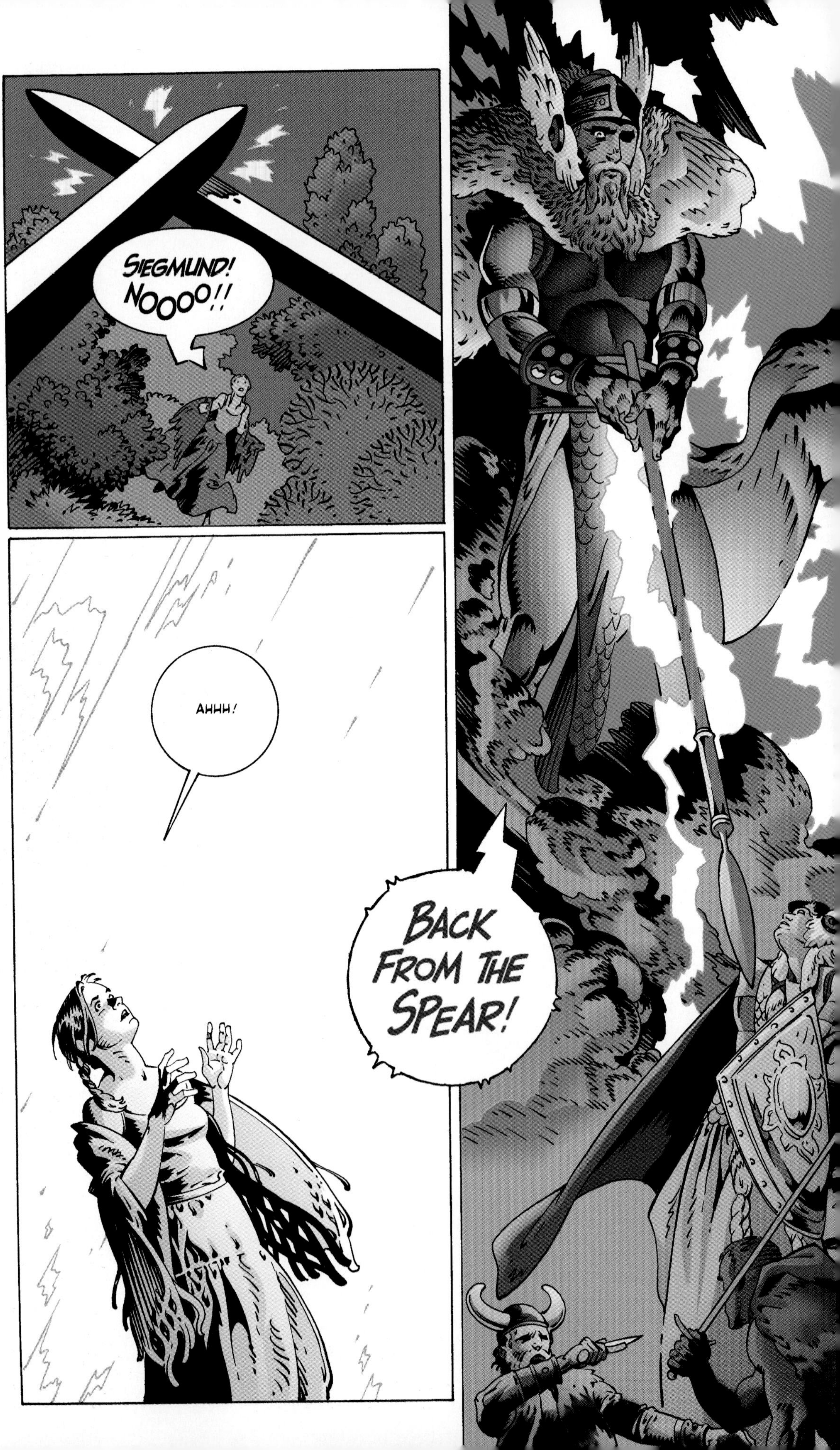
SIEGMUND! NOOOO!!
AHHH!
BACK FROM THE SPEAR!

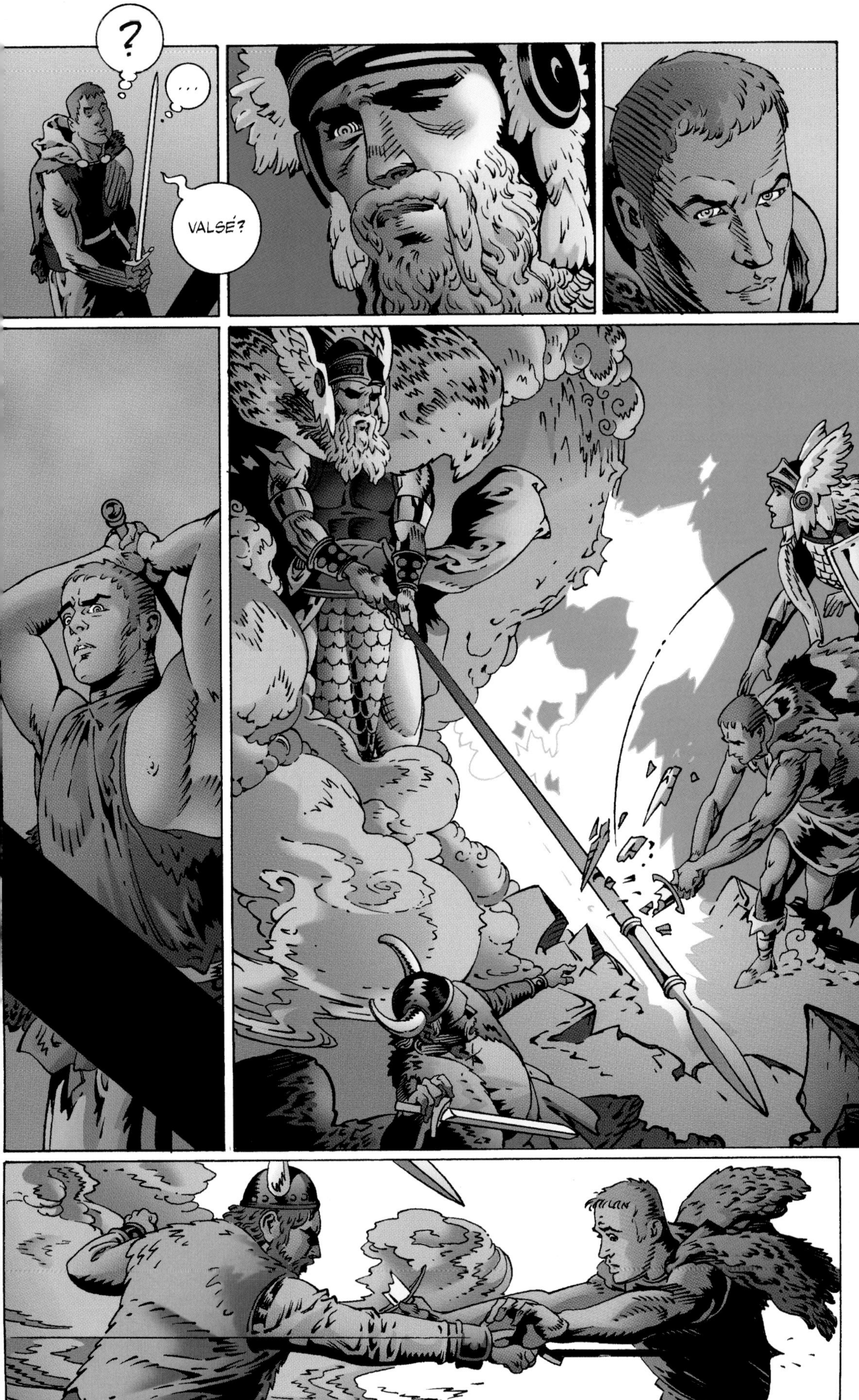
?
...
VALSÉ?

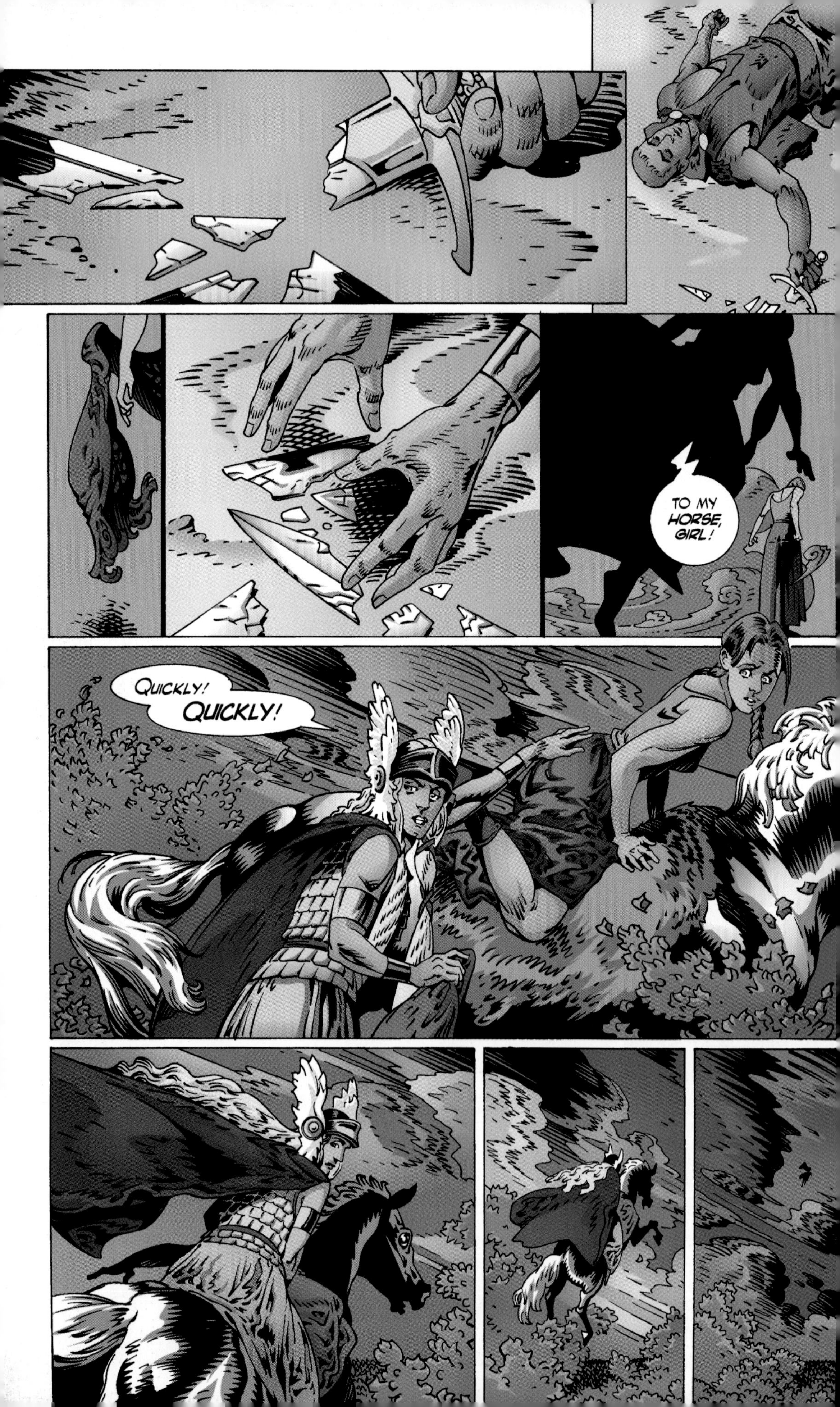
TO MY HORSE, GIRL!
QUICKLY! QUICKLY!

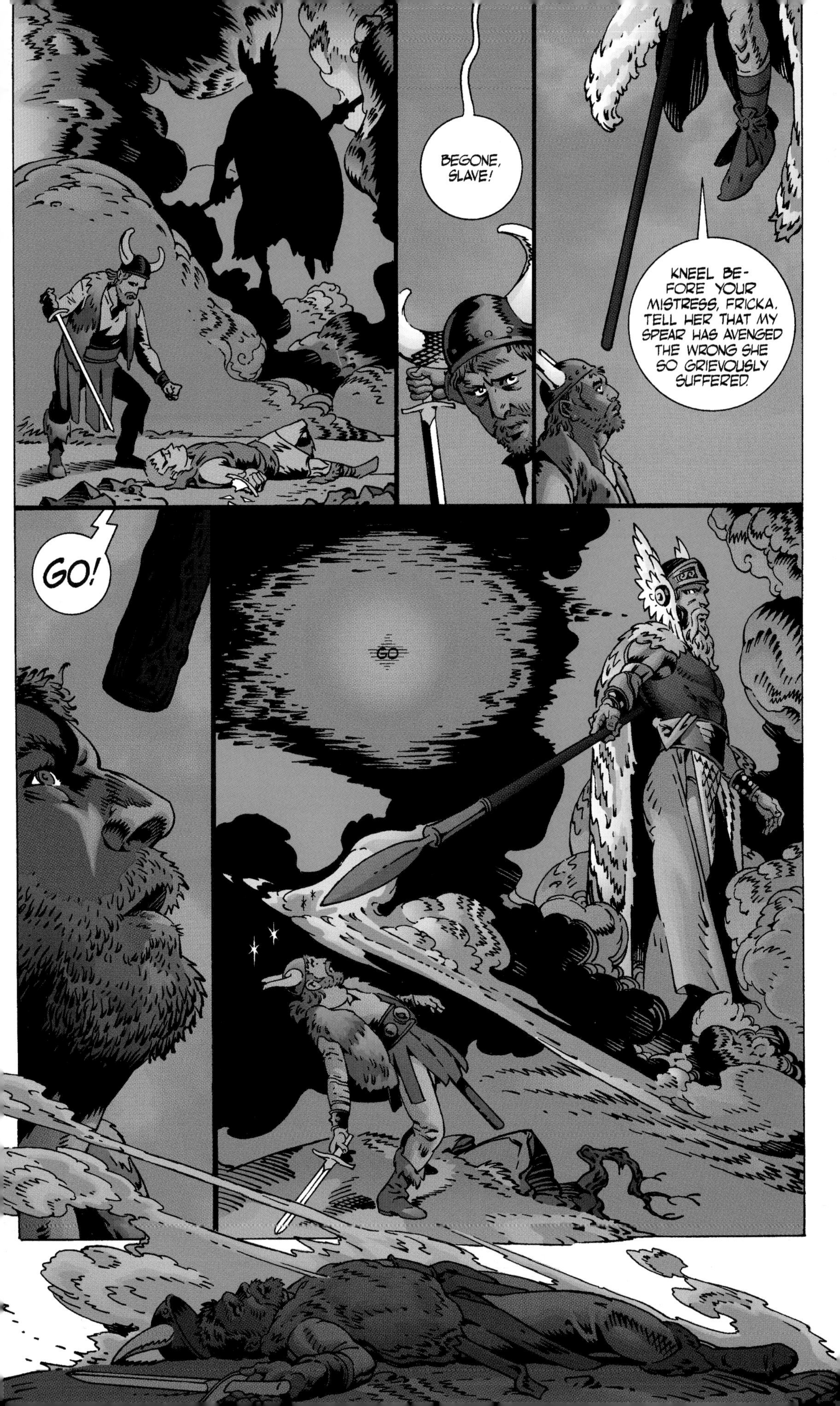
BEGONE, SLAVE!
KNEEL BEFORE YOUR MISTRESS, FRICKA. TELL HER THAT MY SPEAR HAS AVENGED THE WRONG SHE SO GRIEVOUSLY SUFFERED.
GO!
GO

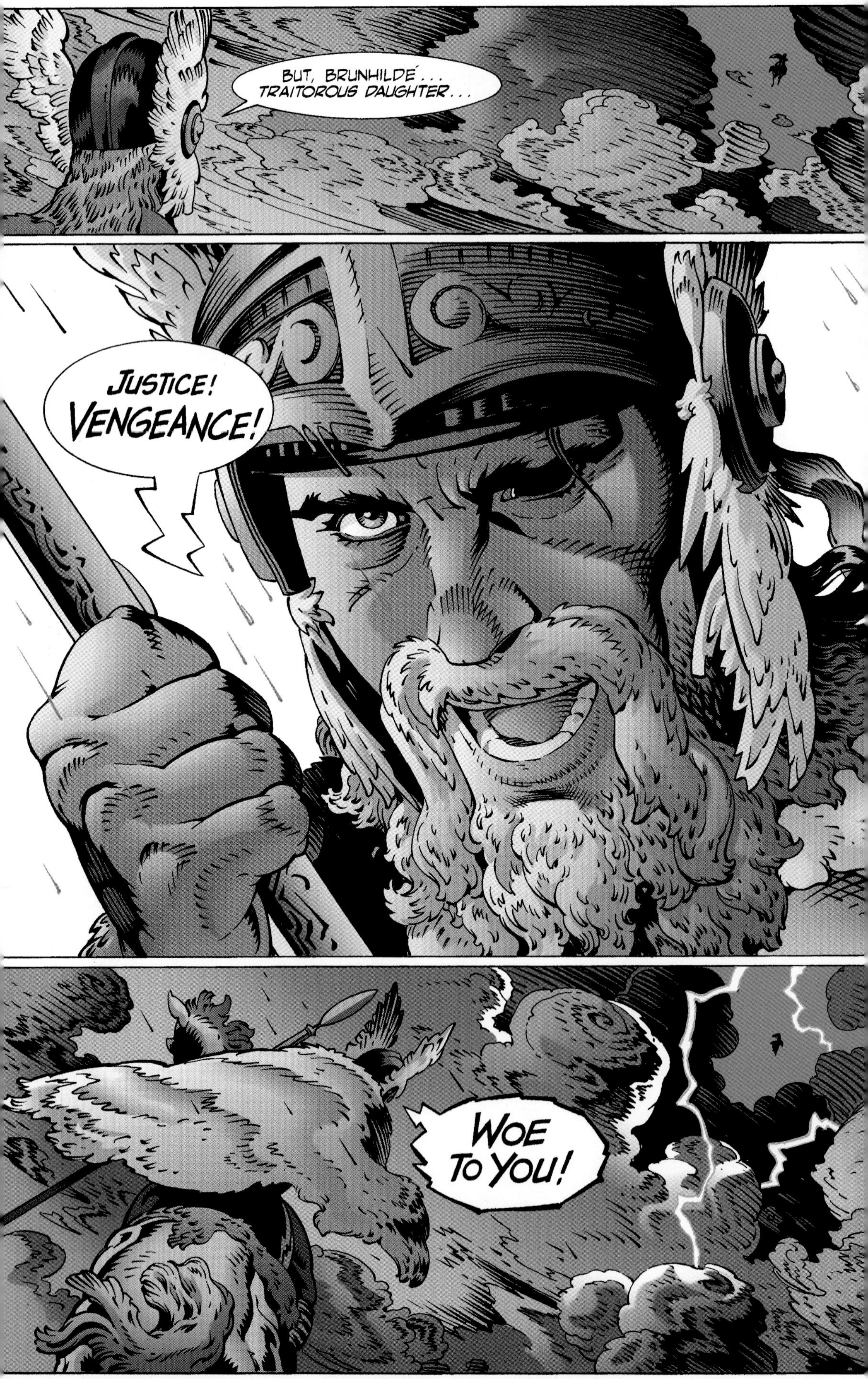
BUT, BRUNHILDE...
TRAITOROUS DAUGHTER...
JUSTICE! VENGEANCE!
WOE TO YOU!

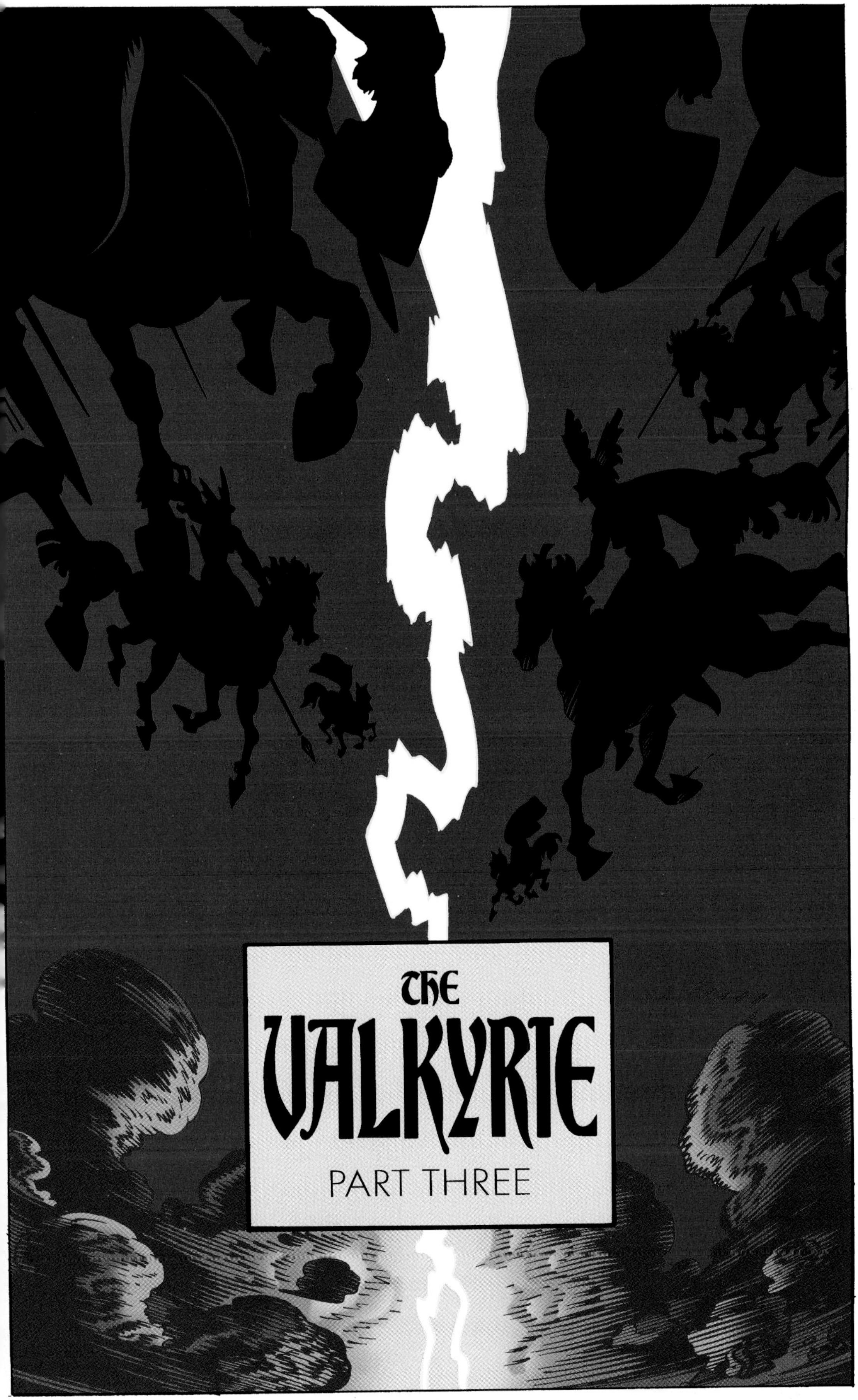
THE
VALKYRIE
PART THREE

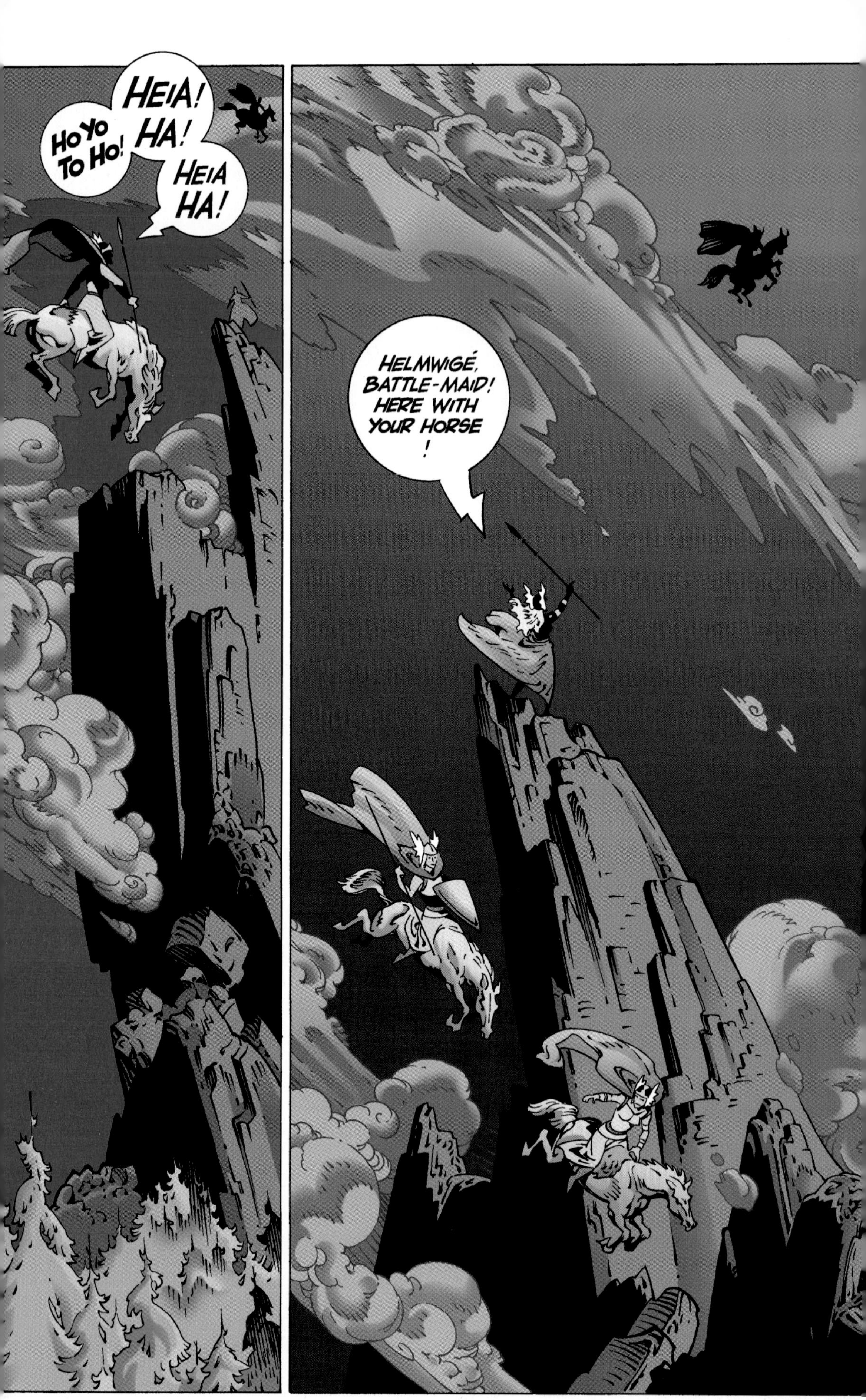
HO YO TO HO!
HEIA! HA!
HEIA HA!
HELMWIGÉ, BATTLE-MAID! HERE WITH YOUR HORSE!

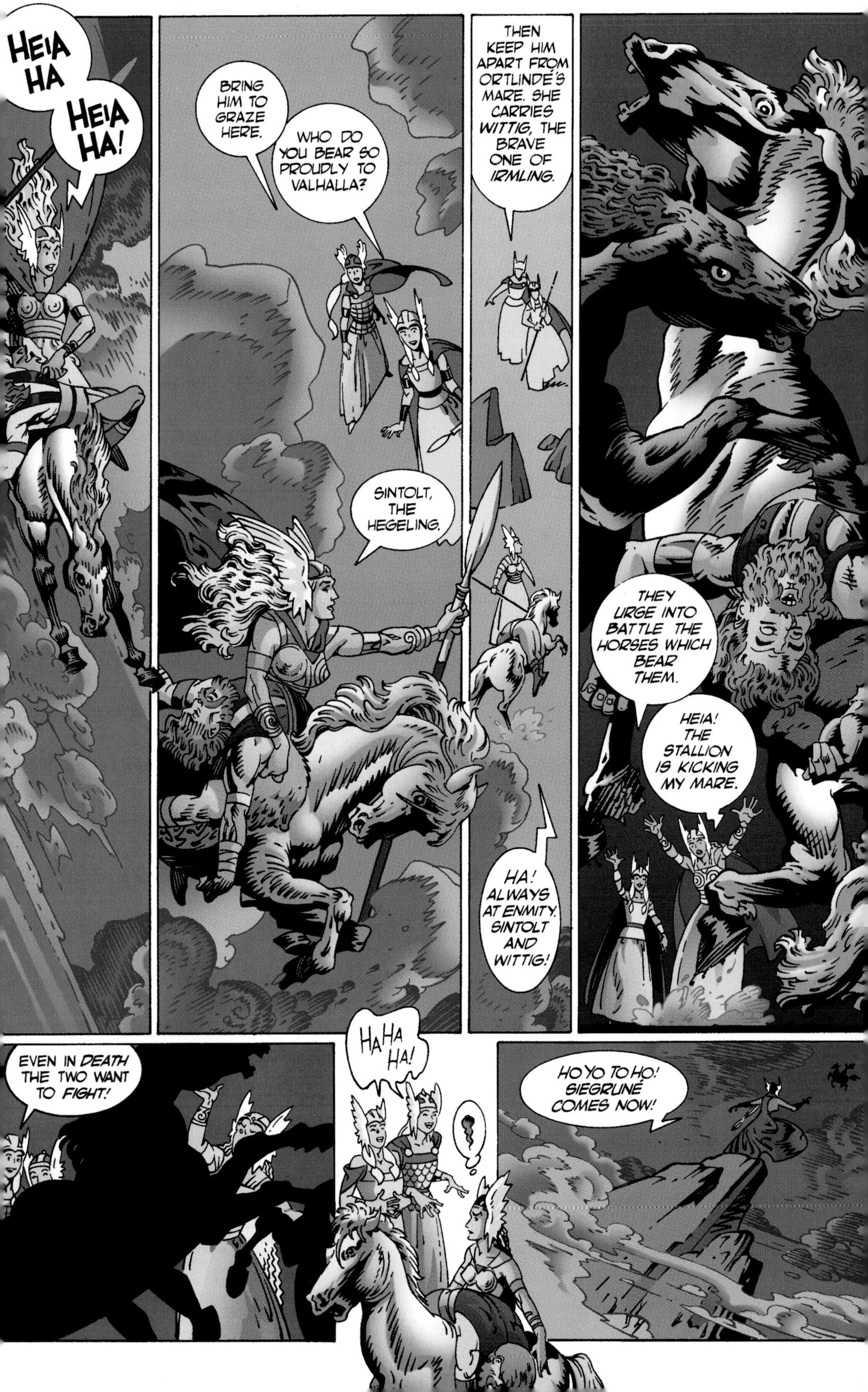
HEIA HA
HEIA HA!
BRING HIM TO GRAZE HERE.
WHO DO YOU BEAR SO PROUDLY TO VALHALLA?
SINTOLT, THE HEGELING.
THEN KEEP HIM APART FROM ORTLINDE'S MARE. SHE CARRIES *WITTIG*, THE BRAVE ONE OF *IRMLING*.
HA! ALWAYS AT ENMITY, SINTOLT AND WITTIG!
THEY URGE INTO BATTLE THE HORSES WHICH BEAR THEM.
HEIA! THE STALLION IS KICKING MY MARE.
EVEN IN *DEATH* THE TWO WANT TO *FIGHT*!
HA HA HA HA!
HO YO TO HO! SIEGRUNÉ COMES NOW!

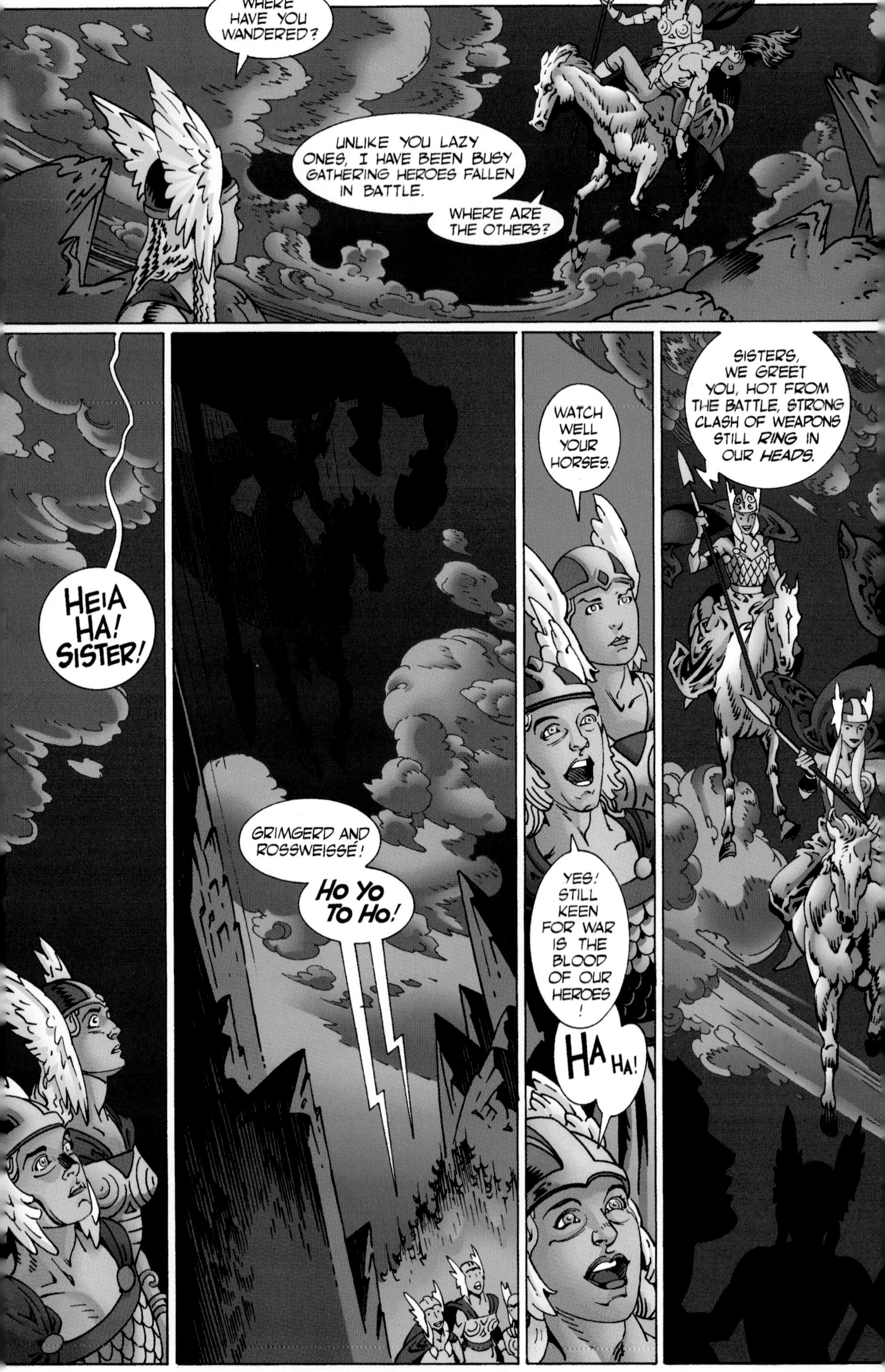

WHERE HAVE YOU WANDERED?
UNLIKE YOU LAZY ONES, I HAVE BEEN BUSY GATHERING HEROES FALLEN IN BATTLE.
WHERE ARE THE OTHERS?
HEIA HA! SISTER!
GRIMGERD AND ROSSWEISSE!
HO YO TO HO!
WATCH WELL YOUR HORSES.
YES! STILL KEEN FOR WAR IS THE BLOOD OF OUR HEROES!
HA HA!
SISTERS, WE GREET YOU, HOT FROM THE BATTLE, STRONG CLASH OF WEAPONS STILL RING IN OUR HEADS.

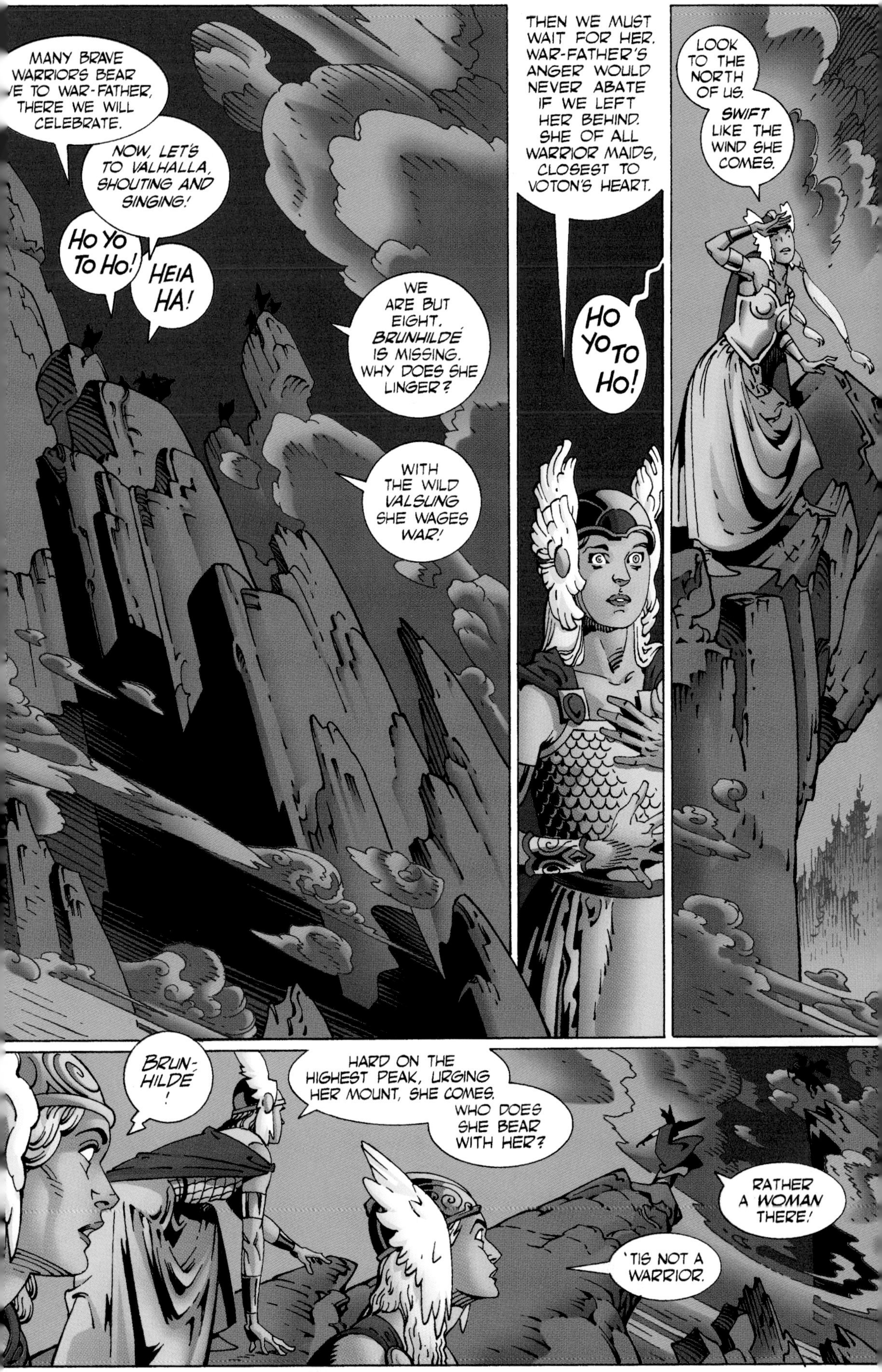

MANY BRAVE WARRIORS BEAR WE TO WAR-FATHER, THERE WE WILL CELEBRATE.
NOW, LET'S TO VALHALLA, SHOUTING AND SINGING!
HO YO TO HO!
HEIA HA!
WE ARE BUT EIGHT. BRUNHILDÉ IS MISSING. WHY DOES SHE LINGER?
WITH THE WILD VALSUNG SHE WAGES WAR!
THEN WE MUST WAIT FOR HER. WAR-FATHER'S ANGER WOULD NEVER ABATE IF WE LEFT HER BEHIND. SHE OF ALL WARRIOR MAIDS, CLOSEST TO VOTON'S HEART.
HO YO TO HO!
LOOK TO THE NORTH OF US. SWIFT LIKE THE WIND SHE COMES.
BRUN-HILDÉ!
HARD ON THE HIGHEST PEAK, URGING HER MOUNT, SHE COMES.
WHO DOES SHE BEAR WITH HER?
'TIS NOT A WARRIOR.
RATHER A WOMAN THERE!

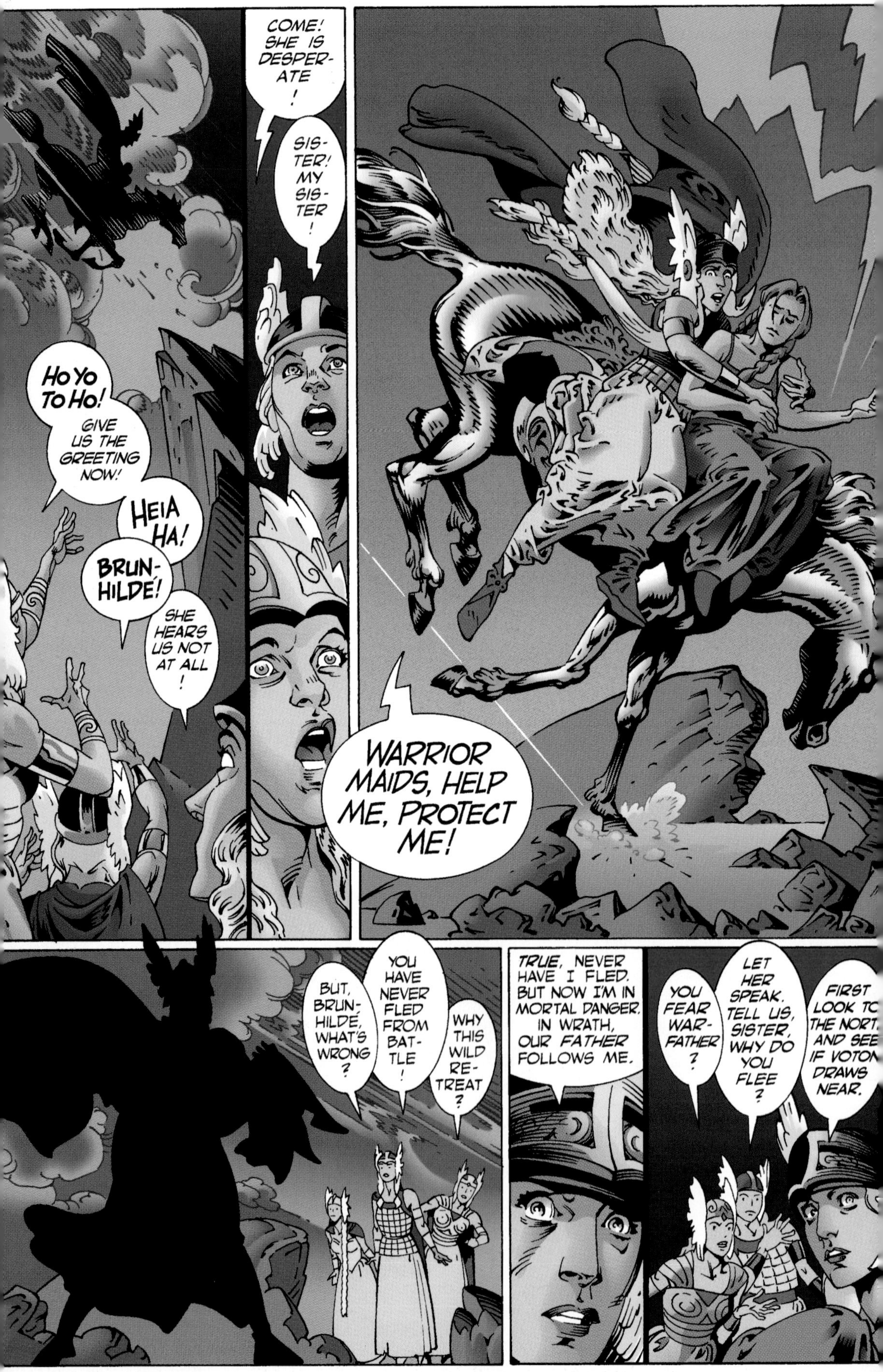

Ho Yo To Ho! GIVE US THE GREETING NOW!
HEIA HA!
BRUN-HILDE!
SHE HEARS US NOT AT ALL!
COME! SHE IS DESPER-ATE!
SIS-TER! MY SIS-TER!
WARRIOR MAIDS, HELP ME, PROTECT ME!
BUT, BRUN-HILDE, WHAT'S WRONG?
YOU HAVE NEVER FLED FROM BAT-TLE!
WHY THIS WILD RE-TREAT?
TRUE, NEVER HAVE I FLED. BUT NOW I'M IN MORTAL DANGER. IN WRATH, OUR FATHER FOLLOWS ME.
YOU FEAR WAR-FATHER?
LET HER SPEAK. TELL US, SISTER, WHY DO YOU FLEE?

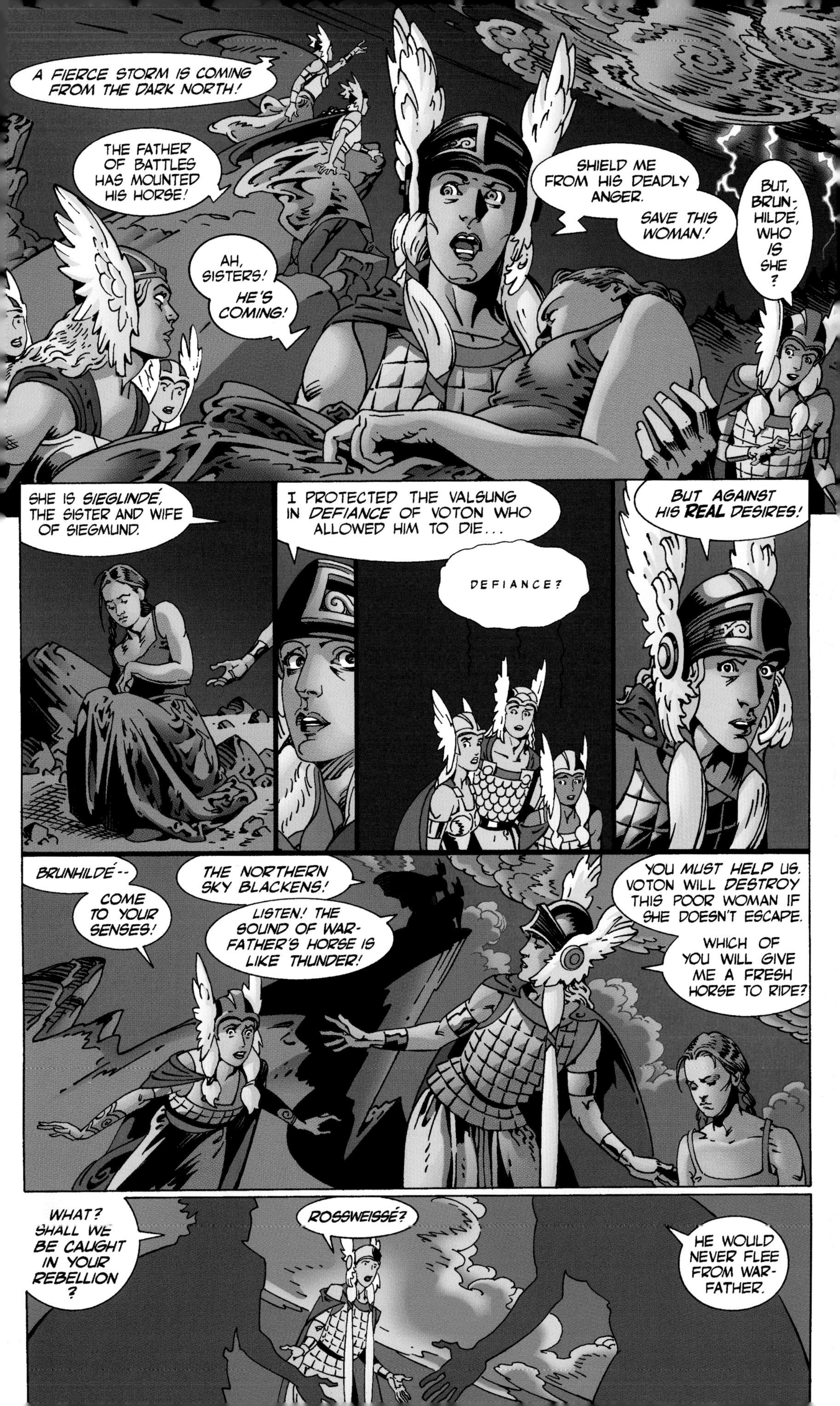
A FIERCE STORM IS COMING FROM THE DARK NORTH!
THE FATHER OF BATTLES HAS MOUNTED HIS HORSE!
AH, SISTERS!
HE'S COMING!
SHIELD ME FROM HIS DEADLY ANGER.
SAVE THIS WOMAN!
BUT, BRUN-HILDE, WHO IS SHE?
SHE IS SIEGLINDE, THE SISTER AND WIFE OF SIEGMUND.
I PROTECTED THE VALSUNG IN DEFIANCE OF VOTON WHO ALLOWED HIM TO DIE...
DEFIANCE?
BUT AGAINST HIS REAL DESIRES!
BRUNHILDÉ--
COME TO YOUR SENSES!
THE NORTHERN SKY BLACKENS!
LISTEN! THE SOUND OF WAR-FATHER'S HORSE IS LIKE THUNDER!
YOU MUST HELP US. VOTON WILL DESTROY THIS POOR WOMAN IF SHE DOESN'T ESCAPE.
WHICH OF YOU WILL GIVE ME A FRESH HORSE TO RIDE?
WHAT? SHALL WE BE CAUGHT IN YOUR REBELLION?
ROSSWEISSÉ?
HE WOULD NEVER FLEE FROM WAR-FATHER.

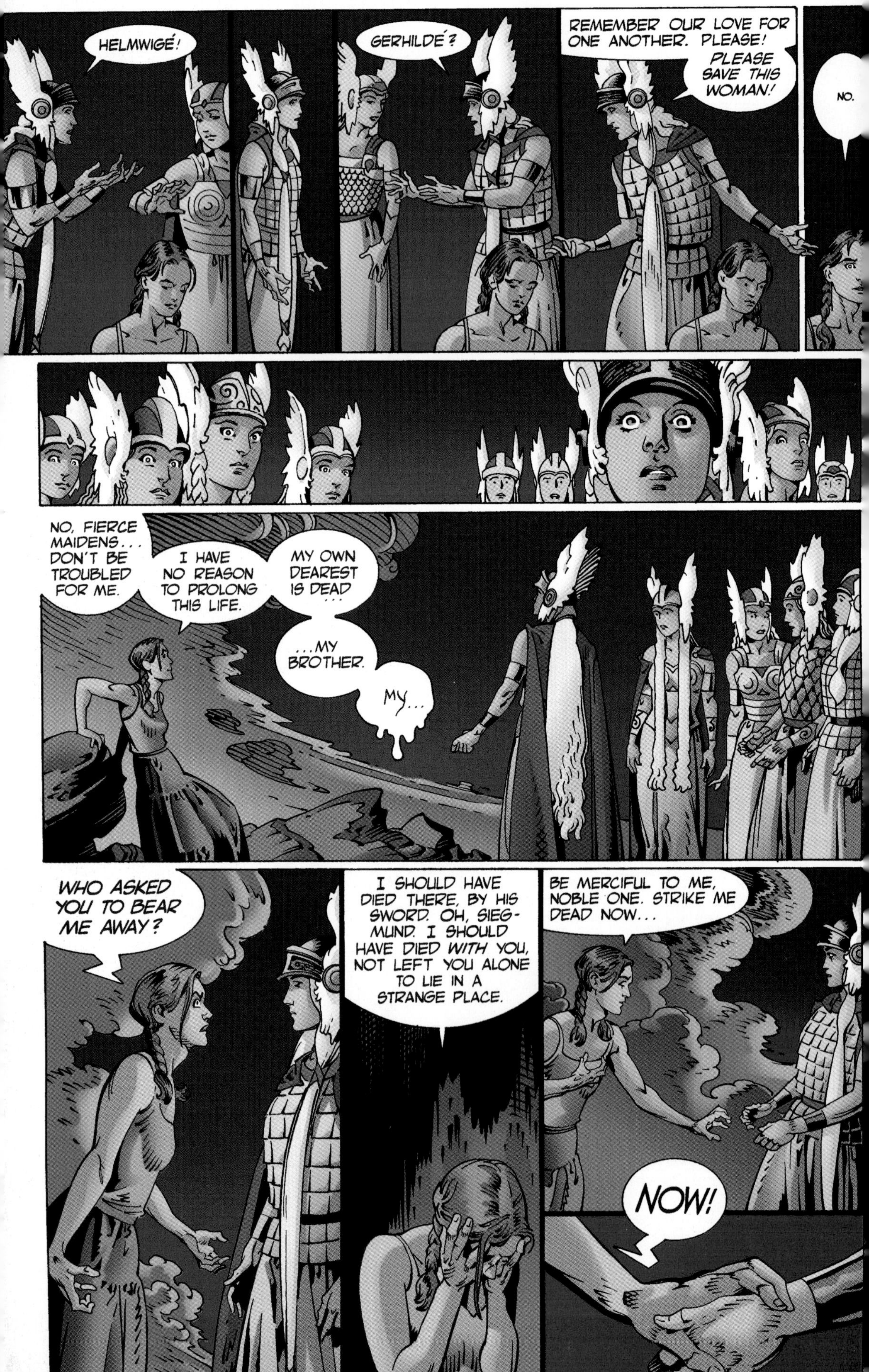
HELMWIGÉ!
GERHILDÉ?
REMEMBER OUR LOVE FOR ONE ANOTHER. PLEASE!
PLEASE SAVE THIS WOMAN!
NO.
NO, FIERCE MAIDENS... DON'T BE TROUBLED FOR ME.
I HAVE NO REASON TO PROLONG THIS LIFE.
MY OWN DEAREST IS DEAD...
...MY BROTHER.
MY...
WHO ASKED YOU TO BEAR ME AWAY?
I SHOULD HAVE DIED THERE, BY HIS SWORD. OH, SIEG-MUND. I SHOULD HAVE DIED WITH YOU, NOT LEFT YOU ALONE TO LIE IN A STRANGE PLACE.
BE MERCIFUL TO ME, NOBLE ONE. STRIKE ME DEAD NOW...
NOW!

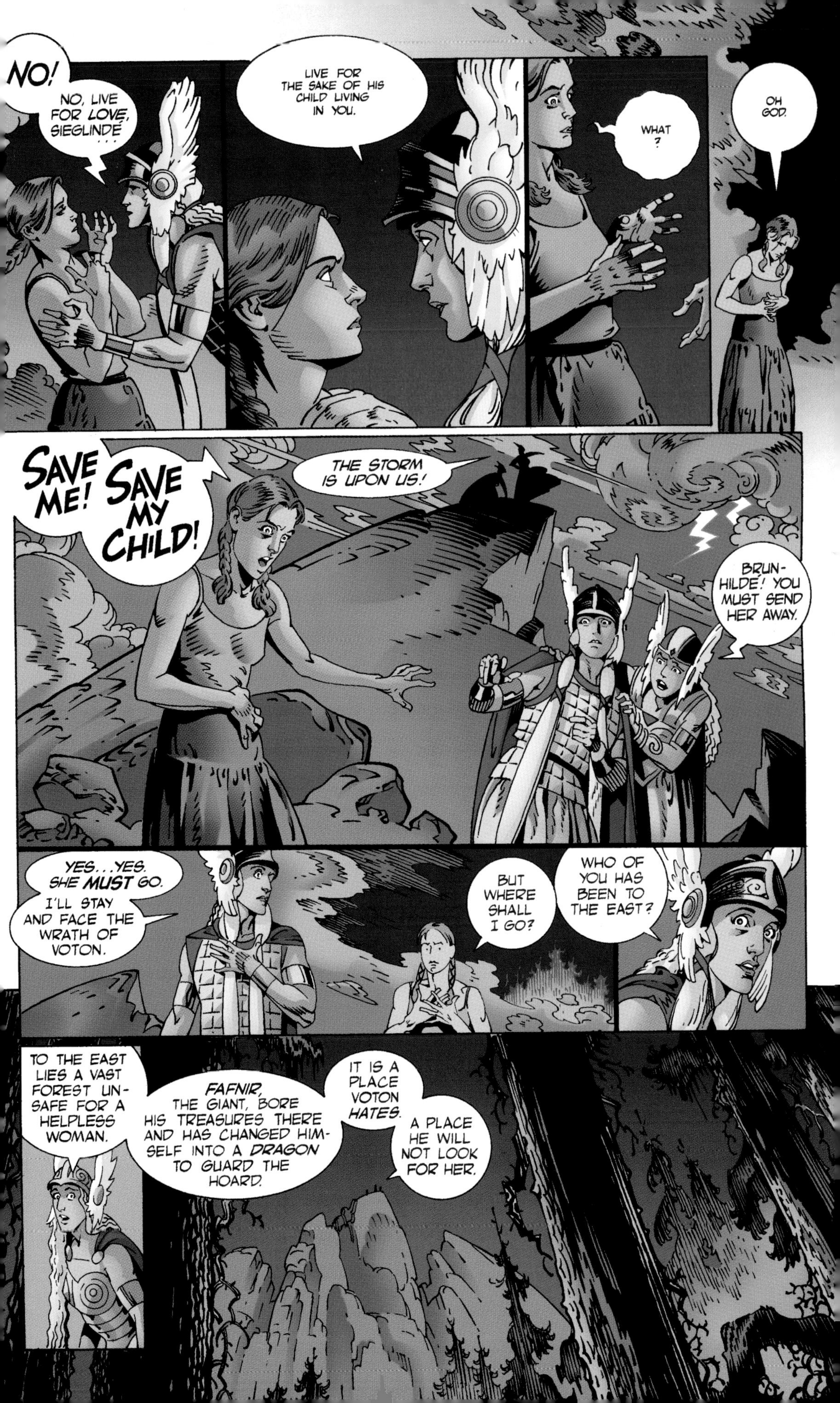

NO!
NO, LIVE FOR LOVE, SIEGLINDE . . .
LIVE FOR THE SAKE OF HIS CHILD LIVING IN YOU.
WHAT ?
OH GOD.
SAVE ME! SAVE MY CHILD!
THE STORM IS UPON US!
BRUN-HILDE! YOU MUST SEND HER AWAY.
YES... YES. SHE MUST GO.
I'LL STAY AND FACE THE WRATH OF VOTON.
BUT WHERE SHALL I GO?
WHO OF YOU HAS BEEN TO THE EAST?
TO THE EAST LIES A VAST FOREST UN-SAFE FOR A HELPLESS WOMAN.
FAFNIR, THE GIANT, BORE HIS TREASURES THERE AND HAS CHANGED HIM-SELF INTO A DRAGON TO GUARD THE HOARD.
IT IS A PLACE VOTON HATES.
A PLACE HE WILL NOT LOOK FOR HER.

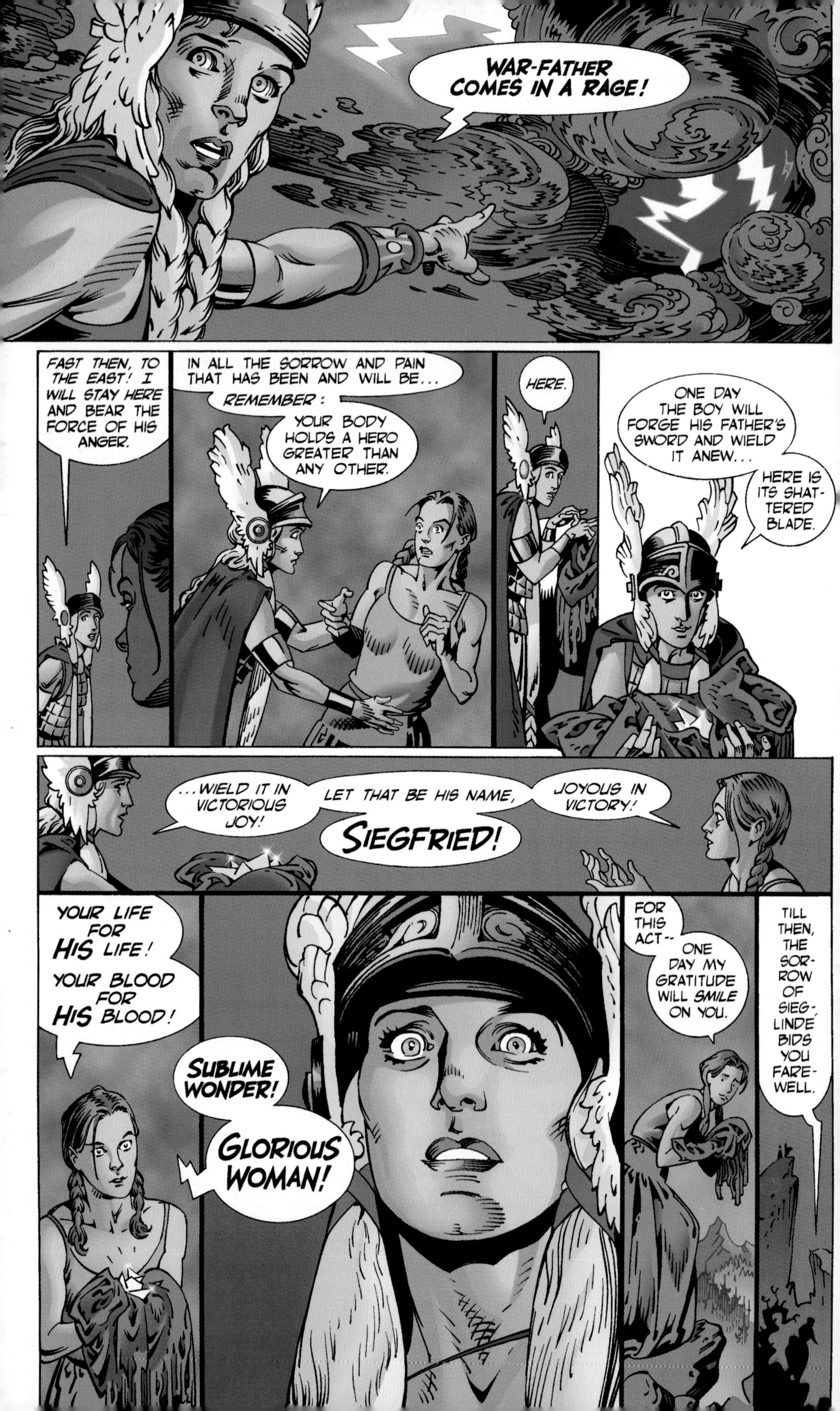
WAR-FATHER COMES IN A RAGE!
FAST THEN, TO THE EAST! I WILL STAY HERE AND BEAR THE FORCE OF HIS ANGER.
IN ALL THE SORROW AND PAIN THAT HAS BEEN AND WILL BE...
REMEMBER:
YOUR BODY HOLDS A HERO GREATER THAN ANY OTHER.
HERE.
ONE DAY THE BOY WILL FORGE HIS FATHER'S SWORD AND WIELD IT ANEW...
HERE IS ITS SHATTERED BLADE.
...WIELD IT IN VICTORIOUS JOY!
LET THAT BE HIS NAME,
JOYOUS IN VICTORY!
SIEGFRIED!
YOUR LIFE FOR HIS LIFE!
YOUR BLOOD FOR HIS BLOOD!
SUBLIME WONDER!
GLORIOUS WOMAN!
FOR THIS ACT--
ONE DAY MY GRATITUDE WILL SMILE ON YOU.
TILL THEN, THE SORROW OF SIEGLINDE BIDS YOU FAREWELL.

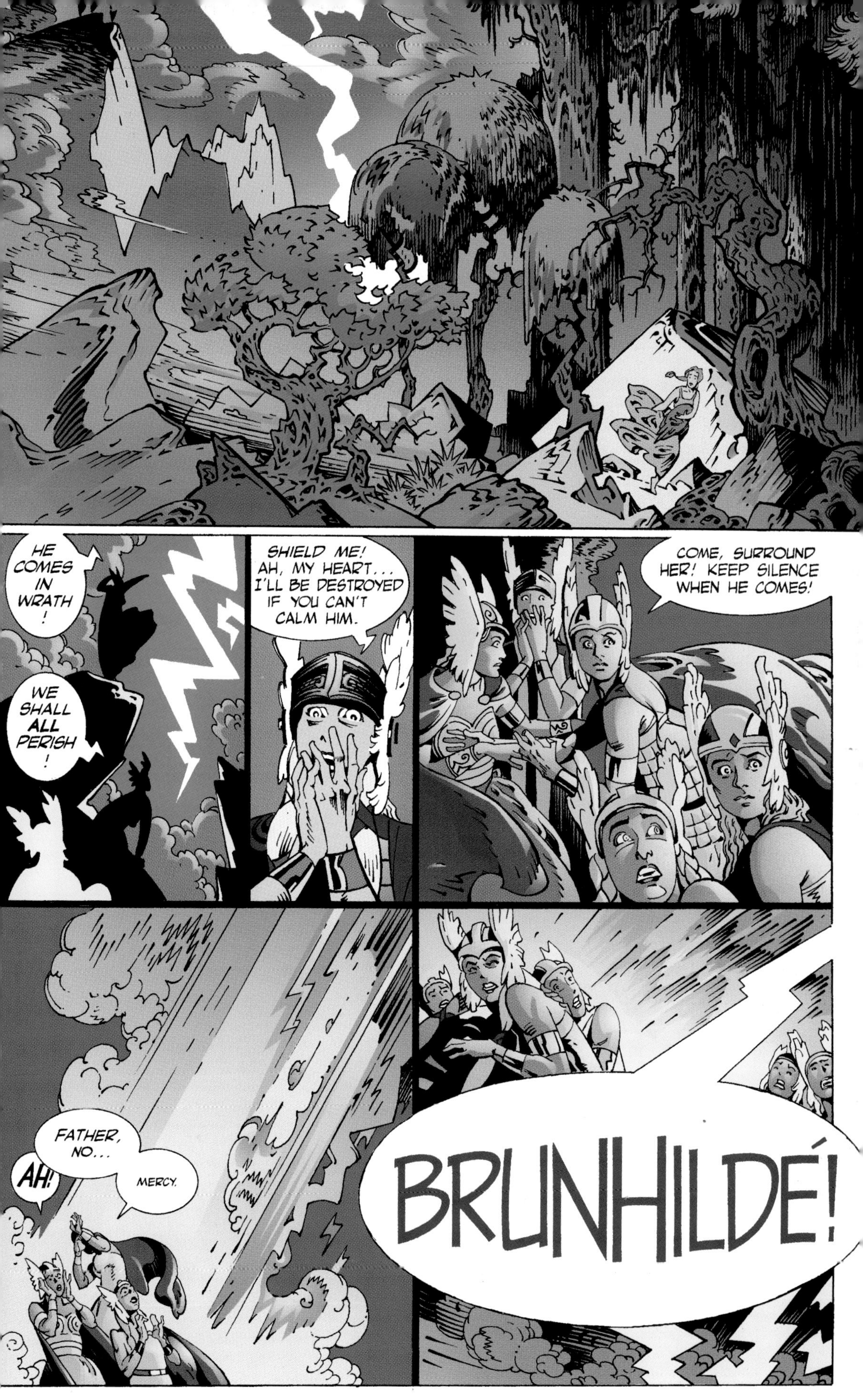
HE COMES IN WRATH!
WE SHALL ALL PERISH!
SHIELD ME! AH, MY HEART... I'LL BE DESTROYED IF YOU CAN'T CALM HIM.
COME, SURROUND HER! KEEP SILENCE WHEN HE COMES!
FATHER, NO...
AH!
MERCY.
BRUNHILDÉ!

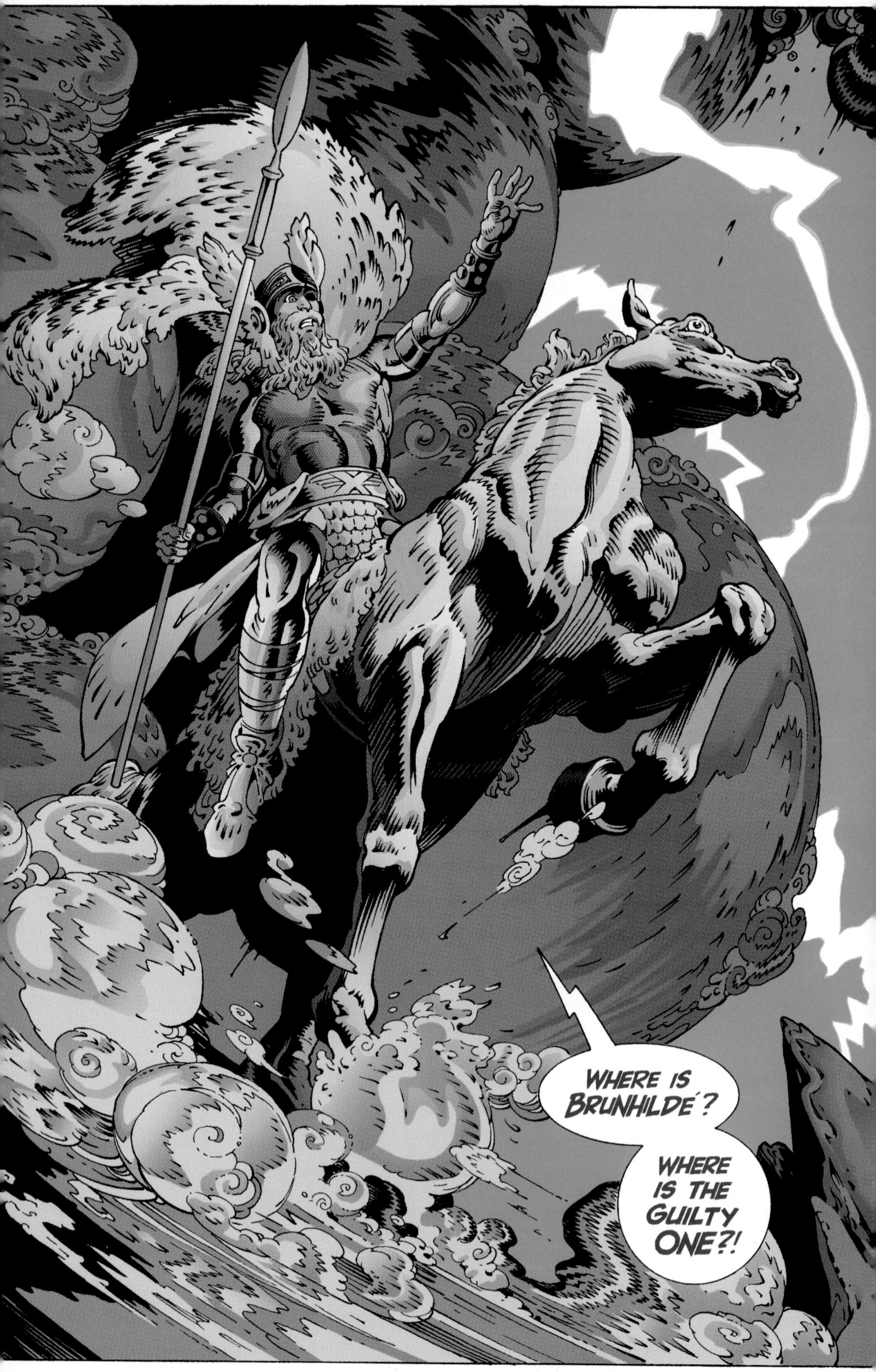
WHERE IS BRUNHILDÉ?
WHERE IS THE GUILTY ONE?!

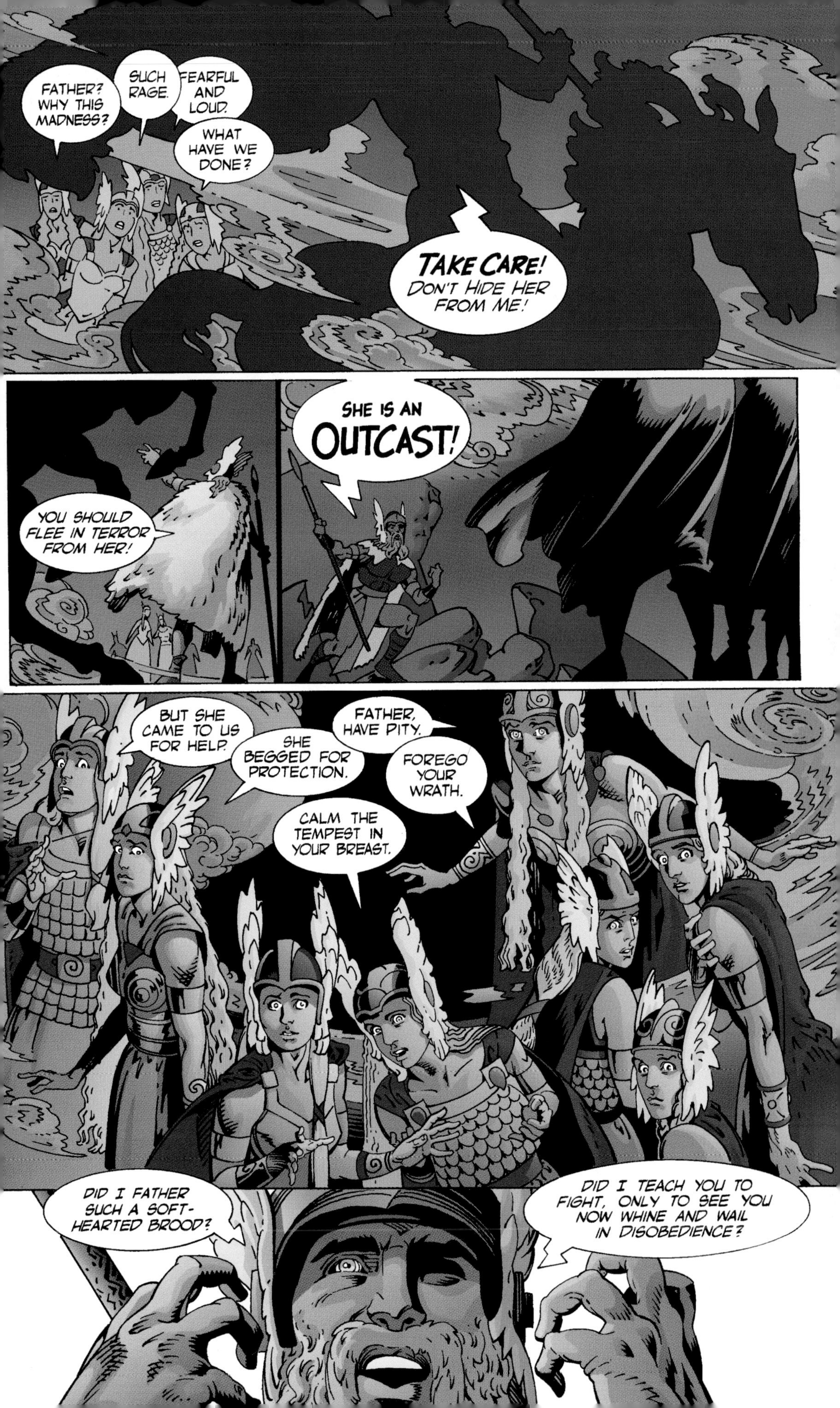
FATHER? WHY THIS MADNESS?
SUCH RAGE.
FEARFUL AND LOUD.
WHAT HAVE WE DONE?
TAKE CARE! DON'T HIDE HER FROM ME!
YOU SHOULD FLEE IN TERROR FROM HER!
SHE IS AN OUTCAST!
BUT SHE CAME TO US FOR HELP.
SHE BEGGED FOR PROTECTION.
FATHER, HAVE PITY.
FOREGO YOUR WRATH.
CALM THE TEMPEST IN YOUR BREAST.
DID I FATHER SUCH A SOFT-HEARTED BROOD?
DID I TEACH YOU TO FIGHT, ONLY TO SEE YOU NOW WHINE AND WAIL IN DISOBEDIENCE?

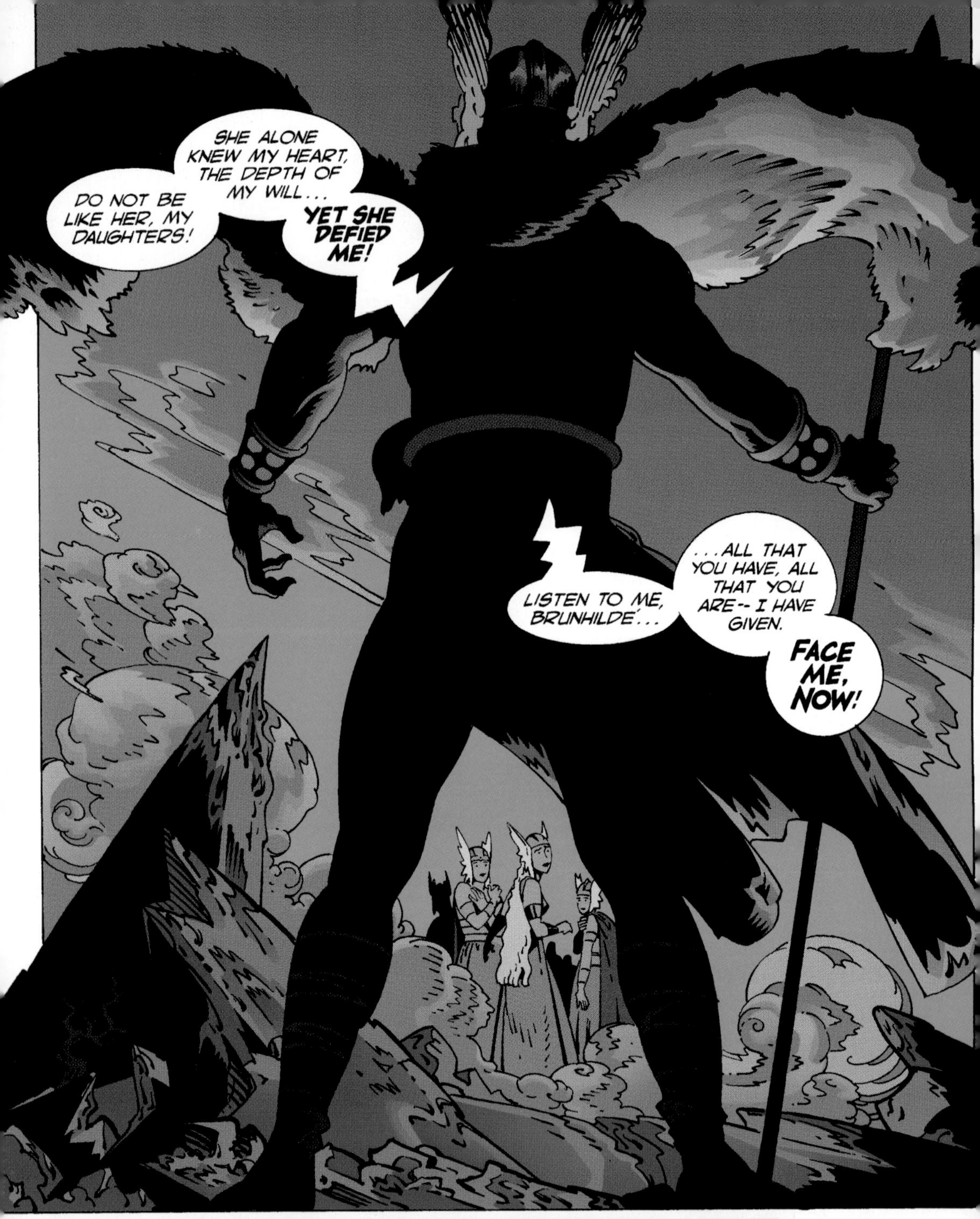
DO NOT BE LIKE HER, MY DAUGHTERS!
SHE ALONE KNEW MY HEART, THE DEPTH OF MY WILL...
YET SHE DEFIED ME!
LISTEN TO ME, BRUNHILDE...
...ALL THAT YOU HAVE, ALL THAT YOU ARE-- I HAVE GIVEN.
FACE ME, NOW!

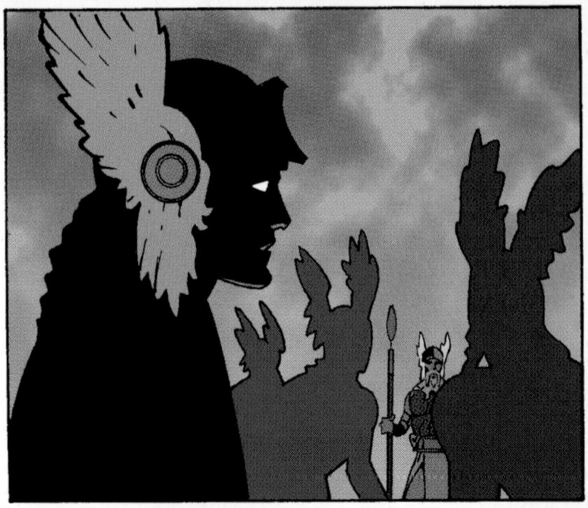

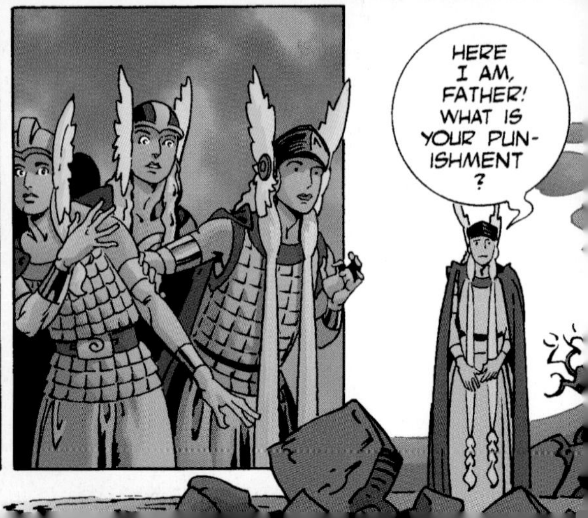
HERE I AM, FATHER! WHAT IS YOUR PUNISHMENT?

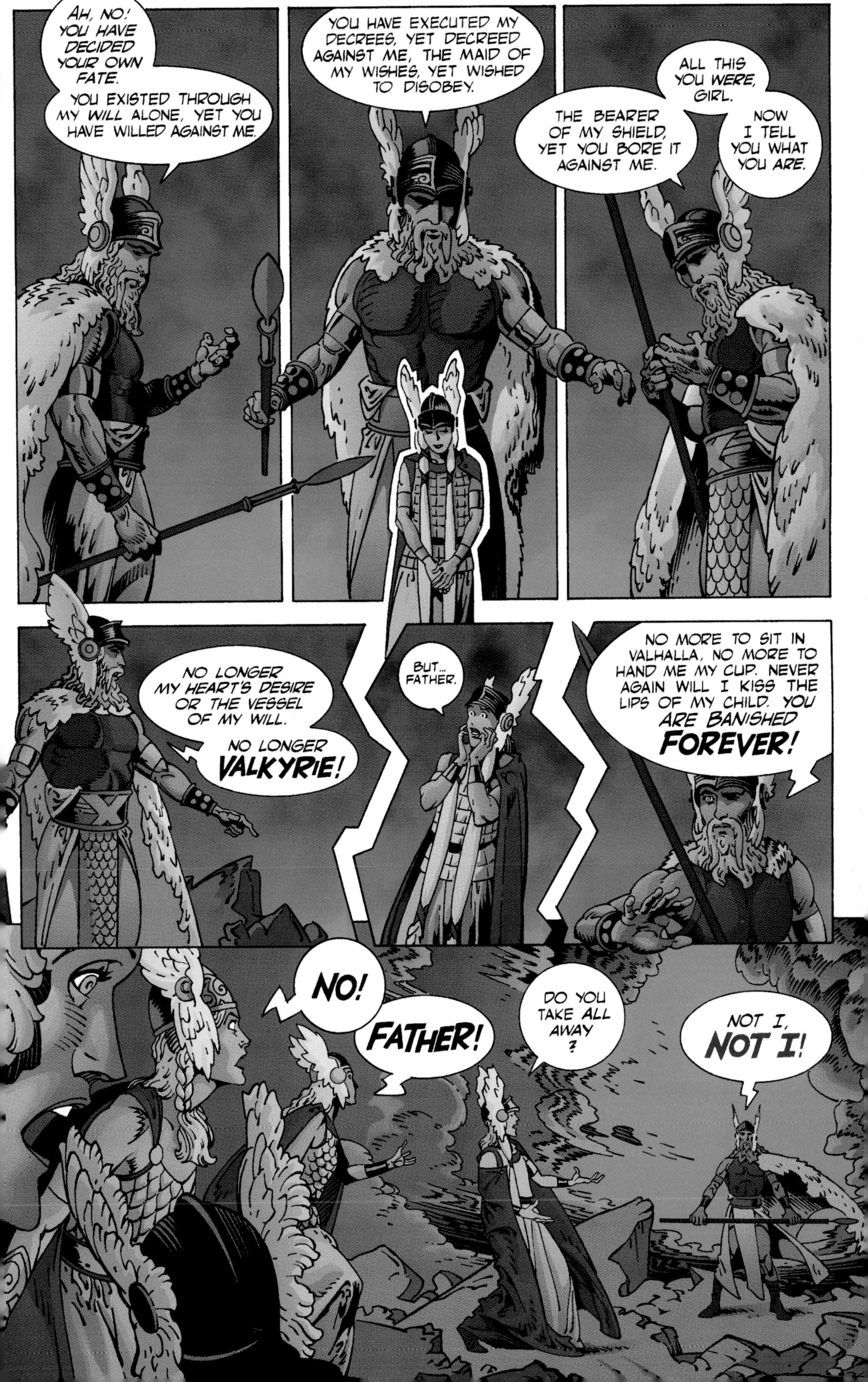
AH, NO! YOU HAVE DECIDED YOUR OWN FATE.
YOU EXISTED THROUGH MY WILL ALONE, YET YOU HAVE WILLED AGAINST ME.
YOU HAVE EXECUTED MY DECREES, YET DECREED AGAINST ME, THE MAID OF MY WISHES, YET WISHED TO DISOBEY.
THE BEARER OF MY SHIELD, YET YOU BORE IT AGAINST ME.
ALL THIS YOU WERE, GIRL.
NOW I TELL YOU WHAT YOU ARE.
NO LONGER MY HEART'S DESIRE OR THE VESSEL OF MY WILL.
NO LONGER VALKYRIE!
BUT... FATHER.
NO MORE TO SIT IN VALHALLA, NO MORE TO HAND ME MY CUP. NEVER AGAIN WILL I KISS THE LIPS OF MY CHILD. YOU ARE BANISHED FOREVER!
NO!
FATHER!
DO YOU TAKE ALL AWAY?
NOT I, NOT I!

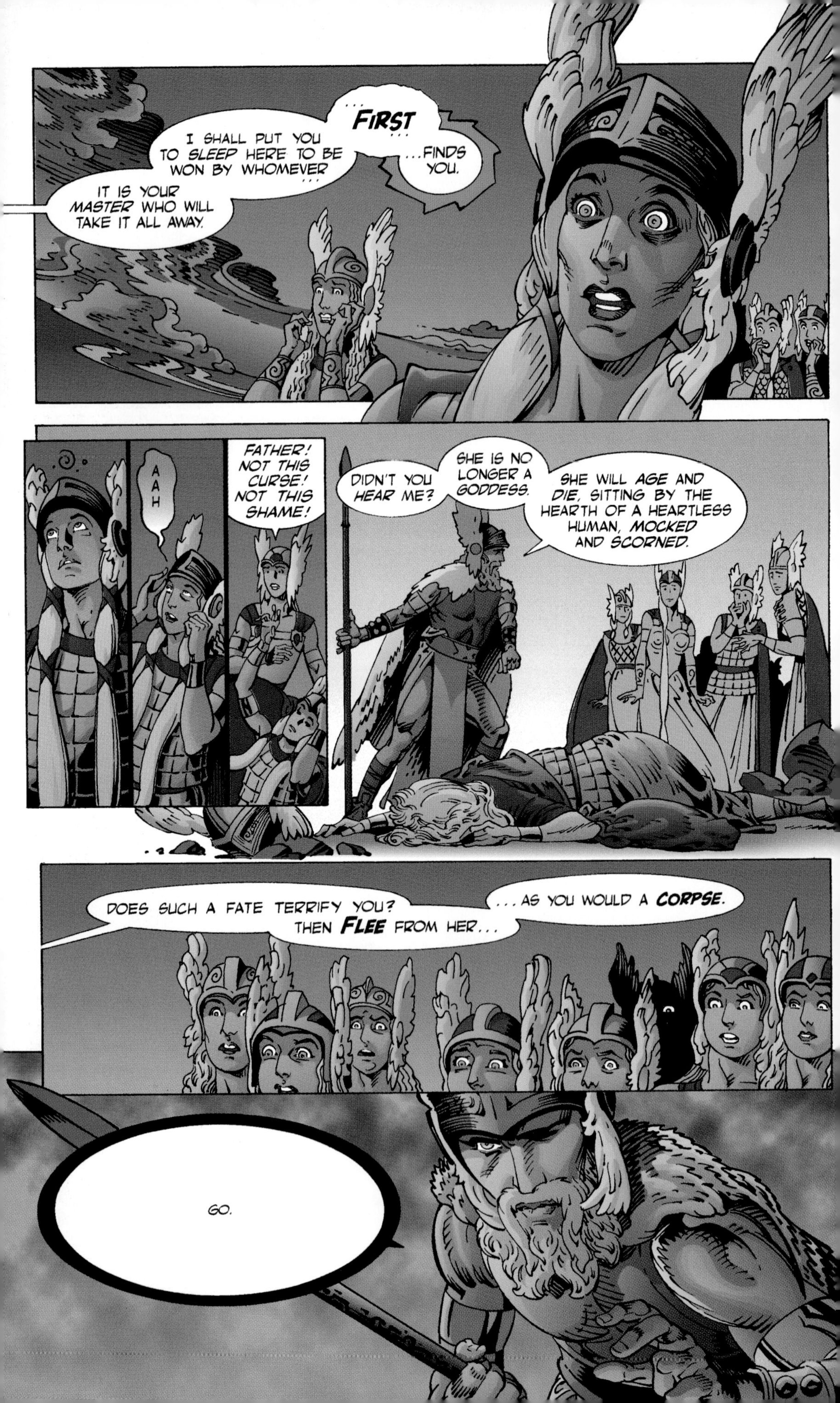
IT IS YOUR MASTER WHO WILL TAKE IT ALL AWAY.
I SHALL PUT YOU TO SLEEP HERE TO BE WON BY WHOMEVER . . .
. . . FIRST . . .
. . . FINDS YOU.
A A H
FATHER! NOT THIS CURSE! NOT THIS SHAME!
DIDN'T YOU HEAR ME?
SHE IS NO LONGER A GODDESS.
SHE WILL AGE AND DIE, SITTING BY THE HEARTH OF A HEARTLESS HUMAN, MOCKED AND SCORNED.
DOES SUCH A FATE TERRIFY YOU? THEN FLEE FROM HER . . .
. . . AS YOU WOULD A CORPSE.
GO.

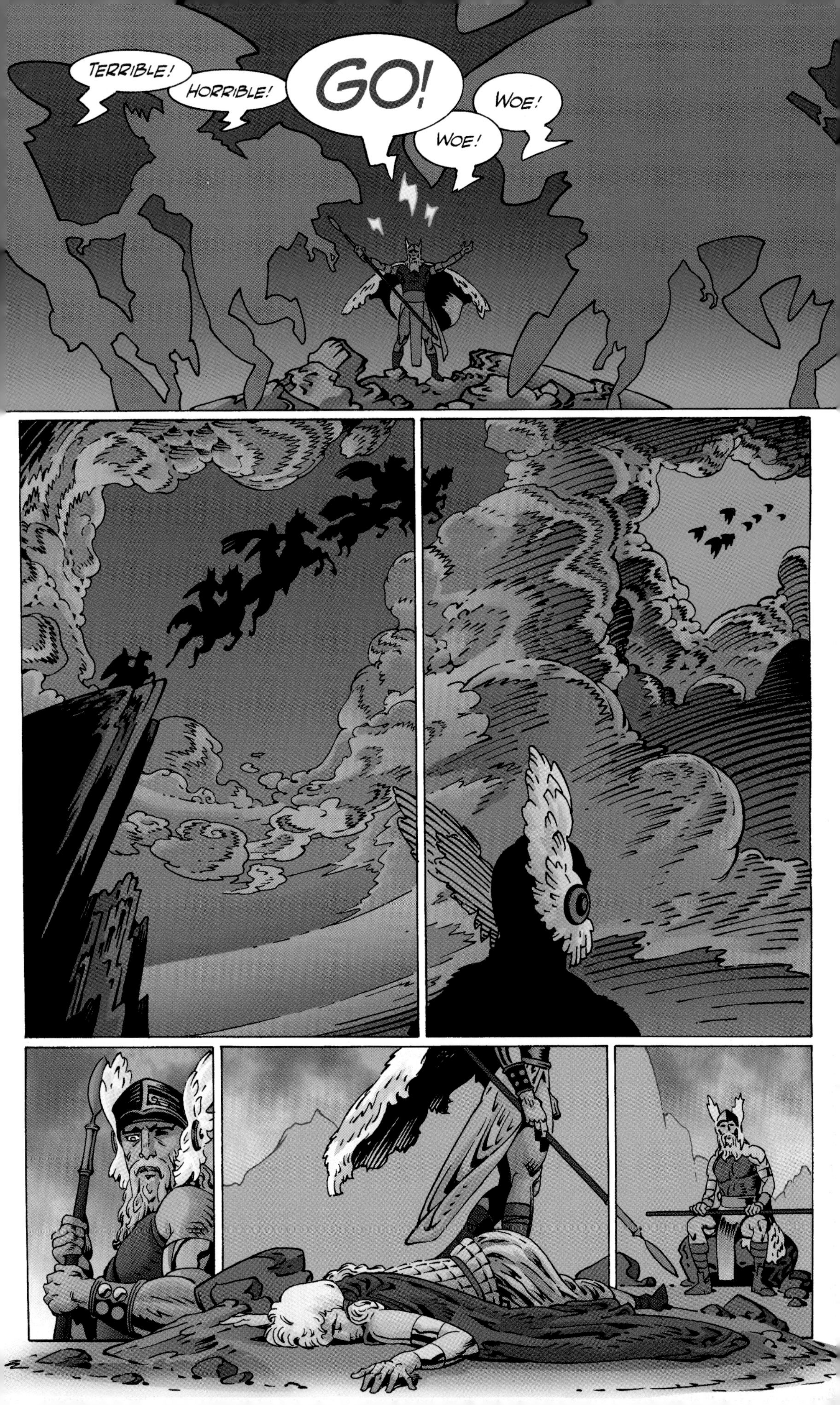

TERRIBLE!
HORRIBLE!
GO!
WOE!
WOE!

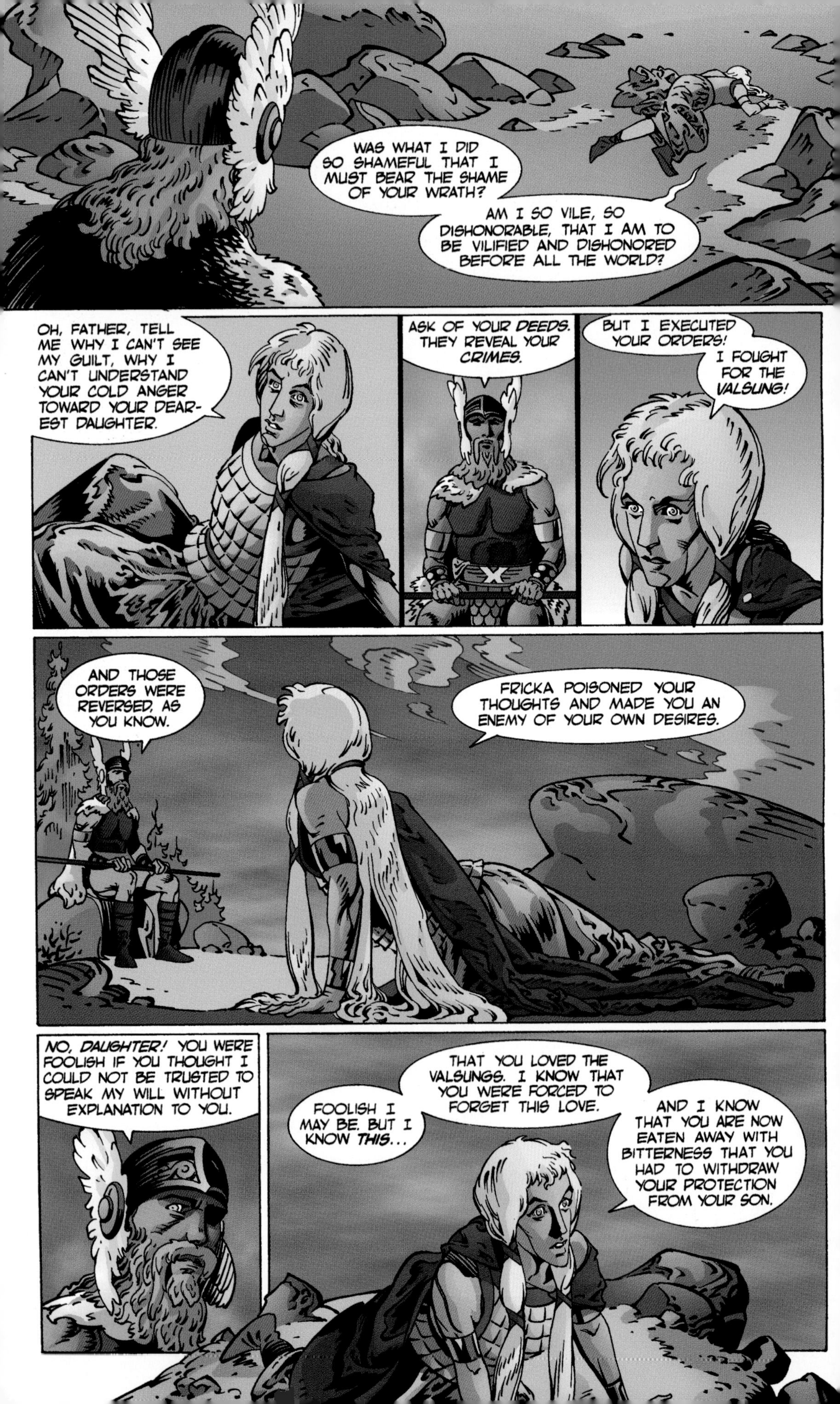
WAS WHAT I DID SO SHAMEFUL THAT I MUST BEAR THE SHAME OF YOUR WRATH?
AM I SO VILE, SO DISHONORABLE, THAT I AM TO BE VILIFIED AND DISHONORED BEFORE ALL THE WORLD?
OH, FATHER, TELL ME WHY I CAN'T SEE MY GUILT, WHY I CAN'T UNDERSTAND YOUR COLD ANGER TOWARD YOUR DEAREST DAUGHTER.
ASK OF YOUR DEEDS. THEY REVEAL YOUR CRIMES.
BUT I EXECUTED YOUR ORDERS!
I FOUGHT FOR THE VALSUNG!
AND THOSE ORDERS WERE REVERSED, AS YOU KNOW.
FRICKA POISONED YOUR THOUGHTS AND MADE YOU AN ENEMY OF YOUR OWN DESIRES.
NO, DAUGHTER! YOU WERE FOOLISH IF YOU THOUGHT I COULD NOT BE TRUSTED TO SPEAK MY WILL WITHOUT EXPLANATION TO YOU.
FOOLISH I MAY BE. BUT I KNOW THIS...
THAT YOU LOVED THE VALSUNGS. I KNOW THAT YOU WERE FORCED TO FORGET THIS LOVE.
AND I KNOW THAT YOU ARE NOW EATEN AWAY WITH BITTERNESS THAT YOU HAD TO WITHDRAW YOUR PROTECTION FROM YOUR SON.

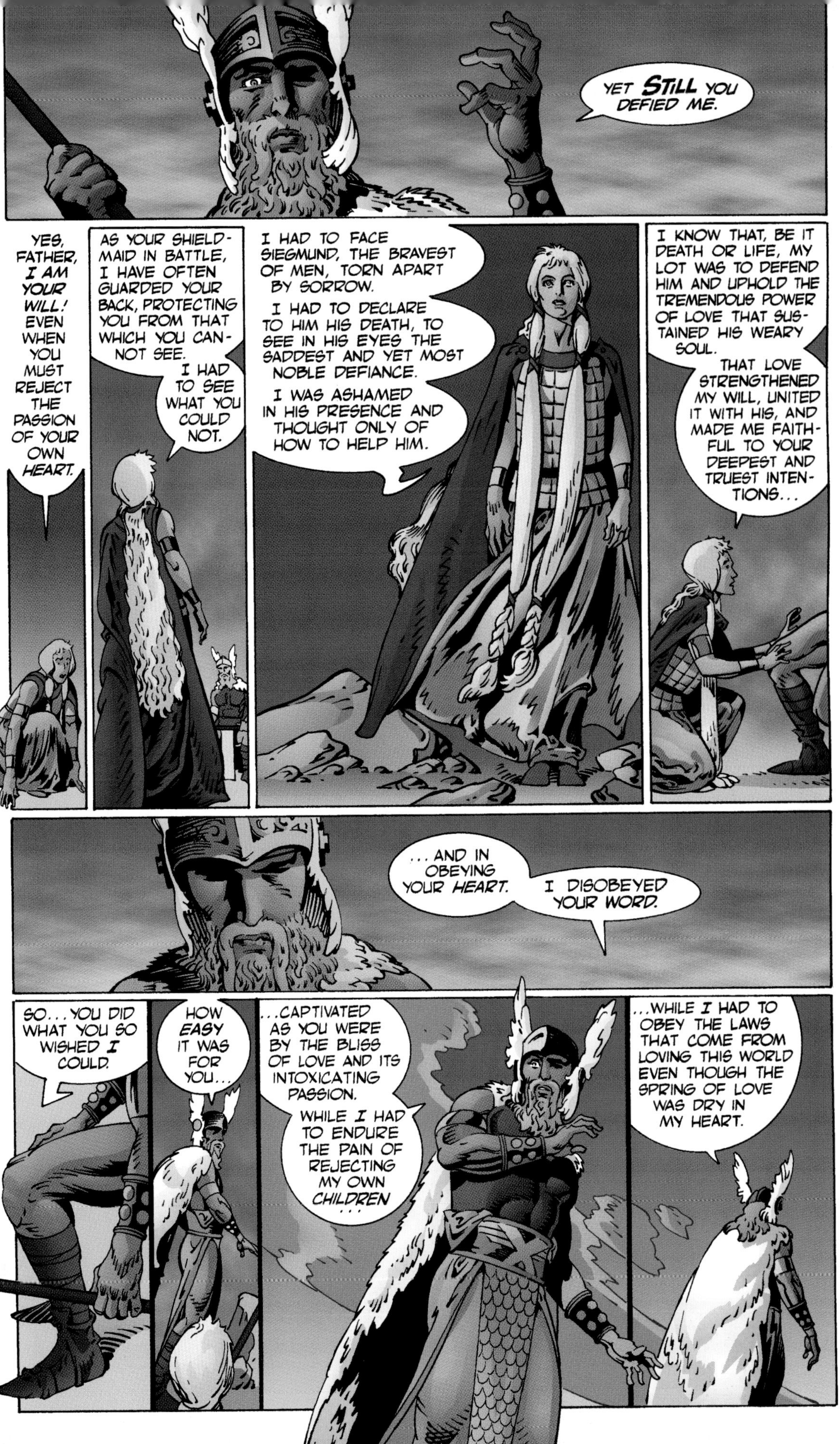
YET STILL YOU DEFIED ME.
YES, FATHER, I AM YOUR WILL! EVEN WHEN YOU MUST REJECT THE PASSION OF YOUR OWN HEART.
AS YOUR SHIELD-MAID IN BATTLE, I HAVE OFTEN GUARDED YOUR BACK, PROTECTING YOU FROM THAT WHICH YOU CANNOT SEE.
I HAD TO SEE WHAT YOU COULD NOT.
I HAD TO FACE SIEGMUND, THE BRAVEST OF MEN, TORN APART BY SORROW.
I HAD TO DECLARE TO HIM HIS DEATH, TO SEE IN HIS EYES THE SADDEST AND YET MOST NOBLE DEFIANCE.
I WAS ASHAMED IN HIS PRESENCE AND THOUGHT ONLY OF HOW TO HELP HIM.
I KNOW THAT, BE IT DEATH OR LIFE, MY LOT WAS TO DEFEND HIM AND UPHOLD THE TREMENDOUS POWER OF LOVE THAT SUSTAINED HIS WEARY SOUL.
THAT LOVE STRENGTHENED MY WILL, UNITED IT WITH HIS, AND MADE ME FAITHFUL TO YOUR DEEPEST AND TRUEST INTENTIONS...
...AND IN OBEYING YOUR HEART.
I DISOBEYED YOUR WORD.
SO... YOU DID WHAT YOU SO WISHED I COULD.
HOW EASY IT WAS FOR YOU...
...CAPTIVATED AS YOU WERE BY THE BLISS OF LOVE AND ITS INTOXICATING PASSION.
WHILE I HAD TO ENDURE THE PAIN OF REJECTING MY OWN CHILDREN...
...WHILE I HAD TO OBEY THE LAWS THAT COME FROM LOVING THIS WORLD EVEN THOUGH THE SPRING OF LOVE WAS DRY IN MY HEART.

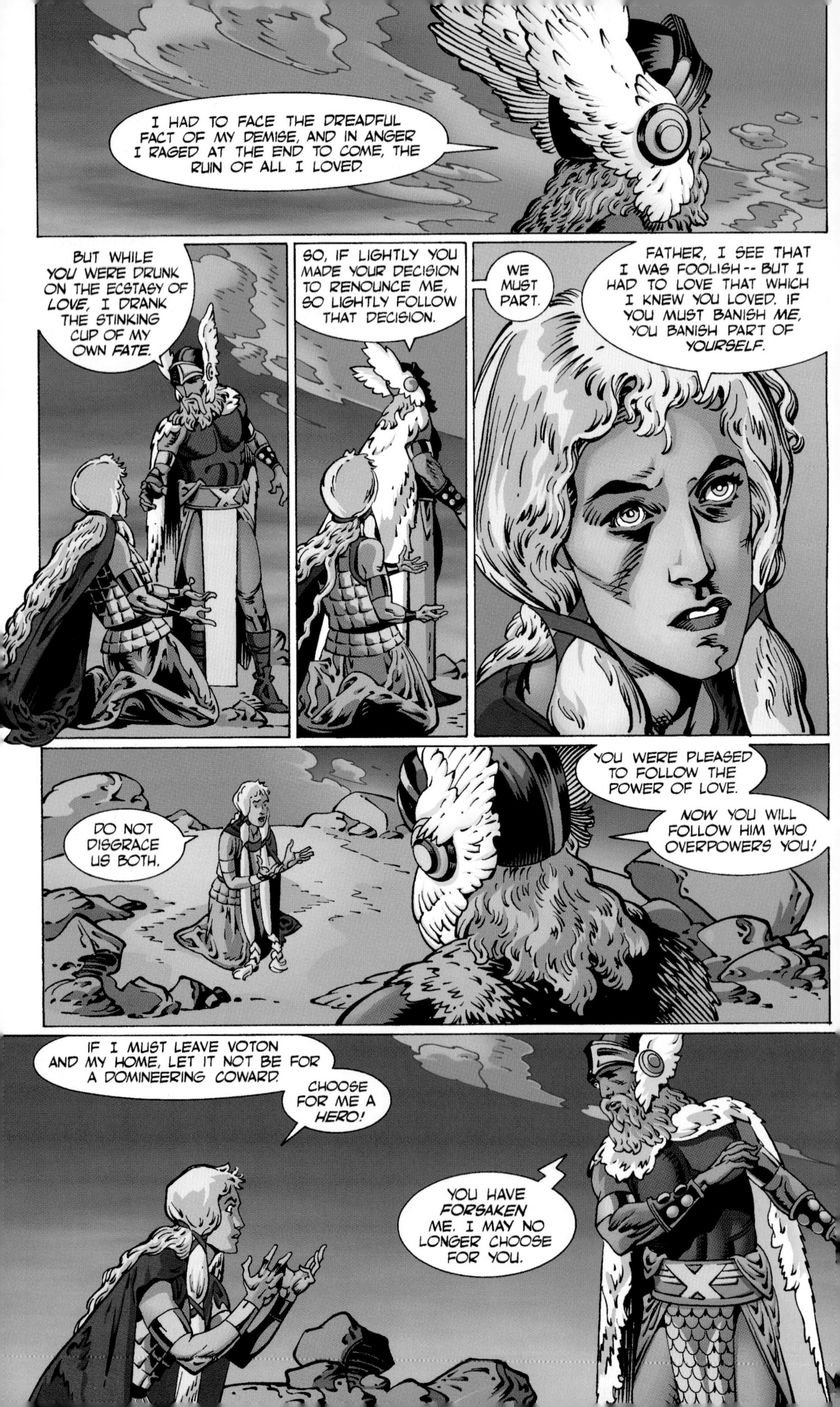
I HAD TO FACE THE DREADFUL FACT OF MY DEMISE, AND IN ANGER I RAGED AT THE END TO COME, THE RUIN OF ALL I LOVED.
BUT WHILE *YOU* WERE DRUNK ON THE ECSTASY OF *LOVE*, I DRANK THE STINKING CUP OF MY OWN *FATE*.
SO, IF LIGHTLY YOU MADE YOUR DECISION TO RENOUNCE ME, SO LIGHTLY FOLLOW THAT DECISION.
WE MUST PART.
FATHER, I SEE THAT I WAS FOOLISH -- BUT I HAD TO LOVE THAT WHICH I KNEW YOU LOVED. IF YOU MUST BANISH *ME*, YOU BANISH PART OF *YOURSELF*.
YOU WERE PLEASED TO FOLLOW THE POWER OF LOVE.
NOW YOU WILL FOLLOW HIM WHO OVERPOWERS YOU!
DO NOT DISGRACE US BOTH.
IF I MUST LEAVE VOTON AND MY HOME, LET IT NOT BE FOR A DOMINEERING COWARD.
CHOOSE FOR ME A *HERO*!
YOU HAVE *FORSAKEN* ME. I MAY NO LONGER CHOOSE FOR YOU.

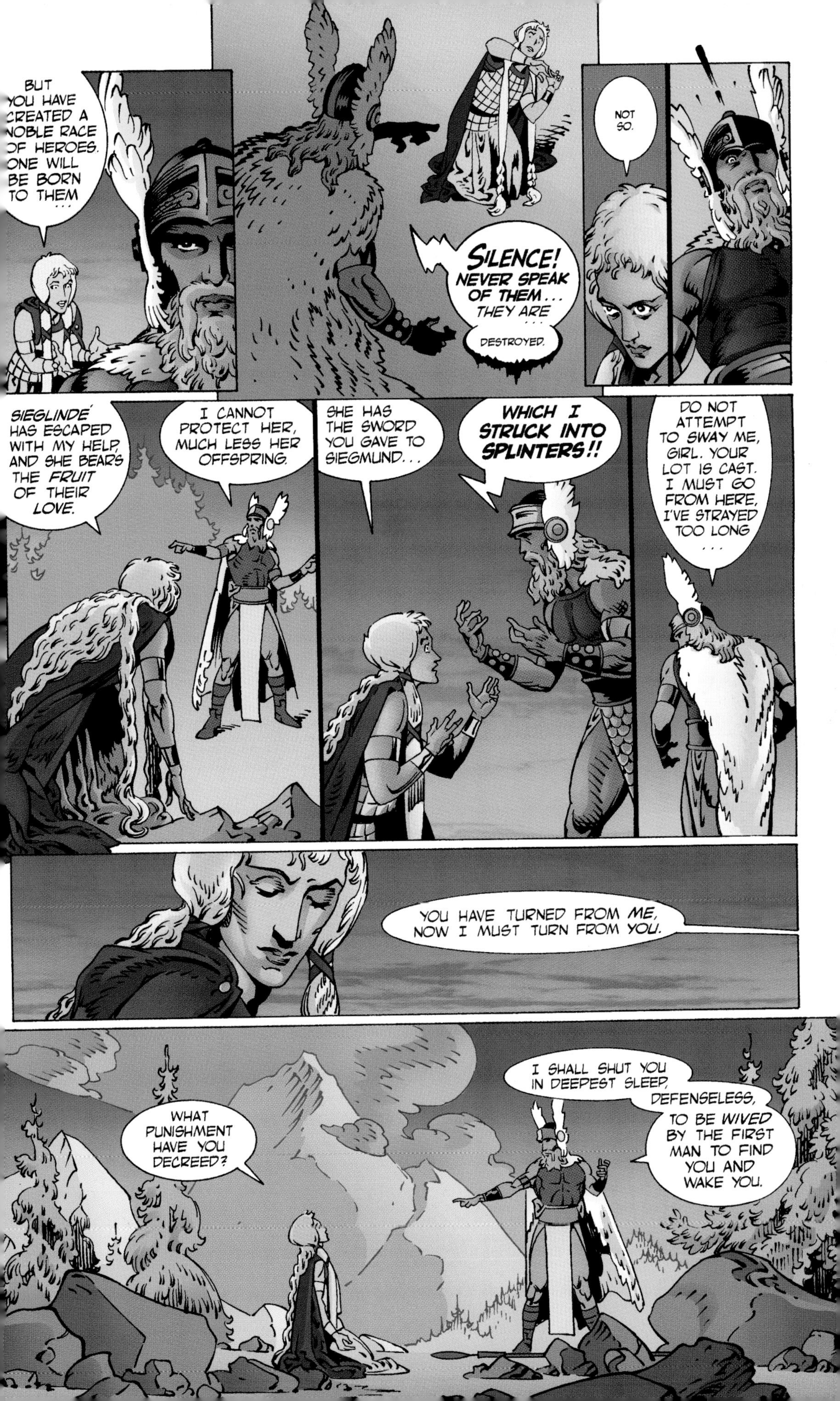
BUT YOU HAVE CREATED A NOBLE RACE OF HEROES. ONE WILL BE BORN TO THEM . . .
SILENCE! NEVER SPEAK OF THEM . . . THEY ARE . . .
DESTROYED.
NOT SO.
SIEGLINDE HAS ESCAPED WITH MY HELP, AND SHE BEARS THE FRUIT OF THEIR LOVE.
I CANNOT PROTECT HER, MUCH LESS HER OFFSPRING.
SHE HAS THE SWORD YOU GAVE TO SIEGMUND . . .
WHICH I STRUCK INTO SPLINTERS!!
DO NOT ATTEMPT TO SWAY ME, GIRL. YOUR LOT IS CAST. I MUST GO FROM HERE, I'VE STRAYED TOO LONG . . .
YOU HAVE TURNED FROM ME, NOW I MUST TURN FROM YOU.
WHAT PUNISHMENT HAVE YOU DECREED?
I SHALL SHUT YOU IN DEEPEST SLEEP,
DEFENSELESS,
TO BE WIVED BY THE FIRST MAN TO FIND YOU AND WAKE YOU.

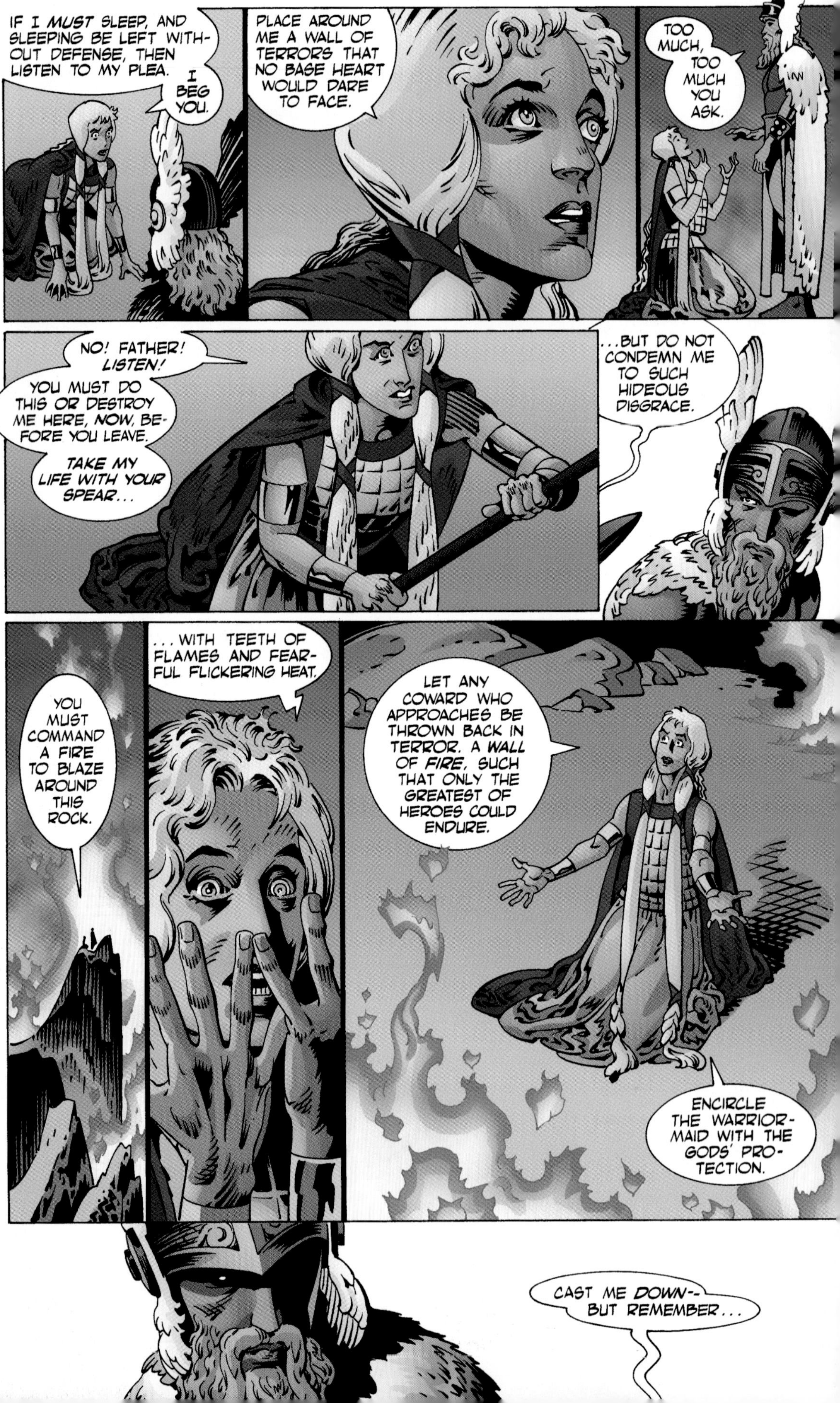
IF I *MUST* SLEEP, AND SLEEPING BE LEFT WITHOUT DEFENSE, THEN LISTEN TO MY PLEA.
I BEG YOU.
PLACE AROUND ME A WALL OF TERRORS THAT NO BASE HEART WOULD DARE TO FACE.
TOO MUCH, TOO MUCH YOU ASK.
NO! FATHER! *LISTEN!*
YOU MUST DO THIS OR DESTROY ME HERE, *NOW*, BEFORE YOU LEAVE.
TAKE MY LIFE WITH YOUR SPEAR...
...BUT DO NOT CONDEMN ME TO SUCH HIDEOUS DISGRACE.
YOU MUST COMMAND A FIRE TO BLAZE AROUND THIS ROCK.
...WITH TEETH OF FLAMES AND FEARFUL FLICKERING HEAT.
LET ANY COWARD WHO APPROACHES BE THROWN BACK IN TERROR. A *WALL* OF *FIRE*, SUCH THAT ONLY THE GREATEST OF HEROES COULD ENDURE.
ENCIRCLE THE WARRIOR-MAID WITH THE GODS' PROTECTION.
CAST ME *DOWN*--BUT REMEMBER...

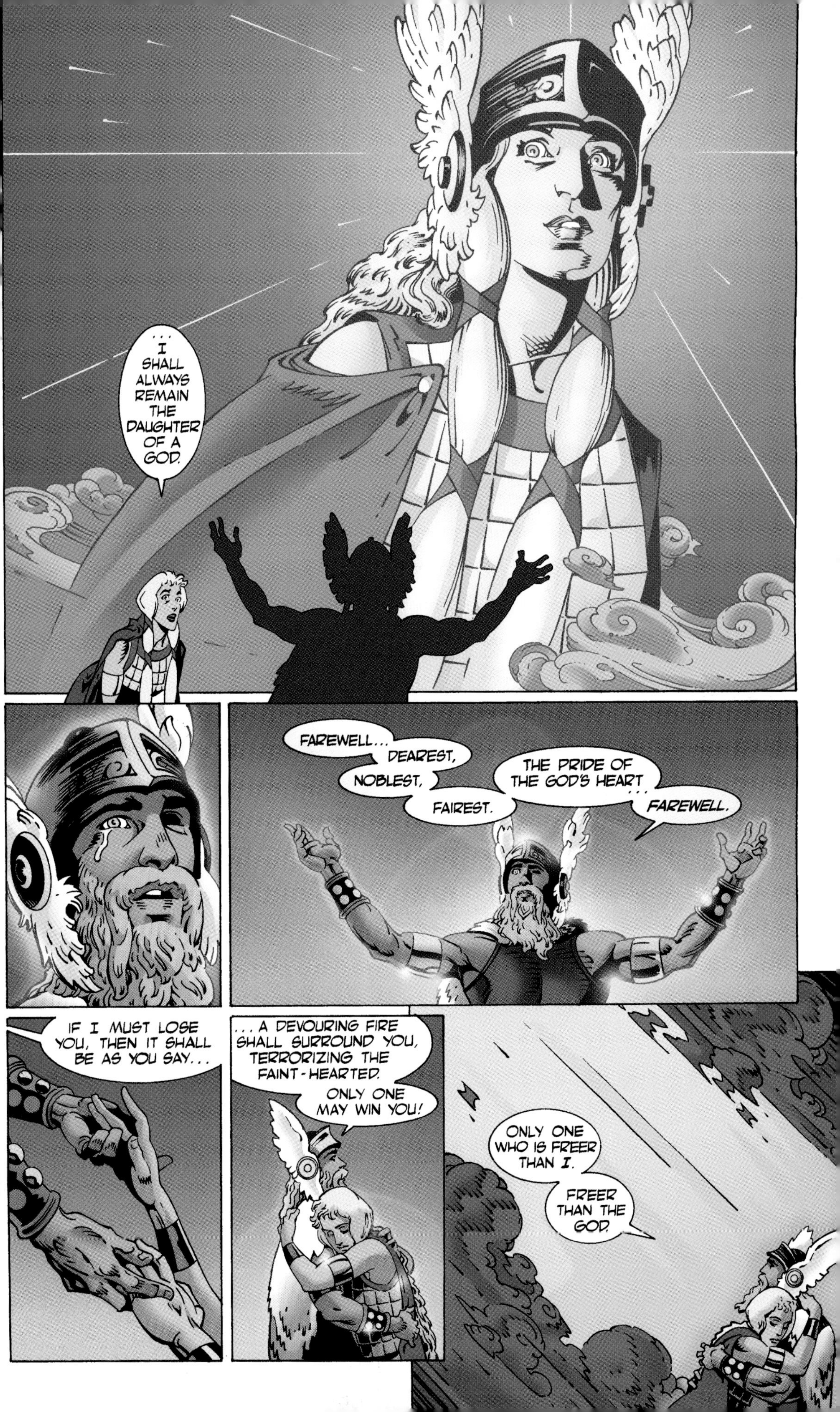

. . . I SHALL ALWAYS REMAIN THE DAUGHTER OF A GOD.
FAREWELL...
DEAREST,
NOBLEST,
FAIREST.
THE PRIDE OF THE GOD'S HEART . . .
FAREWELL.
IF I MUST LOSE YOU, THEN IT SHALL BE AS YOU SAY...
... A DEVOURING FIRE SHALL SURROUND YOU, TERRORIZING THE FAINT-HEARTED.
ONLY ONE MAY WIN YOU!
ONLY ONE WHO IS FREER THAN I.
FREER THAN THE GOD.

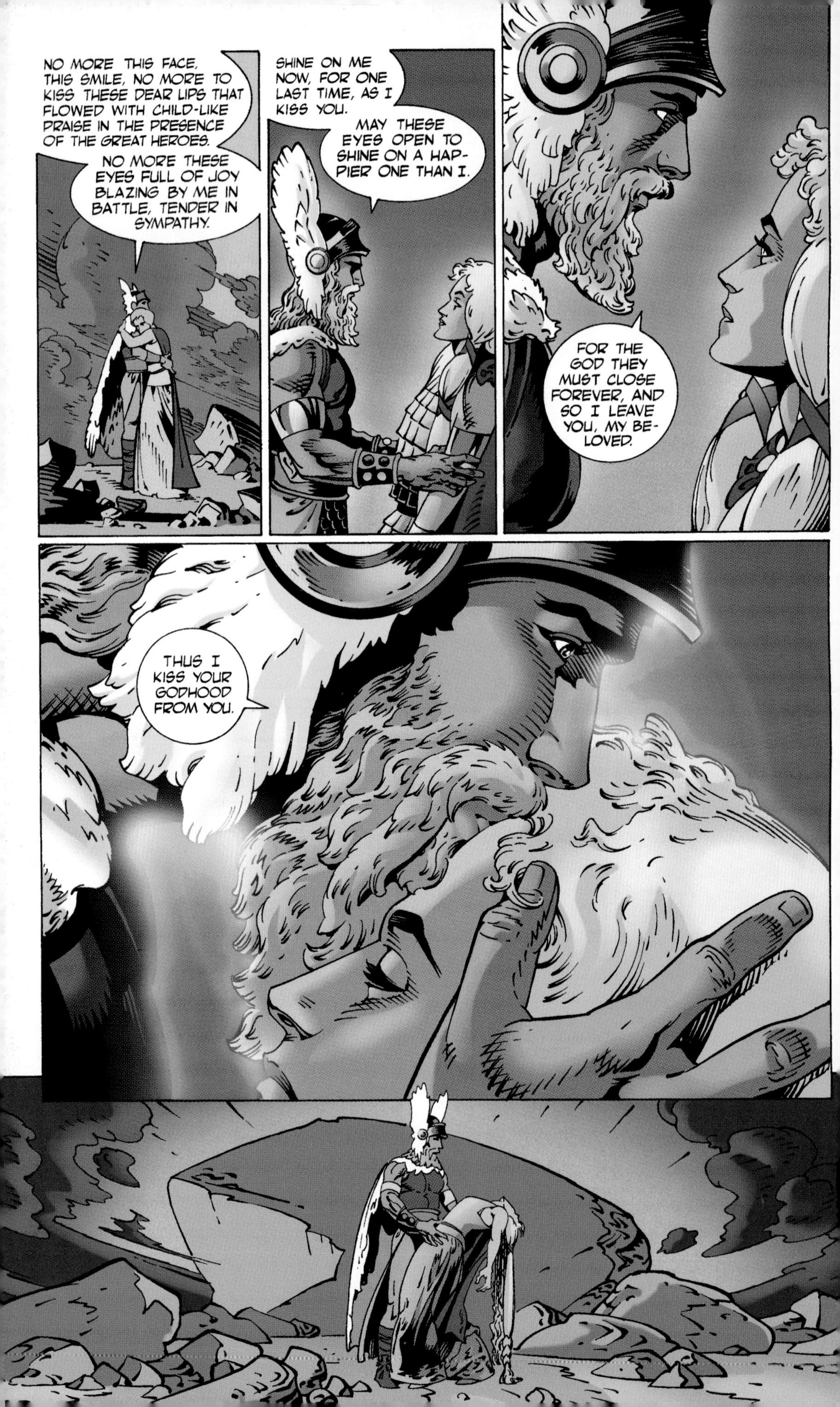
NO MORE THIS FACE, THIS SMILE, NO MORE TO KISS THESE DEAR LIPS THAT FLOWED WITH CHILD-LIKE PRAISE IN THE PRESENCE OF THE GREAT HEROES.
NO MORE THESE EYES FULL OF JOY BLAZING BY ME IN BATTLE, TENDER IN SYMPATHY.
SHINE ON ME NOW, FOR ONE LAST TIME, AS I KISS YOU.
MAY THESE EYES OPEN TO SHINE ON A HAP-PIER ONE THAN I.
FOR THE GOD THEY MUST CLOSE FOREVER, AND SO I LEAVE YOU, MY BE-LOVED.
THUS I KISS YOUR GODHOOD FROM YOU.

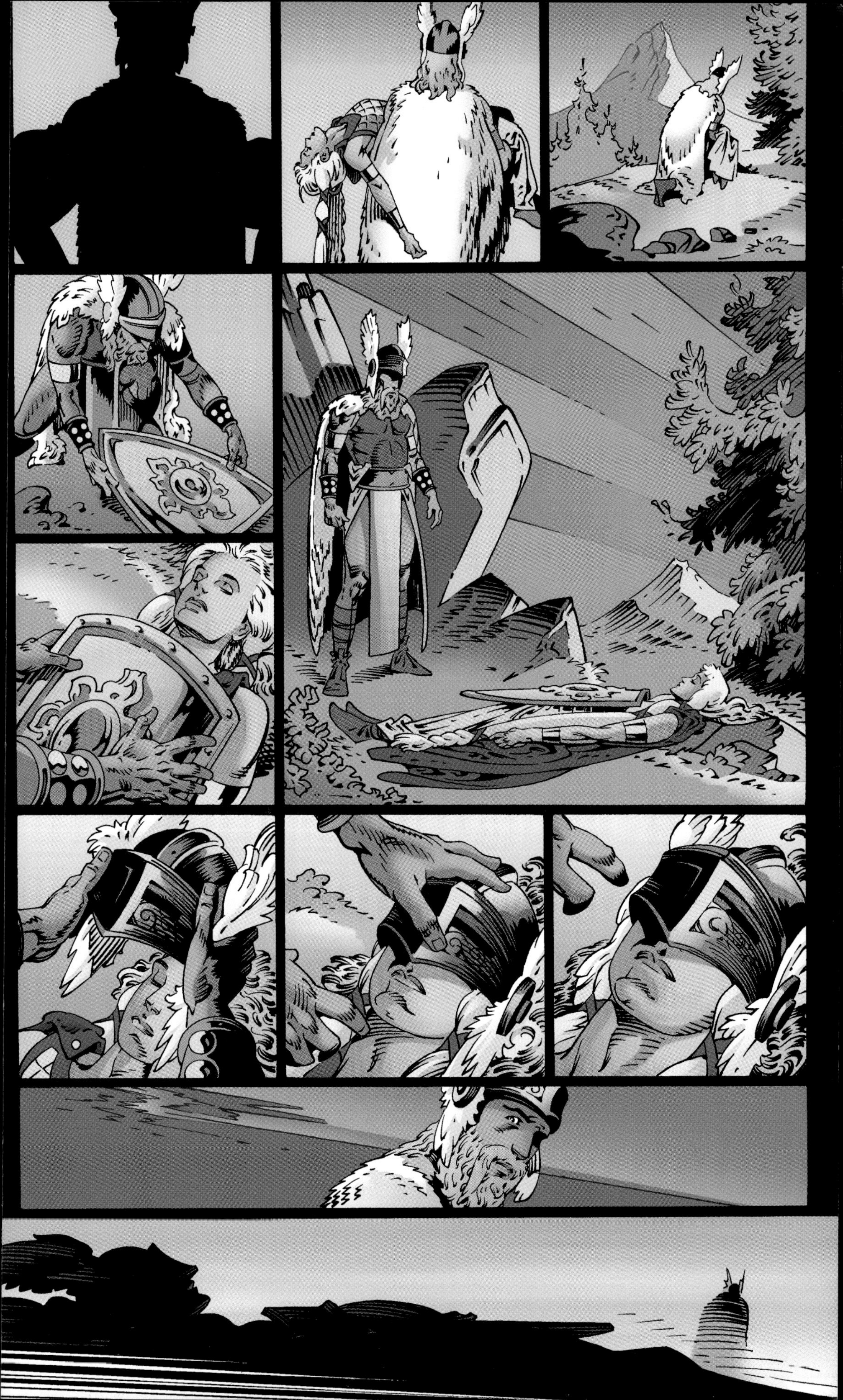

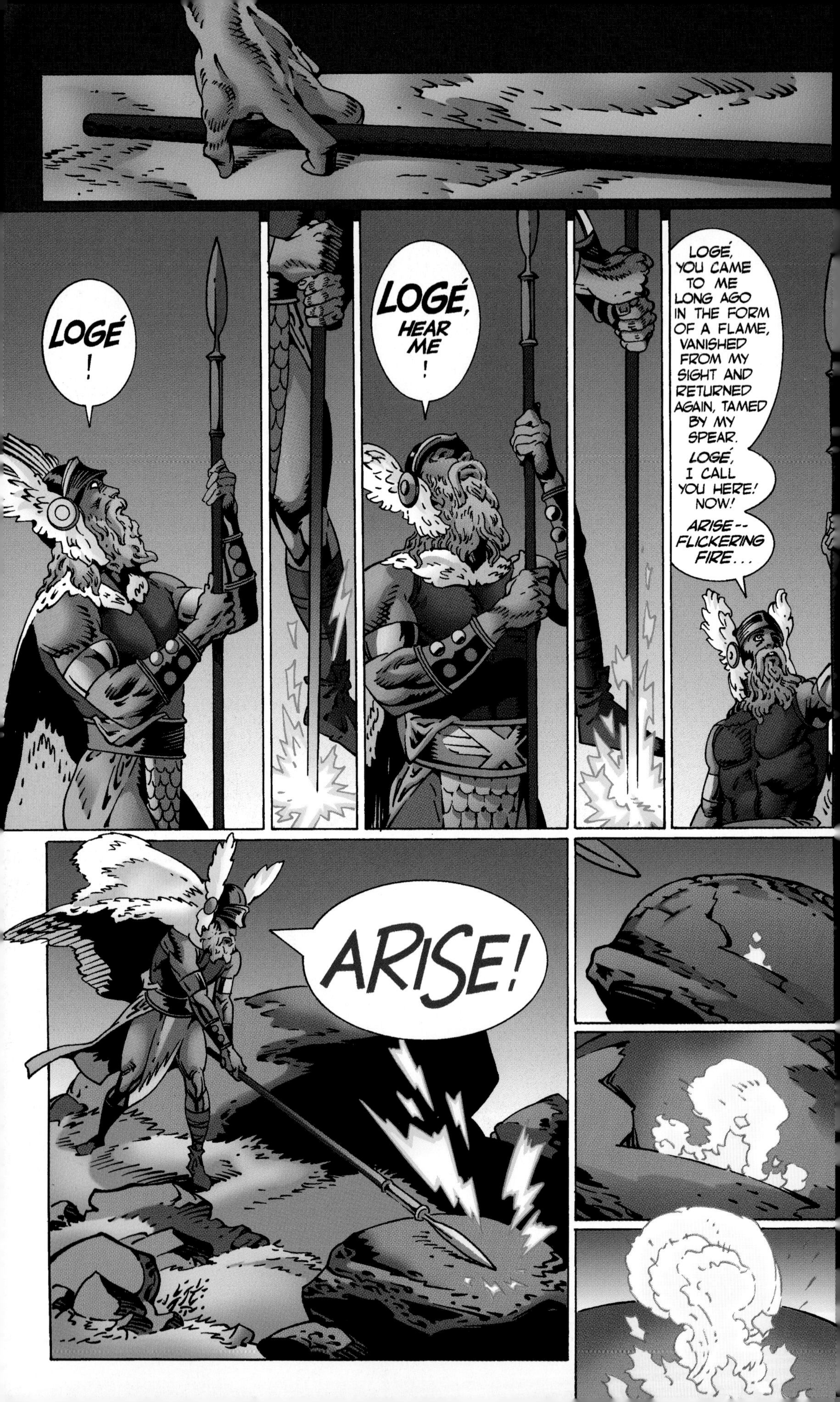
LOGÉ!
LOGÉ, HEAR ME!
LOGÉ, YOU CAME TO ME LONG AGO IN THE FORM OF A FLAME, VANISHED FROM MY SIGHT AND RETURNED AGAIN, TAMED BY MY SPEAR. LOGÉ, I CALL YOU HERE! NOW! ARISE-- FLICKERING FIRE...
ARISE!

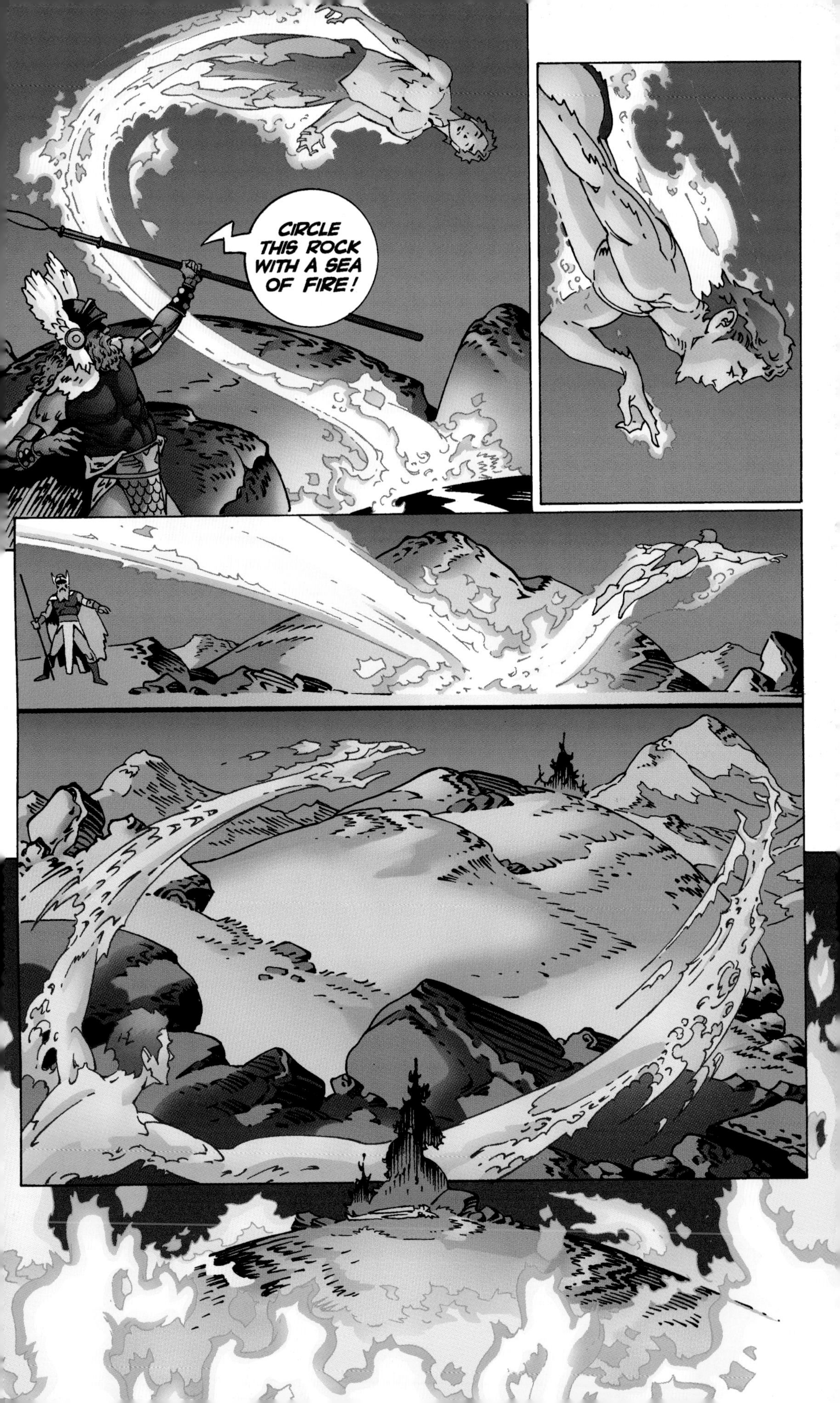
CIRCLE THIS ROCK WITH A SEA OF FIRE!

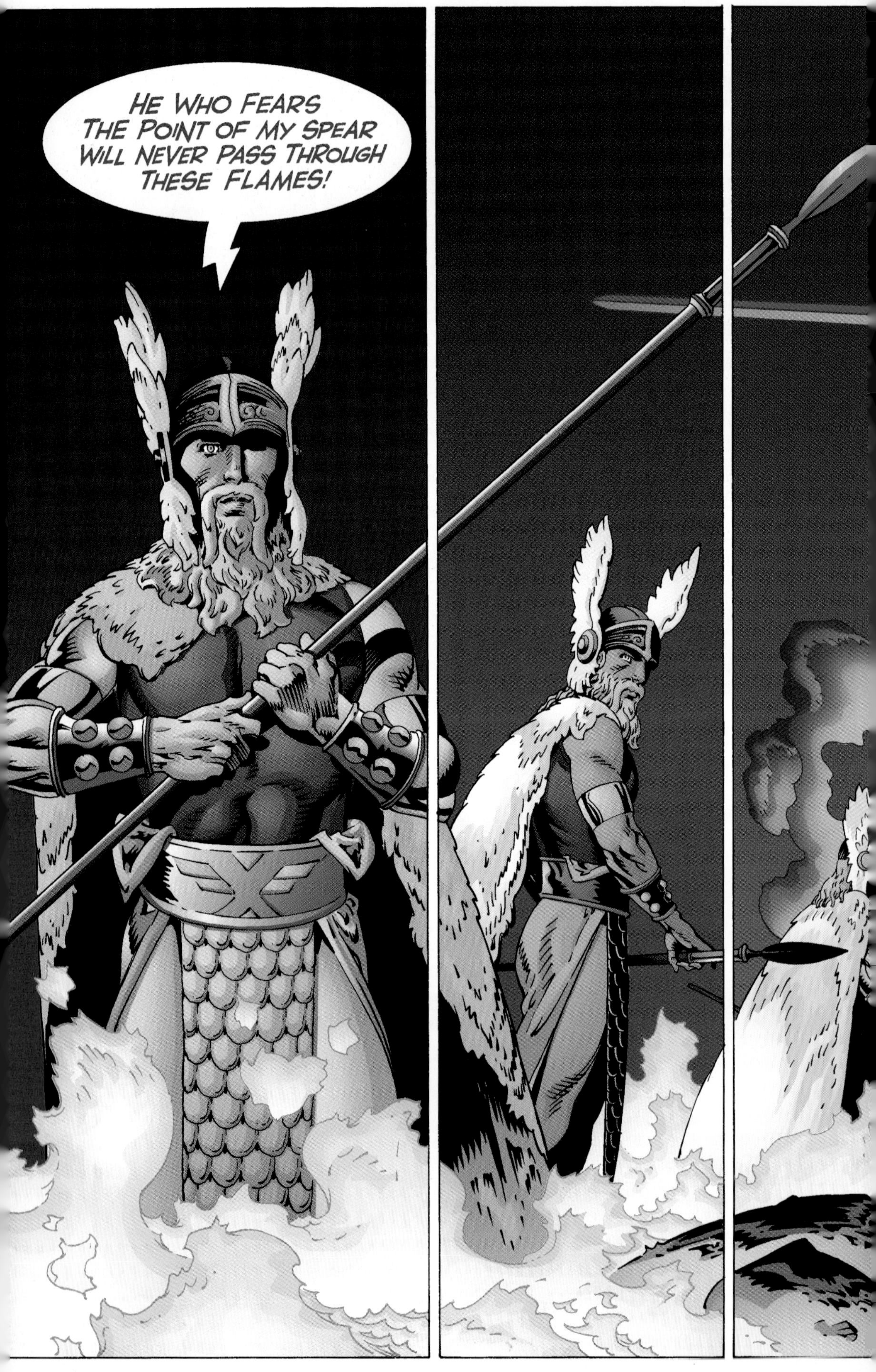
HE WHO FEARS THE POINT OF MY SPEAR WILL NEVER PASS THROUGH THESE FLAMES!

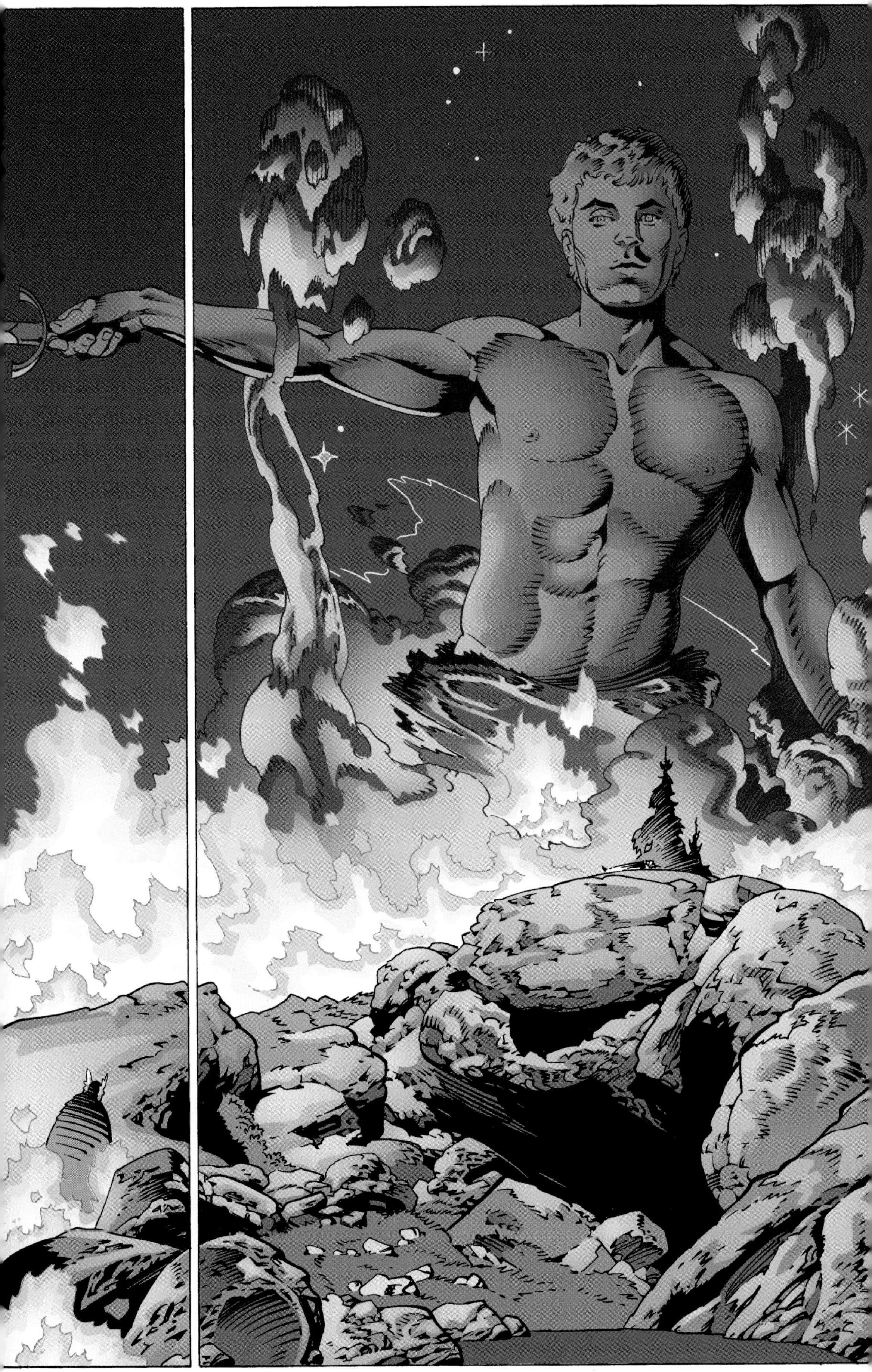

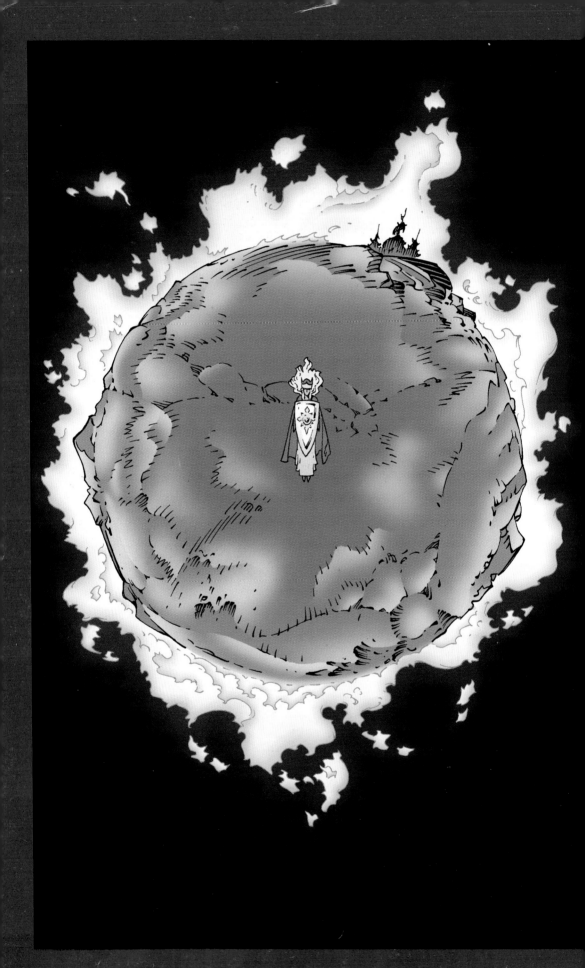